MODERN LEGAL STUDIES

Policing in a Changing Constitutional Order

Professor Neil Walker

D1331487

London
Sweet & Maxwell
2000

Published in 2000 by
Sweet & Maxwell Limited of
100 Avenue Road London NW3 3PF.
http://www.sweetandmaxwell.co.uk
Typeset by J&L Composition Ltd,
Filey, North Yorkshire
Printed in England by Clays Ltd, St Ives plc

A CIP catalogue record for this book
is available from the British Library.

ISBN 0421 633700

No natural forests were destroyed to make this product,
only farmed timber was used and re-planted.

©

For my parents, Bill and Kitty

Preface

Since Lawrence Lustgarten's seminal work, *The Governance of the Police*, was published in the Modern Legal Studies Series in 1986, much has changed both in the institutional pattern of British policing and in its constitutional backdrop. Lustgarten's purpose, in which he was conspicuously successful and which I share, was to provide "a systematic treatment of policing within the broad framework of public law." (v) In utilising the concept of "governance" rather than the more narrow term "accountability", he rightly emphasised the sheer variety of ways in which law helps to shape policing, performing an enabling as much as a restraining function.

The present work takes Lustgarten's text as an empirical and analytical point of departure. Part one charts the interwoven development of the legal and social frameworks of policing up to the 1980s, and then beyond to the new millennium. It also locates the idea of police governance deep within the constitutional foundations of the state, seeking to develop a more elaborate conceptualisation of the nature and forms of legal influence over the bedrock internal security function of the state. Part two concentrates on how the basic tripartite template of local police governance—central government, local government and the police themselves—has been altered in recent years, not only in England and Wales, but in the markedly different social and constitutional circumstances of Scotland and Northern Ireland. Part three deals with the governance of other forms of policing—national, supranational and private—which have emerged or expanded in the wake of the social and constitutional changes set out in part one. Finally, part four returns to broader conceptual issues, suggesting that, if assessed cumulatively, the changes of recent years demand new ways of conceiving of policing, of constitutionalism, and of the relationship between the two, in which the role of the state is no longer axiomatic.

While writing this book, and, indeed, in thinking about its issues for years beforehand, I have benefited from the advice, encouragement, inspiration, stimulation and practical assistance of many colleagues. I am particularly grateful to Malcolm Anderson, Stephen Bennett, Didier

Bigo, Monica den Boer, David Bradley, Douglas Brodie, Johnny Connolly, Adam Crawford, Peter Cullen, Pete Duff, David Garland, Bill Gilmore, Chris Himsworth, Tony Jefferson, Les Johnston, Trevor Jones, Richard Kinsey, Ian Loader, Barry Loveday, Carole Lyons, Charles Raab, Robert Reiner, Jim Sheptycki, David Smith, Mark Telford and Roy Wilkie. I am grateful, too, to Mark Telford and, especially, to Lynne Allan, for editorial assistance, and to Amanda Walton for secretarial assistance. Thanks are also due to Aberdeen University Law Department for the provision of sabbatical leave: as is so often the case, what was intended to provide time and space to begin a new book, in fact became indispensable to finishing the previous one. A succession of editors at Sweet & Maxwell also indulged my tardiness, in particular Tony Hawitt, whose steady faith in the project was invaluable. One reason for the inordinate delay in finishing the project was the difficulty of bringing together my two major intellectual interests—police governance and constitutional theory—for the first time in a systematic fashion. Whether I have ultimately succeeded or failed, I also owe a huge debt of gratitude to another group of colleagues within constitutional theory from whom I have gained so much over the years. However, as my list of acknowledgements is already too long, I will save my individual thanks to these colleagues until the (already delayed) next book. Finally, my heartfelt thanks to Gillian, Lewis and Ross, whose love and support sustains me.

I took account of material available to me before June 1, 2000, although in a few places I was able to incorporate slightly later developments and references.

Neil Walker
Aberdeen, July 2000.

Contents

Table of Cases

Table of Statutes

Table of Statutory Instruments

PART I

HISTORICAL AND
CONCEPTUAL BACKGROUND

Chapter One

Policing In the Constitutional Order

All policing systems are profoundly influenced by the constitutional order in which they are situated. For some—mainly lawyers—this is a self-evident truth, hardly worthy of comment. For others—mainly non-lawyers—it is more debatable, or even demonstrably false. The present chapter avoids categorical claims about the connection between law and policing,[1] and instead offers a preliminary assessment of the different ways in which constitutional arrangements may be relevant to policing. In so doing, it sets the scene for a more detailed treatment of the relationship between policing and the constitution in the U.K. today.

In this introductory analysis, we proceed by addressing two questions. First, quite briefly but crucially, why is policing in principle of constitutional interest and significance? Secondly, and at rather greater length, by

---

[1] Such claims can have important political consequences. For example, Reiner makes the telling point that the civil liberties lobby has often made precisely the same assumptions in concluding that increased legal controls on police behaviour will be reflected in less police wrongdoing as has the law and order lobby in concluding that every increase in police powers will deter more crimes. In neither case is the rational deterrence model remotely justified by the evidence, but continued unreflective reliance upon it tends to polarize political debate in the pursuit of implausible policy objectives. Those who do not subscribe to such a naive legalistic-bureaucratic conception of police behaviour and who are more appreciative of the complexities of the relationship between legal/constitutional background and police practice may be divided into interactionists, or culturalists, on the one hand, and structuralists on the other (see Dixon, 1997, chap.1). For the former, the occupational culture is the primary determinant of police behaviour, and rules will only work to the extent that they are sensitive to the demands of this culture. For the latter, the detailed structure of legal rules is of key significance, with vague or permissive legal rules and inadequate sanctions and enforcement mechanisms all contributing to the gap between legal ideal and profane reality. See also Reiner (1992), pp. 211–217, and Brogden, Jefferson and Walklate (1988) pp. 164–170. See also section 2(B)(v) below. The present study does not seek to join the debate at the level of general sociological theory, but instead works on the assumption that culture and structure are both significant, providing a complexly interrelated set of influences on police behaviour.

what means may constitutional law influence policing practices and arrangements?

1. Two Constitutional Paradoxes of Policing

Constitutions, the unwritten British constitution included, are both enabling and constraining. They constitute power as legal authority in the form of the organs of state, and set limits to that authority. This duality of function lends constitutions a paradoxical quality; they seek to control the very agents they empower and to delimit the very institutions they create. Likewise, constitutional*ism*, understood as a set of values or attitudes underpinning the commitment to constitutional law and government, is often depicted as centring upon the idea of limited government[2]; yet what is being limited is the power of the state, and constitutional law is just as central to the process of "coercive self-organisation,"[3] through which the state secures a dominant role within society, as it is to the restriction of that role.

That empowerment and constraint are two sides of a single constitutional coin is more than just a logical paradox. The presence of these opposing dynamics generates tensions within the constitutional order; a series of puzzles with which constitution-builders and constitutional theorists from the authors of *The Federalist* onwards have grappled in their attempts to unlock the secrets of good government.[4] These tensions affect each of the three organs of government traditionally recognised in constitutional law—legislature, executive and judiciary. Responsibility for the making and unmaking of laws which set limits upon the capacity of the state rests with those whose role and loyalties in the system of government may encourage them instead to promulgate legislation that minimises constraints upon public power. Those charged under the constitution with the execution of public policy within legal limits may on occasion be both able and willing to stretch, or even violate those limits in the name of bureaucratic self-interest or ideological commitment. A

---

[2] Recent discussions of this vast topic include Griffin (1990); Walker (1996b); MacCormick (1993).

[3] MacCormick (1993) p. 128.

[4] *The Federalist* was a series of eighty-five papers published in 1787–8 in which Alexander Hamilton, James Madison and John Jay expounded a general theory of government which supported the ratification of the new Constitution of the United States. See Madison, Hamilton and Jay (1987).

similar conundrum affects the judicial branch; the judges are entrusted with ensuring that the constitution means what it says, but their role as authoritative interpreters of fundamental law means that the validity or persuasiveness of their own pronouncements cannot be challenged, and so they may with impunity deny that law its best interpretation.

There is a sense in which the paradox of policing—or, to be more accurate, the set of paradoxes associated with policing—represents the paradox of the constitutional order writ small. Policing, as one prominent theorist puts it, "implies the set of activities directed at preserving the security of a particular social order"[5]. Historically, this executive function has had both a specific dimension and a general dimension. As the main domestic mechanism for the distribution of non-negotiably coercive force,[6] the police are the sharpest instrument of state power; in imposing and safe-guarding its "specific order", they fortify the position of those interests and constituencies that are socially and politically predominant within the state. At the same time, the police are mandated to secure "general order"; that is, through preserving the public peace and enforcing the universal precepts of the criminal law, they also seek to secure the maintenance of public tranquillity and safety in the interests of *all* sections of society.[7] In both aspects of their remit, the police should act as ultimate guarantors of the efficacy of the constitutional order. In protecting the state, they under-gird the key institutional configuration established by constitutional law. In providing a level of general security, they establish an environment within which the range of constitutionally-endorsed individual and collective entitlements and freedoms—including the right to life, liberty and security of the person; the right to privacy; and freedom of conscience, expression, assembly and association—may be fully enjoyed.

Just as constitutional practice in general can betray constitutionalism, however, so the practice of policing is capable of posing a threat to the preservation of specific and general order—and in turn to the underlying constitutional order. This is due partly to the coercive power of the police, which provides them with the wherewithal to affect adversely—whether by commission or by omission—the security of the state, or of wider interests represented within the social order. It is also partly in consequence of the tensions which may exist between the more specific and the more general function of the police, and also within the more general function. The

---

[5] Reiner (1994) p. 718.

[6] Bittner (1971) p. 46.

[7] The analysis of the police as defenders of both specific order and general order is offered by Marenin (1982).

protection of elite interests may be at the expense of the interests of wider social constituencies, or vice-versa, while in the pursuit of their more general function, the police may give undue preference or priority to the rights and interests of some wider constituencies over others.

In a nutshell, it is the capacity of the police to use force and their complex dual mandate which marks them out as indispensable to the protection of the institutions and interests endorsed by the constitutional order; yet it is these same attributes which makes them more liable than any other agency within the executive branch of the state to endanger or corrupt that order. As both guardian of, and threats to, the constitutional order, police institutions have an inherently double-edged, paradoxical quality. This basic paradox of the *police function* can only be resolved by fashioning a regulatory framework which encourages the police to use their special position to promote a high overall level of societal security and a satisfactory accommodation between its different aspects, rather than permitting them to undermine security generally or to give undue priority to some of its aspects at the expense of others.

This is a daunting enough challenge, but it is made all the more formidable by the fact that the very source from which it must be addressed gives rise to a further paradox of *police governance*. That is to say, the state (central and local), through its constitutional order, is not only the ultimate author of any solution to the regulatory puzzle of policing, but is also, in its intimate and complex relationship to the police and the police mandate—as beneficiary of the production of specific order—an integral part of the problem to be addressed. Accordingly, the state should be required not only to seek to empower and constrain the police in a manner which is best calculated to resolve the paradox of the police function, but also, as part of that regulatory strategy, reflexively to acknowledge its own position as an interested party, and so to embrace measures which preclude or limit its ability to influence the performance of the police function unduly in its own favour. In short, the state must develop a framework of governance which both serves to enable and constrain the police effectively and to constrain the state's own capacity to interfere unduly on its own behalf. [8]

---

[8] The paradox of governance is by no means uniquely applicable to policing. Broadcasting, for example, is another area where the state should be required to take active regulatory steps to secure certain broader interests and values, such as the dissemination of high quality news and entertainment and the avoidance of racial bias or incitement, and prevented from influencing the content of broadcasting in its own favour. See *e.g.* Gibbons (1998).

2. Constitutional Influences upon Policing

If these, in a very general sense, are the puzzles and paradoxes of policing with which the constitutional lawyer is confronted, what are the constitutional mechanisms through which influence may be exerted? Broadly speaking, the constitutional order may shape policing by two means. First, the overall framework of constitutional law and practice affects the way in which any specific area of regulation, policing included, may be addressed. Secondly, there is the body of rules through which the direct regulation of policing is sought.

(A) THE OVERALL FRAMEWORK

A number of general features of the overall framework of constitutional law have a bearing upon the regulation of policing. In the first place, there are matters of *constitutional form,* in particular the status of constitutional law and the question of entrenchment of a particular constitutional scheme. Secondly, there is *constitutional doctrine,* those rules pitched at such a broad level of generality as to impinge upon policing within their general coverage of public law. Thirdly, at the highest level of abstraction, there are matters of *constitutional principle,* general normative axioms which influence the content or interpretation of more specific precepts. Finally, there is *constitutional technique*; this refers to those general styles and methods of governing which, although not usually considered as matters internal to the constitutional order, nevertheless provide the mechanisms through which constitutional objectives tend to be pursued, so influencing the pattern of constitutional practice just as closely as any of the other general features.

(i) Constitutional Form

The formal status of constitutional law within a particular jurisdiction sets broad limits on what is possible by way of legal regulation of policing. As is well-known, the United Kingdom is almost unique in the contemporary world in not possessing a written constitution.[9] Its constitutional law may be found in a number of written sources—statutes, case-law, works of authority and so on—but there is no "documentary

---

[9] Israel is the only other prominent exception.

constitution"[10] which sets out the most important rules regulating the system of government. This absence has important consequences. Without a written constitution set apart form the staple sources of law there can be no species of domestic law superior in status to the rest. Typically, the superior status of such law would be reflected in and confirmed by its entrenchment against change, or by a requirement that a special procedure be followed in order for it to be validly altered; and such a procedure would be more onerous than for ordinary legislation, perhaps requiring a qualified majority within a legislature or legislatures, or a referendum majority, or, indeed, elements of both representative and popular endorsement.[11] Instead, ultimate constitutional authority in the United Kingdom rests with the ordinary legislator, the Queen-in-Parliament, who is competent to make or unmake any law on any matter.

The British constitution, therefore, is an extremely flexible affair. While this confers the advantage of easy adaptability, it rules out certain arrangements which have a considerable impact upon policing in other jurisdictions. For instance, it rules out an entrenched system of protection of fundamental rights. Since the promulgation of the first modern Bill of Rights in 1791 in the form of the first ten amendments of the United States Constitution, such codes have become familiar entries in the index of written constitutions. Neither are they entirely unfamiliar within British jurisprudence. In 1951 the United Kingdom became the first state to ratify the Council of Europe's Convention on Human Rights (ECHR) which contains provisions relevant to a wide range of police practices, including arrest, search of persons and property, detention following arrest, interrogation, seizure of goods, taking of fingerprints, photographs and body samples, regulation of public meetings and processions, surreptitious surveillance, automatic processing of personal data, and use of force.[12] However, although the U.K. Government undertakes in international law to secure to everyone within its jurisdiction the rights laid down in the ECHR[13] and is subject to the compulsory jurisdiction of the European Court of Human Rights in Strasbourg,[14] the ECHR was not until recently recognised in domestic

---

[10] Munro (1999) p. 3.

[11] As proposed under art. 69 of the Draft Constitution of the United Kingdom produced under the auspices of the Institute for Public Policy Research (IPPR). See IPPR (1991). For discussion of this and other recent attempts to formulate a new constitutional settlement for the United Kingdom, see Brazier (1993), (1998).

[12] For discussion, see Alderson (1984).

[13] Art. 1, ECHR.

[14] Art. 46, ECHR.

law. The Human Rights Act, 1998—one of the flagship measures in New Labour's rolling programme of constitutional reform—has now corrected this omission. However, the form of recognition under the 1998 Act is weak, involving only a requirement to interpret other legislation (past and future) in a way which is compatible with Convention rights "so far as is possible to do so",[15] and so falling short of full incorporation. This somewhat tentative strategy together with the status of the 1998 Act as ordinary law under the prevailing constitutional orthodoxy leaves the newly domesticated catalogue of rights vulnerable to override, amendment or repeal by later legislation.

Of even more immediate relevance to broad issues of police governance, the flexible constitution also rules out certain structural options in the allocation of constitutional authority. To begin with, the splitting of executive and legislative powers between distinct organs of government—a major element of the classical constitutional doctrine of the separation of powers—is precluded in a constitutional system which pivots on the single axis of the legislative supremacy of Parliament, and which consequently grants executive power to whomever can control the legislature. Thus the framework of checks and balances between the two major governmental institutions which, under the separation doctrine, might curb the excesses and correct or modify the errors of each in the development and implementation of a system of policing, is ruled out.

Equally, as sovereignty is the indivisible property of the Queen-in-Parliament, the establishment of a federal arrangement in which general and regional levels of government are each constitutionally guaranteed a significant degree of authority is excluded by constitutional fiat. This structural limitation of the unitary constitution[16] is directly pertinent to the design of policing institutions, since in federal systems there is usually a pronounced decentralisation of policing arrangements with only a limited national capacity permitted. This is normally achieved through vesting residual legislative authority in the states or provinces, including the general policing remit, and requiring the federation to found upon one of its constitutionally enumerated heads of authority to justify any particular exercise of police power.

The Tenth Amendment of the United States Constitution, for example, specifically reserves to the states all powers not otherwise allocated under the Constitution, including the majority of policing functions.

---

[15] Human Rights Act 1998, s.3(1).
[16] See Walker (2000a).

Only 10 per cent of U.S. law enforcement personnel work for federal agencies,[17] the authority for which includes provisions such as the exclusive power of Congress to regulate commerce amongst the states and to establish post offices.[18] Unlike the American model, the German Basic Law of 1949 was drafted against the background of the global development of professional policing systems within states, yet a similar scheme is in place. Governmental powers not explicitly allocated elsewhere, which again include the main policing tasks, are reserved to the Länder under Article 30, while the federation is empowered to carry out specific functions in matters such as border controls, national and international co-ordination against crime, and protection of the basic democratic order of the federation or Länder.[19] As in the United States, the series of specialist federal jurisdiction accounts for no more than a small minority of overall police strength, in this case 15 per cent.[20]

Under the Canadian Constitution, which contains more centralising features than many federal systems, residual powers lie with the national level of government rather than the local level. Nevertheless, even in this unusual case policing remains primarily a provincial function[21] by virtue of the exclusive provincial power over the administration of justice.[22] National functions are again marginal. National security policing is justified under the peace, order and good government power[23] and the defence power,[24] while the power to police specific matters such as drugs crime and environmental crime derives from the federal Parliament's power to enforce its own statutes.[25]

How important is the absence of a federal option under present constitutional arrangements in the U.K? As we discuss later, the U.K. has a decentralised system of policing which is closely tied to the structures of local government, but there has been a secular trend towards greater central government control and influence. As a unitary state the United Kingdom can supply no constitutional guarantees for its decentralised system of policing just as it cannot guarantee the constitutional status of

---

[17] See S. Walker (1992), p. 38.
[18] Constitution of the United States, Art. 1, S. 8.
[19] Basic Law, Art. 73.
[20] Cullen (1992) p. 17.
[21] See Hogg (1992) pp. 504–510. Constitution Act 1867, s.92.
[22] Constitution Act 1867, s.92.
[23] Constitution Act 1867, s.91.
[24] Constitution Act 1867 s.91(7).
[25] *A-G. Alberta v. Putnam* [1981] 2 S.C.R. 267. The power of enforcement is specifically included in each federal head of authority under the Constitution.

local government, and has no basis in constitutional doctrine for discriminating between those functions which are properly central and those which are properly provincial.

This inability to underwrite a territorial division of authority applies as much to more ambitious schemes of regional devolution—past and present—as to the traditional forms of local government. Thus, under the peace, order and good government power in the Government of Ireland Act of 1920,[26] responsibility for the regulation of policing was transferred to the devolved Northern Ireland Parliament at Stormont. However, the reversibility of this transfer was confirmed by the return to direct rule from Westminster in 1972.[27] Equally, in the various statutory schemes of the New Labour Government for the devolution of both legislative and executive authority to Scotland[28] and to Northern Ireland,[29] which are discussed in detail in Part Two of the book, and for the devolution of executive authority to Wales[30] (and, potentially, to the English regions[31] or cities[32]), power devolved in respect of policing is power ultimately retained—in strict constitutional theory at least.

The link between federalism and the effective entrenchment of the tradition of decentralised policing has been made explicit in recent, more radical, proposals for the reform of the British Constitution which have remained on the drawing board. The Institute for Public Policy Research (IPPR), for example, has suggested in its Draft Constitution that, with the exception of national security matters,[33] policing should be the settled responsibility of the Scottish and Irish Assemblies in their own areas.[34] The special majority procedure for constitutional amendment which the IPPR advocated as part of its proposed new constitutional order would serve to protect this division

---

[26] Northern Ireland Act 1920, s.4(1).

[27] Northern Ireland (Temporary Provisions) Act 1972.

[28] Scotland Act 1998.

[29] Government of Ireland Act 1998.

[30] Government of Wales Act 1998. A transfer of Home Office policing functions to the Welsh Assembly would be competent by Order in Council under s.22(1)(a), although no such order has yet been made.

[31] The beginnings of a process of regional devolution are evident under the Regional Development Agencies Act 1998; see Hazell and O"Leary (1999); Hazell (1999); Walker (2000a).

[32] Following the introduction of an elected Mayor to London under the Greater London Authority Act 1999, provision is to be made for other areas to decide by referendum whether to follow suit; see Local Government Bill 2000, Part II. This trend may complement, or, more likely, rival the trend towards regional devolution; see n. 31.

[33] IPPR Draft Constitution, art.126.

[34] IPPR Draft Constitution, art. 54.2.5.

of authority.[35] The IPPR example also demonstrates the flexibility of the federal device, in that it is not premised upon a classically symmetrical federal constitution in which all territorial units within the state are subject to the same institutional design and the same division of federal and regional jurisdiction. In theory at least, the division and decentralisation of authority within a federal arrangement which is "lop-sided" in a manner rather similar to the piecemeal devolution programme sponsored by the New Labour Government, can be just as secure as in the classical model of federalism.

The IPPR draft indicated other policing matters which may be the subject of special protection, depending upon the formal status accorded to constitutional law. Non-discrimination in employment policy, mechanisms of democratic accountability, an independent element in complaints procedure and an effective system of compensation for victims of police misconduct or inefficiency, are all matters deemed important enough to be given special protection within its text.[36] In each case, no attempt is made at detailed regulation, which underlines the argument that the value of a system in which constitutional law is of superior status to ordinary law is that it facilitates the framing of an authoritative message as to the main principles to be observed and long-term priorities to be pursued.

Before leaving the topic of constitutional form, we should note that our argument about the consequences of the flexibility of the British constitution requires to be qualified in three respects. First, as the initiatives of New Labour demonstrate, retention of the classical foundations of the British Constitution need not rule out reforms pertinent to policing, such as systemic protection of fundamental rights and extensive devolution of power, which are more commonly associated with the tradition of written, entrenched constitutional arrangements. In legal terms, there will always remain a crucial distinction between what is possible under the two types of system. It is at least arguable, however, that in terms of *realpolitik* the difference is of less significance.

In the second place, in any case the doctrine of parliamentary sovereignty which underpins the flexible constitution is not immutable, but is susceptible to modification even within the existing constitutional order. Thirdly, the traditional doctrine, even if not challenged head-on, does not entirely exclude the development of arrangements whose

---

[35] IPPR Draft Constitution, art. 69. For discussion, see Bradley (1994).
[36] IPPR Draft Constitution, art. 125.

source is other than the Queen-in-Parliament but which nonetheless involve the exercise of public authority affecting the interests of the United Kingdom. These last two qualifications are taken together as they both have implications for the development of a European dimension in British policing arrangements.

In the classical Diceyan formulation, parliamentary sovereignty not only establishes the absolute freedom of the Queen-in-Parliament to make and to repeal laws, but also prohibits any other body from over-riding or setting aside the legislation of Parliament.[37] Britain's member-ship of the European Union, established by the European Communities Act 1972, is clearly inconsistent with the second limb of the traditional sovereignty doctrine, as United Kingdom law recognises that Community organs are entitled to make law which may have the effect of supersed-ing domestic law. Further, the British courts have recently begun to acknowledge that the new order of European law also affects the first limb,[38] although precisely how and with what ultimate consequences remains a matter of considerable uncertainty.[39] What is certain, however, is that the relationship between the United Kingdom and the wider European Union is beginning to assume at least some of the character-istics of a federation.[40]

As yet, policing and criminal justice matters do not fall within the direct ambit of Community law, and thus there is no immediate scope for the domestic constitutional arrangements for policing to be challenged from Brussels in line with the general European shift in our understand-ing of sovereignty. However, as successive treaties have extended the jurisdiction of the E.U., it would be imprudent to assume that this will remain the case indefinitely, particularly since the Member States have already registered their interest in co-operation in this area. Under Title VI of the Maastricht Treaty on European Union 1993, as amended and extended by the Treaty of Amsterdam 1997, they have committed them-selves to working together within the area of "Justice and Home Affairs" generally, although, strictly speaking, this arrangement remains some-what distinct from the E.U.'s existing supranational order. Nevertheless,

---

[37] Dicey (1959) p. 40.

[38] See for example, *R. v. Secretary of State for Transport, ex p. Factortame (No.2)* [1991] 1 A.C. 603; *R. v. Secretary of State for Employment, ex p. E.O.C.* [1994] 2 W.L.R. 409.

[39] For discussion, see *e.g.* Wade (1996); Allen (1997); MacCormick (1999) chap.6.

[40] See *e.g.*, Van Bogdandy (2000). Although with the development by the European Court of Justice of the doctrines of direct effect and supremacy of Community law and its often generous approach to Community competence, the federal trend is more pronounced in the legal sphere than in the political sphere. See Hartley (1994), chap.l: Weiler (1981).

the Community institutions are involved to some extent and the policing provisions[41] have led to the creation of the Europol Drugs Unit and, more recently, Europol—a Union-wide policing agency. Despite the unitary structure of the United Kingdom, therefore, legal developments at the margin between Community law and international law have planted the seeds of a new range of policing institutions which, when brought to fruition, may stand alongside the domestic policing institutions in a proto-federal relationship. In chapter eight we examine this new European dimension in greater depth while in the final chapter we discuss how the development of new sites of public authority more generally is altering the texture of the State's traditional claim to internal and external authority over policing and other vital functions.

(ii) Constitutional Doctrine

In all constitutional systems there are to be found rules or doctrines of sufficient generality to influence a number of different spheres of regulation. These doctrines may be legal or non-legal in nature. Both subgroups are relevant to an assessment of the constitutional context of British policing.

An instructive example of a legal rule of broader scope which profoundly affects the regulation of policing is the prerogative power of the Crown to keep the Queen's Peace within the realm. In *R v. Home Secretary, ex parte Northumbria Police Authority*,[42] the Court of Appeal decided that under a broad interpretation of section 41 of the Police Act 1964, the Home Secretary was entitled to supply plastic baton rounds and CS gas to local police forces from a central store. The court further held that absent statutory authority, the prerogative power to maintain the peace would in any case have justified the Home Secretary's actions, despite the fact that section 4 of the 1964 Act explicitly confers upon another party, namely the police authority, the power to "provide . . . equipment as may be required for police purposes of the area".

The deeper significance of this decision as an illustration of broader constitutional influence over the regulation of policing arises from certain characteristics of the peace-keeping prerogative, at least as interpreted by the Court of Appeal. The Revolution Settlement of 1688 made it clear that prerogative powers, as these special legal attributes of

---

[41] Treaty on European Union, Arts. 29–30.
[42] [1988] 1 All E.R. 556.

the Crown which are not enjoyed in common with private persons, were henceforth to be treated as a residual category. However, the rule that no new prerogatives could be created and existing ones could be abrogated by statute has always sat uneasily with the fact that many prerogative powers are broadly conceived, resist easy definition, and so are easily extended or adapted.

The *Northumbria* decision epitomises this tension. There was no consensus over the doctrinal source of the prerogative to maintain the peace. One member of the court linked it to a more general right to prevent crime and administer justice,[43] while another viewed it as a "sister prerogative"[44] to the war prerogative, securing against domestic threats to order whereas the latter is concerned with external threats. The absence of a clear basis in principle inevitably leaves the scope of the doctrine unclear. The court in *Northumbria* stated that the peace-keeping prerogative covers not only actual outbreaks of disorder but also apprehended outbreaks, but did not attempt to specify how remote or immediate the apprehension may be. The answer rather depends upon to which of the more general prerogatives the peace-keeping prerogative is more closely linked. If it is to the war prerogative, then the urgency and seriousness of the apprehension of disorder is at a premium. If, on the other hand, there is a closer link to the administration of justice prerogative, then the efficient management of the criminal justice system—a somewhat broader notion—is the key consideration.

The open-ended quality of the decision is also evident in the position taken by the court on the relationship between prerogative and statute. As already noted, the residual character of modern prerogative powers means that they can be abolished or restricted by statute. Where this is done explicitly, no difficulty arises. Where, as in the dispute in question, a statutory scheme dealing with the same subject-matter as a prerogative power has been established but no attempt has been made to address the pre-existing prerogative power, the law is less clear. The *Northumbria* decision sought to distinguish between cases in which the statute confers directly upon individuals rights or benefits which would be undermined if the Crown's prerogative power was retained, and cases in which it does not. Only in the former circumstance, the court argued, should the statute be construed as having abrogated the prerogative power.[45] On this reasoning, in the absence of a direct link to individual rights the mere

---

[43] Croom-Johnson L.J., at 563–565.
[44] Nourse L.J., at 575.
[45] Purchas L.J., at 570–573.

fact that the prerogative power is capable of disturbing or frustrating a particular statutory allocation of competencies between public agencies, as in the 1964 Act, is not considered sufficient to limit the prerogative power.

The enduring influence of the prerogative in the face of a public law statute reflects the common law foundations of the legal systems of the United Kingdom. The common law has often been viewed as a more fundamental source of legal values than legislation[46] (a tendency underscored by the absence of the "higher legislation" of a written constitution); and as a sub-category of the common law pitched at a high level of generality, the prerogative power is in a particularly elevated position within the internal hierarchy of our law.[47]

A rather similar form of influence is exerted by certain non-legal doctrines of the constitution. It is beyond dispute that constitutional conventions are the most important non-legal source. As rules of political behaviour which are not enforceable by the courts, their prominence is a further indicator of the flexibility of the British constitution and of its capacity to undergo substantial restructuring without resort to legal revolution. As we discuss in the next chapter, arguably the key constitutional rule of British policing—the doctrine of constabulary independence—is itself underpinned by convention. For present purposes, we are concerned with conventional doctrines which deal with general matters of government, but the ramifications of which are sufficiently broad to affect the regulation of policing.

The doctrine of ministerial responsibility is of particular significance in this respect. Individual ministerial responsibility requires Ministers to account to Parliament for anything they or their department do within their field of competence. There cannot be full ministerial responsibility for the actions of the police, as the chief constable and the police authorities, among others, have a significant degree of independent legal authority over local policing. The relevant Home Office ministers, however, are responsible to Parliament for those matters over which they have statutory or common-law authority. These range from the setting of national objectives to the provision of central services, while in the case of London the Home Secretary has accepted a much more detailed responsibility for the Metropolitan Police in the absence, until very

---

[46] See, *e.g.*, the discussion in Atiyah (1985); Cross (1987). On the recent revival of common law constitutionalism, see Hunt (1997) and chapter four.

[47] Peace-keeping is not the only head of prerogative power which impinges upon policing. Until they were placed upon a statutory footing by the Security Service Act 1989 and the Intelligence Services Act 1994, the only legal authority for the security and intelligence services was the prerogative power to defend the realm. Wade and Bradley, (1993) p. 560. See also chapter seven.

recently,[48] of a separately constituted police authority for the area.[49] The application of the doctrine of individual responsibility to the regulation of policing inevitably highlights some of the difficulties traditionally associated with constitutional conventions. This is particularly so in respect of the enforcement of responsibility. Ministerial responsibility, or accountability, may be divided into "explanatory accountability" and "amendatory accountability"[50]. Under the former, the minister is expected to meet reasonable requests for information from a Member of Parliament, but there is no effective means by which Parliament can compel a Minister or an official to answer to it or its committees. Certainly, as is generally the case when conventions are flouted, a political penalty may be paid by an unduly reticent Government. However, in an area such as policing, where there is a considerable grey zone in the allocation of responsibility between government and other agencies, a ministerial reluctance to divulge information can more easily be defended in terms of limited competence, thereby deflecting political criticism of the Government.

The uncertainties surrounding the sanctions associated with amendatory accountability are perhaps even greater. Amendatory accountability requires ministers to take remedial action or otherwise to bear responsibility to Parliament for acknowledged errors. In its ultimate form, amendatory accountability involves ministerial resignation, but there is deep and persistent controversy as to the circumstances in which this is required. No-one who had undertaken the most cursory examination of ministerial non-resignation in the twentieth century could seriously hold the view, once widely subscribed to, that a minister is obliged to resign for any significant policy failure or mismanagement within his department. However, it is more difficult, if not impossible, to set out the precise circumstances in which a minister would now be obliged to resign.[51]

In recent years, particularly in the context of a series of high-publicity breaches of prison security which have severely embarrassed the Home Office, a distinction between "policy" and "operations" has begun to be advanced as a basis for isolating the responsibility of the Minister from that of his officials.[52] Although, as we shall see in the context of the

---

[48] Greater London Authority Act 1999, s.312, amending s.101 of the Police Act 1996. See further chapter four.

[49] See Marshall (1984), pp. 119–122.

[50] Turpin (1994), pp. 134–144. See also Marshall (1984), pp. 77–79.

[51] See *e.g.*, Tomkins (1998).

[52] Turpin (1994), pp. 139–141.

jurisdictional debate between chief constables and local police authorities, this is a notoriously blurred boundary,[53] when applied to ministerial responsibility it may be a more serviceable distinction for policing than for many other policy areas. The statutory remit of central Government is confined to matters which, at least presumptively, fall within the policy domain, a tendency reinforced by the Police and Magistrates" Courts Act, 1994.[54] On the other hand, even if we negotiate the basic definitional hurdle, policy *responsibility* remains a notoriously elusive animal. What constitutes policy failure rather than policy success is often a matter of dispute between the two sides of the House of Commons, and the high constitutional focus upon individual ministerial responsibility can easily be lost in the glare of general party political controversy. This is rather underlined by the fact that, short of voluntary resignation, the only sanction available to enforce amendatory accountability is a motion of censure against a minister. In practice, such a motion is likely to be construed by cabinet colleagues as one of confidence in the Government as a whole, in which case the conduct of the Minister will be embraced within the protective cloak of collective responsibility.

Prerogative powers and constitutional conventions have important attributes in common. Their prominence is integral to the British constitutional heritage of "pragmatic empiricism"[55]—the idea that constitutional practice should evolve slowly, accommodating traditional forms and embodying an experience-based, "common-sense" approach to constitutional decision-making. Both types of constitutional doctrine tend to be executive-friendly, permitting central government considerable latitude in problem-solving without attracting close legal oversight or triggering constitutional crisis. By the same token, both types of doctrine tend to confound or discourage attempts to impose a comprehensive and self-contained statutory design upon any particular sphere of constitutional regulation. Whether this is an appropriate legacy for the regulation of modern policing is a subject to which we will have occasion to return.[56]

---

[53] See chapter two

[54] Now consolidated as the Police Act 1996. See chapters three and four.

[55] McCrudden (1994), p. 325.

[56] With particular regard to the doctrine of constabulary independence. See especially chapter two below.

(iii) Constitutional Principle

It is a matter of some academic dispute whether or not fundamental constitutional principles exist within our law, and, if so, what status attaches to them. If we think of principles as axiomatic norms which guide and inform the more specific rules and doctrines of the Constitution, then the obvious answer is that U.K. law recognises no such animal. We have already seen how the strict doctrine of the sovereignty of Parliament renders impossible the enactment of a higher law restricting what the Queen-in-Parliament may promulgate as legislation. By extension, Parliamentary sovereignty would seem to exclude the possibility of any other type of rule internal to the constitutional order performing a similar role.[57]

Yet some take a less positivist view of the British constitution. From an alternative perspective, the constitution already includes a framework of principles, or at least certain background presuppositions. Indeed, much theoretically fertile and practically suggestive work has been carried out in recent years by commentators, both academic[58] and judicial,[59] seeking to expound and defend a version of this unwritten constitution of principle. For all the rich inventiveness of these contributions, however, it remains difficult to ascribe a definite value to constitutional principles as an ingredient of our constitutional law. Opinions differ as to their justification, source, content and status. For some they are justified in terms of immanent claims and expectations within the constitutional culture,[60] while for others they are defended as general norms of good government.[61] For some, the source of constitutional principles is the judges themselves,[62] for others it may be in the publications of government departments or the pronouncements of parliamentary officers or committees,[63] while for others still it may be in no particular office, but in the objective terms and conditions of the "common-law constitution"[64]. For some the content of these principles may be fairly well-grounded, for example, in rules of central-local government relations,[65]

---

[57] For a robust defence of this position, see Brazier (1992).
[58] See *e.g.*, Elliot (1981); Prosser (1982); McAuslan and McEldowney (1985); Harden and Lewis (1986); Daintith (1991); Harden (1991); Allen (1993).
[59] See *e.g.*, Laws (1993), (1995), (1998); Sedley (1995); Browne-Wilkinson (1992).
[60] See *e.g.*, Harden and Lewis (1986) p. 10.
[61] See *e.g.*, McAuslan and McEldowney (1985) p. 7.
[62] See *e.g.*, Laws (1995), pp. 92–93.
[63] See *e.g.*, Daintith (1991) p. 61.
[64] See *e.g.*, Allen, (1993) ch.1.
[65] See *e.g.*, Elliot (1981).

or of good administration,[66] or for the conduct of public expenditure[67]; for others, they may refer to more abstract values, such as open and accountable government,[68] limited government,[69] freedom of thought and expression,[70] and even democracy itself.[71] For some, such principles are fundamental and unalterable,[72] for others they may be altered by the courts,[73] while for others still they remain in an embryonic state, requiring further refinement before they acquire the status of mature constitutional norms.[74]

If the exponents of constitutional principles cannot agree amongst themselves on these matters, they are unlikely to convince those who are more broadly sceptical of this alternative view. This does not mean, however, that we should entirely discount them in a discussion of a substantive topic of constitutional law such as policing. In the first place, apart from the broader question of the moral justification of our constitutional order, one of the reasons why the idea of constitutional principles has such broad appeal is that it appears to offer a more satisfactory explanation for certain specific features of public law than can be provided from a positivist starting point. Presumptions of statutory interpretation offer a particularly instructive example. A statute is presumed, in the absence of clear words, not to deprive someone of property without compensation, not to impose a tax, nor—to cite two examples more relevant to policing—to exclude the jurisdiction of the courts, or to enact retrospective legislation. On one view, such principles reinforce parliamentary sovereignty, the presumptions merely reflecting the background parliamentary intention. On another view, this is a legal fiction, and these presumptions instead represent a shared constitutional morality—a minimum floor of principle on which the vast edifice of statute law is built.[75]

In the second place, and of greater topical significance, constitutional principles may figure significantly in schemes for constitutional reform.

---

[66] See e.g. Daintith (1991) p. 51.
[67] ibid. pp. 51–52.
[68] See e.g., Harden and Lewis (1986) p. 9.
[69] See e.g. McAuslan and McEldowney (1985) p. 8.
[70] See e.g. Laws (1995), p. 84.
[71] See e.g. Harden (1991) p. 503.
[72] ibid. p. 504.
[73] See e.g. Allen (1993) ch.3.
[74] See e.g. Daintith (1991) p. 52.
[75] Mitchell, for instance, argues that such presumptions of interpretation "indicate the broad acceptance in normal times of general and fundamental constitutional ideas, which were once translated in theory, but not in practice, into restrictions upon Parliament in the name of natural law, or other names". (1968) p. 66.

Even those who doubt their existing credentials may find room for the articulation of general constitutional principles within a new constitutional settlement.[76] Norms such as those governing central-local relations and open and accountable government have an obvious relevance to policing. We return to a fuller examination of the importance of principle in the final chapter.

(iv) Constitutional Technique

A final broad constitutional influence on the regulation of policing is represented by developments in constitutional technique. Unlike the other cases, the capacity of constitutional technique to exercise a pervasive influence does not depend upon structural arrangements or general rules and principles *within* the constitutional order. Rather, it is due to the systematic effect upon constitutional law and practice of wider political doctrine and programmes and broader trends in statecraft.

The key word is "systematic". Although all public policy initiatives presuppose a particular constitutional context and may be shaped more or less explicitly to suit that context, the causal relationship tends to be one way. Many such initiatives do little or nothing to alter the wider constitutional order, and of those which do make an impact in constitutional terms, it is important to distinguish between these consequences which are discrete, and those which strike a more general chord. For example, every section of every statute which addresses civil liberties, whether concerned with public order, data protection, official secrecy or anti-terrorist measures, may be characterised as having constitutional implications, in the sense that it alters, however minutely, the balance of power between individual and state. Beyond the morass of detail, however, it is arguable that at least some of these changes contribute to and reflect a broader trend, such as a general erosion of personal rights and freedoms, or a reduction of the categories to whom they are applicable.[77]

This is one type of systematic effect, albeit one the identification of which requires both a high level of abstraction from the minutiae of the law, and the adoption of a perspective which may be vigorously disputed by other constitution-watchers. Changes in constitutional technique involve a rather different type of systematic effect, more closely grounded

---

[76] See *e.g.* Brazier (1992),pp. 283–287.

[77] An argument made about constitutional developments under Margaret Thatcher's three Conservative administrations by Ewing and Gearty (1990).

in everyday constitutional practice. What we are here concerned with are those parts of a political programme or philosophy which refer, in a reflexive manner, to the very foundations and mechanisms of state power and public authority. The political theory underpinning any particular programme of social and economic policies often suggests answers to some of the key questions which exercise constitutional analysts. These include the proper allocation of power between public and private domains, and, relatedly, between state and market; the internal structure of the state, including the degree and forms of central direction, and the use of "quasi-market" methods; the meaning and weight given to the principle of democracy, including the relationship between its component concepts such as participation, representation and responsiveness, and between these and other values in public administration such as efficiency and expertise.

New answers to these questions profoundly transformed constitutional technique after 1979, when the Conservatives embarked upon the longest unbroken spell of government of the 20th century.[78] The economic liberalism of the New Right spawned a "new public management"[79]; and in turn, a "new public sector vocabulary" including themes such as "privatisation, contracting-out, market-testing, internal markets, enabling authorities, prior options, and so on"[80]. Alongside this discourse, a parallel language with a more explicitly constitutional tone has developed which reflects changing institutions and methods of government. FMI, Next Steps, Citizen's Charter, quangocracy, the skeletal state, government by contract, government by audit; these are some of the ideas and initiatives around which the new constitutional technique has evolved.[81] These trends have had profound implications for the regulation of policing, particularly in more recent years, and are explored in some depth in our discussion of the contemporary history of British policing in chapters three and four.

(B) The Regulation of Policing

While matters of constitutional form and broader patterns of constitutional doctrine, principle and technique provide important, and often

---

[78] Se *e.g.* Daintith (1991).
[79] See *e.g.* Hood (1991); Rhodes (1997)
[80] Drewry (1994) p. 156.
[81] See *e.g.* Harden (1992); Oliver (1999); Freedland (1999).

neglected background factors, the most significant constitutional influence upon policing is clearly the body of legal rules which bears directly and exclusively upon police institutions and practices. This body of rules may be dissected and analysed in any number of ways, but for introductory purposes it is useful to examine the manner in which it addresses the following basic issues. First, what different *types* of police practice does it recognise, and what distinguishes its treatment of one type from another? Secondly, how does it define the *scope* of policing? Thirdly, what basic *organisational structure* does it provide for? Fourthly, what *regulatory strategy* does it embody? Fifthly, what *techniques of enforcement* does it provide for or presuppose? We shall consider each of these in turn.

(i) Types of Police Practice

In order to identify the basic pattern of regulation of the general range of police practices, we first need criteria for distinguishing the various main types of practice. Reiner has developed a typology which groups police decisions according to whether they relate, first, to general policy or individual cases, and, secondly, to law enforcement or internal organisational matters.[82] Variation along these two dimensions produces a matrix of four different types of police decision. Matters of general policing style refer to the broad law enforcement policies pursued by the police organisation. As Lustgarten argues, these may include the fundamental method of policing—reactive or community-based, hard or soft, etc., the functional or territorial pattern of deployment of manpower, and the emphasis given to particular offences.[83] The focus of law enforcement at the individual level, for Reiner, is the decision to use or not to use legal powers such as stop and search, detention or arrest. As regards internal organisational matters, he distinguishes between house-keeping decisions and personnel management decisions. House-keeping decisions relate to internal organisational policy, and include matters as diverse as controls on petrol consumption and policy concerning the acquisition of weaponry and other resources. On the other hand, personnel management decisions relate to individual officers, and concern issues such as career development, redeployment and discipline.

Reiner's typology provides a useful conceptual tool, with three caveats. In the first place, his typology would be more complete if, as the heading

---

[82] Reiner (1993), pp. 6–13.
[83] Lustgarten (1986), pp. 19–20.

of the present sub-section suggests, it applied to police practices in the round, and not only to police decisions. The law is, and ought to be, just as concerned with non-decisions or omissions, and with the unintended, and often quite remote, consequences of decisions, as with decisions themselves. For example, the question of the liability of a police officer in tort or delict for negligence may concern aspects or consequences of conduct, such as failure over a protracted period to detect an offender[84] or arrest a suspect,[85] which are not aptly described as the subject-matter of a specific decision. Equally, internal disciplinary offences, such as conduct likely to bring discredit on the police force, or incivility towards a member of the public, need not necessarily be tied to a discrete decision, but may arise out of the general flow of operational practice.

Secondly, as Reiner readily acknowledges,[86] these various types of practice cannot be sealed off from one another. Policy decisions, whether of the law enforcement or the house-keeping variety, may have an impact on concrete operational incidents. For example, the general policing style or method adopted can affect the number and distribution of stop and searches, the availability of a particular piece of equipment can affect detection techniques, and the targeting of a particular crime or the weight of deployment in a particular neighbourhood can affect the likelihood of arrest in specific cases. Conversely, in matters where there is no or little explicit policy direction or where such guidance is ignored or qualified in practice, the pattern of individual actions and decisions can amount to a *de facto* policy. There is also a close connection between law enforcement and organisational matters at both policy and individual levels. At the policy level, house-keeping decisions about the purchase of equipment, shift patterns, opening hours for substations, etc., provide a framework which influences the formation and impact of law enforcement policy. At the individual level, career development may depend upon operational performance, and may be blighted by operational misconduct. For example, under section 67 of the Police and Criminal Evidence Act 1984, failure to comply with the Codes of Practice regulating stop and search, search and seizure, detention and questioning of suspects, identification parades and tape-recording of interviews, all of which are incidental to law enforcement, constitutes an offence under the Discipline Code—an instrument of personnel policy,

---

[84] *Hill v. Chief Constable of West Yorkshire* [1989] A.C. 53.
[85] *Osman v. Ferguson* [1993] 4 All E.R. 344; [1998] 5 B.H.R.C. 293. See further chapter four.
[86] Reiner (1993) p. 7; see also Lustgarten (1986) pp. 20–22.

which, while having legal status, is in the main applied and adjudicated upon within the organisation.

Thirdly, not only are policy and operational practices mutually influential, but the boundary between them is hazy. There is no precise level of abstraction at which a decision or practice crosses the operational divide and becomes a matter of policy. The policy/operational distinction is best viewed, not as a dichotomy, but as a spectrum of possibilities, with a large category of intermediate decisions or practices *more or less* about operations or policy. Take, for example, the case of a policy decision by a chief constable to reduce police numbers in the city centre in order to re-open suburban police stations in the evenings. Such a decision would inform and constrain the options available to the city centre area commander or control-room operator when deploying officers to particular incidents. For instance, if officers were required simultaneously to respond to a fight in a pub and attend a domestic dispute, hard choices about the level and priority of allocation of scarce resources might have to be made. In turn, these hard choices would inform and constrain the on-the-spot operational decision of the officers actually deployed to the two incidents. For example, although much of course depends upon the precise circumstances, a speedy and high-level deployment might make identification of suspects, corroboration and arrest a more likely option in either case, while a slower and more limited deployment would more likely lead to more modest forms of containment, mediation etc. Within this decision-making chain, while the decision of the chief constable is clearly located at the policy end of the spectrum and those of the officers attending the two incidents are clearly located at the operational end of the spectrum (although, in line with our previous analysis, the operational decision is ultimately influenced by the policy decision), the deployment decision by the area commander is located at an intermediate point; it both allows considerable scope for policy choice and carries fairly immediate implications for concrete operational decisions affecting individual members of the public.

As we shall see in later chapters,[87] these interconnections and overlaps place severe obstacles before any attempt to use the policy/operational distinction to coherent effect when crafting the rules of police governance. In turn, this has traditionally encouraged the polarisation of the debate between, on the one hand, those who wish to defend the "operational" independence of the police professional, and who feel

---

[87] See especially chapters two, four, seven and ten.

justified in defining the operational domain expansively, and on the other, those who wish to assert the "policy" prerogative of the politicians, and who feel equally justified in defining the policy domain expansively. Yet even if the policy/operational distinction is a difficult one to apply for normative purposes—and I will argue that this difficulty can be overstated—the analytical value of Reiner's scheme remains. Indeed one of its benefits is precisely to demonstrate the complex interplay of the different dimensions of policework. This is a consideration to which we return shortly below, but first, and more fundamentally, we focus on the way in which his typology helps to illuminate the limited and differentiated role of law as a means of shaping policing.

To begin with, the typology highlights the restricted reach of the law. Insofar as rules have a bearing on internal organisational matters, they tend, with the notable exception of the Discipline Code, not to be legal rules. Police organisations, like all other bureaucratic organisations, have their own internal rule-books—Force Standing Orders, Force Memoranda, etc., which establish how various housekeeping decisions are taken and who takes them, and which regulate matters of personnel management—often in fine detail, as in the case of staff appraisal and counselling schemes. On the other hand, the law clearly has a prominent role in the law enforcement domain, both at the policy and the individual operational level. Even here, however, it is by no means exclusive, as the internal rule-book also contains a vast array of standard operating rules stipulating what procedures individual officers should follow across the range of operational situations—from completing arrest forms to reporting serious incidents to a superior officer of a particular rank.

Secondly, where law does have a role, it is not always one of direct regulation, although this does not make its contribution any less important. This is illustrated by the manner in which Reiner's category of general law enforcement policy is addressed by the law. As we shall see in chapter two, one of the most important insights of the recent literature on police governance has been to demonstrate how the prominence of the doctrine of constabulary independence, with its accent on the legal autonomy of each individual constable, has tended to obscure awareness of the different types of decision-making which occur in policing, so contributing to a general understatement of the law's regulatory potential in the debate about how law enforcement policy is and ought to be made.[88] The law does not and

---

[88] See *e.g.*, Reiner (1993) pp. 8–10; Jefferson and Grimshaw (1984) chaps.2–4; Grimshaw and Jefferson (1987) ch.1; Bradley, Walter and Wilkie (1986) chap.4; Brogden, Jefferson and Walklate (1988) ch.7; Goldsmith (1990).

should not seek to direct law enforcement policy, but it has a vital indirect and facultative role to play in setting out the mechanisms of policy-making and policy-monitoring and in establishing the internal structure and powers of the agencies involved.

Evidently, therefore, the role of law in regulating policing is complex, diverse[89] and restricted, themes which we explore further below in our discussion of regulatory strategies and enforcement techniques. But the themes of complexity and diversity in particular suggest some further broad conclusions. On the one hand, they highlight the need for the regulation of policework to be treated in a holistic manner, with an awareness of how one part of the package can affect the others. We try to be sensitive to this need throughout the book. On the other hand, law's deep complexity and broad diversity obliges us in a book of limited length to concentrate on those parts of the law which are of primary significance in the constitutional ordering of policing. Again Reiner's scheme is useful, for while it suggests an element of mutual causality between the different spheres of activity and of regulation, it clearly identifies the level of general law enforcement policy as the major influence in shaping the overall pattern of contemporary policing. Accordingly, while we pay attention to some aspects of individual liability in tort in our discussion of contemporary trends in chapter four, the reader will have to look to one or more of a number of other more specialist sources for a comprehensive treatment of the law relating to individual police powers and misconduct.[90] Our emphasis instead is upon the mechanisms and agencies of policy-making and policy-monitoring over the broad, and ever-broadening range of policing activities.

(ii) The Scope of Policing

As one commentator has remarked, "[had] one asked the question "who polices" 20 years ago, one would have been met with blank incomprehension by British police and public alike"[91]. Until recently, it was mistakenly assumed that the public police, more particularly the local territorial police under the general regulatory umbrella of the Home Office or equivalent department in the devolved nation and regions,

---

[89] For a seminal comparative and theoretical analysis of the diverse modes and functions of law in policing, see Dixon (1997).

[90] For England and Wales, see, *e.g.*, Lidstone and Palmer (1995); Reiner and Leigh (1994). For Scotland, see, *e.g.*, Ewing and Finnie (1988) chap.3; Murdoch (1995).

[91] Johnston (1993) p. 772.

exercised a monopoly over the policing function, and the dearth of scholarly research on other forms of policing suggested that this view was also widespread in academic circles. A combination of changing macro-economic conditions, commercial practices, cultural patterns and government attitudes has meant that considerable expansion of the non-Home Office sector has since taken place. These developments have attracted the attention of students of policing, and in so doing have also stimulated their awareness of and interest in those non-public parts of the policing enterprise which are of an older vintage.

The non-Home Office forces include, on the public side of the fence, specialist nationalist forces, police sections of broader public organisations and municipal policing; and on the private side of the fence, they include various forms of commercial policing and a similarly diverse pattern of voluntary self-policing or civil policing.[92] In chapter nine, we look at the development and constitutional grounding of these activities in some depth. For now, it is sufficient to indicate that given the diversity of forms of policing, the extent to which policing activity is legally recognised as such assumes great significance. As noted earlier, the law both enables and constrains policing activity. In the paradigm case of Home Office policing, a particular range of powers is granted to police officers and a particular structure of controls is imposed, including individual controls and a framework of public accountability. Beyond the writ of Home Office policing, policing activities may take place without some or all aspects of the regulatory framework deemed appropriate in the former case, which begs the question whether and on what grounds such divergence is justifiable. The law, by setting the institutional boundaries of the public police where it does, makes an implicit but resonant judgment about the level of recognition which different modes of policing deserve and the degree and quality of supervision and control they require.

(iii) The Organisational Structure of Policing

The constitutional framework of policing not only defines the institutional limits of policing, but also dictates the internal structure of that institution. Although localism is still commonly assumed to be one of the key enduring traits of the British police, it is instructive to note that under

---

[92] See in particular, Johnston (1992b), (1993), (1995), (2000) chaps. 8–9; Jones and Newburn (1998).

Bailey's comparative scheme of classification, the U.K. system is only moderately decentralised.[93] Compared to the United States which can boast around 2,500 forces, or—to confine ourselves to European comparisons—Belgium with approximately 250 forces, the United Kingdom with only 52 territorial police forces exhibits a relatively closely integrated policing system. Moreover, as we explain in chapters two and three, the secular trend has been towards greater centralisation, a movement strongly reinforced by the legislative reforms of the 1990s.

Why does the degree of centralisation of the policing system matter? On the one hand, it is arguable that any modern policing system requires certain devices of central control and co-ordination. There are financial, logistical, operational and political reasons for this.[94] The provision of central services in matters such as training, information technology and forensic science facilities produces economies of scale and avoids duplication of effort by   smaller units. Common radio and computer systems facilitate the co-ordination of effort between different territorial or functional units. National, or even supranational, operational units or initiatives may be required to tackle crime which is national or international in its organisation or implications—including terrorism, money-laundering and drug-trafficking. Even in the case of predominantly local crime, a degree of central direction allows for the pooling of operational knowledge and the dissemination of good practice. Last, but by no means least, central influence can provide political balance. By monitoring the activities of local units, it can provide a check against corruption or partisanship or against an undue populism which disregards the interests of local minorities. On the other hand, as the 1962 Royal Commission on the Police recognised,[95] localism has a number of virtues. Just as central organisation and influence can check local excesses, so local organisation and influence can resist centripetal forces. Localism also has democratic advantages. The grant of influence to local bodies allows for the wider involvement of citizens in public life. It also enhances the prospects of decisions being taken which reflect local needs and conditions.

The degree of centralisation of the police, therefore, is a significant structural feature, but one which warrants careful evaluation. Neither centralism nor localism is an unqualified good; rather, a careful balancing of the two is required. Moreover, the degree of centralisation is only

---

[93] Bailey (1985) p. 59.
[94] Reiner and Spencer (1993) pp. 183–186.
[95] Royal Commission on the Police, (1962). Although a dissenting memorandum by Dr A.L. Goodhart did advocate the creation of a national force; *ibid.* pp. 157–179

one factor bearing upon the overall character of policing within a society. Bayley has argued persuasively that although centralisation is influenced by wider social and political factors—in particular that traditions of centralisation are linked to violent resistance in the phase of state formation, centralisation is not itself a determinant of the character of the contemporary political regime, but is compatible with more or less authoritarian or liberal political systems.[96] Nor is there evidence to suggest that centralisation *per se* is a determinant of other important outcomes, such as the degree of legitimacy or effectiveness of the police—however measured.

One reason for this is the intervention of other structural variables. Within the category of centralised police structures, Bayley distinguishes between single systems, such as Ireland or Poland, and multiple systems, such as France or Finland.[97] Arguably, the existence of more than one national system of policing has some of the same effects in dispersing power and diversifying influence as does decentralisation.[98] France and Finland are also examples of co-ordinated systems, where one force has sole or predominant jurisdiction over any area. Bayley draws a further distinction between these and multiple uncoordinated systems, such as Italy or Belgium, where there is substantial overlapping of authority between the various forces.[99] Joint jurisdiction may offer a further safeguard against the over-concentration of power.[1] A final general structural feature bearing upon the distribution of authority within the policing system is the career structure. Whereas the British police has a single-tier entry system, the continental model favours a two-tier system of commissioned officers and ordinary recruits. The existence of two internal constituencies separated by education, training, experience, current responsibilities and career prospects, may provide a further antidote to the development of a monolithic power structure.[2]

Even with these embellishments, structure remains of limited independent significance. In the final analysis, the structural organisation of the police is only one matter addressed within the overall regulatory

---

[96] Bayley (1985) chaps. 3 and 8.

[97] *ibid.* pp. 53–59.

[98] Journes (1993) p. 287

[99] Bayley (1985) pp. 57–60.

[1] For instance, the fact that in Italy the Carabinieri and the Guardia have joint jurisdiction everywhere is seen by some Italians as a safeguard of freedom. See Bayley (1985) p. 657; Barzini, (1964) pp. 215–216. 91; Journes, (1993) p. 287.

[2] Although the importance of the two-tier entry system as a factor contributing to this cultural division should not be overstated See n.27 below.

strategy or policing. It is to discussion of this underlying strategy that we now turn.

(iv) Regulatory Strategy

Of course, the idea that within any jurisdiction there is in place a single coherent strategy for the regulation of policing overstates the rationality of the legal system. The development of the law in this area, as elsewhere, is a political process, involving competition between competing visions and interests. Positions may be internally incoherent. Equally, the compromises struck between different positions may reflect their mutual incoherence. Legal change may also be incremental and opportunistic, not clearly linked to any underlying big idea. Even when a government has a comprehensive long-term project which informs its legislative programme, as was arguably the case with the Conservatives under Margaret Thatcher,[3] there is little prospect of the wholesale transformation of any particular area of law in accordance with that project. Rather, successive generations are more likely to graft their own particular contribution onto a legal edifice which retains elements inspired by quite different approaches.

Nevertheless, it is possible to pose a number of questions the answers to which may supply the general outline of a regulatory strategy, insofar as one exists, and also highlight its main tensions and inconsistencies. One set of questions concerns the range of the agencies involved in the regulatory network. A second concerns the nature of the power relations between these agencies. A third concerns the underlying purpose or purposes of regulation.

Institutional architecture

It is received wisdom within both the professional and the academic community that the general pattern of the regulatory network governing policing in the United Kingdom is defined by the so-called tripartite structure—the triangular relationship between chief constable, Home Office (or devolved equivalent) and local police authority. Since the end of the nineteenth century the powers and duties of these three agencies *inter se* have been central to the system of police governance. This remains the case, as in reflected in the organisation of Parts I and II of

---

[3] See Daintith (1991).

the book. However, note should be taken of various trends which modify the significance of the tripartite structure.

In the first place, the centrality of the tripartite structure rather depends upon that other shaky pillar of received wisdom about British policing—the predominant role of the Home Office police.[4] In the expanding non-Home Office sectors, the tripartite structure is less firmly established. Local government is marginalized in specialist national policing, central government is marginalized in municipal policing, while neither level of government exerts a significant influence over private security or self-policing activities.[5] In the second place, even within the Home Office realm, the drift towards national policing initiatives, both through the emergence of new agencies, such as the National Criminal Intelligence Service and the National Crime Squad, and through the expansion into general policing services of old agencies such as the security and intelligence services, has taken place with uneven reference to the tripartite template.[6]

Yet while the tripartite structure has been marginalized in some areas of policing in recent years, it has also been supplemented by the development of other supervisory agencies. For example, the Police Complaints Authority for England and Wales[7] and the Police Ombudsman for Northern Ireland[8] are two bodies which are more closely involved in the oversight of individual police behaviour than either central government or the local police authority, and which are unassociated with any of the traditional power centres within the tripartite structure. On the other hand, the strengthening of the role of the Inspectorate of Constabulary and the expansion of the remit of the Audit Commission illustrate the development of new efficiency controls on the part of agencies associated with central government[9] Likewise, the emergence of local consultative committees demonstrates new forms of involvement in police governance at the local level.[10] Indeed, if, as some have suggested, tripartitism is conceived of as a broad arrangement involving central and local government generally rather than a narrow arrangement involving particular institutions of

---

[4] See section 2(B)(ii) above.
[5] See chapter nine
[6] See chapter seven
[7] See chapter four.
[8] See chapter six.
[9] See chapters three and four.
[10] See chapters three and four.

local and central government,[11] these types of development may be seen as reinforcing rather than qualifying the general pattern. Whichever way recent trends are interpreted, however, it is clear enough that tripartitism continues to describe the basic outline but not the detailed contours of the police regulatory map.

Accountability relationships

What of the balance of power within the qualified tripartite structure? Accountability is the main currency of political power relations in a representative democracy, as it addresses the key question of the manner in which agencies that are given responsibility for performing certain functions on behalf of their fellow citizens, such as the police, are made answerable for their performance to those fellow citizens.[12] Accordingly, although we warned in the preface against the tendency to reduce all constitutional questions of police governance to the issue of accountability, it is neither surprising nor inappropriate that most discussion of this aspect of the regulatory approach tends to be couched in the language of accountability.

Morgan usefully distinguishes between three different models of accountability in terms of the degree of autonomy allowed to the chief constable and the manner in which influence may be exercised by the accountees.[13] The chief constable is most autonomous under the *stewardship* model. As a steward, he is delegated general responsibility for policing but is expected to provide a full explanatory account of his activities to the accountee, and is required to have his performance audited against a set of predetermined general standards. In particular, he must satisfy the accountee that his delegated functions are being carried out honestly and competently. The ends towards which the steward ought to be working are treated as self-evident and uncontroversial. At the other end of the spectrum is the *directive* model. Here control over policy ends, which are viewed as contentious, remains firmly in the hands of the local and/or

---

[11] See, for example, Oliver (1987) p. 12. The broader definition also tended to be used by Conservative Home Secretaries of the reform period of the early 1990s, in particular Kenneth Clarke and Michael Howard, when discussing the institutional redesign of policing. See chapters three and four.

[12] Day and Klein (1987), pp. 6–7.

[13] Morgan (1985), pp. 7–9. Morgan's scheme builds upon Marshall's earlier analysis, with the stewardship model closely based upon the "explanatory and co-operative style" and the directive model closely based upon the "subordinate and obedient" style (Marshall (1978), pp. 61–63). However, Morgan's identification of three basic models within his typology provides a more sensitive overall explanatory framework.

central democratic element. The main purpose of giving account is prospective rather than retrospective. It enables the accountee to engage in an informed evaluation and, where necessary, redirection of policy, rather than merely to sanction past performance. Between these two poles lies the *partner* model. The theme here is one of dialogue and negotiation between accountor and accountee. The flow of information is two-way and emphasis is placed on the joint resolution of policy objectives, which again may be contentious.

As is true of regulatory strategy more broadly, the accountability arrangements which apply in a particular system are unlikely to conform neatly to any particular model. In the United Kingdom, the stewardship model is perceived by many as depicting most closely the actual state of affairs.[14] However, signs of the partner model may be present in initiatives such as Consultative Committees and the new joint planning framework. Alternatively, the strong role of central government within that planning framework, together with other additions to its legal arsenal, might suggests the growing prominence of the directive model.[15] The models, therefore, are merely ideal types, but they remain useful as an indicator of the predominant strategic pattern underpinning any particular set of accountability arrangements and as a means of identifying and exploring divergent elements within these arrangements.

Morgan's typology, however, can only tell us so much about power relations within the tripartite system. Within each type, there may be significant variations of emphasis. Additionally, other variables such as those associated with police organisational structure,[16] may affect the operation of all types. Moreover, in its basic form, Morgan's approach is blind to the distinction between central and local levels of government. The key issue addressed by his model is professional independence versus democratic control, but democratic control is itself a fiercely contested prize. As the trend within the tripartite relationship towards greater power at the centre and declining power at the local level illustrates, it is quite possible for democracy to be enhanced at one level while it is reduced at the other; indeed, there may be a direct causal link between the two processes. Accordingly, while Morgan's scheme provides an important point of departure in our discussions of accountability, it requires to be supplemented by other concepts and categories.

---

[14] See *e.g.* Morgan (1985) p. 7; Bradley *et al* (1986) ch.4; Brogden, Jefferson and Walklak (1988) chaps 7–8.

[15] See chapter four.

[16] See section 2(B)(iii) above.

Underlying purposes

The third, and most fundamental level of analysis of regulatory strategy concerns the underlying purposes of regulation. A regulatory strategy may seek to achieve three different types of objectives, which vary in accordance with the extent to which they may be abstracted from the activity regulated.[17] At the most abstract level, it may seek to achieve objectives or uphold values which have a wider significance than the activity which is the immediate object of regulation. In particular, its aim may be to further certain values associated with a democratic polity, such as participation or responsiveness to public needs, because these are believed to be worthwhile ends in themselves, regardless of the specific object of regulation.[18] At the intermediate level, it may seek to influence the outcomes of the activity regulated in accordance with certain general standards and without reference to the substantive ends of that activity. For instance, it may typically aim to secure the effectiveness and efficiency of the regulated activity, or the equitable treatment of those affected by the activity.[19] Finally, and most concretely, it may seek to shape the ends of the regulated activity.

There are clear links between these different levels of strategic purpose. Particular regulatory features may advance purposes at more than one level simultaneously. For example, the emphasis upon police responsiveness to local and central government within the tripartite structure both serves democratic purposes and may contribute to overall effectiveness. This is so because it is axiomatic to the doctrine of policing by consent that the police require a steady flow of information from all sections of the public in order to achieve acceptable standards of performance in preventing and detecting crime; that this information flow depends upon mutual trust, and that this is at least partly dependent upon public confidence that the police are democratically answerable for their actions.[20] Another example of linkage is the recent promotion of a more exacting performance culture through the technique of monitoring police practice against pre-established measurable indicators.[21] At one level, this is a way of ensuring responsiveness to the democratic will of central

---

[17] For a sophisticated analysis of different tiers of values targeted by regulatory procedures, see Galligan (1996).

[18] For detailed exploration of the relationship between policing and democracy, see Jones, Newburn and Smith (1994).

[19] For analysis of these intermediate variables, see Baldwin (1987).

[20] See *e.g.* Kinsey, Lea and Young (1986) chap.6; see further, chapter four, section 3(B).

[21] See chapters three and four.

government and its agents. At the most concrete level, however, it is arguable that it may also directly affect the substantive ends towards which policework is directed, as the emphasis on measurable outputs favours those activities, such as crime detection, which are amenable to quantifiable analysis, over more intangible objectives, such as providing public reassurance as to the security of the neighbourhood.[22]

In some instances, strategic purposes at different levels may appear to be in tension with one another. To return to the relationship between democracy and effectiveness, for example, many would argue that external consultation and supervision can lead to undue interference with professional expertise and inadequate security of sensitive information, both of which are prerequisite to high standards of performance. Similarly, some forms of democratic involvement in policing may be criticised for undermining the commitment to equitable standards of treatment and service in the name of popular control.[23]

What general conclusions can we draw about the relative priority given to these various purposes in the development of the constitutional framework for policing in recent years? It is undoubtedly the case that the main debate has revolved around the relationship between the high-level democratic values and the intermediate concerns with effectiveness, efficiency and equity. Moreover, although, as pointed out earlier, it would be unwise to make strong claims about the coherence and integrity of purpose underpinning the police regulatory system, it would appear that the present statutory regime, with its emphasis upon the stewardship model, tends to accentuate the significance of the intermediate concerns. Democratic values are also firmly inscribed in the system, but there is a tendency—underlined by recent reforms[24]—to justify them primarily in instrumental terms, particularly as ways of bolstering effectiveness and efficiency. The emphasis upon intermediate concerns is still further highlighted by the absence of explicit concern with the regulation of substantive ends. Nevertheless, regulation at the higher levels undoubtedly affects indirectly the choice and pursuit of particular policing policies, a set of influences which, as indicated above, has been reinforced by recent developments.

We shall return to this debate about the fundamentals of regulatory strategy at various points throughout the book. For now, we can sum up the rudiments of the existing regulatory strategy. It is based upon a tri-

---

[22] See Waddington (1999) chap.8.
[23] See for example, Jones, Newburn and Smith (1994) chap.l; Oliver, (1987);(1997).
[24] See chapter four.

partite institutional structure, although there are a number of significant elaborations and qualifications to this design; it favours the stewardship model of accountability, although again with qualifications, particularly in respect of the growing power of central government; and finally it is underpinned by a philosophy which seeks a pragmatic balance between democratic values and the more grounded virtues of effectiveness, efficiency and equity of treatment and service.

(v) Techniques of Enforcement

It is generally the case that rule-makers give insufficient attention to matters of enforcement.[25] In the prevalent culture of legal instrumentalism,[26] law is often viewed as a tool of social engineering of limitless versatility and enforcement is treated as unproblematic. This very attitude is one of the reasons why implementation failure is so rife. Like many of the subjects of public law, the police operate within large and complex organisations. Even if the willingness of the higher echelons to conform to the letter and intention of the law could be guaranteed, the obedience of their juniors could not. Many commentators have documented the cultural heterogeneity of the police, particularly the "schism" between senior management and the rank-and-file—a phenomenon which is by no means restricted to two-tier entry systems.[27] Furthermore, in an operational context dominated by dispersed patrol-work and instant decision-making, those junior officers minded to do things their own way have plenty of opportunity so to do. Yet there appears to be little appreciation of this within political discourse on regulation, and little attempt to anticipate and counter the problems which might arise.

For example, the stewardship model of accountability is highly dependent upon the supply of information to the accountee in order for monitoring to work effectively; but how is the accuracy and comprehensiveness of the information to be ensured? The directive model, and, to a lesser extent the partner model,[28] challenges the professional autonomy of all ranks, and so may be resisted within the constabulary; but how, therefore, are we to ensure that the democratic will is not subverted?

---

[25] See Baldwin (1994), p. 173.

[26] See Cotterrell (1992).

[27] For example, the gap between rank-and-file culture and management culture reported in the single-tier British system (Holdaway, 1983; Walker 1994a), would appear to be no less significant than that reported in the two-tier Dutch system (Punch, 1983).

[28] But see chapter four, section 3(B).

It could be argued that the growing emphasis upon a measurable performance culture[29] does attempt to tackle the problem of monitoring compliance, but this merely highlights another difficulty associated with the design of effective enforcement techniques; that is to say, the options available are constrained by, and in turn constrain, the broader regulatory strategy. Thus, the use of performance indicators is premised upon a particular model of police effectiveness as well as a particular enforcement strategy. It is impossible to have one without the other.

Accordingly, if we aim to subject the proposition with which we opened this chapter to serious examination, then as we engage more deeply with the various aspects of the constitutional regulation of policing in the pages that follow we must remain vigilant as to the implications of regulatory choice for questions of implementation. An analysis which begins with questions of enforceability is likely to err on the side of prudence, unable to conceive of any viable constitutional framework other than one which runs with the grain of dominant interests. On the other hand, an analysis which does not end with questions of enforceability threatens to become detached from the realities of enabling and constraining the exercise of public authority, and so to be equally incapable of generating an effective framework of constitutional regulation.

---

[29] See chapters three and four.

Chapter Two

The Foundations of Modern Tripartitism

In the summer of 1993 three major inquiries into policing reported within a few days of each other.[1] Their cumulative effect was to set in train a reform process which would modify significantly the constitutional settlement of the previous 30 years, while retaining some of its fundamental premises and structures. In the present chapter we examine the roots and branches of that long-standing constitutional settlement — paying particular attention to the core idea of constabulary independence, while in the chapter that follows we analyse the social and political pressures that gradually came to challenge it.

1. The Making of a Royal Commission

Most commentators agree that the 1962 Royal Commission on the Police (the Willink Commission)[2] represented a watershed in the development of the constitutional framework for British policing.[3] It was the first Royal Commission to examine the constitutional position of the police for more than 40 years, and almost 40 years later remains the last such body to have done so. Like many Royal Commissions, it was born of the crisis of the moment, but in seeking to alleviate current anxieties it also engaged with matters of more fundamental and long-term significance.

---

[1] Home Office (1993a); (1993b); Royal Commission on Criminal Justice (1993).
[2] Royal Commission (1962).
[3] See *e.g.* Marshall (1965); Reiner (1992a) chap.2; Lustgarten (1986) chap.3

(A) Public Controversy

Immediate public and political concern derived from a series of incidents dating back to the mid-1950s in which policing methods had been controversially exposed and police relations with other constitutional actors had become strained. In 1956, disciplinary proceedings were taken against the Chief Constable of Cardiganshire on the basis of his alleged failure to administer the force properly. In 1957, the Chief Constables of Brighton and Worcester faced criminal charges of corruption and fraud respectively, in the latter case resulting in conviction and imprisonment. In the same year the assault of a youth by a policeman in the Scottish town of Thurso together with allegations that the assault subsequently was not properly investigated by the police led to the establishment of a tribunal of inquiry. In 1959, Captain Popkess, the Chief Constable of Nottingham, was suspended by his local police authority because he refused to provide them with a report into a criminal investigation he had undertaken into allegations concerning a local councillor. Finally, a "Whitehall farce"[4] provided the immediate catalyst for the appointment of the Royal Commission. Brian Rix, a comedy star, had been stopped for speeding by PC Edmond of the Metropolitan Police. A civil servant, Mr Garratt, intervened on behalf of Rix, upon which Garratt and Edmond became embroiled in an argument. Mutual assault allegations followed, and when the Metropolitan Commissioner eventually settled out of court in favour of Garratt, public anxiety was expressed that the Home Secretary had been prepared to make £300 of public money available to finance the settlement and that this settlement was not accompanied by internal disciplinary proceedings against Edmond.

Two factors endowed these incidents with a wider significance. In the first place, they stood out clearly on a rising tide of general public anxiety about policing. While we should be careful not to overestimate the degree of public backing for the new police at any point since its inception in the early nineteenth century, there is evidence to suggest that that oft-quoted sociological phenomenon, the post-war consensus, had in some measure embraced the institutions of policing, so marking the high point in the long struggle to legitimate the coercive apparatus of the state in the eyes of the working classes.[5] The subsequent wavering of public support and confidence in the years immediately prior to the Royal

---

[4] Reiner (1992a) p. 75
[5] See *e.g.* Reiner (1992a) pp. 57–73.

Commission is attributable to two factors. From the mid-1950s onwards, the recorded crime figures began to rise in a steep curve, fuelling fears that the police were no longer competent to fulfil their historical mandate. At the same time, there was a growth in confrontational policing. The flowering of the self-styled youth cultures of the 1950s, the emergence of racial tensions and disturbances in London and the provinces, the rise of political demonstrations of increasing militancy over issues of great sensitivity to the state, including the Suez crisis and the international build-up of nuclear weapons; all of these factors led to a more frequent, intense and visible challenge to the authority of policing, played out before a growing mass-media audience. Each of the *causes celebres* reported above gave eloquent expression to these burgeoning anxieties about effectiveness and legitimate authority.

The incidents in question also served to dramatise the specifically constitutional dimension to the new debate on policing. As the Royal Commission itself explicitly acknowledged, they served to highlight concerns about the adequacy of accountability arrangements for policing, uncertainty surrounding the general constitutional position of the police, and reservations as to the fairness and effectiveness of the method of dealing with complaints against the police.[6] In turn, these concerns were rooted in certain underlying dynamics and unresolved tensions which had marked the history of police governance.

(B) A CONSTITUTIONAL PATCHWORK

The constitutional framework which had evolved since the early nineteenth century to regulate the New Police was a patchwork affair which reflected the gradual and uneven acceptance of the modern policing idea in the United Kingdom. The system of police governance it bequeathed was by no means uniform. Within England and Wales it varied markedly between the London Metropolitan Police, the borough forces and the county police, while Scotland was different again.[7] The distinctive arrangements reflected different — and in each case contested — forms of accommodation between internal and external accountability, and between central and local influence.

Since its inception, the Metropolitan Police had been accountable to the Home Secretary alone, with no role for local government despite

---

[6] Para. 11
[7] See chapter five.

recurrent pressure for local involvement from the late nineteenth century onwards.[8] In the founding legislation, the terms of the relationship between the Home Secretary and the Metropolitan Police Commissioner were uncertain, a state of affairs which the Home Secretary exploited to assert a controlling remit until well into the present century. As regards the borough forces, local government through the agency of the watch committee occupied a position of strength within the framework of governance to rival that of the Home Secretary in London. In contrast, in the counties no organ of government, local or central, exercised a comparable level of influence. Democratic local government took longer to develop in rural areas and the external accountability of the police focused instead on the local judiciary, although through his power to approve appointments and to impose uniform administrative rules, the Home Secretary from the outset wielded more influence than he did in urban areas. Overall, however, the chief police officer was a more powerful and autonomous figure in the counties than in urban England and Wales—metropolitan or provincial.

If these significant historical variations are one sign of unresolved tensions within the project of police governance prior to the 1964 Act, so too are the development of two long–term tendencies which cut across sectoral distinctions. The secular trends in question concern the gradual centralisation of power and the consolidation of the professional autonomy of the local police around the developing concept of constabulary independence.

(C) TOWARDS AN INTEGRATED POLICE SERVICE

The seeds of the centralising movement were evident in the early police legislation and developed significantly as the twentieth century progressed. The powers granted to central government in the nineteenth century, in particular inspection and withdrawal of grant aid,[9] together with other early unifying trends such as the gradual consolidation of forces into larger units, laid the foundations for the assertion of central authority. The First World War and the police strikes which coincided with its end provided the impetus and the opportunity for central government to develop the two related roles which would define its contribution to police governance for the greater part of the century and

---

[8] Lustgarten (1986) p. 36.
[9] County and Borough Police Act 1856.

provide institutional confirmation of the idea of "the police as a service, an integrated system, rather than a collection of separate forces each concerned with its merely local requirements and personnel".[10]

The first such role was that of basic co-ordination of an integrated pattern and process of police governance. It was only in the special circumstances of the First World War, the state primed to combat an external security threat and, internally, concerned to harness the complex of economic, cultural and political forces required to manage, sustain and legitimise a concerted "war effort", that it began to make systematic efforts to nurture a *national* "policy community"[11] with regard to policing. Gradually, through "setting up committees, issuing circulars and holding conferences",[12] the Home Office began to incorporate chief constables, and to a lesser extent the officers and members of local government within a "stable, integrated policy network"[13] in which ideas and information could be exchanged and common lines of policy identified or formulated. Central government's new co-ordinating role was quickly consolidated in the legislation passed in response to the police strikes—the Police Act 1919—with the establishment of the Police Department within the Home Office and of the Police Council as a consultative and advisory body representing local, national and professional interests in the formulation of national regulations.

The Police Department and Police Council were also central to the second main role assumed by central government, namely the setting of national minimum standards in certain areas of police provision. Where previously central regulation had been restricted to the counties, the 1919 Act extended the power of the Home Secretary to make rules relating to pay, terms and conditions of employment, promotion and discipline to all forces. And as the standard-setting capacity of the centre within the developing national policy community became established, the new police department used its position of structural advantage to deepen and widen its power base. The financial and logistical arguments in favour of centralisation were invoked in the inter-war years to justify the establishment of a Police College, District Police Training Centres, forensic science laboratories and wireless depots. At the operational level, too, governmental anxiety about the "enemy within" in the form of the

---

[10] Critchley (1978) p. 190.
[11] For exposition of the idea of a policy community, see, *e.g.*, Richardson and Jordan (1979); Rhodes (1985); (1997) chap.2
[12] Lustgarten (1986) p. 43
[13] Rhodes (1985) p. 23

organised working class led the police department to encourage local forces to take firm action to protect property and the free flow of commerce against the tactics of those engaged in industrial action, hunger marches or other forms of political demonstration.[14] With the return to war conditions in 1939 the co-ordinating and standard-setting functions of the centre received a further boost. And in the aftermath of the Second Word War, legislation to strengthen the power of the centre to compel amalgamations of small forces shifted the balance of power still further, reducing the size and heterogeneity of the national policy community and providing the Home Secretary with an additional lever of influence in the development of substantive police policy.

If there is a single causal thread running through this accretion of central authority it is the tendency of national government to respond to the opportunity provided by political crisis by assuming a more direct form of control over policing. As we saw in the opening chapter, the two key police functions of maintaining general order and specific order are ones in which the central state possesses a strong interest. For both economic reasons, given the historically limited financial revenue of the centre, and political reasons, given the long tradition of locally organised policing,[15] the British central state was neither able nor willing to assume close control over these interests during the early generations of the New Police. As the central state began to develop a more direct regime of governance generally, as the scale, scope and technical and logistical complexity of policing increased, and as the threat posed by other organised political interests, including the local state itself (see below) sharpened, things began to change.

(D) CONSTABULARY INDEPENDENCE AND PROFESSIONAL AUTONOMY

The other long-term trend in police governance—the emergence of the doctrine of constabulary independence—has attracted more coverage, and been the subject of greater controversy, than any other aspect of the constitutional position of the British police. It remains central to contemporary attempts to understand—and to change—the world of police governance. For these reasons, analysis of the career of the con-

---

[14] See *e.g.* Geary (1985); Weinberger (1991); Ewing and Gearty (2000) especially chaps. 3–6.
[15] See *e.g.* Lustgarten (1986) chap.3.

cept of constabulary independence deserves, and receives, extended treatment.

The doctrine of constabulary independence, which in its most developed form suggests that police officers are responsible for their actions to the law and only to the law,[16] is of uncertain origin and has never been free of controversy. There is no doubt, however, that over the first half of the twentieth century it emerged as the major premise, if often unstated or under-argued, upon which conventional understandings of the limits of political involvement in policing rested. In so doing, the doctrine came to represent in the modern constitutional order the paradigm of the state's response to the underlying paradox of police governance identified in chapter one. It will be recalled that this concerns the difficulty of reconciling the role of the state as interested party and as regulatory source; of ensuring, on the one hand, that as a body whose security and other interests are capable of being significantly affected by the police, the state does not exploit constitutional arrangements to exert inappropriate political influence over the police, and on the other, that the state provides a regulatory structure calculated to ensure that the police act in balanced and effective pursuit of their mandate. By building a protective legal framework around the sphere of police action, the doctrine of constabulary independence announces a firm recognition of the first of these imperatives—setting the boundaries of state interference in the domain of policing. And by presenting that same legal framework as a form of positive guidance for the police, the doctrine of constabulary independence, albeit in a less systematic fashion, also recognises the second imperative—facilitating the fair and effective pursuit of the police mission.

It is important from the outset that the emergence of the doctrine of constabulary independence be viewed both as a fundamental and plausible response to the broader paradox of police governance—in the sense that it grasps and seeks to offer serious answers to the essential features of that paradox—but also as a response which in the final analysis is unconvincing and incomplete. On the one hand, the fundamental and plausible problem-solving thrust of the doctrine means that, despite the uncertainty of its legal pedigree and considerable disagreement surrounding its precise ambit, we should not be surprised that constabulary independence displays a certain resilience; that we should be slow to conclude that constabulary independence is a radically novel departure,

---

[16] R. v. *Metropolitan Police Commissioner, ex parte Blackburn* [1968] 2 Q.B. 118, at 136, *per* Lord Denning, M.R.

or one that we can make sense of only as the product of a particular historical conjuncture, or, indeed, that, it could ever be removed from the conceptual map of police governance without transforming the entire topography and requiring a new key. These points merit particular stress because many (but not all[17]) witnesses, including influential commentators such as Marshall,[18] Lustgarten[19] and Reiner[20] have tended to emphasise the historically *discontinuous* character of the emergence of constabulary independence and its roots in the peculiar legal and political circumstances of inter-war Britain. And while, as we shall see, their analysis tells an important part of the story, it should not be at the expense of the broader historical and constitutional context provided by the inescapable paradox of police governance.

Yet, on the other hand, it is precisely on account of the fundamental character of the issues at stake that an appreciation of the limitations of the constabulary independence doctrine is also vital.[21] If the independence doctrine is indeed deep-rooted, resilient and central to the conceptual map of police governance, then its shortcomings and inadequacies as a response to the underlying paradox of police governance will inevitably cast a long shadow. As is argued at length below, the history of the doctrine of constabulary independence is in important respects a history of failure to come to terms with the requirements of legitimate governance of the police.

(i) The Protean Form of Constabulary Independence

The authors cited above are undoubtedly correct in their explanation of the emergence of the doctrine of constabulary independence in its modern form to focus upon a movement in the balance of power between the watch committee and the chief constable which developed critical momentum in the inter-war years. Whereas there are a number of well documented earlier cases in which the will of the watch committee prevailed in clashes with the chief constable,[22] by the middle of the twenti-

---

[17] Dissenting voices, including Jefferson and Grimshaw (1984) chap.2, and Brogden (1982) chap.2, argue that the doctrine was accorded some recognition in the 19th century.

[18] See *e.g.* Marshall (1965) chap.2; Marshall and Loveday (1994).

[19] (1986) chap.3.

[20] See, *e.g.* (1991) chap.2

[21] Commentators on either side of the debate on the historical origins of the independence doctrine, including Marshall, Lustgarten, Reiner, Jefferson, Grimshaw and Brogden, are amongst the most incisive critics of the doctrine.

[22] See *e.g.* Lustgarten (1986) pp. 37–41.

eth century the authority of the urban chief constable, while still not matching that of his county equivalent, was markedly more pronounced, and was strongly underscored by the constabulary independence doctrine. Although the historical record remains patchy,[23] the available evidence suggests that a broad mix of occupational, political and legal factors contributed to this change.

Occupationally, the relative autonomy of the police from local control was encouraged by developments in the police function and in police understanding and presentation of their function. As Clifford Shearing has argued, although the New Police sought to distinguish themselves from their predecessors by developing a "future-orientated mode of policing"[24] with vigilant crime prevention as its main focus, in fact their inability to develop the requisite information channels and to overcome the obstacles set by the modern "institutions of privacy"[25] meant that they gradually reverted to a responsive style. And as reactive, crime-fighting became more central to their mandate, including from the 1860s the development of specialist CID units, a particular conception of policework as a skill drawing upon experience, technical expertise and internal organisational solidarity, and so divorced from political considerations, gained ground. While this implies a narrowing of the police function from a broader, proactive sense of order maintenance, in another respect the police function widened significantly as the New Police became more entrenched. As a full-time resource with coercive powers, the police were uniquely well placed in a context of expanding government to assume the role of "stand-in authority"[26] over a range of official activities wherever there was no alternative agency in place or available.

The combined effect of these functional developments was gradually to create a "professional" distance between police and the centres of local government power. As a quick-response, crime fighting and order restoring facility, the police sought to develop and project a distinctive sense of craft expertise, one guided in its day-to-day activities less by the aspirations of the local "community" as a social and political collectivity and more by the serial demands of those more assertive sections of the local population minded to submit complaints of crime or disorder. And as a wide-ranging surrogate authority, the police gradually assumed statutory

[23] *ibid*. p. 43.
[24] Shearing (1996) p. 87.
[25] Stinchcombe (1963).
[26] Cohen (1985) p. 37.

responsibility independent of local government over matter as diverse as liquor licensing, weights and measures and explosives.[27]

In political terms, the assertion of police independence is connected to the rise of democratic local government. The inter-war years saw the full maturing of the idea of the local state as an integrated multi-functional level of government accountable to a broad democratic constituency.[28] It was contended above that the increasingly reactive work pattern of the New Police did not fit a model in which they were under the directive control of local government, but this did not mean that there did not remain a close homology of interests between police and local state, nor, as intimated, that the watch committee did not exert significant influence over policy or prevail in particular disputes with the constabulary. The broadening base of local government, and, in particular, the rise of municipal socialism, changed this. Where previously, the main, working-class targets of repressive policing had lacked a political voice, and the aspirations of social order of those dominant social groups typically represented in or taken account of by watch committees, including the mercantile class and the new manufacturing and professional classes, were, generally speaking,[29] mutually compatible,[30] compatibility was no longer the norm. As local government became more representative of the spectrum of political choices, the choices involved in policing between different patterns of resource allocation, different balances of competing interests and different overall conceptions of social order began to register more strongly and more transparently within the domain of politics. Where previously, the political arena of urban local government had marginalised or suppressed certain interests and thus avoided or minimised conflict over policing, now it threatened to institutionalise such struggle. In these circumstances, the moulding of the doctrine of constabulary independence is explicable as a way of distancing the police from the site of political struggle over the ends and means of policing, and in particular from those interests which did not share the definitions of order favoured by the local *bourgeoisie* who had long dominated the watch committee and set the policing agenda.

Moreover, this gradual immunisation of the police from the stresses

---

[27] See *e.g.* Lustgarten (1986) p. 47; Steedman (1984) pp. 53–55.

[28] Alongside democratisation, there was a significant shift in local government from production orientated services to social services, where the overlaps and interconnections with policing are arguably greater; see Loughlin (1996) pp. 52–55.

[29] But see Brogden (1982) chap.2; Jefferson and Grimshaw (1984) chap.2.

[30] See *e.g.* Lustgarten (1986) pp. 39–41.

of local politics gelled with the other long-term trend described earlier—the developing national political interest in an integrated police service, with co-ordination and standard-setting functions provided from the centre. If central government was developing a growing influence over local policing in the early and middle years of this century, the traditional economic and political objections to its assuming direct authority nevertheless remained. In these circumstances, an approach which resisted effective local political opposition and consolidated the position of the professionals who could, by and large, be relied upon to share the conservative priorities of the central state in defining and maintaining order, provided an attractive alternative.[31]

This brings us, crucially, to the legal dimension of constabulary independence. The fashioning of this doctrine by the judiciary is an example of a particular kind of "discursive manoeuvre"[32] which often accompanies the development of the common law. A variety of historical threads are drawn together to form a legal doctrine which derives much of its legitimacy and credibility from its apparent discursive continuity with established tradition, but which is also a device fashioned to address a new set of problems.

The key judicial moment in the modern development of the constabulary independence doctrine is undoubtedly the 1930 High Court decision in *Fisher* v. *Oldham Corporation*.[33] Mr Fisher raised an action in tort claiming that he had been falsely imprisoned by the local constabulary. The action was taken, not against the police officers in question, but against their employer, the local corporation and watch committee, presumably on the basis that they possessed the deeper pockets. However, in order to extend the principle of vicarious liability to the case in point, Fisher had to satisfy the court that the corporation and the police officers were related as master and servant.

McCardie J.'s refusal to concede the applicability of the master-servant relationship or the tortious liability of the local authority [34] is interesting both for the reasons that he adduces for the decision and also for the uses to which his decision was subsequently put. The judge's sources were historical and, in more strictly doctrinal terms, comparative. Historically,

---

[31] Lustgarten (1986) pp. 45–46
[32] Garland (1985) p. 172.
[33] [1930] 2 K.B. 364.
[34] In due course, the decision was effectively overturned by statute, s.48 of the Police Act 1964, treating the chief constable as vicariously liable in tort for the actions of constables and requiring the police authority to meet any resulting financial liability; see now Police Act 1996, s.88.

he could point to two separate, but at points intertwined, lines of development. There was, first, the "not . . . delegated . . . but . . . original authority"[35] exercised by the constable when acting as a peace officer. By original authority is meant an authority which vests directly in the constable both at statute and at common law. The notion of direct statutory authority is self-explanatory, but direct common law authority merits closer examination. At one level, it denotes the legal tradition of the constable as "citizen in uniform", in which the constable shares with all other citizens—or, more accurately, subjects—various common law rights and duties associated with arrest, prosecution and peace-keeping. Yet the common citizenship of the constable would appear to vary inversely with the extent to which the constable attracts specific statutory rights and duties and draws upon an organisational structure and set of resources not available to the ordinary citizen. To that extent, the claim to common citizenship has represented a steadily declining asset as the New Police have become more closely regulated, more elaborately organised and more extensively funded.

Yet underlying this conception of policing as good citizenship, and representing the second strong historical thread in McCardie J.'s judgment, is the idea of the public nature of the constable's function. The constable is but the specialist repository of the general peace-keeping responsibility—a responsibility which serves the broad public interest in general order. In turn, this idea of the constable as public functionary traces its roots to the thirteenth century conception of the office as one which, although locally situated, involves a generic responsibility to maintain the King's order.[36]

If these two themes—original authority and national public function—argue for some degree of legal independence from the paymasters of local government, in *Fisher* this line was reinforced by the citation of two types of comparative judicial authority. Reliance was placed on direct Commonwealth precedents,[37] inspired by early American authority,[38] concerning the absence of municipal liability for the civil wrongs of police officers. If anything, however, the court was more heavily influenced by the indirect English authority of *Stanbury v. Exeter Corporation*,[39]

---

[35] at 372.

[36] At 371–2, drawing upon *Enever v. The King* [1906] 3 C.L.R. 969 (High Court of Australia).

[37] *McCleave v. City of Moncton* (1903) 32 S.C.R. 106; *British South Africa Co. v. Crickmore* S.A.L.R. [1921] A.D. 107.

[38] *Buttrick v. City of Lowell*, (1861) 1 Allen (Mass.)172.

[39] [1905] 2 K.B. 838.

in which the position of a livestock inspector as an officer performing duties "of a public nature", and as such not attracting the vicarious liability of the local authority who appointed him to the post, was held to be "almost exactly analogous to the case of the police officer".[40]

The logic of McCardie J.'s judgment is far from impeccable.[41] He was evidently influenced in his determination that the constable was not a servant of the borough by his failure to appreciate that the relevant statutory background[42] empowered the watch committee to give orders to members of the constabulary.[43] Of more direct relevance to subsequent developments in the doctrine of constabulary independence, the judge seems to have drawn too readily the conclusion that to concede liability in tort would imply overall control of the law enforcement actions of constables by the watch committee, and that, conversely, the absence of tortious liability guaranteed the absence of such control.[44] Yet, if these lines of argument are discounted, the various historical and doctrinal fragments assembled in *Fisher* still represent a not inconsiderable legal case for extending to the police a degree of independence from local government with regard to the particular matter of tortious liability. What is more, even if the automatic inference from the absence of tortious liability on the part of the police authority to its incompetence to direct law enforcement cannot be justified, as we explain below a persuasive case can be made on quite separate grounds for the denial of political control of law enforcement decisions, and for the invocation of the doctrine of independence to achieve that end.

Far less compelling, however, is the way in which the concept of constabulary independence has been still further extended on the basis of the

---

[40] At 842, *per* Wiils J.

[41] See especially Marshall (1965) chap.3; Lustgarten (1986) pp. 55–61. One eccentric feature of the judgment is the suggestion that a police constable is "a servant of the state" (at 371) rather than the local authority. Whatever this might mean, s.2(6) of the Crown Proceedings Act 1947 makes it clear that it does not mean that a police officer is a Crown servant, as he or she is neither directly or indirectly appointed by the Crown nor wholly paid from central government funds; see also Watt (1999) pp. 307–309.

[42] County and Borough Police Act 1856, s.7.

[43] [1930] 2 K.B. 364, at 370.

[44] At 377–378. Neither of these linked propositions is sustainable in a categorical sense. There are some offices in which a master-servant relationship and vicarious liability co-exist with considerable independence of action on the part of the servant, while there are other offices in which detailed subordination to a superior obtains notwithstanding the absence of a master-servant relationship (e.g. military servants). That is to say, the absence of a master-servant relationship and of vicarious tortious liability is neither a necessary nor a sufficient condition of independence of office; see Marshall and Loveday (1994) pp. 298–299.

ostensible authority of *Fisher*. In the years between *Fisher* and the 1962 Royal Commission, the view gradually gained support that the doctrine of constabulary independence did not confine its ambit to the narrow private law matter of the local police authority's immunity in tort, nor even to the limited public law proposition that the local police authority should not control law enforcement decisions, but that it might also imply the *general* freedom from external control of constabulary decision-making, including the decisions of the chief constable. This development, which clearly resonates with the occupational and political developments discussed above, is first evident in the statements and attitudes of politicians and other public agencies; for example, in the reports of departmental committees, in Parliamentary statements made on behalf of Government,[45] in evidence to the 1962 Royal Commission,[46] and, crucially, in the Report of the Commission itself.[47] Only thereafter, did the extension of the doctrine of constabulary independence to the discretion of the chief officer receive its judicial *imprimatur*.[48]

Undoubtedly, the discursive manoeuvre involved in the extension of the constabulary independence doctrine to the decision zone of the chief was more strategic and less fully supported by the weight of authority than that involved in its original application to the master and servant context. The legitimate transferability of the doctrine between different legal contexts and different ranks tended to be assumed rather than argued. As we have seen, *Fisher* foreshadowed and encouraged this by implying that the answer to the question of control of law enforcement decisions in public law could be "read off" from the answer to the question of tortious liability in private law. As far as the occlusion of the further distinction between operational law enforcement decisions and the decisions of the chief constable is concerned, this is only flimsily supported by the assertion that the chief constable remains a constable at common law. Such an assertion fails to appreciate that the crucial point is not that the chief constable retains the powers and duties of his operational colleagues, but that the functions of his or her office involve much more besides. As a matter of legal form, the chief constable has

---

[45] 213 H.L. Debs 5s, (1958), *per* Lord Chesam.

[46] In particular, from the Association of Chief Police Officers; Royal Commission on the Police (1962) para. 72.

[47] See especially chaps. 4–5.

[48] Most significantly, in *R* v. *Metropolitan Police Commissioner, ex parte Blackburn* [1968] 2 Q.B. 118, discussed in chapter three. For an earlier re-affirmation of constabulary independence in the narrower tort context, see *Att.-Gen. for New South Wales* v. *Perpetual Trustee Co.* [1955] A.C. 457.

always possessed the basic constabulary powers of arrest, search, etc., but this pales into insignificance alongside his or her unique and distinctive responsibility for developing broad policy of general application in the force, including allocation of manpower to particular territories and units, general crime priorities, and strategies of crime prevention, crime detection and order maintenance. Accordingly, whatever arguments are adduced to justify the legal independence of the ordinary constable, they cannot be sufficient in themselves to justify a similar autonomy for the chief officer.

(ii) Constabulary Independence and the Paradox of Police Governance

Clearly, then, the doctrine of constabulary independence developed in new ways in the twentieth century and was part of a definite trend, supported by central government and the police themselves, towards the greater professional autonomy of forces from local government influence. Yet, as intimated earlier, underneath this conjunctural shift in legal doctrine and in the balance of political power resides a set of abiding concerns with the paradox of police governance which affect all states with developed systems of policing.[49] The main arguments which might justify the doctrine of constabulary independence as it had developed by the time of the Royal Commission are all in their different ways connected to the aspiration that the regulatory framework for policing, on the one hand, should not enable or encourage the central and local state in exercising their responsibilities for police governance to do so in a manner which unduly favours their own interests, and on the other hand, should facilitate the balanced and effective pursuit of the police mandate between and across all social groups and their different conceptions of social order. As we shall see, some of these arguments are more persuasive than others, and may be more supportive of a narrow rather than a broad conception of constabulary independence. Yet it is noteworthy that all such arguments have commanded some measure of support and have benefited from some degree of mutual nourishment through their common and enduring link to the governance paradox. The case for a broad conception of constabulary independence, in other words, is embedded in the deep soil of conventional wisdom. Its critique, therefore,

---

[49] See Waddington (1999) pp. 188–191, reviewing American, Commonwealth and continental experience.

involves unearthing and disentangling some very strong and tightly interwoven roots within our political culture.

The idea of constabulary independence contains both negative and positive dimensions. The negative dimension emphasises that *all other candidate authorities have to defer to law* as the sole or primary basis for holding the police to account. The positive dimension, already implicit in the negative dimension, is that *law alone is a sufficient authority* to provide the sole or primary basis for holding the police to account. It follows that the justification of the doctrine rests upon one of two arguments: either that all other forms of authority over policing—which may be gathered under the general label of *political* authority—are entirely illegitimate; or that even if these various forms of political authority are not entirely illegitimate, some measure of reliance upon them would produce less acceptable results than would be produced by exclusive or primary reliance upon the authority of law. Let us now test these alternative arguments by exploring in greater depth the negative and positive dimensions of the independence doctrine.

(iii) The Contested Legitimacy of Political Authority

In historical terms, the negative dimension of the doctrine is traceable to the source of constabulary independence which viewed the constable as a functionary operating in the general public interest rather than under the influence or instruction of any particular political master. In conceptual terms, the negative dimension concentrates on the dangers and deficiencies of political authority by tackling head-on the problem of self-interested political interference in police governance—the first strand of the paradox of police governance. In so doing, it acknowledges the entire spectrum of concerns about political involvement in policing.

To begin with, it recognises the danger of abuse of power for *personal ends*. A politician may from motives of greed, ambition, rivalry or personal enmity exert undue influence over police officers to secure, for example, that no police action is taken against that politician or another person with connected interests as the suspected perpetrator of a crime; that the politician or other with connected interests benefits from the illicit proceeds of crime; or that another person with conflicting interests becomes the unjustified object of police attention. A politician, secondly, may exploit influence over the police to serve *narrow political interests*. For example, political leverage over police officers may be used to prevent investigations or arrests which would be embarrassing or disabling to the politician's party or faction and detrimental to the party or factional interest, or to encourage investigations or secure arrests which would be embarrassing or disabling to a rival party or faction and so conducive to the interests of the politician's own party or faction.[50]

Thirdly, at a deeper level, politicians may seek to use the police as a means to defend the security and well-being of the governing regime—whether central or local—against difficulties associated with or consequential upon choices made or programmes pursued in other policy areas. That is to say, politicians may use the police in pursuit of a cross-sectoral *compensatory strategy*; for example, where they seek to influence the deployment of the police in favour of a confrontational industrial relations policy, which may in turn be connected to the government's macro-economic policy, or in favour of an intolerant approach to "new age travellers", which may in turn be connected to the government's social welfare policy. This shades into a fourth form of political involvement, where the police may be used as a means *to ensure the security of the underlying political order*. Of course, as noted in chapter one, it is a key historical role of the New Police to protect the "specific order" of the state against insurrection and various other forms of destabilisation or systemic challenge. It is an inevitable part of the police function, and within certain limits it is a legitimate role. However, such limits must be specified and respected to ensure that a corrupt or undemocratic regime is not sustained by force or that legitimate criticism and opposition is not discouraged or repressed. Where the police are too closely influenced by the representatives of the specific order of the state, these limits may be transgressed.

Fifth and finally, and again overlapping with the two previous categories, there is a broader form of influence by which politicians seek to secure in the policing and security sector the interests of a particular constituency they represent, or the objectives or priorities favoured by a particular political ideology they espouse. This broader category of *interest representation or ideological commitment*[51] may, for example, involve seeking

---

[50] Fear of these two types of political interference lie at the root of Marshall's later (1978, 1984) reversal of his original position (1965) in favour of greater democratic control of police discretion.

[51] "Ideology" here is used in its neutral sense as a set of ideas that reflects collective beliefs and values rather than in its alternative sense as a set of ideas that is false, misleading or held for the wrong reasons; see Freeden (1996) chap.1. The precise balance and relationship between interest representation and ideological commitment depends upon the theory of politics to which one subscribes. Economic theories of democracy and public choice approaches would stress interest representation over ideological commitment, while

to make certain types of crime, suspect or victim a priority, or concentrating police resources upon particular types of neighbourhood or socio-economic or cultural groups, or encouraging the police to adopt different ways of relating to the local population, whether stressing "communitarian" involvement, "liberal" detachment or "authoritarian" control.

As noted above, the strongest thesis in favour of constabulary independence involves the claim that direct political authority over and interference in policing is in no circumstances legitimate. In turn, this depends upon one of two propositions; *either* that all forms of political authority over policing are morally unacceptable *or* that, even if no such categorical denunciation is warranted, it is nevertheless not possible to distinguish between acceptable and unacceptable forms of political authority sufficiently to endorse one without also inviting the other. Neither of these propositions, it may be submitted, is sustainable, both relying upon variations of what Lustgarten nicely terms "the fallacy of the seamless web".[52]

As regards the first possibility, we have already remarked upon the way in which, due to its historical roots, the doctrine of constabulary independence tends to elide the distinction between the chief constable and junior officers, and so by extension, between the different forms of political encroachment upon their respective domains of action and decision-making. As we shall argue, direct political control of the law enforcement decisions of junior operational officers is never justified, but that does not imply equivalent condemnation of political influence over decisions of senior police policy-makers. To be sure, there is no morally relevant difference between a politician interfering with the decision of a chief constable or that of his most lowly constable in order to achieve narrow personal or political advantage. Both are decisions which directly affect particular members of the public, and are equally reprehensible, equally to be avoided, and equally well-targeted by the doctrine of constabulary independence. However, if we proceed to the other forms of political involvement, this easy symmetry disappears. As regards each of the other

---

broader sociological conceptions of politics would stress the importance of ideological commitment; see Dryzek (2000) chap.2. The contrast between the two should not be over-stated, however, since interest representation may be the product of ideological commitment and vice versa. While the analysis that follows does not strictly depend upon any particular view of the relationship between interests and ideology, it assumes that they are closely interwoven.

[52] Lustgarten (1986) p. 65.

three forms of political involvement—compensatory cross-sectoral strategy, the defence of specific order and the pursuit of broad interests or ideological commitments—action and decision-making may likewise be pitched at the operational level and affect particular individuals. Yet, in each of these three areas, there is an additional and quite different sphere of police action and decision-making pitched at a more general policy level, and so apt to engage more senior officers, including the chief constable, in a quite distinctive type of practice.

The recognition of this distinction by no means implies that all chief level decisions in these areas, unlike junior operational decisions, need not be protected from political interference. Indeed, in the areas of compensatory cross-sectoral strategy and influence over specific order, it is submitted that direct political interference is unacceptable regardless of the level at which it is pitched—and, moreover, that interference pitched at the broader policy level is likely to have more egregious results. Granted, as *consequences* of the overall pattern of policing within a political order, neither compensatory adjustment to government initiatives in other sectors nor protection of specific order are necessarily illegitimate— the latter, indeed, is in some measure inevitable. Yet insofar as these consequences are the effective and intended results of active political intervention,[53] such intervention cannot be legitimate unless its shape and purpose is crystallised as general law—for example in the form of anti-terrorist or public order legislation. For reasons (expanded upon shortly) associated with the formal virtues of the rule of law, politicians should have the legislative courage of their convictions if they wish to exert legitimate influence over the police for reasons of compensatory strategy or specific order, although even legislation itself offers no *guarantee* of legitimacy. Direct political intervention in pursuit of a non-legislative policy of cross-sectoral compensation or protection of specific order, on the other hand, poses an immediate threat of self-interested interference on an arbitrary and unaccountable basis with the life-chances of individuals and groups who challenge or impede these interests.

---

[53] An alternative—and morally more confused—scenario, has central government benefiting from the pursuit of specific order or a compensatory policing strategy in circumstances where active political intervention is disputed, as in the 1984–85 miners strike. In that instance, the co-ordination of mutual aid between forces was achieved through the National Reporting Centre at Scotland Yard, a facility run by the Association of Chief Police Officers. However, much contemporary political and academic commentary was sceptical about the degree of independence of this quasi-national body from central governmental control (*e.g.* Fine and Millar (1985)). Reiner's subsequent documentation of the recollections of chief constables involved in the strike suggests that this scepticism was not entirely unfounded (1991, pp. 182–192). See further, chapter three, section 2.

The issues of legitimacy raised by political influence which represents particular broad interests or ideological commitments, however, are more subtle and complex than those raised in the other four categories. Here, the balance between professional independence and democratic politics is at its most delicate. On the one hand, the questions of resource allocation, value preference and optimal method of service delivery which shape the higher reaches of police policy-making are the normal stuff of democratic politics in many other fields of public policy, where they are typically influenced by broad forms of interest representation and ideological commitment. There is no reason in democratic theory, then, why such policy matters[54] and the normal ways of addressing them should be any less appropriate to the political arena in policing than in those other fields. On the other hand, however, considerations of fairness counsel against the unqualified application of this approach. To begin with, even within the broad policy sphere, narrow and exclusionary forms of interest representation or ideological commitment are not conducive to discovering a fair balance between different constituencies and different conceptions of order. As such a balance is essentially elusive and necessarily controversial, however,[55] this is not so much an indictment of the presence of politics in high policy-making as a plea for a political process which discourages sectionalism and the assertion of the "tyranny of the majority".[56] Considerations of fairness sound much more insistently at a second level, militating against taking such broader policy considerations into account in individual questions of law enforcement—concerning the decision to arrest, detain, search or use other executive powers, or even to investigate in response to a specific complaint. [57] That is to say, the types of sectional political bias generated by interest representation or ideological commitment—whether based on considerations of ethnicity, gender, social class, locality, etc., are no more acceptable as a basis of discrimination in matters of individual law enforcement than are these forms of unfairness generated by personal interests, narrow political interests, compensatory strategy or considerations of specific order. In each category, the basic good of impartiality and like treatment of like cases is equally threatened if extraneous political considerations are

---

[54] These, of course, are precisely the questions pertaining to the balance between different conceptions of order in pursuit of the mandate, which, in terms of the second strand of the paradox of police governance, require active direction, whether legal or political. See subsection (D)(iv) below.

[55] See further, subsection (D)(iv) below.

[56] See e.g. Johnston (2000), pp. 87–88. See further, chapter four, section 3.

[57] See Lustgarten (1986) p. 164.

allowed to interfere with professional judgement in law enforcement, however justifiable or otherwise such extraneous political considerations may be within a more general decision-making sphere.

Consideration of this final category of political influence, therefore, both challenges the thesis that political interference is entirely illegitimate and offers it renewed support. On the one hand, the illegitimacy thesis is clearly challenged by the argument that, as a matter of political morality, political interference in broad policy decisions in the name of interest representation or ideological commitment is not in principle objectionable. On the other hand, as even this type of political influence remains unacceptable at the level of individual law enforcement, the question of the feasibility of separating the legitimate sphere of policy decision-making from the illegitimate sphere of operational decision-making is highlighted. That is to say, as the categorical moral objection to political interference recedes, so the practical objection comes to the fore.

As we saw in chapter one, the distinction between policy and operations is a notoriously difficult one to draw. High-level policy decisions, often in conjunction with other management decisions located in the middle range of the policy/operations spectrum, provide the framework of opportunities and constraints within which even the most concrete law enforcement decisions are made. Accordingly, even if executive law enforcement decisions affecting suspects, victims and other directly affected parties in ways which raise in acute manner issues of fairness and impartiality between different individuals and the social constituencies of which they are members are not *dictated* by policy considerations, they may nevertheless be *influenced* by such considerations—say as regards the allocation and availability of resources for effective response and investigation—and by the interests and ideological commitments which underpin them. Yet such influence is very much a matter of degree and proportion, and should not encourage categorical judgements about the need to protect one value—impartiality—to the exclusion of others. We should not, therefore, succumb to that variant of the seamlessness fallacy which holds that as authoritative democratic involvement at any point in the thickly interconnected world of police organisational decision-making risks impugning the impartiality of particular law enforcement decisions, the only guarantee against such contamination is a total embargo on such involvement. The more pertinent and measured question concedes in principle the legitimacy of democratic involvement within the limited parameters identified above, and asks whether the dangers and drawbacks associated with such a concession are outweighed by the dangers and drawbacks of allowing instead full rein to the doctrine of constabulary independence. That is to say, the case for a broad version of constabulary independence cannot in the final analysis rest on an *absolute* critique of political authority, but instead must turn on the *relative* merits of exclusive reliance on the law as the highest form of authority as against a framework which allows some recognition of other forms of expression of democratic will.

(iv) The Asserted Legitimacy of Legal Authority

This requires us to turn our attention to the positive dimension of constabulary independence—the idea that the law is capable of holding constables—chief or otherwise—comprehensively to account. As argued in chapter one, there is no need to accept the "legalistic-bureaucratic"[58] conception of the relationship between policing and the law, which sees law as the major determinant of policing, to appreciate that law is nevertheless significant as both a constraint upon and influence over police conduct, and so a key factor in addressing the paradox of police governance. The theme of comprehensive accountability to law is closely linked to the second major historical root of the doctrine, which views the constable as an original authority in law. Conceptually, like the negative dimension of the doctrine, this positive dimension concentrates on the first strand of the paradox of police governance—the problem of political self-interest. As we shall see, however, as it must, the positive dimension also addresses, albeit somewhat less systematically, the other strand of the paradox—namely the need actively to guide pursuit of the mandate in a way which achieves a satisfactory balance between various interests and conceptions of order.

The idea of law as a bulwark against political intervention in its various guises is well captured in Marshall and Loveday's claim that the irreducible core of the independence doctrine is "that police officers cannot be given unlawful orders by those who appoint and dismiss them and that, insofar as the duties of constables are prescribed by statute or common law, they cannot be instructed not to perform them."[59] Two aspects of this proposition deserve to be drawn out. First, it specifies that political interference is most likely to fall foul of the independence doctrine when it involves a direction to an individual officer to break or disregard

---

[58] Dixon (1997) p. 1.
[59] (1994) p. 298.

an authoritative legal rule, which is precisely how interference in an operational law enforcement decision would manifest itself—so endorsing the view that this type of interference is the most demonstrably unjust. Secondly, it implies that the injunction against breach or disregard acts as a constraint upon and protection for *all* police officers, regardless of rank; a constraint upon chief officers whose power of hire and fire and general disciplinary power over different levels of police staff places them in a position to give orders and wield influence, but also upon operational officers who, whether under orders or not, would act in breach or disregard of an authoritative legal rule; a protection for senior officers who are disinclined to succumb to illegitimate direction from an external political authority—despite that external authority having the corresponding power of hire and fire and general discipline over the chief—and also for junior officers who are disinclined to carry out the unlawful orders of their superiors. In other words, the requirement of fealty to the law blocks off both available channels of illegitimate political influence, direct control exercised by external political sources and indirect control mediated through senior officers.

But what special qualities does law possess to make it an *effective* barrier against illegitimate political interference? As noted in chapter one,[60] the absence of a framework of fundamental constitutional law rules out some of the deeper forms of legal protection against the problem of political self-interest. The separation of executive and legislative power, which seeks to ensure that the current managers of the state apparatus do not have direct control of the reins of legislative authority, is not possible in a constitutional system which vests supreme legislative authority in the institution of Parliament and—in consequence—supreme, executive authority in those who command the confidence of Parliament. Yet while this, and other, constitutional buffers against overweening political power such as territorial division and dispersal of authority and fundamental rights protection may be unavailable or, even if available, unentrenched[61] due to the peculiarities of our constitutional form, other less constitutionally elevated legal protections are available.

The criminal law (both as a constraint on police conduct and as a direction to the police as to the public conduct they should seek to constrain), the law of police procedural powers and duties, the framework of police discipline and public complaints, and the rules of civil liability in

---

[60] See chapter one, section 2(a)(i).
[61] See *e.g.* Human Rights Act 1998.

tort, all offer some protection against political interference. Together, they provide the basic framework of rules in terms of which the independent judgement of the constable in law enforcement is asserted. The value of these protections, moreover, lies not only in the content of the rules but also in the very form that they take. Legal regulation comes in an (increasing[62]) variety of modes, but in at least some of these we may discern certain characteristics associated with a formal, neo-Diceyan conception of the "rule of law"[63] which seek to provide surety against unrestrained political power.

Built into the texture of many of the rules we recognise as legal rules— legislative rules in particular—are some or all of the attributes of prospectivity, stability, openness, uniformity, certainty and clarity of purpose, and accessibility and independence of adjudication. In a general sense, each of these formal attributes contributes to the classical liberal constitutionalist equation between *government through law* and *limited government*.[64] More specifically, each formal attribute to some extent counterbalances the risk of the state abusing its influence over policing. Prospectivity allows individuals to plan their lives to avoid infractions of the law and the unwanted attention of police and state, and acts as a check against self-interested retroactivity on the part of state officials. Stability, and the requirement to observe certain procedures when changing the law, acts as a check against expedient refinement and opportunistic amendment. Openness aids accountability by increasing public awareness of legal rights and responsibilities and exposing the state's efforts to apply and modify the law to some level of scrutiny. Uniformity militates against formal differentiation of treatment within specified legal categories, and so offers some reduction, albeit limited (see below), of the risk of an approach to police regulation which would allow preferential treatment of some constituencies— whether the state itself or constituencies favoured by the state. Finally, both certainty and clarity of purpose and accessibility and independence of adjudication have supportive functions, bolstering the various values enumerated above; certainty and clarity of purpose, because vagueness is the enemy of forward planning, consistency, transparency and equal treatment; accessibility and independence of adjudication, because these facilitate the vindication of rights and the enforcement of safeguards, and thus the practical realisation of the virtues of the rule of law.

---

[62] See *e.g.,* Cotterrell (1993)

[63] See *e.g.,* Jowell (1994) especially pp. 62–64.; Craig (1997); Raz (1979) chap.11.

[64] See *e.g.,* Barendt (1998) chap.1; MacCormick (1993); Vile (1967); Vincent (1987) chap.3,

But the protection afforded by law knows certain limits. First, despite the rhetoric of the rule of law, much law which delimits police practice in fact lacks formal precision and clarity of meaning, so allowing a high level of discretion to those charged with its interpretation and application. Public order crimes in particular are notoriously open-textured and may be construed in a manner which accommodates the various types of illegitimate political consideration discussed above without falling foul of the requirement not to break or disregard legal rules.[65] In the second place, in any case even the clear and intended meaning of legal rules may reflect or endorse the illegitimate self-interest of the state. To be sure, the presence of the formal qualities of the rule of law offers certain safeguards against such a tendency. As a general proposition, the more the balance between legality and official discretion is struck towards the formal pole, the less scope there is for the state to abuse its influence over policing and security. But in the final analysis, legal formalism alone cannot frustrate the will of a government of sufficient determination and popularity. For example, the accumulated catalogue of legislation over the past 25 years aimed at combating terrorism in Northern Ireland[66] arguably places too great an emphasis on the specific order of the state at the expense of individual rights of privacy, liberty and property. Arguably, too, both of these limitations—the license allowed to official discretion and the statist bias of legislation—are exacerbated by the absence of entrenched constitutional guarantees concerning the separation and dispersal of powers and the defence of fundamental rights.[67]

If law is in some respects an inadequate shield against illegitimate political interference, what of its credentials in addressing the other strand of the governance paradox—the need to provide positive regulatory guidance in pursuit of the police mandate? Given their tendency to rely on the distorted image of the chief as indistinct in legal powers and responsibility from any other constable, the defenders of constabulary independence tend to avoid or to marginalize the question of the broader policy dimension in police decision-making. There is, nevertheless, a loose congeries of arguments which are drawn upon from time to time by those who have faith in the directive power of law over police

---

[65] See *e.g.*, Lustgarten (1987).

[66] Beginning with the Prevention of Terrorism (Temporary Provisions) Act 1974, which passed all its legislative stages in two days.

[67] Although, as the experience of jurisdictions (such as the USA) with structural and substantive constitutional protections indicates, such protections themselves by no means guarantee the eradication of statist bias in legislation and in official discretion with regard to policing.

policy,[68] which, like the arguments for the protective role of law, tend to rely at different points on both the content of law and its formal qualities.

The least subtle variation of this thesis holds that the law is an adequate guide to police policy inasmuch as it exhorts the police towards maximum law enforcement. If policing aspires to universal law enforcement in an ideal world, then a maximalist policy appears attractive as an optimal strategy in the real world. But this assumes that law enforcement has a linear quality, that the only policy question is *how much* enforcement, rather than what methods of enforcement should be preferred, or which crimes, victims or offenders should be given priority. Once it is conceded that the "units" of law enforcement are not identical, then important policy choices re-surface and particular emphases and priorities become unavoidable. Furthermore, to introduce a theme which is often associated with maximum law enforcement, these questions are not adequately answered simply by citing the quasi-market in public policing—the pattern of demand in complaints to the police.[69] As crime levels and clear-up rates testify, demand invariably exceeds supply, and so selectivity is inevitable. Further, to the extent that supply is nevertheless influenced by the pattern of demand, there is no particular reason why the law of the market-place should be endorsed. The pattern of demand is a function of the variable social confidence and articulateness, and of the thresholds of tolerance and trust in the police of particular groups, and should not be seen as a neutral guide to public priorities.

If the maximalist approach founders on its inability to discriminate between different types and patterns of law enforcement, a second approach purports to tackle this difficulty directly by giving priority attention to the more central areas of the criminal law. Yet taken literally, this is meaningless, since the law does not supply internal rules of priority. Such rules of priority might instead be supplied externally, by reference, for example, to consensual public opinion. But if this is the case, then the idea of central law enforcement simply becomes a surrogate for popular morality, of no independent conceptual significance or legiti-

---

[68] See in particular Jefferson and Grimshaw (1984) pp. 143–148, whose discussion provides a basis for the argument that follows. These authors discuss their various alternatives as "the range of the possible, rather than descriptions of particular, observed police strategies" (143) for developing an acceptable conception of the police mandate, but there is no doubt that the various strategies discussed for many years figured prominently within professional discourses in defence of the tradition of constabulary independence and the Royal Commission's model of tripartitism; see *e.g.*, Anderton (1981); Pike (1985) chap. 8; Newing (1987); Oliver (1987); (1997).

[69] See *e.g.*, Kinsey, Lea and Young (1986) pp. 163–164.

macy. Further, on closer inspection, consensual public opinion itself does not take us very far. There may be rough agreement across social groups about the pecking order of serious crimes, but victimisation studies and other public opinion surveys have consistently revealed considerable disagreement over detailed priorities.[70] And, it may be recalled, it is precisely this scope for disagreement between different constituencies over policing priorities which makes the interpretation of the police mandate unavoidably policy-driven and controversial. The idea of central law enforcement does not resolve the problem of contested priorities over police policy, it merely glosses over it.

A final law-based strategy for directing police policy focuses on the idea of equality before the law. In one sense of the term, this flows from the model version of the formal rule of law. With its universalising framework, its public and transparent nature, and in its qualities of accessibility and independent adjudication, the law should encourage consistency and impartiality in the police officer's dealings with the public. According to this formal idea of equality, the law should be blind to the social or other characteristics of victims or suspects of crime, and so the custodians of the law should treat all social categories in like manner. Yet this has proved to be an elusive aspiration. Operational officers not only possess considerable latitude in the interpretation of their legal powers, but also possess significant practical discretion due to their working in "regions of low visibility"[71] and in contexts which may require prompt and uncorroborated decision-making. As operational officers also typically come into differential contact with different groups, this permissive framework may provide the space within which they may cultivate stereotypes and develop or reinforce occupational prejudices. Even if they are not subjected to external political pressures to compromise their impartiality, therefore, the influences of occupational culture may lead to discriminatory behaviour by operational decision-makers on the basis of sex, gender, race or moral preference.[72]

As we shall see in later chapters, the extent to which and the ways in which the British police discriminate has become a deeply controversial issue in recent years, but even if direct discrimination in individual cases could be eliminated, this would not cure the broader inadequacies of a strategy of formal equality before the law. As with the maximalist and the priority strategy, formal equality of individual treatment cannot supply a

---

[70] See e.g., Kinsey (1985); Jones, MacLean and Young (1986).
[71] Van Maanen (1983) p. 377.
[72] See e.g. Reiner (1992a), pp. 156–169.

coherent overall framework for the allocation of scarce resources. It may demand an even-handed approach to individual cases *once* addressed, but it cannot provide criteria to decide which cases should be addressed in the first instance. Additionally, even if, for the sake of argument, this were not the case, and different social groups (however classified) were somehow accorded equal priority in the allocation of policing resources, such a result could by no means be viewed as an uncontroversial extrapolation of a policy of law enforcement from a basic idea of accountability to law. A formal norm of equal treatment would inevitably operate against a background of unequal victimisation rates in terms of sex, age, race, and so on, and thus would be vulnerable to the familiar charge levelled by radical critics of the function of law in a socially and economically unequal society; that *formal* equality of treatment merely serves to sustain or exacerbate *substantive* inequality of outcome. This danger is underlined by the fact that victimisation and offender rates "are not independent of each other."[73] If, as is well-documented of unequal societies, high levels of crime typically take place *within* disadvantaged communities,[74] the price of ensuring equality of treatment for a disadvantaged class of victims might be disproportionate concentration on offenders from the same class. Moreover, if, as some writers have suggested, a more radical version of equality were to be sponsored which sought positive police discrimination in favour of disadvantaged groups as victims or offenders in order to compensate for wider inequalities,[75] while this might answer some of the criticisms of the regressiveness of formal equality, it could not, of course, be presented any more plausibly than the formal version as an uncontroversial policy implicit in the value framework of our legal system. Neither would a more radical policy easily resolve the problem of crime within social categories and the internal incoherence with which that threatens any strategy of equality aimed at both victims and offenders.

It seems, therefore, that the idea of comprehensive accountability to law implicit in the doctrine of constabulary independence is even less convincing in asserting that police policy may be generated through the framework of law than in positing that framework as a foolproof protection against illegitimate political interference. Rather, the unwarranted

---

[73] Jefferson and Grimshaw (1984) p. 162

[74] See e.g. Kinsey, Lea and Young (1986)

[75] For example, Jefferson and Grimshaw's conception of "socialist justice", (1984) pp. 163–164. For criticism, see Jones, Newburn and Smith (1994), pp. 28–31; Marshall and Loveday (1994) pp. 315–316.

claims made on behalf of the directive capacity of the law threatens a "policy vacuum"[76]—a zone free of any form of external regulation or direction in which the cultural preferences and sensibilities of the police themselves are instead allowed to flourish.[77]

This overview of the main components of constabulary independence allows us to demonstrate why it is plausible, even attractive, as an integrated solution to the paradox of police governance, yet also why it is in the final analysis inadequate. Its plausibility lies in its propensity: first, to trade on the difficulty of distinguishing clearly between different categories of political influence over policing—between influences upon chief officers as opposed to ordinary constables, and, relatedly, between influences upon policy decisions as opposed to operational decisions—and so to present political influence as a single issue demanding a single response, namely outright condemnation and the erection of watertight legal barriers against its threat; and secondly, to discover, or assume, in law the capacity to offer positive guidance in pursuit of the mandate. Its ultimate inadequacy lies in its failure to concede that however difficult, the task of distinguishing between legitimate and illegitimate forms of political influence over policing is both possible and necessary; that, in any case, the law is not proof against illegitimate political interference; and that any positive guidance offered by the law in pursuit of the mandate is intrinsically inadequate.[78]

2. The Royal Commission's Response

(A) THE RECEIVED FRAMEWORK

Underlying the critical incidents of the late 1950s, therefore, were a number of problematic features of the system of police governance which the Royal Commission was bound to address. At the most basic level, the Royal Commission was confronting a system which was inherently controversial, reflecting two perennial conflicts: between local and central control on the one hand, and between professional autonomy and democratic governance on the other. Indeed, one notable feature of the

---

[76] Goldsmith (1990) p. 96.

[77] See in particular Brogden, Jefferson and Walklate (1988) chap.7; Grimshaw and Jefferson (1987)

[78] The means by which politics may be acknowledged and regulated as a complementary source of influence or guidance is considered in detail in chapter four.

series of incidents that precipitated the inquiry is that they highlighted no single tendency, but the whole range of concerns associated with the two perennial conflicts. Thus, the actions taken against the Chief Constables of Cardiganshire, Brighton and Worcester illustrated the dangers of professional autonomy, as did the *Thurso* case, and in some respects the Rix, Garratt and Edmond affair. But this last incident also revealed some of the problems associated with central political interference, while the Popkess affair was graphically instructive about the dangers of local political control.

As we have observed, the tensions caused by these two underlying conflicts expressed themselves in a number of more specific characteristics of the system of police governance. First, reflecting a failure to agree the "one best way", there was marked *variation* in governance arrangements between jurisdictions and between town and county. Secondly, there was the long-term tendency, encouraged by the structural advantage of the central state as the fount of political authority, towards *centralisation* of governmental influence over policing in matters of co-ordination and standard-setting. Thirdly, and linked to centralisation to the extent that both implied a corresponding reduction in the influence of local government over policing, there was an increase in the authority and *professional autonomy* of the police themselves, most clearly evident in the doctrine of constabulary independence.

A fourth and final characteristic of the scene encountered by the Royal Commission was closely connected with the other three. This was a basic *underspecification* of the legal relations which constituted the system of police governance. We have already seen how the pivotal doctrine of constabulary independence was characterised by vagueness and drift, and thus the key relationships between police and local government and between police and central government both possessed an uncertain and fluid character. Equally, the relationship in policing matters between the two levels of government lacked precision, in part an indirect casualty of the fuzziness of the independence doctrine and in part because the direct statutory framework failed to specify in detail the respective jurisdictions and terms of mutual influence between local and central state.[79]

---

[79] See generally, *Royal Commission on the Police* (1962) chap. VII. For example, the Inspectorate of Constabulary was a key player in managing the relationship between central and local government, while the Secretary of State could wield much influence over police authorities through his power to withhold all or part of the police grant. Yet the powers of the Inspectorate and the conditions under which the grant was payable were set out in only the most general terms.

Underspecification is in some measure attributable to the underlying and unresolved tensions between centre and locality and between democracy and independence. Yet it would be wrong to view under-specification purely as a function of conflict. Sunstein has argued that underspecified, or, as he puts it, "incompletely theorized agreements play a pervasive role in law and society . . . as they allow people to develop frameworks for decision and judgment despite large-scale dis-agreements."[80] Thus the vagueness at the heart of the police governance system can also be viewed in a more constructive light, as a means of facilitating a level of informal mutual accommodation between parties with a different understanding of or role in police governance. The rela-tionship between the two dimensions of underspecification—disagree-ment and accommodation—is complex and context-specific. For the moment, it is sufficient to note that underspecification is always a pre-carious vehicle for mutual accommodation, dependent upon a minimum floor of reciprocity and common understanding. The series of incidents which preceded the Royal Commission, and more importantly, the underlying anxieties about the legitimacy and effectiveness of the police role which these incidents served to dramatise, suggest that this mini-mum floor was becoming progressively less stable as that landmark approached.

(B) THE NEW CONSTITUTIONAL SETTLEMENT

How did the Royal Commission, and the Conservative administration charged with giving legislative expression to its report in the form of the Police Act 1964, address the various problematic features of the existing regime of police governance? To begin with, they took certain steps to reduce the variability of the statutory framework. The distinction between town and county in England with regard to the relationship between chief constable and police authority was ended. The new police authorities, unlike the old watch committees, had no powers of direction over the chiefs. The new unitary system of police authorities in which elected members outnumbered magistrates by a ratio of two to one[81] reflected a compromise between the two models it replaced; namely the watch committees, composed exclusively of local councillors, and the standing joint committees in the counties, half of whose members were

---

[80] Sunstein (1996) pp. 35–36
[81] Police Act 1964, ss. 2(2) and 3(2).

elected and half of whom were magistrates. Yet uniformity was not systematically pursued. The special position of the Metropolitan Police was preserved, while the Scottish system remained distinctive in important ways, and, indeed, was separately legislated for in 1967.[82]

In the second place, the trend towards centralisation was acknowledged and encouraged, albeit ultimately rather tentatively. Some specific new provisions were proposed and introduced to augment the existing co-ordination and standard-setting role of the centre. These included increased resources and powers of supervision for the Inspectorate of Constabulary and new powers on the part of the Secretary of State to call for reports from chief constables on matters pertaining to the policing of the area,[83] to secure collaboration between forces,[84] and to require amalgamations between forces without restriction as to the population of the areas affected.[85] However, the boldest recommendation of the Royal Commission, that the Secretary of State should assume a statutory responsibility for the efficiency of the police was rejected by Henry Brooke, the Home Secretary responsible for the Parliamentary passage of the 1964 Act. In favouring instead the framing of a more modest obligation to exercise "his powers in such a way as appeared to him best calculated to promote the efficiency of the police",[86] the Home Secretary was anxious that the centre should not overreach itself, and in particular that it should not seek "responsibility without power".[87]

In the third place, the trend towards recognition of the autonomy of the police was also consolidated. The Report considered the evolution of the doctrine of constabulary independence at some length,[88] but decided to let sleeping dogs lie. In an oddly fatalistic discussion, despite their obvious scepticism about the developing conventional wisdom which equated the chief with ordinary constables under the *Fisher* doctrine and despite their sympathy with some of the dissenting voices, the Commissioners appeared resigned to accepting the incremental drift of the common law. The 1964 Act duly maintained the tradition of statutory silence on the subject of constabulary independence, but did provide important indirect support for the idea of professional autonomy by

---

[82] Police (Scotland) Act 1967; see chapter five.
[83] Police Act 1964, s.38.
[84] *ibid.*, s.13.
[85] *ibid.*, ss.21–24
[86] *ibid.*, s.28.
[87] 677 HC Deb. 5s, Col. 688.
[88] Royal Commission on the Police (1964), chap.IV.

introducing a provision that each police force should be "under the direction and control"[89] of its chief constable.

The Commission's endorsement of the century-long shift towards centralisation and professional autonomy was reflected in their approach to the third main player within the tripartite system, the police authority. While responsibility for the key areas of co-ordination, standard-setting, efficiency and operational direction and control was by and large allocated to the other two main players, the police authority was to retain its own distinctive remit.[90] It was to retain responsibility for the infrastructure of the local police, through its duties to provide and equip an adequate force. It was allowed to retain a set of personnel responsibilities, relating to the appointment, discipline and dismissal of senior officers.[91] Further, its responsibility was acknowledged over two potentially broader areas—fostering good relations between the police and the public and, even more importantly, providing advice and guidance to the chief constable about local problems.[92] To facilitate the performance of their advisory function, the police authorities were to be statutorily entitled to receive annual and other reports from the chief constable on matters pertaining to the policing of the area.[93]

Yet, as a number of commentators have remarked,[94] despite the fact that the Commissioners explicitly conceded that there were certain aspects of policing policy, such as the general concentration of resources or disposition of the force or the means used to control public protest, which remained the proper concern of the police authority,[95] they failed to fill out the bare bones of their important recommendation on the authority's policy remit. They did not specify in detail how, short of the now apparently excluded option of policy *direction*, the police authority was to substantiate that role. For instance, neither the Commissioners nor the 1964 Act stipulated which matters would be the legitimate subject of advice, or what the procedures for consultation should be. Arguably, this lack of detail weakened the force of the recommendation, and left the

---

[89] Police Act 1964, s.5(1)

[90] Royal Commission on the Police (1962) para. 154.

[91] Police Act 1964, ss.5–6. However, it was also recommended (paras. 186–188) that the powers of watch committees in relation to the appointment, promotion and discipline of subordinate ranks be transferred to chief constables, and that watch committees cease to have an appellate function with regard to discipline. These recommendations were duly implemented in the 1964 Act, ss.7 and 37.

[92] Royal Commission on the Police (1962) paras 162–164.

[93] Police Act 1964, s.12.

[94] See *e.g.* Marshall and Loveday (1994) pp. 300–301; Loughlin (1996) p. 166.

[95] Royal Commission on the Police (1962) paras. 88–91.

police authority without a secure foothold from which to contribute to policy-making.

This example of legislative omission returns us, naturally, to the final defining characteristic of the contemporary regime of police governance—the underspecification of statutory responsibilities. For all that the Royal Commission and the ensuing legislation set out many of the detailed obligations of the various parties to the tripartite systems more fully and more systematically than ever before, arguably it failed to resolve many of the broader and more fundamental questions about boundaries and relationships. This failure appears to have been linked not only to the general prudential justification for underspecification discussed above, but also to the particular conceptual minefield presented by the doctrine of constabulary independence. We have already noted how the Commissioners were not prepared to confront the limitations and obscurities of the doctrine, but instead bound themselves to accepting it as an unalterable baseline for thinking about police governance.[96] However, in fudging this key issue, the Commissioners also undermined their capacity to describe in confident brushstrokes the general allocation of responsibilities within the renewed tripartite system. The decision not to allocate overall responsibility for an efficient policing system to the centre, which had the consequence, *inter alia*, of limiting the answerability of ministers to Parliament, was clearly linked to the concern that a general political responsibility for efficiency might be at odds with the broad professional autonomy permitted by the independence doctrine. Equally, that the Commissioners were squeamish about the prospect of "rough parliamentary hands [being] laid on the delicately balanced relationship"[97] between police and local police authority and "shirked the job"[98] of establishing a clear statutory mandate for the police authority, was undoubtedly connected to their concern that too robust an assertion of the involvement of police authorities in the policy process might encroach upon the uncertain and expansive boundaries of constabulary independence.

As we shall discover in the next chapter, the Commissioners' reluctance to dispense with the strategy of underspecification was not without consequence. The strained working relations under the police governance system which precipitated the 1962 report were to recur in more serious form, exposing the omissions and confusions of the new

---

[96] See esp. , *ibid.*, para. 81.
[97] Marshall and Loveday (1994) p. 311.
[98] *ibid.*, p. 301.

system. Further, and ironically, the fact that the new regime of police governance was more systematic in some of its detailed specification promised to exacerbate, rather than alleviate, the more basic failure to resolve the broader questions definitively. After the 1964 Act, law, conceived of as a narrow instrumental resource, was in more plentiful supply to the parties to the tripartite system as they pursued the fundamental conflicts of police governance that law, conceived of instead as a broad normative guide, had left unresolved.

Chapter Three

The Royal Commission Model in Context

Any attempt to assess the success of the tripartite model instituted by the 1964 Act and to explain why the pressures towards change became irresistible by the early 1990s is fraught with difficulty. Should a shelf life of thirty years be viewed as a vindication of the modern settlement, or as evidence of its structural weakness? Should the unparalleled levels of public controversy surrounding the police in the years since the Royal Commission deliberated be interpreted as an indictment of their conclusions? Should we look to the long stretches of harmony, or instead to the increasingly abrasive notes of disharmony, which attended relations within the triumvirate of central government, local police authority and chief constable under the 1964 Act as the barometer of its effectiveness?

There is no simple answer. There is no straightforward index of the success of modern tripartitism. Its relationship with the general public profile of policing is complex, shifting and indirect, and evidence of harmony or disharmony within the constitutional triangle tells us very little about the *quality* of the key relationships. If we want to understand the trajectory of modern tripartitism, we must develop a more rounded and less reductionist perspective, one which is sensitive to the dynamic quality of a framework of governance in an area so closely influenced by the overall balance of political forces within the state.

In this vein, we set out to examine three related dimensions of the tripartite relationship from the perspective of each party. First, there are the resources, legal or otherwise, available to the parties, which define their capacity to act. Secondly, there are the various strategic priorities of the three parties. What are the aspirations of the three parties as regards the scope and nature of their influence over the conduct of policing? Thirdly—the issue which tends to attract most attention—how do the various parties relate to one another? In what follows we examine, with reference to the three dimensions of capacity, priorities and triangular relations, the three defining phases in the post-1964 order: the early consolidation of the new ascendancy of the chief constables and central government; descent into crisis in the late 1970s and 1980s; and the fashioning of a reform agenda in the early 1990s.

1. Consolidation

If the Royal Commission and the 1964 Act planted the seeds of conflict, a long period elapsed before the first shoots appeared. For Lustgarten, indeed, the initial fifteen years was a "period of quiescence approaching the comatose".[1] Why was this so, and why did it come to an end?

Basically, the period of harmony was attributable to two factors. First, the enhanced aspirations of two of the parties—chief constables and central government—were satisfactorily accommodated within the new constitutional settlement. Secondly, the diminished capacity under the settlement of the third party—the police authorities—was mitigated by their correspondingly reduced ambition and the absence of circumstances which set their interests and perspective in direct opposition to those of the other two parties.

In the last chapter we explored at length how an expansive definition of constabulary independence evolved over the course of the twentieth century, eventually receiving the endorsement of the Royal Commission. In the central example of its tendency to underspecification,[2] the 1964 Act endorsed the independence doctrine *sub silentio* rather than by active pronouncement, yet in the years that followed the courts took a strong initiative in underlining the freedom of the police in general and the chief constable in particular from external interference. *R v. Metropolitan Police Commissioner, ex parte Blackburn*[3] is a watershed in this regard. In the first of a series of actions against the capital police force, Raymond Blackburn sought mandamus to require the Commissioner to adopt a more vigorous approach to the monitoring of London casinos and the prosecution of illegal gaming. In rejecting Mr Blackburn's claim, the Court of Appeal struck two telling blows in favour of chief constabulary discretion.

---

[1] Lustgarten (1986) p. 74.
[2] See chapter two, section 2.
[3] [1968] 2 Q.B. 118.

First, the court made it clear that the appellant's attempt to give more body to the somewhat anaemic concept of accountability to law[4] by resort to the long-standing but rapidly expanding jurisdiction[5] of the courts to review the exercise of executive discretion of accountability could meet with only limited success. While confirming that the police had a public duty to enforce the law, which they could be judicially required to perform, the court asserted that short of complete non-enforcement the chief officer retained a broad discretion over methods and priorities.[6] However, while this was the fundamental *ratio* of the case, and formed an important base point for the line of judicial review decisions which followed, the case is better known for Lord Denning's extended *obiter* in which he addressed the tripartite system directly and confirmed that the chief officer was the servant neither of the police authority nor of central government.[7] Lustgarten has argued convincingly that this passage owes much more to assertion than to argument and is replete with basic legal errors, not least a failure to appreciate the manner in which the constitutional position of the Metropolitan Commissioner differs from that of his chief constable colleagues.[8] However, the sloppy reasoning which underlies the decision is not unconnected with its having assumed such importance. In essence, Lord Denning's judgment is merely an "uncritical repetition of the familiar inferences from *Fisher* v. *Oldham*"[9]—a first *judicial* journey along the well-trodden short-cut from tort law and employment law, through the private/public boundary fence, to the fundamentals of police governance. Yet it is precisely the confident and categorical tone of the Master of the Rolls and his unswerving sense of direction which makes his contribution such a significant endorsement of the constitutional *zeitgeist*.

Later case law has tended to concentrate on the judicial control of police discretion without direct regard to the tripartite relationship and has endorsed the first *Blackburn* decision with only minor qualifications. Mr Blackburn took the Metropolitan Commissioner back to court in the 1970s,[10] and again in the 1980s,[11] seeking to challenge various restrictive

---

[4] See chapter 2, section 1(D).

[5] On the exponential development of administrative law in general and judicial review in particular from the 1950s onwards, see, for example, De Smith, Woolf and Jowell, (1995) ch.1.

[6] At 136, *per* Lord Denning M.R; at 148, *per* Edmund Davies L.J.

[7] At 136.

[8] Lustgarten (1986) pp. 62–67.

[9] Marshall and Loveday (1994) p. 300.

[10] *R* v. *Metropolitan Police Commissioner, ex parte Blackburn (No.3)* [1973] Q.B. 241.

[11] *R* v. *Metropolitan Police Commissioner, ex parte Blackburn, The Times* March 7, 1980 (CA).

enforcement regimes and prosecution policies under the Obscene Publications Act 1959. While the court did not necessarily approve of the
Commissioner's priorities, they reinforced the point, particularly in the
latter case, that in the context of general law enforcement policy they
will not interfere with the discretion of the chief officer provided there
is no self-imposed policy of total non-enforcement.

Challenges by way of judicial review of the law enforcement discretion of the chief officer with regard to concrete incidents rather than
general policy and practice have been no more successful. In *R. v.
Oxford, ex p. Levey*[12] the victim of a jewellery shop theft failed to persuade the court to declare *ultra vires* the policy of the chief constable
requiring the force control room to be informed prior to a police vehicle entering the Toxteth area of Liverpool, a policy which Mr Levey
claimed led to the premature termination of the pursuit of the suspect in
the instant case. Here the court drew a distinction between "methods"
and "standards" of law enforcement. Methods were a matter over which
chief constables exercised a non-reviewable discretion, provided that the
methods chosen were not tantamount to the abdication of all responsibility for enforcement of a particular law in a particular area, or required
a lower standard of law enforcement.[13]

On its facts, the *Oxford* case did not in the final analysis reveal a "no-
go" policy, but what of a more directive policy decision which seeks to
remove the effective discretion of the street constable by requiring or for-
bidding arrest, or some other exercise of legal power, in a predefined
type of situation? Such an eventuality would appear to expose the internal incoherence of constabulary independence as a double-layered concept, since it suggests that the policy autonomy of the chief cannot be
respected without encroaching upon the autonomy of the ordinary constable in the execution of the law, and vice versa. In such circumstances,
it is clear that the law will—and should—respect the independence of
the ordinary constable.[14] Yet, paradoxically, judicial deference to the
authority of the individual constable may reinforce rather than qualify
the independence of the chief officer. In the *Central Electricity Generating
Board* (C.E.G.B.) case,[15] the Board had applied for an order of mandamus
against the chief officer's refusal to act to remove protesters obstructing

[12] (1987) 151 L.G. Rev. 371.
[13] *per* Sir John Donaldson, M.R.
[14] *Fisher v. Oldham Corporation* [1930] 2 K.B. 364. See generally chapter two, section 1(d).
[15] *R v. Chief Constable of Devon and Cornwall, ex parte Central Electricity Generating Board*
[1981] 3 W.L.R. 961.

78

the exploration of the site of a possible nuclear power station. In declining to grant the order, the majority of the court were persuaded by the argument that it is for the constable on the spot to exercise authority against the protesters, as only that officer is in a position to assess whether the factual conditions which are prerequisite to the lawful exercise of the necessary powers have been met.[16]

It would seem, therefore, that from the mid-1960s onwards the case-law on constabulary independence offers chief constables two layers of protection; direct insulation, in terms of theirs own sphere of independent action, and further indirect cover by reference to their *absence* of responsibility within the executive law enforcement sphere of the ordinary constable. Admittedly, even now, despite the weight of case-law[17] and the absence of any legislative intervention to the contrary, an argument could be made that, on a close reading, the judicial authority for a strong doctrine of constabulary independence amounts to no more than "the piling on of *obiter* upon *obiter*".[18] However, such academic quibbles surely do not challenge Lustgarten's judgement that the doctrine has "embedded itself in the lore and learning of both judges and police, and it is inconceivable that, without parliamentary intervention, the courts would resile from the position they have reached".[19]

If this rich seam of judicial law-making consolidated the statutory independence granted to chief constables under the 1964 Act, other institutional and cultural factors enhanced their power. Successive Home Secretaries were vigorous in the use of their improved powers of amalgamation,[20] resulting in fewer chief constables with higher profiles and with larger bureaucracies and budgets under their command. This increase in organisational scale combined with a new emphasis upon technologically-grounded expertise in police work and the growth of a more general managerial culture within local government administration to produce an increasingly robust professional ideology within the police.[21]

---

[16] See esp. Lawton, L.J., at 835.

[17] Other unsuccessful applications include *Kent* v. *Metropolitan Police Commissioner, The Times,* 15 May 1981 (a challenge to the Metropolitan Police Commissioner's 28–day ban on public processions after the Brixton Disorders); *Adams* v. *Metropolitan Police Commissioner* [1980] R.T.R. 289 (an attempt to obtain a declaration concerning the Commissioner's discretion not to prosecute for alleged traffic violations). For recent developments inspired by EU law, see chapter four, section 2(C)(ii).

[18] Reiner (1991) p. 18.

[19] Lustgarten (1986) p. 67.

[20] As early as 1969, the number of forces in England and Wales had been reduced from 117 (at the passage of the 1964 Act) to 47.

[21] See *e.g.* Holdaway (1977)

The significance of the emergence of this, as indeed of any professional ideology, is that it provided senior police officers—both individually and collectively through the increasingly influential Association of Chief Police Officers (ACPO)[22]—with a status, and a self-understanding, as privileged exponents of their craft, and so less inclined to defer to external opinion.

This enhanced professionalism also provided a defining feature of relations between the chief and the Home Office after the 1964 Act. We noted earlier that the emergence of an embryonic uniform police service in the first half of the twentieth century was marked by the assumption of a central role in co-ordination and standard-setting, and by the development of policy networks which included local points of influence.[23] After 1964 this network thickened considerably, with central government and the chiefs, each supported by enhanced legal powers and by its own body of professional advisors, consolidating their position as prime movers and close collaborators in the development of policy detail. Their joint influence ranged from the highly formal context of statutory consultative machinery and the preparation of delegated legislation, through the semi-formal, "soft law" of circulars,[24] to a web of more informal exchanges and dependencies.

Where did the consolidation of the power of the Home Office and police professionals leave the local police authority? In strictly legal terms, they may have been deprived of explicit powers of policy direction, but they did retain significant authority over personnel, force infrastructure and the receipt of information—although even these powers were subject to the veto of the Home Secretary. In practice, however, the evidence suggests that the new authorities adopted a marginal and largely deferential attitude towards their statutory role. For the most part, authorities did not use their information-gathering powers very extensively, did not dwell upon potentially sensitive areas such as public complaints, did not offer policy advice, and merely rubber-stamped requests for more resources.[25] There appeared to be a higher level of involvement in the narrowly focused area of senior appointments, although there is nothing to suggest that authorities sought to utilise their power to hire

---

[22] ACPO was formed in 1948 by a merger of two earlier bodies, a County Chief Constables Club founded in 1858, and a Chief Constables Association founded in 1896 for city and borough chiefs.

[23] See chapter two, section 1(C).

[24] See, for example, Brogden (1982) pp. 114–116.

[25] See, for example, Marshall (1973); Banton (1974); Brogden (1977); Kettle (1980).

as a way of exercising prospective influence over policy.[26] Rather than major strategic issues, police authorities were more pre-occupied with the "dignified" aspects of policing—the kind of public ceremony and organisational ritual which barely scratches the surface of police work.[27]

Why were police authorities prepared to adopt such a supine role? In part it may have been an acceptance, in accordance with the "rule of anticipated reactions",[28] that any attempt by them to flex their legal muscles would likely end in defeat. But given the uncertainty of their legal position, such an acceptance seems unnecessarily fatalistic. In part, too, therefore, their attitude may have been the self-exclusion of the under-informed and amateur before the formidable informational resources and professional expertise of the chief constable-Home Office axis,[29] a contrast underscored by the increasing scale at which police authorities and their forces were expected to operate in the new regime. And the modesty of police authorities may have been reinforced by the fact that one third lacked the basic democratic mandate and responsibility of the elected politician, while, after local government reorganisation and the introduction of joint committees in 1974, even the elected two thirds in many cases lacked the unity of purpose and directness of popular accountability of a police authority whose boundaries were co-terminus with those of a single local authority.[30] Yet most importantly of all, it seems in retrospect, the initial acquiescence of police authorities in this new uneven balance of power was bound up with the continuing absence of a sustained critical discourse about policing within British society and politics. It is to the development of such a critical discourse that we now turn.

2. Polarisation

The late 1970s and early 1980s marked a radical departure in police-public relations in Britain, and proved to be a watershed in the operation of the 1964 model of tripartitism. This statement, which is similar to

---

[26] See Regan (1983).

[27] See, e.g., Loveday (1983).

[28] Friedrichs (1937) p. 16.

[29] On the significance of (the lack of) independent information sources and administrative back-up, see Loveday (1985); Simey (1988); McLaughlin (1994); Jones, Newburn and Smith (1994).

[30] See e.g., Loveday (1991).

countless other general observations of the period, contains two significant assumptions which, if unpacked and justified, provide the explanatory key to the emergence of a new political climate around police
accountability. In the first place, there is the assumption that over the
longue durée of police history, we can talk meaningfully about radical
departures within a narrow time-frame. Secondly, there is the assumption that a radical departure in police-public relations, if such it was,
would in any case have had direct and immediate consequences for the
framework of accountability.

As we saw in chapter two, in the late 1950s a combination of public
and political anxieties about policing created the climate within which a
Royal Commission was established. Yet research undertaken by the
Commission itself suggested the resilience of high levels of respect for the
police across all social classes. Over the following twenty years, however,
police legitimacy declined markedly, especially in the eyes of young people, ethnic minorities and economic marginals.[31] That this decline led to
a qualitative shift in the character of police-public relations around the
turn of the 1980s depended upon a two-stage process.

To begin with, the decline in legitimacy developed its own momentum, involving the mutual reinforcement of a wide range of factors. Corruption scandals in the Metropolitan Police and elsewhere sullied the
constabulary image as a disciplined bureaucracy. A series of miscarriages
of justice in murder and, later, in terrorist cases threatened the reputation
of the British police for adherence to the rule of law. The increasing use
of aggressive units and military tactics and technology in the contexts of
mass picketing and public disorder undercut their traditional commitment to minimal force. Widespread resort to incident-centred car patrol
in place of general foot-patrol threatened to replace the motto of service
and prevention with that of force and reaction. An increasingly open ideological affiliation in the 1970s with the "law and order" politics of the
Conservatives and declining relations with certain groups such as young
blacks and industrial pickets, challenged the ideal of an impartial police
force—a neutral dispenser of justice above politics and apart from society. Recorded crime increased fivefold in 20 years and was increasingly
perceived as the tip of the iceberg of overall crime, reinforcing existing
doubts about the efficacy of the police in their core task of security
provision.[32]

---

[31] See *e.g.,* Policy Studies Institute (1983).
[32] For an excellent overview of these trends, see Reiner (1992a) chap.2. See also Reiner
(1992b);(1994);(1995).

These various trends fed closely off each other. For instance, the rise in crime prompted resort to reactive, "fire brigade" policing, which increased the physical and social distance between police and community and loosened the co-operative bonds on which public support and assistance for policing depends, in turn further blighting the effectiveness of policing as a crime-fighting facility. The use of more aggressive tactics for policing crowds and public spaces encouraged a cycle of increasingly abrasive confrontation. Scandals associated with police rule-breaking were events around which public campaigns critical of policing were organised, and this also led to general distrust and specific flashpoints between the police and particular groups.

If this self-reinforcing process raised the temperature of police-public relations, it took a number of critical incidents to bring matters to the boil. The riots in the spring and summer of 1981 involving the police and young ethnic minority populations in London, Liverpool, Bristol and elsewhere provided the crucial catalyst, leading to the establishment of a high profile Committee of Inquiry under Lord Scarman.[33] Various confrontational industrial disputes culminating in the miners' strike of 1984–85 provided a second defining moment, consolidating a new and less consensual phase of police-public relations.[34]

Why, and how, did this transformation in police-public relations affect the accountability system? Whereas most of the incidents which precipitated the 1962 Royal Commission were directly concerned with the operation of the system of police governance, this was not the case with the new trends. Yet they did have a clear and cumulative impact upon the operation of the governance system. In particular, they altered the attitudes and relationship of two of the main tripartite players—police and police authorities.

As noted above, one of the significant shifts of the 1970s was the overt politicisation of police representation, including certain high profile chief constables and the Police Federation. This reached its apogee in 1979 with the Federation's clear, if implicit electoral support for the law and order policies of the Conservative government-in-waiting.[35] The politicisation process was not exempt from the close interaction which characterised the relationship between the various dimensions of change in this period. In particular, the self-raising of the police profile was closely connected with the wish to convey the right sort of security-conscious,

---

[33] Scarman (1981); for contemporary commentary, see Cowell, Lea and Young (1982).
[34] See, *e.g.*, Fine and Millar (1985).
[35] See, *e.g.*, Reiner (1981).

budget-justifying public message about the rise in crime rates. It was, however, also connected, in a mutually reinforcing fashion, with the trend towards focused local campaigns of opposition to controversial police incidents and strategies. As the police defended their position with greater vigour against "do-gooders" and "politicians",[36] so, paradoxically, they increasingly made themselves "fair game" as political targets.

Although police monitoring and campaign groups at some remove from local government were also present at the birth of this critical movement and remained a significant influence,[37] gradually the local authorities themselves and their police authorities moved centre stage, and the tripartite system became both a site of struggle and a renewed object of political critique and reform attempts. Racist behaviour, corruption, violence against prisoners, discriminatory policing of public marches and assemblies, deaths in custody; these were some of the themes around which a more general politicisation of the tripartite relationship took place.[38] Nationally, the Labour Party took up the cause of greater democratic accountability to local authorities, first through two unsuccessful private member bills in 1979 and 1980 sponsored by Jack Straw in an earlier incarnation as an opposition backbencher, and later in official party policy. Locally, the exclusion of London from the 1964 Act provided a campaigning flagship in a location where controversial incidents were disproportionately concentrated. After its victory in the 1981 local elections, the Labour administration of the Greater London Council (GLC) set up its own police committee and support unit, which quickly became a major nerve-centre of oppositional politics. These same elections also threw up a number of Labour administrations on the left of the party in the other metropolitan centres of England. Radically opposed to the Thatcherite agenda, this new wave of municipal socialism saw it as its mission to make local government the vehicle to recover from the overweening centre control of those institutions, such as the police, whose actions directly affected the interests of local communities.

Reinforcing the link between the crisis of legitimacy and stresses within the governance structure, these same metropolitan areas played host to the major policing incidents associated with the urban disorders and the miners strike. For example, the riots of 1981, as well as raising the temperature another few notches in London, also acutely politicised

---

[36] These are two of the categories of the lay public of which, according to Reiner (1992a) pp. 120–121), the police develop stereotypical conceptions.

[37] See *e.g.*, Brogden, Jefferson and Walklate (1988) chap. 8; Jefferson, McLaughlin and Robertson (1988); McLaughlin (1994).

[38] See *e.g.*, Spencer (1985a).

the relationship in Merseyside and Greater Manchester between the respective chief constables, Kenneth Oxford and James Anderton, and their police committees, which were critical of police attitudes to ethnic minorities in general and their handling of the disorders in particular.[39] In 1984, the miners' strike was the occasion for more acute and sustained conflict between chief constables and their police authorities.[40] The tensions were nationwide, extending even to areas far removed from the strike action but encouraged, under the mutual aid arrangements, to send considerable policing support. Yet it was in the striking heartlands, Lancashire, Yorkshire, Derbyshire and Nottinghamshire, that the breakdown in relations was most acute between chief constables firmly committed to securing the free passage of working miners and local authorities apprehensive at the cost and public order implications of such tactics and ideologically sympathetic to the cause of the strikers.

At this juncture, the problem of underspecification which had been built into the foundations of the 1964 Act reared itself. In the period of post-act consolidation, the police authorities' poverty of aspiration meant that the fuzzy definition of the legal landscape had few practical consequences. Now, with some authorities seeking to assert their autonomy from and opposition to the chief constables and frustrated at the lack of any clear legal mandate to develop a strategy, the gaps and incoherence left by the Royal Commission settlement were exposed.

In Greater Manchester, the police authority sought to reduce its financial commitments during the strike by ordering the removal of the police band. The chief, James Anderton, regarded this order as an invasion of his command, but backed down after the Chief Inspector of Constabulary and the Home Office refused to support this view. Clearly, they did not consider the making of music at ceremonial occasions to fall within chief constabulary independence, despite its broad extension across operational and policy elements, or within the chief's statutory power to direct and control the force. Yet on what basis were the police authority justified in making the order? Granted, they had a formal power to approve expenditure not already earmarked by law, but if the principle of he who pays the piper calls the tune were to apply to all such expenditure, then the police authority, particularly through refusing to provide for various forms of operational equipment, could frustrate, qualify or otherwise affect many decisions regarded as falling within the exclusive

---

[39] See *e.g.,* Anderton (1981); Simey (1996).
[40] See *e.g.,* Spencer (1985b); Lustgarten (1986) chap.8; Oliver (1987) chap.15; Reiner (1991) pp. 182–192.

domain of constabulary independence. If, on the other hand, this principle did not apply generally, on what basis should it apply to any particular case, such as the present one?

Matters were even more complicated in South Yorkshire. Over the first few months of the strike the police authority aired a number of grievances about the local force's policing response, particularly their involvement in mutual aid and their intensive policing of a heavily picketed coking depot at Orgreave, the isolation of which the miners perceived to be vital to the enduring success of their action. The police authority devised a number of strategies to register their displeasure, curb the activities of the constabulary, and force the Home Office to pick up a larger share of the bill. Having withdrawn the chief constable's delegated authority to incur any expenditure in connection with the mining dispute without their prior approval, the police authority refused a subsequent request by him for a considerable sum of money to police Orgreave over the course of a week. The chief constable complained to the Home Office, and the Attorney General, as the Government's chief law officer, raised an action of judicial review to challenge the police authority's refusal. A compromise solution was found before the court could rule, but again the blurred lines of the statute and common law make it difficult to predict how the case would have been resolved. Palpably, this was a more direct encroachment upon the command of the chief constable than was attempted in Greater Manchester, yet it remains difficult to justify restriction of the clear and specific financial authority of the police authority in the name of the hazy and general common law and statutory powers of the chief.[41] Another line of argument is that this particular use of the police authority's financial powers would be at odds with their own broader responsibility to secure the maintenance of an adequate and efficient police force, but for a court to reach such a conclusion would require a more robust judicial attitude to the interpretation of value-laden terms such as "adequate" and "efficient" than is the norm within administrative law.[42]

---

[41] Furthermore, as the Attorney General's role is to assert public rights, it is difficult to see why he should have standing to assert the chief constable's exclusive powers of direction and control under s.5 of the 1964 Act. Surely, as Lustgarten argues (1986, p. 122), that should be a matter for the chief constable alone.

[42] This is not to deny that the courts continue, in practice, to apply variable thresholds of intervention by way of judicial review of the exercise of public power, and that they remain inclined in the exercise of their discretion to be more favourably disposed to the needs and concerns of some authorities, such as those associated with state security (including the police), than to others such as local government. See, for example, Griffiths (1997),

Later the same year, a further legal stand-off occurred between the tri-partite parties in South Yorkshire. The police authority devised a cost-cutting package which included a plan to dispose of the entire mounted section and half the dogs section of the local force. Once more, the question of encroachment on the operational command of the chief constable was raised. The interference may have been less apparent than the attempted embargo on policing at Orgreave, but it remained a hard case. Unlike the Greater Manchester Police Band, there was a direct link between the capacity of the mounted and dogs sections and the general effectiveness of the police in carrying out their core tasks, not least in the context of policing a major strike. A further tangle in the legal knot was supplied by the Home Secretary, who threatened to instigate his own court action against the police authority. It seems unlikely that this third party intervention would have clarified the uncertain articulation of police authority and chief constabulary powers, as the Home Secretary's own powers are no more definite. Denied direct responsibility for the overall efficiency of the police in the 1964 Act, and also lacking particular responsibility for establishment or equipment, his capacity to raise such an action, still less to succeed in it, would at that time have seemed tenuous.[43] In any event, for a second time the parties negotiated a solution before the courts could pronounce. The difficulties of the 1964 Act had been further exposed, again without attracting a judicial resolution.

3. Steering from the Centre

If the measure of tripartitism was simply the degree of overt harmony or disharmony between the parties, then the mid-1980s marked the nadir of this system of governance. On this crude empirical test, things had

---

chap.10; see also section 1 above. Relatedly, in a famous series of cases the courts have developed the idea of a fiduciary relationship between local government and local tax-payers, placing the former under a duty to spend money efficiently and with due regard to economy; see *e.g., Roberts* v. *Hopwood* [1925] A.C. 578; *Prescott* v. *Birmingham Corporation* [1955] chap.10; *Bromley L.B.C.* v. *Greater London Council* [1983] 1 A.C. 768; see also Loughlin (1996) chap.4. Running these two trends together, we should perhaps not be surprised if the courts were to adopt an unusually robust supervisory approach towards the police authority's exercise of its financial powers over the local force.

[43] Although now much strengthened following *R.* v. *Secretary of State for the Home Department, ex parte Northumbria Police Authority*, [1988] 1 All E.R. 556, discussed in chapter one, section 2(a)(ii).

never been so bad, and, it is fair to say, were not again subsequently. Why did relations "improve", and with what implications for the underlying health and direction of the system of governance?

In the short-term, restoration of harmony was achieved not by fundamentally restructuring and reallocating legal powers and responsibilities amongst the triumvirate, but by reshaping aims and expectations. For the most part, the new confrontational politics had remained confined to the metropolitan heartlands of municipal socialism, the habits of deference proving resilient elsewhere. It required, then, only a limited surgical incision to restore the surface equilibrium, and this was provided by the abolition of the metropolitan county councils under the Local Government Act 1985. In one fell swoop, the most long-standing, committed, reflective and articulate opponents of the skewing of tripartitism towards the constabulary and the political centre were removed—by the political centre. They were replaced by joint boards, drawn from and financed through the district councils which covered the old metropolitan area.[44] As with joint boards generally in local government, these new hybrids lacked the direct accountability, the ideological unity, the organisational coherence and the radicalising experience of the unitary structures they replaced. Unsurprisingly, they have proved far more biddable to the preferences and demands of chief constables than their predecessors.[45]

Another development which had the effect of reshaping the attitudes of the "community" constituency within the tripartite relationship was the introduction of local consultative arrangements in the wake of the Scarman Report.[46] Police authorities were now required to make arrangements for obtaining the views of people in local areas about matters concerning policing and for securing the co-operation of the local population with the police in preventing crime. These new responsibilities were met through the establishment within each force of a number of local police-community liaison committees. While these new structures served to broaden the base of public involvement in local policing, their membership and functions militated against any serious challenge to a police-centred agenda. The liaison committees tended to be drawn from the local "great and good"—from constituencies who lack experi-

---

[44] It was not, however, an entirely bloodless coup, as many Labour-controlled district councils at first threatened not to meet their new responsibilities; see McLaughlin (1994) p. 105

[45] See e.g., Loveday (1991).

[46] Initially introduced by Home Office Circular (54/1982) and subsequently formalised as s.106 of the Police and Criminal Evidence Act 1984. See now, Police Act 1996, s.96

ence of adversarial contact with the police and a critical perspective on police professional ideology. And in the absence of a legal mandate to assert a more independent role, the liaison committees were apt to be treated as junior partners within a new consultative framework. What limited impact they have made has been as forums for the articulation of community preferences, for local conflict-resolution, for educating the community in the needs and demands of policing, and for the development of a more co-operative approach to crime prevention. All in all, while the new consultative mechanism had—and retains—the potential to shift the balance of power within police governance towards the local community, in its early years at least[47]—and against the background of the existing asymmetry of power—it tended, rather, to reinforce police control. Key sections of the local community were co-opted to the police standpoint, while the *appearance* of root and branch reform served to reduce the momentum of the campaign for more radical reform of police governance.[48]

In other respects, too, the late 1980s saw a gradual reshaping of expectations and orientations away from the confrontational politics of the earlier part of the decade. The absence of any further flashpoints on the same scale as 1981 and 1984–85 made a difference. So, too, did the retreat of chief constables and other representative associations from a position of close alignment to the Conservative Party on law and order. There was to be no repeat of the partisan politicking of the 1979 general election, and even though the chiefs in general vigorously defended their impartiality during the miners strike,[49] the abrasive climate surrounding the dispute doubtless reminded many police representatives of the wisdom of political discretion. The modernisation of the Labour Party and its new commitment, first under Neil Kinnock and then under John Smith and his shadow Home Secretary Tony Blair to be "tough on crime and tough on the causes of crime"[50] also began to shift anti-establishment attitudes in socialist local government.

Yet the gradual reintegration of the local government point of the tripartite structure was only part of the changing political landscape. There were larger movements afoot in the late 1980s—again largely at the level of ideas and beliefs rather than concrete rights and responsibilities—which

---

[47] On the place of local consultative arrangements within the revised tripartite system, see chapter four.

[48] See in particular Morgan (1992).

[49] See Reiner (1991) pp. 182–192.

[50] Tony Blair's first national soundbite—and still perhaps his most notorious.

cut more deeply across existing relationships and provided a template for the statutory reforms of the 1990s. In particular, there were twin and related movements towards greater centralisation and towards a more managerialist culture in the governance of policing.

It was earlier remarked that in times of crisis the opportunity may be taken to consolidate greater control at the centre. It was also noted that the gradual establishment of a national policing "policy network" was not about crude "top-down" control, but about the development of a national framework of dialogue and mutual understanding. [51] In the 1980s, we can observe the accentuation of both trends.

Although the National Reporting Centre,[52] which co-ordinated mutual aid arrangements during the miners' strike, remained under the ultimate control of the constituent forces, there is evidence of some central influence and interference.[53] We have already seen how the landmark decision of the Court of Appeal in the *Northumbria* case[54] made it possible for central government conceptions of efficient resource deployment to prevail over those of the local police authority in the context of the provision of plastic bullets for riot control. Alongside these bold new prints of central encroachment there were more subtle markers of influence. The 1964 Act had given the Home Office the power to approve the short-list of candidates for the office of chief constable or his assistants or deputy, and this was one of a number of tools increasingly used by the centre as a means of moulding a policing elite with broadly the same professional orientation. Senior training and career development, too, became well-tuned instruments of socialisation. By the end of the decade, almost all chief constables had undergone the *rites de passage* of attendance at the Senior Command Course, the Bramshill Special Course and secondment to one of the growing number of key central units.[55] These factors meant that between the Home Office and the chiefs, whether individually or collectively—with ACPO's profile continuing to rise with the development of its in-house policy facility in 1990[56]—the trend towards an underlying concurrence of interests and

---

[51] See chapter two, section 1(C).

[52] Later renamed the Mutual Aid Centre.

[53] See Reiner (1991) pp. 182–192.

[54] *R. v Secretary of State for the Home Department, ex parte Northumbria Police Authority* [1988] 1 All E.R. 556. See also chapter one, section 2(A)(ii).

[55] Reiner (1991) chap.2. On the growth of central units, see chapter seven.

[56] For an analysis which demonstrates that the rise of ACPO is in one sense a centralising tendency—given its preference for national standardization, but in another sense a decentralising tendency—given ACPO's own reliance on "bottom-up" policy making, see Savage, Charman and Cope (1996). See also Charman and Savage (1998).

co-operation of effort, already quickened since 1964, became increasingly pronounced.

The new managerialism—or New Public Management—of the 1980s was a final crucial and complicating factor in this mix. The return of the economically liberal Conservative Government in 1979 signalled a more sceptical attitude towards the public sector. The new administration sought so far as possible to adapt private sector managerial imperatives of effectiveness and efficiency to the demands of the public sector. At first, the police were shielded from this process. They were "doubly different"[57] from private enterprise. If the simple fact of their membership of the public sector no longer guaranteed them immunity from market disciplines, then their special constitutional position and political role did allow at least some retention of privileges. The police could, and frequently did, invoke notions of constabulary independence, low performance visibility and necessary on-the-spot discretion to resist reduction of their job to the cold, documented logic of value-for-money. Perhaps more pertinently, the 1979 Government had made a manifesto commitment to loosen the public purse-strings on law and order and substantially to increase police pay. Their unflinching support for the constabulary was both ideological—a public pledge of their uncompromising approach to crime, and strategic—a loyalty bonus to the institution which had to deal with some of the more divisive social consequences of Government policy.

In the final analysis, however, this could only delay the subjection of the police to managerial audit. As we have seen, the end of the post-war Golden Age of policing was as much about decreased effectiveness as declining legitimacy. Policing was an increasingly expensive activity which increasingly failed to deliver in terms of the performance indicators most closely associated with its core activity of crime control. As early as 1983, the Home Office, as part of its departmental response to the broader Financial Management Initiative, produced a circular which called upon forces, under the supervision of the Inspectorate of Constabulary, to set clear and measurable priorities and objectives which reflected the wishes of the public.[58] The involvement of the Inspectorate, which has a statutory responsibility to report on force efficiency, became

---

[57] McLaughlin and Murji (1997) p. 86.
[58] Home Office Circular 114/1983. This gave an early boost in the UK to Policing by Objectives (PBO) systems, whose most articulate British exponent has been Tony Butler (1984; 1992b).

a regular theme of central managerial initiatives throughout the 1980s, and by the end of the decade, it was a main player in applying financial management techniques to the police.[59] So, too, was the Audit Commission. Created in 1982[60] specifically to evaluate local government management in terms of the "three Es" of economy, efficiency and effectiveness, it began a series of critical studies of police managerial practice in 1988 and strongly reinforced the need for rational management techniques and quasi-market disciplines.

By the early 1990s, the development of the new managerialism in policing was critically poised, and was beginning to have contradictory effects upon the system of governance. On the one hand, it underscored the movement towards greater co-ordination from the centre. Against a background of increasing central control over finance and personnel, the Home Office, the Inspectorate, the Audit Commission and ACPO were increasingly speaking the language and applying the techniques of financial management and performance assessment. This was providing an outline strategy of "rule at a distance"[61]—with local constabularies constrained less by direct orders and more by incorporation within an approach which imposed its own set disciplines and suggested its own priorities. To adapt a phrase, central government was deploying its considerable authority not so much in "rowing" the police organisation, but in "steering" it on a course of fiscal probity.[62]

On the other hand, the new managerialism opened up a new channel of tension between the centre and the chief constable. The unconditional generosity of the early Thatcher years was gone, and the police could not be entirely willing partners in a process which remorselessly tested their professionalism against measurable levels of productivity.[63] Yet, from that same managerialist perspective, the process of overhauling the police had hardly begun. In many ways, the police organisation, with its radical variation between forces, inflexible rank structure, high job security, still

---

[59] See *e.g.,* Reiner (1991) pp. 29–31.

[60] Local Government Act 1982.

[61] Rose and Miller (1992a).

[62] The language is that of Osbourne and Gaebler (1993), as applied to the police by Shearing (1996). See also Walker (1999a).

[63] See, for example, Butler's (1992a) warning that the PBO framework which he championed risked been applied by bodies such as the Audit Commission as a way of developing and measuring quantitative indicators of performance and promoting a narrow conception of value-for-money, rather than being utilised to develop and measure *quality* of service; see also Walker (1994a); Waddington (1999) chap.8.

expanding budget, conservative occupational culture and unclear lines of fiscal responsibility and public accountability, remained a dinosaur.[64]

New battle lines were being drawn up. Whereas the greatest challenge to the professional independence of the police in the 1980s had come from left-wing police authorities, in the 1990s it came in the more subtle form of a new centrally-endorsed philosophy of public management. Once again, the tripartite system was found wanting before these new political forces, but on this occasion the response was one of reform rather than retrenchment.

---

[64] McLaughlin and Muncie (1997) pp. 96–97.

PART II

THE TRIPARTITE SYSTEM RECAST

Chapter Four

The New Framework of Police Governance

It is a measure of how far and how quickly the tide had turned in the politics of policing that the re-election of John Major's Conservative Government in 1991 was greeted with consternation in some senior police circles. The profession was becoming increasingly nervous of the new managerialism, and their fears were fuelled the following year with the announcement of a busy reform agenda. The Sheehy Inquiry into Police Responsibilities and Rewards[1] was joined by an internal Home Office review into police reform[2] and an additional Home Office survey of core and ancillary police tasks.[3] The first two of these provided the raw material from which the Police and Magistrates' Courts Act 1994 was eventually wrought. Now consolidated within the Police Act 1996, this provides the contemporary legal framework of police governance for England and Wales.

In the present chapter we examine the philosophy and details of the new provisions, and how these relate to recent developments in case-law. We also address the early operation of these arrangements in the reconstituted police authorities and assess their potential to provide a more legitimate framework for the governance of local policing.

1. Police Governance Recalculated

(A) THE REFORM BLUEPRINT

Although the new legislation was the result of not one but two reviews, and although political and professional opposition led to watering down

---

[1] Home Office (1993a).
[2] Home Office (1993b).
[3] Home Office (1995a).

of some of the key proposals, it is still possible to see an overall strategy at work. Reiner has dubbed this the "calculative and contractual"[4] approach, and while this may not capture its full essence, it does sound the appropriate notes of managerialism and marketization.

The "contractual" element was pursued in the Sheehy Report. It proposed 272 employment and organisational initiatives, including the simplification and reduction of the rank structure; fixed-term appointments for new recruits and promoted ranks alike; reduction of starting salaries; introduction of performance-related pay for all ranks; a severance programme to eradicate "top-heaviness" in promoted ranks; and the abolition of many forms of overtime and allowance payment. The aim was to produce a leaner and more flexible organisation, one which would "provide reward structures which reward good performance and address bad" and, more generally, which should "enhance the ability of the police service to manage itself and its staff effectively".[5]

As we shall see, Sheehy's attack on the "closed shop" of British policing engendered such bad feeling between Government and profession that, initially at least, it overshadowed the proposals in the White Paper on Police Reform. Yet it was the latter set of proposals which promised the more radical change and the more elaborate reform. Where Sheehy was concerned with internal organisational matters, the White Paper focused on the general governance framework. Both, however, were ultimately concerned with effectiveness and efficiency. The White Paper conveyed the clear message—echoing the well-known approach to public sector reform of its ministerial sponsor Kenneth Clarke—that the institutional architecture should in the final analysis be viewed and assessed in instrumental terms. That is to say, it was less concerned than previous conceptions of police governance[6] with the articulation of the various underlying democratic values associated with the traditional public sphere—participation, representativeness, responsiveness, etc.,—for their own sake, and more concerned with their effectiveness as tools to achieve a better police force; "to build a partnership between the police and the public to deliver what people want most, *a country which is safer to live in*".[7]

The rigorous instrumentalism of the White Paper displayed itself in an approach which was both deep and narrow; deep in its diagnosis of the

---

[4] Reiner (1993) p. 19.
[5] Home Office (1993a) pp. 6–7.
[6] See further, chapter one, section 2(B)(iv).
[7] Home Office (1993b) p. 1

ills of the 1964 system of police governance, but narrow in its vision of the type of alternative which could be developed with the aid of this diagnosis. The White Paper recognised that under the 1964 Act "confusion"[8] about the functions of the Home Secretary, police authorities and chief constables had arisen and there had developed an "entanglement of responsibilities [leading] to uncertain lines of accountability".[9] In the analytical language of previous chapters,[10] these problems could be traced to the strategy of underspecification which had been built into the foundations of the Royal Commission settlement, and, underlying this, its lack of a coherent vision of the overall governance framework and of the place of the parties within it. The institutional framework failed to treat the legal powers and responsibilities of each party as a cohesive whole, or even to match the legal powers of each party to the role to which it was best suited.

To begin with, the Home Office, commonly viewed to have got more of what it wanted than any of the other tripartite parties under the centralising drift of the 1964 Act, could nevertheless point to gaps and anomalies in its legal framework. Given its position as representative of the national democratic will, it was most suited to a broad strategic role in policy-making. Yet central government control over resources and rules—the two main mechanisms by which strategic authority might be exercised—left something to be desired. The Home Office might be the main paymaster—providing 51 per cent of the resources—but the overall size of its contribution was determined elsewhere—by how much the police authority was prepared to pay. The Home Office's rule-making authority might be considerable, but it tended to be concentrated at the "bureaucratic"[11] level of detailed circulars and guidance. Indeed, many of its most significant regulatory powers, such as the determination of establishment (in combination with police authorities), pay and working conditions, sounded at the micro-level rather than the macro-level of policy-making.

A similar mismatch between legal powers and role aspiration was evident in the case of police authorities. As representatives of the local democratic will and joint paymasters, they, too, could with some justification claim a role in the "strategic direction"[12] of the force. Yet although

---

[8] Para. 2.14
[9] Para. 2.17
[10] See esp. chapter two, section 2.
[11] Home Office (1993b) para. 2.14.
[12] Para. 2.15.

they had a duty to obtain the views of the local population about policing, they had little formal influence over policy-making. Equally, in
some areas such as pay, their duty to provide resources carried no corresponding decision-making influence. By the same token, as we saw in
the case of the miners' strike,[13] the various operational support functions
of the police authorities—in particular their general budgetary powers
and specific responsibilities for police and civilian manpower and equipment—gave them some involvement in and influence over "detailed
management issues".[14]

Such management issues, in the view of the White Paper, should
instead fall within the remit of the chief constable. As the senior professional, the chief constable should have general authority over his staff and
should have authority to deploy the resources available as he saw fit. In
fact, however, the chief had no authority over civilian staff and could be
refused particular resources or constrained to use them in a particular
way by the other parties.[15] Even the power of direction over police officers was circumscribed by the kind of organisational rigidities over rank
structure, pay and working conditions which were simultaneously being
criticised by Sheehy.[16]

Apart from the general wastage caused by the miscasting of governance roles, the "entanglement" of responsibilities and "confusion" of
functions identified by the White Paper suggested two more concrete
difficulties associated with the operation of the modern tripartite model.
In the first place, if, due to lack of strategic vision and underspecification
in key areas, the tripartite parties were disappointed in their role expectations, but if, also, due to the greater detail of legal regulation under the
1964 Act, the parties had plentiful particular legal powers to draw upon
as strategic resources,[17] we should not be surprised to find mutual entanglement leading to mutual frustration. In some respects, each party had
what the other wanted and lacked, and so it was little wonder that in circumstances of conflict over resources and policy influence there was a

---

[13] See chapter three, section 2 above. Although the White Paper's critical analysis does
illuminate some of the concrete problems which arose under the 1964 Act, including the
miners' strike, it does not in fact draw upon specific examples to make its points. In contrast, far more space is given over to a forward-looking elaboration of the Government's
reform plans, although not, as noted in the text, to a careful consideration of the alternatives. This approach is clearly a matter of political priorities and impression management.

[14] Home Office (1993b) para. 2.15.

[15] Para. 2.17.

[16] Para. 2.21.

[17] A point anticipated at the conclusion to chapter two.

tendency for each party to use spoiling tactics in seeking to advance its cause, often leading to an unproductive stalemate.[18]

A second and related problem with the underspecification of governance roles concerns confused lines of accountability.[19] In a representative democracy, a satisfactory framework of public accountability requires not only the accountors but also the accountees to be transparently accountable. Yet uncertainty concerning the extent of police policy responsibility of both central and local government meant that their own accountability—the Home Secretary's ministerial responsibility to Parliament for policing[20] and the police authority's answerability to local government and its electorate[21]—was limited and contested. The blurring of lines and attenuation of links presented an unsatisfactorily vague and fragmented pictures and encouraged a culture of avoidance, with the tripartite parties drawn into a pattern of mutual criticism and buck-passing rather than assuming joint responsibility.

The White Paper responded to these perceived shortcomings through the pursuit of three overlapping strategies. First, it sought to provide each of the three parties with a governance role which was internally coherent and to which it was best suited in terms of its authority and expertise. Secondly, it tried to ensure that the performance of each party in its newly clarified role was transparently accountable. Thirdly, it attempted to engender a co-operative rather than a conflictual atmosphere between the three parties. To recall our earlier discussion, however, these various governance strategies were viewed in narrow instrumental terms, as means towards a more effective delivery of policing services, rather than as a self-justifying normative framework for the public sphere. And, as we have observed, the ultimate objective of effective delivery was to be defined so far as possible by reference to the model of private enterprise. In practice, this meant combining the economics of the market place

---

[18] Quite apart from the legal-strategic behaviour evident in high profile cases, such as the inner-city disorders and the miners' strike of the 1980s (see chapter three, section 2), there are other documented cases of long-standing stand-offs between chiefs and their police authorities over matters such as information supply and police attendance at police authority meetings; see *e.g.*, Oliver (1987) chap.15; Kettle (1980); Reiner (1981).

[19] Home Office (1993b) para. 2.22.

[20] See chapter one, section 2(A)(ii).

[21] Arguably, this relationship becomes weaker in the case of joint boards whose own relationship to generic local government is more remote (see *e.g.*, Loveday, 1991). Tellingly in the light of its subsequent proposals, the White Paper took rather the opposite point, arguing that distance encourages independence of decision-making and that "for single county police authorities in particular, their ability to discharge this responsibility as they see fit can be undermined by their status as subordinate parts of local government"; para. 2.18.

with the politics of centralisation. In the absence of a conventional market in policing where the nature and price of the commodity would be determined by competitive supply and demand, the fashioning of a common police product and the supply of methods of assessing its quality and cost effectiveness necessarily presupposed a high degree of central decision-making and standard-setting. This was at the root of the pervasive new rationalism—the imposition of a more "calculative" discipline on all the parties involved in the business of police governance.

Bearing these underlying factors in mind, let us now look at the three governance strategies of the White Paper in greater detail. As regards general role definitions, representatives of central and local government were each to be given a more explicitly strategic role in policy formation while the chief constable was to be allowed greater autonomy in the day-to-day management of the force. The 1980s trend in the role of the Home Secretary from "rowing" towards "steering" was to be reinforced.[22] He was to become less involved in detailed forced management and more concerned with broad strategy. He would establish key objectives for all forces, supported by a small number of national performance indicators.[23] He would be aided in his strategic role by the Audit Commission, with its more detailed approach to performance measurement, and also by the Inspectorate of Constabulary, which would continue to develop its broad responsibility for ensuring force efficiency and to supplement the information available to the Home Secretary with its published reports on force and "thematic" inspections.[24] In establishing and maintaining a strategic national framework, the Home Secretary would also have more systematic oversight of the functions of the police authority. He would have new powers to call for reports from police authorities, to take remedial measures where they had failed their responsibilities, and to ensure that they set adequate budgets. On the other hand, just as the Home Secretary would no longer have detailed financial control over manpower levels, he would no longer be expected to provide a global financial contribution established by reference to local budgetary decisions. Instead, the central contribution to police expenditure would be cash limited. In some areas, however, more specific central initiatives and controls would remain. For financial, logistical and operational reasons, various central services would continue to be provided, and the centre would remain a standard-setter in a number of areas

---

[22] Home Office (1993b) chap.5.
[23] Para. 7.8.
[24] Chap.8.

of detailed police policy where local variation could not be justified.[25] Also in pursuit of economies of scale and reduction of diversity, central government would be able to take advantage of a less cumbersome procedural framework to encourage future amalgamations between police forces.[26]

Perhaps the most radical change was that contemplated for police authorities.[27] For them, the move from detailed management to strategic policy involved a more profound re-orientation. No longer involved in the minutiae of force provision, they were instead to provide the local fulcrum of the new calculative approach. Their new role would require close liaison not only with the chief constable, but also with central government and with the local community. In consultation with the chief constable, they would establish local priorities and a costed plan, and they would set the overall budget for the force. Local objectives and plans would have to fit within the overall national framework, and, as noted above, central government would had new powers over police authorities to secure this, while police authorities were to be offered the reciprocal opportunity "to feed local policing concerns into central policy making at an early stage".[28] Police authorities would continue to be closely involved with the local public, both representing their interests as the "customer"[29] whose views required to be consulted and represented in policy-making, and also, increasingly, encouraging them to offer active support to the police, themselves organisationally devolved into increasingly small units, in pursuit of their local objectives.[30]

The chief constable[31] would no longer be hamstrung by externally imposed decisions on establishment levels and the balance of ranks. Civilians would henceforth be the employees of the chief constable rather than the police authority, and so would join police officers in a "unitary management structure"[32] under the direction of the chief

---

[25] See chapter one, section 2(b)(iii). The example of necessary national standard-setting provided in the White Paper is the requirement on the Home Secretary to issue codes of practice on the exercise of police powers under the Police and Criminal Evidence Act 1984; Home Office (1993b) para.5.9.

[26] Home Office (1993b) chap.10.

[27] ibid. chap.4.

[28] ibid. para.4.14.

[29] ibid. para.4.15.

[30] ibid. chap.6. This part of the White Paper draws upon and reinforces the wider "responsibilisation strategy" (Garland (1997b) p. 189) of the 1980s and 1990s through which successive governments sought to devolve responsibility on to agencies and individuals who had previously relied upon the state itself for protection against crime.

[31] Home Office (1993b) chap.3.

[32] Para. 3.8; but see section 2(b)(v) below.

constable. Equally, professional managerial control demanded that responsibility for providing vehicles, buildings and other equipment be transferred from police authority to chief constable, with a similar transfer of responsibility for police building and premises further to be considered.[33] The chief constable's managerial prerogative would also be strengthened by the introduction of more flexible working patterns, enhanced internal procedures for dealing with officer misconduct and incompetence, and the Sheehy-inspired alterations to the pay and rank structure.[34] Devolution of managerial responsibility would not stop at the level of the chief constable. The White Paper commended and encouraged the trend towards "sectoral policing"[35] which, supported by the Inspectorate, had been gaining momentum over a number of years. Under this, the local commander and command unit were encouraged "to establish clear ownership of the area and in turn allow the local community to identify them as their police officers".[36] The consistent theme, therefore, was of the transfer of managerial authority and responsibility downwards from the politicians to the professionals and from senior to middle ranks.

The manner in which these three reconfigured governance roles were mutually articulated and the centrality of the calculative approach also aided the White Paper's second strategy of enhancing the accountability of the tripartite parties. This would be both horizontal and vertical. Horizontally, the accountability of the force and police authority to the local community would be enhanced by the visibility of the new local objectives and performance indicators. Vertically, there would, in theory, now be an unbroken chain of responsibility from local command units upwards. These were answerable to the chief constable, who was answerable in terms of the local plan and objectives to the police authority, which, in turn, was answerable in terms of the national framework of objectives and performance indicators to the Home Secretary, who, finally, was answerable to the public as a whole for the success of the national framework.

As regards the final strategy of encouraging co-operation and avoiding conflict amongst the tripartite parties, this was to be achieved in different ways. Many of the powers and responsibilities of the parties specifically required or necessarily implied co-operation. The police authority

---

[33] Paras.3.11–3.13.
[34] Explicit cross-reference is made to Sheehy at paras 3.24–3.27.
[35] See, *e.g.*, Dixon and Stanko (1995).
[36] Home Office (1993b) para. 3.21.

would have to work in partnership with the local public, it would have to agree local plans and objectives with the chief constable, and it would be involved in continuous dialogue and negotiation with the Home Office and the Inspectorate over the pursuit and mutual articulation of the local and national agendas. To recall Morgan's typology, in this aspect of the White Paper's blueprint, it is possible to see signs of a general, if far from complete, shift, from the stewardship model towards the partner model of accountability.[37]

As noted in the last chapter, however, we cannot simply "read off" the relationship between the parties from a formal consideration of their legal powers and responsibilities. We must also look to the expectations and aspirations that they bring to their position. And while the White Paper made a concerted effort to match legal profile to role perception, it would have been a hard task to reconcile fully the aspirations of parties with such a history of mutual tensions. In particular, would the police authorities be able and willing to accept a mandate which, although appearing to allow them more direct involvement in policy-making, did so in terms which made them subordinate to central government in a grand and detailed instrumental project to achieve effective policing, while leaving them limited scope to contest with the other parties what the fundamental parameters of effective policing were? The White Paper addressed this difficulty by proposing, in a much more radical and comprehensive manner than had been achieved by the abolition of the metropolitan counties in 1985,[38] to reconstitute the police authorities along less political lines.[39] Only half the members would be drawn from local authorities, the other half comprising magistrates and Home Office appointees, with the crucial role of chair also nominated by the Home Secretary. Naturally, the White Paper sought to justify this in positive rather than negative terms. It presented its plan as an opportunity to bring into the governance framework people with management, financial or other valuable forms of experience and expertise of a type not fully represented in local government,[40] rather than as a means to marginalise the "dangers" of excessive political interference from the town hall. Even on the least cynical reading, however, it cannot but be acknowledged that the latter was an entirely

---

[37] Morgan (1985) pp. 7–9. See chapter one, section 2(B)(iv). See further, section 3 below.
[38] See chapter three, section 3.
[39] Home Office (1993b) para. 4.19–4.29
[40] *ibid.* para.4.22.

foreseeable consequence of the former, and thus something to which the Government was not ill-disposed.[41]

(B) OBJECTION AND COMPROMISE

As pointed out in the opening chapter, regulatory systems such as the tripartite framework of police governance are rarely a pure reflection of any particular political ideology. They are more likely to be the result of an incremental mix and match of different approaches. In this regard, the 1993 proposals provided an unusually clear ideological blueprint, a significant departure from the cumulative wisdom and recurrent compromise which marked the constitutional history of modern policing. Yet its novelty should not be overstated. As we shall see, many of the features and difficulties associated with the old system remained. Further, the Government did not succeed in fully translating the Sheehy and White Paper proposals into legislation.

Significant compromises were made. The various police staff associations reacted against Sheehy, and when the new Home Secretary, Michael Howard, eventually clarified the Government's position in October 1993, there were important concessions. Performance-related pay was dropped for lower-ranking (and, eventually, all) officers, fixed-term contracts were restricted to ACPO ranks, the proposal to reduce starting salaries was dropped, and one of the three ranks to be removed—Chief Inspector—earned a reprieve.

The White Paper proposals drew even wider criticism. Indeed, one key proposed amendment, to allow London its own independent police authority for the first time, although trailed in an indicative statement by the Home Secretary in March 1993,[42] was dropped *in advance of* the White Paper due to backbench Conservative opposi-

---

[41] The evidence is somewhat clouded. In their study of the Act, Jones and Newburn (1997: chap.2) indicate that Kenneth Clarke was strongly committed from the outset to reducing local councillor influence on police authorities, and had to face down considerable opposition from Cabinet, including, ironically, Michael Howard who, as his successor as Home Secretary would be responsible for securing the eventual passage of the legislation. Jones and Newburn interviewed Clarke, and this provides the basis for some fascinating insights into his thinking. While most of his articulated views suggest the positive justification rather than the negative justification for replacing councillors with independent members, in one extended quote (p. 22) he seems to suggest that they are two sides of the same coin, the narrow concern of some police authority councillors with party political matters being portrayed as in part a consequence of their lack of deep knowledge and understanding of the important policing issues.

[42] HC Debs. 23 March 1993, col.765, *per* Kenneth Clarke.

tion.[43] The White Paper itself attracted considerable criticism from police and local authority associations irked by the lack of prior consultation, and, once reduced to Bill form, the proposals ran into further opposition from a wide cross-section of Parliamentarians, particularly in the House of Lords where the proposed legislation was introduced. Police opposition to the centralisation implicit in the introduction in tandem of national objectives and fixed-term contracts for senior officers did not deflect the Government from their strategy. Where the campaign against the Bill was conspicuously successful, however, was in respect of the proposal to reconstitute the police authority with greater central influence and control. A number of amendments were moved which had the effect of watering down this key component of Government thinking and, in some measure at least, reasserting the independence of the police authority. As we shall see in the closing section of the chapter, one of the most intriguing question surrounding the implementation of the new scheme would be the ramifications of this significant modification of the Government's grand design to reconceive police governance in more instrumental terms.

2. The New Legal Framework

In this section we examine the final legal form of the new tripartite framework. We follow the same order as above, discussing central government, police authorities and chief constables in turn.

(A) CENTRAL GOVERNMENT

As with the 1964 Act, the new legislative framework falls short of conferring upon the Home Secretary a general responsibility for the efficiency of policing. However, in a modification of the compromise formula negotiated in 1964, the Home Secretary must now exercise his specific powers in such manner and to such extent as appears to him to be best calculated to promote not only the *efficiency* of the police, as before, but also their *effectiveness*.[44] Clearly, this extension is in line with the new managerialist ethos of central co-ordination and supervision of a quasi-market performance culture, although it is not obvious how

---

[43] *Independent*, 26 May 1993.
[44] Police Act 1996, s.36.

precisely it extends the overall jurisdiction of the Home Secretary.[45] As regards the specific legal responsibilities of, or associated with the Home Secretary and central government, these may be categorised as follows: strategic policy-making; influence over and oversight of police authorities; influence over and oversight of chief constables; budgetary powers; the responsibilities of the Inspectorate; detailed regulation; central services; and alteration of force areas.

(i) Strategic Policy-making

The centrepiece of the Home Secretary's new strategic authority is the power, after consulting representatives of police authorities and chief constables, to determine national policing objectives[46] by statutory instrument. The earliest objectives set were very broadly stated and uncontentious, but in subsequent amendments they have become slightly more detailed, focusing more upon broad strategy than ultimate outputs and outcomes.[47] The present objectives, which reflect the new emphasis in the Crime and Disorder Act 1998 upon local multi-agency strategies in the prevention and reduction of crime,[48] are[49]: first, to deal speedily and effectively with young offenders and to work with other agencies to reduce offending and re-offending by young people[50]; secondly, to identify and reduce local problems of crime and disorder in partnership with local authorities, other local agencies and the public[51]; thirdly, to target and reduce drug-related crime in partnership with other local agencies, in particular local Drug Action Teams or local Drug and Alcohol Action Teams[52]; and

---

[45] The meaning of the general standard of effectiveness under s.36 could be put to the test in an action of judicial review of the extent of one of the Home Secretary's more specific powers and responsibilities.

[46] Police Act 1996, s.37.

[47] The original order contained four objectives which no longer appear in any shape or form: (1) to maintain or increase detections for violent crimes; (2) to increase detections for burglaries; (3) to respond promptly to emergency calls, and (4) to provide high visibility policing in order to reassure the public. (S.I. 1994/2678). All but the last were retained in the subsequent 1998 order (S.I. 1998/216).

[48] Crime and Disorder Act 1998 ss.5–6; see Crawford (1998a).

[49] Police (Secretary of State's Objectives) Order 1999 (S.I. 1999/543).

[50] This is a slightly modified version of the objective which first appeared in the 1998 order.

[51] This objective appeared in the previous two orders, although not in its present detailed form in the original 1994 version.

[52] In so doing, police authorities are to have regard to the New Labour Government's ten-year anti-drugs strategy; Her Majesty's Government (1999).This is a more detailed version of the objective which first appeared in the 1998 order.

fourthly, in response to the Stephen Lawrence Inquiry,[53] to increase trust and confidence in policing amongst minority ethnic communities.[54] The Home Secretary may also direct police authorities to establish performance targets in order to achieve these national objectives.[55] The direction, which is published,[56] may apply to some or all police authorities,[57] and may impose conditions—which may differ between authorities—with which the performance targets must conform.[58]

(ii) Influence Over and Oversight of Police Authorities

The Home Secretary has a battery of new powers over police authorities which consolidate his status as senior partner in strategic policy-making. The police authority must publish and send to the Home Secretary an annual report relating to the policing of the authority's area, which must include an assessment of the extent to which the local policing plan for the previous year has been carried out.[59] The Home Secretary can also ask for a report on any matter connected with the discharge of the police authority's functions, or otherwise connected with the policing of the area.[60] This widely-drawn power is additional to pre-existing powers to call for reports from the chief constable,[61] and to ask for a local inquiry into any policing matter to be undertaken by a third party appointed by the Home Secretary.[62] The Home Secretary has a similarly broad power to issue codes of practice relating to the discharge by police authorities of any of their functions.[63] The Home Secretary also acquires the more

---

[53] MacPherson (1999) Recommendations 1–2. For a wide-ranging assessment of the Lawrence Inquiry, which delivered a substantial indictment of police response to the murder of a black teenager in South London in 1993, see Bridges (1999).

[54] As first announced in the Home Secretary's Action Plan in response to the Lawrence Inquiry; see Home Office (1999c) p. 3.

[55] Police Act 1996 s.38(1).

[56] *ibid.*, s.38(4).

[57] *ibid.*, s.38(2).

[58] *ibid.*, s.38(3).

[59] *ibid.*, s.9.

[60] *ibid.*, s.43.

[61] See subsection (A)(iii) below.

[62] Police Act 1996, s.49. This is the power under which a number of high-profile inquiries into policing controversies or wrongdoings have taken place, including Lord Scarman's report into the Brixton disturbances (Scarman, 1981), and, most recently, Sir William MacPherson's report into the police investigation of the murder of Stephen Lawrence (MacPherson, 1999).

[63] Police Act 1996, s.39. The first to be promulgated under the new legislation was *Financial Management*, 1993/94 HC Papers 673.

focused power to direct police authorities to take remedial measures pursuant upon a report by an Inspector of Constabulary which concludes that a force is, or, in the absence of remedial action, is likely to become inefficient or ineffective.[64] Such remedial measures include the power to direct a police authority to set a minimum budget for any financial year.[65]

(iii) Influence Over and Oversight of Chief Constables

In contrast to the powers held over police authorities, the powers of the Home Secretary over the chief constable are for the most part of an earlier vintage.[66] The Home Secretary retains a significant array of personnel powers in relation to the chief constables and his assistants. The Home Secretary's approval is required before they can be appointed,[67] and, quite apart from the detailed provisions under the disciplinary regulations,[68] he may require a police authority[69] to exercise its statutory

---

[64] Police Act 1996, s.40

[65] *ibid.*, s.41. This power appears to be at least partly in response to tensions between the Home Office and Derbyshire Constabulary in the early 1990s. On three occasions the Constabulary was refused a certificate of efficiency, upon which payment of the central grant depended, following an adverse report by the Inspectorate of Constabulary concerning the inadequacy of the local budget.

[66] The Metropolitan Police provides a key exception, where reforms introduced by the Greater London Authority Act 1999 have significantly qualified the traditional pre-eminence of the Home Secretary. Ss.315 and 317 of the 1999 Act, inserting s.9B and 9D respectively of the Police Act 1996, stipulate that the Commissioner and Deputy Commissioner posts are to remain Crown appointments made on the recommendation of the Home Secretary, but before making such a recommendation the Home Secretary now must consider any recommendations made by the new Metropolitan Police Authority and any representations made by the new Mayor of London. S.319 of the 1999 Act, inserting s.9F of the 1996 Act, provides that Assistant Commissioners are to be appointed in the same way as non-London chief constables. Further, the same section read together with s.318 of the 1999 Act, which inserts s.9E of the 1996 Act, allocates responsibilities to the Home Secretary and Police Authority as regards the dismissal or resignation of all chief officer ranks similar to those they enjoy in the provinces. See further, subsection (B)(i) below.

[67] *ibid.*, ss.11(1) and 12(1).

[68] *ibid.*, s.50; see subsection (B)(vii) below.

[69] The convoluted procedural pathway whereby the Secretary of State acts not directly but through the police authority, is not new, but remains an interesting example of symbolic legislation. There is no substantive difference between the operation of the provision as it stands and its operation were the chief constable empowered to act directly. We are bound to conclude, therefore, that the present form is retained only to preserve the appearance of the absence of central government control over the tenure of chief constables—an inescapably sensitive issue given the paradox of police governance; see chapters one and two. It should also be noted that the parallel provisions under ss.11(2) and 12(2) of the 1996 Act, which allow the police authority to take the initiative in calling upon the chief constable to retire in the interests of efficiency or effectiveness, also require the approval of the Secretary of State.

power to call upon the chief constable or an assistant chief constable to retire in the interests of efficiency or effectiveness.[70] Before doing so, however, the Home Secretary must allow and consider representations from the chief officer concerned,[71] and where he proposes to require the exercise of the power to compel retiral, he must first appoint an independent inquiry and consider its report.[72]

The Home Secretary's other major power in relation to the chief constable is informational. The Home Secretary can require a report on any matter connected to the policing of the area,[73] and is also entitled to a copy at the earliest possible opportunity of the chief constable's annual report to the police authority.[74] Finally, the Home Secretary can require from the chief constable a periodical return of criminal statistics, which the Home Secretary must lay before Parliament in consolidated form.[75]

(iv) Budgetary Powers

The Home Secretary's control over budgetary matters is significantly altered. Where under the previous system central government had to meet 51 per cent of whatever was spent by the police authority, the new legislation honours the White Paper's pledge to cash limit the amount of police grant made available from the centre.[76] The overall amount of grant and the allocation to each local authority is determined with the approval of the Treasury.[77] The allocation comprises 51 per cent of assessed police costs, a figure calculated in accordance with a formula which takes account of key police activities and certain social, economic and demographic variables to produce a Standard Spending Assessment for each area. While there is no formal provision for consultation with police authorities or chief constables,[78] there is a requirement of publicity, with

---

[70] *ibid.*, s.42(1). As with other provisions of the new legislative framework, "effectiveness" joins "efficiency" as an alternative trigger to action. In theory at least, this broadens the power of central government.

[71] *ibid.*, s.42(2).

[72] *ibid.*, s.42(3). Thereafter, there is a right of appeal to a new police appeals tribunal; *ibid*, s.85(1). See further, White (1998).

[73] *ibid.*, s.44(1)–(3).

[74] *ibid.*, s.44(4).

[75] *ibid.*, s.45.

[76] *ibid.*, s.46.

[77] *ibid.*, s.46(2).

[78] Although undertakings were given by the Government during the passage of the 1994 Act that such consultation would take place; HL Debs, 1993–94, Vol. 552, col. 363, *per* Earl Ferrers.

the Home Secretary obliged to report to Parliament on the reasons behind his budgetary decisions.[79] Separate provision is made for major capital expenditure.[80] Here, the Home Secretary, again acting with the approval of the Treasury,[81] retains the power to make grants subject to conditions.[82] The Home Secretary also has a new power to make grants in respect of police expenditure in respect of national security.[83] This power, which was not anticipated in the White Paper, is a response to the difficulties associated with local funding of major incidents or events of national significance. It is not clear, however, how widely the new provision may be interpreted. Whereas a particular response to an urgent terrorist threat or to a security alarm at a nuclear missile basis would be covered, it is unlikely, to take two notorious examples of inordinate expenditure of recent years, that it would cover the policing of a major industrial dispute or the picketing by animal rights protesters of a port used for the transport of livestock.[84] Finally, these various positive fiscal measures are complemented by the Home Secretary's new power—noted above—to direct a police authority, where an adverse report has been received from an Inspector of Constabulary, to set its annual budget at a minimum level.[85]

While these various provisions significantly increase the control of the Home Secretary over total spending, central influence over the allocation of spending *within* the budget is much reduced. Under the 1964 Act,[86] the Home Secretary retained the ultimate power of approval with regard to force establishment and the provision, maintenance and alteration of buildings, structures and premises, matters which in the first instance lay with the police authority. Under the new framework this detailed regime of control over spending has been dismantled.

---

[79] Police Act 1996, s.46(4) and (6). The rules or formulae that the Home Secretary applies may differ between different authorities or classes of authority (s.46(5)).

[80] *ibid.*, s.47.

[81] *ibid.*, s.47(3).

[82] *ibid.*, s.47(2).

[83] *ibid.*, s.48.

[84] See Uglow (1996) p. 28. The animal rights example involved a legal challenge to the decision of the chief constable to reduce the level of support offered to a cross-channel ferry company against the disruptions of the protesters. See *R. v. Chief Constable of Sussex, ex parte International Trader's Ferry Ltd*, [1996] Q.B. 177 (DC); [1998] Q.B. 477 (C.A.); [1999] A.C. 418 (HL); discussed in subsection 2(C)(ii) below.

[85] Police Act 1996, s.41.

[86] s.4

(v) The Inspectorate of Constabulary

Since its introduction in 1856 the Inspectorate of Constabulary has been an important player in the development of a uniform police force, but never more so than in the decade prior to the present reform watershed.[87] The new legislative framework consolidates and builds upon the developments of the 80s and 90s. The increasing prominence of the Inspectorate adds an extra edge to the perennial debate about their independence or otherwise from the Home Office. Constitutionally, the chief inspector[88] and five inspectors—are independent, appointed by the Crown[89] rather than the Home Office or the police.[90] However, if it is artificial to address the relationship between central government and chief constables in purely legal terms, it is all the more so in the case of the Inspectorate's various relationships with the tripartite parties. In practice the Home Secretary selects the Inspectorate, and he is legally empowered to appoint their assistants and staff officers.[91] Where once the Inspectorate was seen as a sinecure for retired chief constables,[92] in the last 15 years it has become "a fast-track option for highly ambitious chiefs . . . in their prime in career terms",[93] albeit there is now also moderate provision for lay involvement.[94] The professional pedigree and ambitions of the Inspectorate and the fact that their various inspection and advice functions, however objectively approached, take place within an increasingly clear national policy framework established and monitored by central government, entails that they are a vital component in the national policy community. Whereas many have debated whether the Inspectorate are "closer" to central government or the profession, they are perhaps better understood as the key agent in ensuring a close relationship between these two parties.

---

[87] See chapter three, section 3. See also Oliver (1997) chap.6; Hughes, Mears and Winch (1997).

[88] Presently David O'Dowd.

[89] Police Act 1996, s.54(1).

[90] This is a status which the Inspectorate jealously guards. See, for example, the typically terse assertion of autonomy in Her Majesty's Chief Inspectorate of Constabulary (1998) para.12: "The Inspectorate is not part of the tripartite structure and is independent of the police service."

[91] Police Act 1996, s.56

[92] See Reiner (1992a) pp. 242–243.

[93] Hughes, Mears and Winch (1997) p. 307.

[94] The first two part-time non-police Inspectors were appointed in 1991 as part of John Major's Citizen's Charter initiative, and provision has recently been made to "increase their input by 50 per cent" (Her Majesty's Chief Inspector of Constabulary, 1998, para. 139).

The main statutory function of the Inspectorate remains one of inspection and report. The Chief Inspector is required to report to the Home Secretary on the efficiency and effectiveness of every police force,[95] including the Metropolitan Police which was previously excluded.[96] As of 1998, the annual force inspection was discontinued in favour of an 18 month cycle, but its importance was reinforced by the development in the same period of a systematic standards-based approach to review, with more comprehensive use of performance data.[97] The longer cycle for force inspection in part reflects the increasing emphasis placed by the Inspectorate on thematic reviews, which have recently been highly influential in areas as diverse as value-for-money and the policing of ethnic minorities. Thematic inspections are a key tool in pursuit of the Inspectorate's broader statutory remit to carry out such other duties for the purpose of furthering police efficiency and effectiveness as the Home Secretary may direct.[98] This broader remit covers the provision of professional advice on policing to the Home Secretary, police authorities, Home Office officials and police forces, and the general promotion and dissemination of good policing practice. It also extends to advising both the Home Office and police authorities on candidates for senior appointments.[99]

A recent amendment to the 1996 Act gives the Inspectorate an important role within New Labour's potentially far-reaching Best Value initiative, which seeks to make managerial audit more systematic across all aspects of local government.[1] Under this new power, the Inspectorate of Constabulary will work in co-ordination with a new Best Value Inspectorate established within the Audit Commission and may inspect and report to the Secretary of State on a police authority's compliance with the Best Value framework.[2] The new framework—set out in Part 1 of the

---

[95] Police Act 1996, s.54(2). An adverse report can lead the Inspectorate to refuse to grant the force a certificate of efficiency, as was the fate of Derbyshire Constabulary for three successive years between 1992–94.

[96] Although in practice inspections have taken place at the invitation of the Metropolitan Commissioner since 1988.

[97] Her Majesty's Chief Inspector of Constabulary (1998) chap.1.

[98] Police Act 1996, s.54(3).

[99] Home Office (1995b); Her Majesty's Chief Inspector of Constabulary (1998) chap.1. The new Best Value provisions have been given additional impetus by the findings of the Stephen Lawrence Inquiry, which made a number of recommendations to strengthen the role of the Inspectorate; MacPherson (1999) Recommendations 3,4,5 and 8; Home Office (1999c) p. 4.

[1] See Department of the Environment, Transport and the Regions (1998b), see also Boyne (1999).

[2] Police Act 1996, s.54(2A), inserted by the Local Government Act 1999, s.24(2).

Local Government Act 1999—requires the police authority, as a Best Value authority,[3] to secure continuous improvements in the way in which its functions are exercised, having regard to a combination of economy, efficiency and effectiveness.[4] Accordingly, the Inspectorate now has powers of scrutiny over two of the tripartite parties.

The 1996 Act also formalises and extends the requirement of publicity in respect of Inspectorate reports.[5] In practice, these have been published since 1990, but now the Home Secretary is required to publish any report received by him in such manner as he deems appropriate[6] and must send a copy to the chief constable[7] and to the police authority.[8] The inclusion of the police authority within the information loop is significant. In line with its broader statutory responsibilities,[9] the police authority is also now obliged to publish, and to communicate to the Home Secretary, its response to force inspection reports by the Inspectorate. The response should include the police authority's own initial comments on the report, any comments submitted by the chief constable, and any response the police authority might have to these comments.[10] The opening of this channel of communication from police authority to Home Secretary must be viewed in the light of the new powers of the Home Secretary to give directions to police authorities after adverse reports by the Inspectorate.[11] Arguably, the vulnerable position of police authorities within this broader statutory context might persuade them to adopt a defensive approach to their reporting responsibilities.

(vi) Detailed Regulations

The Home Secretary retains a cluster of powers which allow him to make regulations for the detailed government, administration and conditions of service of police officers.[12] Regulations may cover police ranks, qualifications for appointment and promotion of police officers, probationary service, voluntary retirement, suspension from office, duties of

---

[3] Local Government Act 1999, s.1.
[4] *ibid.*, s.3(1). See further, subsection. (B)(ii) below.
[5] Police Act 1996, s.55
[6] *ibid.*, s.55(1), amended by Local Government Act 1999, s.24(3) to include reports on Best Value compliance.
[7] *ibid.*, s.55(3)(b).
[8] *ibid.*, s.55(3)(a).
[9] See subsection (B) below.
[10] Police Act 1996, s.55(4)–(6).
[11] *ibid.*, ss.40–41. See subsection (A)(ii) above.
[12] *ibid.*, s.50.

office and the maintenance of discipline—a category which has been extended under the new legislative framework to cover the conduct, efficiency and effectiveness of members of police forces.[13] In specific recognition of the Sheehy recommendations on new terms of employment for senior officers, provision is also made for regulations to embrace fixed-term contracts for superintendents and higher ranks.[14] Before making regulations in any of the above matters, the Home Secretary must first consult the Police Advisory Board for England and Wales, which is a general policy advisory body representing the interests of police authorities, police forces and police cadets.[15] Regulations may also cover hours of duty, leave, pay and allowances, police clothing, personal equipment and accoutrements.[16] Before making regulations in these matters, the Home Secretary must first consult the Police Negotiating Board for the United Kingdom, which is a forum for discussion and bargaining over "trade union" matters between representatives of central and local government and police officers and cadets.[17] Similar provision is made for the regulation of police cadets[18] and special constables,[19] and in order to ensure that police equipment meets appropriate design specifications and performance standards.[20]

(vii) Central Services

The Home Secretary's authority to provide central services is more widely drawn than before.[21] He may provide and maintain such organisations, facilities and services as he considers necessary or expedient for promoting the efficiency and effectiveness of the police.[22] This may include permanent facilities, such as training colleges, forensic laboratories and the Police National Computer, as well as *ad hoc* arrangements

---

[13] Police Act 1996, s.50(2)(e). See further subsection 2(c) below.

[14] *ibid.*, s.50(6).

[15] *ibid.*, s.63. The Police Advisory Board was first established under the Police Act 1964.

[16] *ibid.*, s.50(2)(j)–(k).

[17] *ibid.*, ss.61–62. The Police Negotiating Board was first established under the Police Negotiating Board Act 1980.

[18] *ibid.*, s.52. The same duties of consultation of the Police Advisory Board and the Police Negotiating Board apply as under s.50.

[19] s.51

[20] s.53.

[21] Although the courts were prepared to interpret its predecessor provision (1964 Act, s.41) in very broad terms; see *R. v. Secretary of State for the Home Department ex p. Northumbria Police Authority* [1988]1 All ER 556. For discussion, see chapter one, section 2(a)(ii).

[22] Police Act 1996, s.57(1).

such as the supply of special riot equipment to a particular force.[23] The Home Secretary has also acquired new powers to charge for the use of common services[24] and to compel all forces to use specified services if he considers this would be in the interests of the efficiency or effectiveness of the police.[25] The Home Secretary retains a complementary power to sponsor research into matters affecting police efficiency and effectiveness, a provision which supplies formal authority for such specialist Home Office bodies as the Police Research Group and the Research and Statistics Directorate.[26] Finally, as discussed in detail below,[27] the Home Secretary can achieve a level of co-ordination by encouraging, or even requiring, mutual aid[28] or collaboration arrangements[29] among forces.

(viii) Alteration of Force Areas

Consistent with a century-long trend, the present legislative framework offers greater encouragement than its predecessor towards the amalgamation and reduction of police forces. The Home Secretary may by order alter the size of police areas,[30] and can thereby abolish any force except the City of London Police and the Metropolitan Police.[31] The Home Secretary can act either on the request of the police authorities for each of the affected areas or on his own initiative, although in the latter event it must appear to him expedient to make the alterations in the interests of efficiency or effectiveness.[32] Before making an order on his own initiative, the Home Secretary must give notice of the intended changes and his reasons for them to local authorities and the police authorities concerned, and also to such other persons as he considers appropriate, and must consider any objections which they might raise.[33] Further, the order must be approved by resolution of both Houses of Parliament.[34] While these represent not insignificant procedural hurdles,

---

[23] As in the *Northumbria Police Authority* case, n. 21 above.
[24] Police Act 1996, s.57(2).
[25] *ibid.*, s.57(3).
[26] *ibid.*, s.58.
[27] See subsection (B)(vi) below.
[28] *ibid.*, s24.
[29] *ibid.*, s.23.
[30] With the exception of the City of London police area; *ibid.*, s.32(1).
[31] *ibid.*, s.32(2).
[32] *ibid.*, s.32(3).
[33] *ibid.*, s.33.
[34] *ibid.*, s.34(3).

they are less onerous than the requirement to hold a local inquiry which obtained under the previous legislation.

(B) POLICE AUTHORITIES

Where possible, it is useful for purposes of comparison to categorise the legal powers and duties of police authorities in a similar manner to those of central government. Accordingly, we may examine police authorities in terms of their strategic policy-making, their influence over and oversight of chief constables and their officers, and their budgetary powers. In other respects, the distinctiveness of the police authority role demands a different classification, and so we also assess police authorities in terms of employment of non-police staff, mutual aid and collaboration and the provision of advice and assistance to international organisations. Before we investigate these various heads, however, an important preliminary matter must be addressed.

(i) Establishment and Membership

As the political debate surrounding the emergence of the new legislative framework underlined, the prior matter of the form and constitution of police authorities is itself significant and controversial. While the Conservative Government's original plans for reforming the police authorities were thwarted, the final legislative solution nevertheless involves a notable shift of power away from local councillors. Their representation, previously two thirds, is reduced to a bare majority. The police authority acquires the status of a body corporate,[35] reflecting and reinforcing its greater independence from the local council(s). The new police authority is also a more streamlined model than its predecessor, normally numbering seventeen,[36] of which nine are councillors,[37] three are magistrates[38] (previously one third) and five are drawn from a new constituency of

---

[35] Police Act 1996, s.3(2).

[36] The Home Secretary may increase this by order; *ibid* s.4(2). He may subsequently vary or revoke such an order only after consulting the police authority and the relevant councils and selection panels; *ibid* s.5.

[37] They must reflect the political balance of the council or councils from which they are drawn; *ibid.*, sched.2, para.4.

[38] Chosen by a local selection panel, or where appropriate a joint committee of local selection panels constituted under s.21(1A) of the Justices of the Peace Act 1979; Police Act 1996, Sched.2, paras. 7–8.

independent members.[39] Originally, the independent members were to have been appointed by the Home Secretary, but as the Bill proceeded through Parliament his role was gradually diluted. In the definitive formula,[40] a local selection panel consisting of a police authority nominee, a central government nominee, and a third member chosen by the other two, identifies a number of provisional candidates, half of whom are then short listed by the Home Secretary. This shortlist, which numbers twice as many candidates as there are vacancies, is then presented to the councillor and magistrate members of the police authority for final selection of the independent members. The chair of the police authority is appointed by the authority as a whole from among its members.[41]

The composition and functions of the police authorities for the London forces has traditionally differed from that of the other forces in England and Wales, but these differences are gradually being removed. The police authority for the City of London Police remains the Common Council of the Corporation of London.[42] The Government agreed to exclude the City of London from the new statutory scheme on the basis that the Common Council voluntarily undertook to reconstitute its police authority and alter its role along the lines indicated in the 1994 Act.[43] As noted earlier, the Metropolitan Police, too, despite initial indications to the contrary, retained its existing police authority— the Home Secretary.[44] Under non-statutory arrangements a new Metropolitan Police Committee was established in 1995, but it was appointed by the Home Secretary and its role was merely advisory.[45] The New Labour Government, however, set out to correct an anomaly of which they had been deeply critical during the long years of opposition. It also sought to link this reform directly to its constitutional reform agenda.[46] A referendum was held in May 1998, which strongly approved the idea of a reconstituted Greater London Authority (GLA) with a directly elected Mayor and Assembly. A Bill was then introduced specifying the structure and functions of the new GLA, including the constitution of a police authority along similar lines to the provincial

---

[39] Police Act 1996 Sched.2, para.1.
[40] *ibid.,* Sched.3.
[41] *ibid.,* Sched.2, para.9.
[42] *ibid.,* s.101(1).
[43] See *e.g.,* Oliver (1997) pp. 94–95
[44] 1996 Act, s.101(1).
[45] See *e.g.,* Oliver (1997) pp. 91–93.
[46] Department of Environment, Transport and the Regions (1999a); see also Loveland (1999).

authorities[47] and with similar functions.[48] The trend towards uniformity was reinforced by the Home Secretary's Action Plan following the Lawrence Inquiry, which called for the Bill to be amended to strengthen the role of the new Metropolitan police authority,[49] including a voice in the appointment of senior officers.[50] The new legislation acknowledges that the Home Secretary retains a special responsibility for the national and international functions of the Metropolitan Police, and to that extent the balance of power within the tripartite relationship remains more favourable to the centre than in the case of the provincial forces.[51] No longer, however, is the broader remit of the Metropolitan Police to serve as a pretext for excluding local influence entirely.[52]

(ii) Strategic Policy-making

The outer shell of the police authority's general legal responsibility under the new framework shows only modest change from the old. Whereas under the 1964 Act the function of the police authority was to secure the maintenance of an adequate and efficient police force, it is now to secure the maintenance of an efficient and effective force.[53] Yet, while the introduction of the standard of effectiveness alongside that of efficiency is a familiar feature of the new legislation, the precise sense of which remains elusive, in the present context it is at least broadly indicative of the shift in police authority priorities away from the detail of force infrastructure and towards issues of strategic planning. Whereas the bare bones of the 1964 duty were filled out with reference to responsibility for the size and rank distribution of the police force and the provision and maintenance of buildings, structures, premises, vehicles, apparatus, clothing and equipment, all that has been swept away and replaced by responsibility for setting local policing objectives

---

[47] Based on Department of Environment, Transport and the Regions (1999a), para.5.140; see Greater London Authority Act s.310, inserting s.5A–C of the Police Act 1998, and Sched.26 of the 1999 Act, inserting Sched.2A of the 1996 Act.

[48] Greater London Police Authority Act 1999, inserting s.6(5) of the Police Act 1996.

[49] Home Office (1999c), responding to MacPherson (1999) Recommendation 6.

[50] See n. 66 above.

[51] Greater London Authority Act 1999, Sched.27, para. 104, inserting s.98A of the Police Act 1996. This permits the Home Secretary to enter into agreements with the police authority with regard to the force's performance in matters relating to (a) the protection of prominent persons or their residences, (b) national security, (c) counter-terrorism, or (d) the provision of services for any other national or international purpose.

[52] Home Office (1993b) para. 11.5.

[53] Police Act 1996 s.6(1).

and performance targets and agreeing an annual police plan with the chief constable.

Local policing objectives must be set annually before the beginning of the financial year by the police authority[54] after consulting both the local chief constable and the Scarman-inspired local consultative committees,[55] whose role is thereby strengthened under the new legislative framework.[56] The local objectives may reflect the national policing objectives set by the Home Secretary or they may identify other local priorities, but in any event they must be framed so as to be consistent with the national objectives.[57] The police authority may also establish performance targets to implement their objectives, and like the latter, the performance targets may be established in compliance with a direction from the Home Secretary or they may be independently established.[58]

A local policing plan setting out the proposed arrangements for the policing of the area for the next year is issued at the same time as the annual policing objectives.[59] The plan sets out the authority's priorities for the year, the financial resources expected to be available and the proposed allocation of those resources.[60] It also includes particulars of the local and national policing objectives and related performance targets, and now of any action proposed by the police authority for the purpose of complying with the new Best Value framework.[61] Unlike the other local strategy documents, it is the chief constable who takes the drafting initiative,[62] but the final decision rests with the police authority, although they must consult with the chief constable before publishing[63] a plan which seeks to depart from his draft.[64]

In seeking to secure the maintenance of an efficient and effective police force the police authority is obliged to "have regard to" the

---

[54] *ibid.*, s.7(1).
[55] *ibid.*, s.7(3).
[56] *ibid.*, s.96.
[57] *ibid.*, s.7(2).
[58] *ibid.*, s.6(2)(c)
[59] *ibid.*, s.8(1).
[60] *ibid.*, s.8(2).
[61] *ibid.*, s.8(2)(d), inserted by Local Government Act 1999, s.24(1). This means that Best Value annual local performance plans (1999 Act, s.6) which must be prepared by all Best Value authorities, including police authorities, and which reflect the findings of the five-yearly fundamental performance reviews (s.5), will effectively become part of the local policing plan; see also Home Office (2000b), which contains statutory guidance under s.5(5)–(7) of the 1999 Act requiring local police authorities to set targets in relation to domestic burglaries, robberies and vehicle crime.
[62] *ibid.*, s.8(3).
[63] *ibid.*, s.8(5). A copy of the plan must also be sent to the Home Secretary.
[64] *ibid.*, s.8(4).

various local and national strategy documents and directives,[65] and also to any code of practice[66] issued by the Home Secretary.[67] On the one hand, this serves to reinforce the subordination of the police authority to the Home Secretary within the strategic planning framework. On the other hand, it implies a standard less than slavish obedience, although any authority who failed to comply with a national norm would presumably be vulnerable in an action of judicial review to the charge of failure to take account of a relevant consideration.

(iii) Influence Over and Oversight of the Local Force

Clearly, the strategic capacity of the police authority provides significant scope to influence the actions of the local police force, but this is supplemented by more specific powers. Like the Home Secretary, the police authority has significant powers over police personnel and to request information.[68] The police authority retains the power to appoint the chief constable and his assistants,[69] but subject to the approval of the Home Secretary,[70] which in practice means that the police authority makes its choice from a short list drawn up by the Home Office. The significance of this power is enhanced by the adoption of the Sheehy recommendation to restrict appointments at senior ranks to fixed terms of between four and seven years.[71] The police authority may also call upon the chief or his assistants to retire in the interests of efficiency or effectiveness,[72] although it must first hear representations from the officer concerned and then seek the approval of the Home Secretary for the course of action it proposes.[73]

The chief constable is also obliged to submit to the police authority, and to publish[74] an annual report on the general policing of the force area.[75] More broadly, the police authority may require the chief consta-

---

[65] Police Act 1996, s.6(2). These include directions by the Home Secretary in the light of an adverse report by an inspector of constabulary under s.40.

[66] Issued under s.39 of the 1996 Act.

[67] *ibid.*, s.6(3).

[68] On the special position of the Metropolitan police authority, see subsection (a)(iii), n. 66 above.

[69] Police Act 1996, ss11–12.

[70] *ibid.*, s.11(1).

[71] *ibid.*, s50(6) .

[72] *ibid.*, s.11(2).

[73] *ibid.*, s.11(3).

[74] *ibid.*, s.22(2).

[75] *ibid.*, s.22(1).

ble to submit a report on any matter connected with the policing of the area.[76] If, however, the chief constable is of the view that the report would contain information which in the public interest ought not to be disclosed or which is not needed for the discharge of the functions of the police authority, the question of the legitimacy of the request may be referred to the Home Secretary for final decision.[77]

(iv) Budgetary Powers

In setting its budget the police authority can look to a number of sources of revenue and capital expenditure.[78] The main source, is central police grant, representing 51 per cent of assessed revenue costs—an amount cash-limited by central government. The balance of revenue expenditure is made up of Revenue Support Grant (administered by the Department of Environment, Transport and the Regions), nationally pooled non-domestic rates, and council tax. Only the council tax element, which comprise less than 10 per cent of all revenue, is drawn directly from the local tax payer. It is collected by police authorities from their constituent local authorities by means of a precept.[79] As noted above,[80] the police authority may also receive from central government capital grants and grants for expenditure on safeguarding national security. Over and above the council tax contribution police authorities may receive grants from local authorities,[81] which may be subject to conditions[82] and so earmarked for specific purposes or projects. They may also receive payment for "special police services,"[83] which the chief constable is entitled to provide on request.[84] More controversially, reflecting the wider move towards the marketization of police functions,[85] police authorities are now empowered to accept gifts of money and gifts or loans of other property[86] on terms which include commercial sponsorship.[87]

---

[76] *ibid.*, s.22(3).

[77] *ibid.*, s.22(5).

[78] All receipts should be paid into a police fund, established under s.16 of the Police Act 1996.

[79] Police Act 1996, s.19.

[80] subsection 2(a)(iv).

[81] Police Act 1996, s.92.

[82] *ibid.*, s.92(3).

[83] See *Harris* v. *Sheffield United Football Club Ltd* [1988]1 Q.B. (C.A.) 77.

[84] Police Act 1996, s.25.

[85] See chapter nine.

[86] Police Act 1996, s.93(1).

[87] *ibid.*, s.93(2).

If police authorities have had to defer to central government over the determination of the overall level of the budget, they have conceded influence to the other tripartite party, the chief constable, over detailed spending questions. As already noted, the police authority no longer has specific control over establishment, buildings and other equipment. All else being equal, however, this would not be sufficient to deprive the police authority of effective control of spending. As the paymaster, the police authority continue to hold all the financial cards. Further, the local policing plan, over which the police authority retains ultimate authority, must deal with the allocation of resources, and as the White Paper acknowledges,[88] this returns considerable influence to the police authority over issues such as the balance between ranks. On the other hand, the Financial Management Code of Practice promulgated under the new legislation[89] makes it clear that day-to-day financial management should be delegated to the force provided that the chief constable can demonstrate that the force has adequate control systems in place and provided the police authority satisfies itself that expenditure is being controlled within approved budgets and monitors any shift in priorities from the approved local plan.[90]

(v) Employment of Non-police Staff

In a similar vein, the new legislative framework transfers direction, control,[91] engagement and dismissal[92] of civilian staff—now comprising some 30 per cent of all police-related personnel—to the chief constable, although the police authority will continue as the formal employers of such staff.[93] Exceptions may be agreed between the police authority and the chief constable in order to allow the police authority to retain managerial control over certain key staff.[94] Equally, the police

---

[88] Home Office (1993b) para. 3.6.

[89] Police Act 1996 s.39.

[90] Her Majesty's Government (1994).

[91] Police Act 1996 s.15(2).

[92] *ibid.,* s.15(4).

[93] *ibid.,* s.15(1). This represents a change of policy from the White Paper, which intended that civilians henceforth be formally employed by the chief constable; Home Office (1993b) para. 3.8.

[94] *ibid.,* s.15(3). For example, a treasurer, or a clerk (whose appointment is statutorily required under s.16), or other staff employed specifically to support the police authority in the exercise of its statutory responsibilities, including its strategic direction and monitoring of the local force.

authority may appoint non-employees to carry out certain duties on its behalf.[95]

(vi) Mutual Aid and Collaboration

This is an area which, unsurprisingly, involves a complex meshing of powers and responsibilities of all three tripartite parties. As in other areas, the police authority is paymaster but has only limited control over the terms and circumstances of co-operation. The new statutory regime continues to allow, and in some circumstances to require chief constables and police authorities to act mutually. Chief constables may ask one another for manpower or other assistance to allow them to meet any special demand on their resources.[96] Payment will normally be made by the police authority of the receiving force for such assistance, and where this cannot be agreed by the police authorities involved, it falls to be determined by the Home Secretary.[97] The Home Secretary may also take a more active role, directing that mutual aid arrangements should be made where he believes it to be expedient in the interests of public safety or order and where he is satisfied that voluntary aid arrangements cannot be made, or cannot be made in time.[98] By far the most prominent example of mutual aid in recent years was the nationally co-ordinated police operation to address the miners" strike of 1984–85.[99] While, in formal terms, this fell within the voluntary category of mutual aid, it took place in the shadow of the Home Secretary's reserve power of intervention.[1]

Collaboration agreements are a close cousin of mutual aid. If two or more chief constables believe that any police function can more efficiently or effectively be discharged by members of those forces acting jointly, they may make an agreement for that purpose.[2] Such an agreement requires the approval of the police authorities involved, who may also independently resolve to make joint provision of premises, equipment or other materials or facilities for their forces where they believe

---

[95] *ibid.*, s.17.
[96] *ibid.*, s.24(1).
[97] *ibid.*, s.24(4).
[98] *ibid.*, s.24(2).
[99] See chapter three, section 2 above. For a fuller analysis of the legal foundations of mutual aid, see Lustgarten (1986) chap. 8.
[1] On central influence over police operations during the miners" strike, see Reiner (1991) pp. 182–192.
[2] Police Act 1996, s.23(1).

this to be advantageous.[3] As with mutual aid, the Home Secretary has the backstop power to allocate costs where these cannot be agreed by the police authorities involved,[4] and also to direct that a collaboration agreement be made between chief constables or between police authorities.[5]

Collaboration agreements provided the original legal foundation for many regional and national policing initiatives. The regional crime squads, which date from 1965, provided the early flagship of collaboration, and the National Criminal Intelligence Service (NCIS) was also established on a collaborative basis in 1992. As we shall see,[6] these important structures have been developed and refined under a separate legal framework in the Police Act 1997. Other important centralising projects continue to take place under the umbrella of collaboration, such as regional training, and, in a more operational vein, the anti-terrorist unit and political surveillance under the aegis of Special Branch.

(vii) Advice and Assistance to International Organisations

The arrangements by which British police officers may be engaged in activities abroad or in international assistance by other means are reinforced under the new legislative framework.[7] A police authority, acting with the authority of the Home Secretary,[8] may provide advice and assistance to an international organisation or institution or to any other person or body engaged in policing activities outside the United Kingdom,[9] including the secondment of local officers to international units.[10] This reflects the trend towards the internationalisation of policing, and, in particular, permits the temporary employment of British police officers in new supranational units such as Europol.[11]

---

[3] Police Act 1996, s.23(2). Formal agreements do not prejudice more informal co-operation between police authorities and external agencies; s.23(7).

[4] *ibid.*, s.23(3).

[5] Provided any representations made by the parties concerned have been considered; *ibid.*, s.23(5).

[6] See chapter seven.

[7] This was formerly provided for only under the more restrictive terms of the Police (Overseas Service) Act 1945 and the Overseas Development and Co-operation Act 1980. These powers are saved by s.26(8) of the Police Act 1996.

[8] Police Act 1996, s.26(3).

[9] *ibid.*, s.26(1).

[10] *ibid.*, s.26(2).

[11] See chapter eight.

(C) CHIEF CONSTABLES

Historically, the doctrine of constabulary independence, both in its general formulation and in its specific application to the office of chief constable, was a creature of the common law. Its nurturing did not require—arguably, could not have withstood—much by way of statutory elaboration of the chief constabulary role.[12] Recent developments, however, contain at least the beginnings of a challenge to the broadest interpretation of the independence doctrine. First, the new statutory framework does develop a fuller conception of the chief constabulary role, one which stresses its complex interdependence with the other tripartite parties. Secondly, wider developments in the form of our constitutional order in the 1990s have provided new angles from which our courts can probe the implications of chief constabulary independence.

(i) Statutory Developments

The chief constable remains responsible for the direction and control of the local force,[13] a formulation which echoes the received modern understanding of his common law authority. In addition, the chief constable now possesses a greater range of specific statutory powers as ballast for this general authority. The chief continues to be responsible for appointments and promotions of all officers below the rank of assistant chief constable,[14] and is a key figure in the extended post-Sheehy regime for monitoring conduct and exercising discipline within the force.[15] As noted above,[16] the chief now possesses similar powers—transferred from police authorities—to direct and control and to hire and fire civilian employees.[17] The chief has also acquired from the police authority detailed powers of financial management in respect of manpower, buildings and other equipment.

On the other hand, in exercising these enhanced powers, chief constables are subject to closer control of the terms of their employment and their obligation to provide information to the other two tripartite

---

[12] See chapter two, section 1(D).
[13] Police Act 1996, s.10(1).
[14] *ibid.,* s.13(3).
[15] *ibid.,* s. 50; The Police (Conduct) Regulations 1999, SI. 1999 No. 730.
[16] See subsection (b)(v).
[17] Police Act 1996 s.15.

parties is extended.[18] And in the increasingly prominent field of trans-force, national and international co-operation, their authority tends to be trumped by that of the police authority, and more emphatically, by the Home Secretary.[19] Most tellingly of all, however, the chief constable's flagship statutory power of direction and control is explicitly qualified by an obligation "to have regard to" the local policing plan issued by the police authority.[20]

To what extent, if at all, does this qualification encroach upon the constabulary independence of the chief constable? Just as with the obligation of the police authority to follow the strategic direction of the Home Secretary,[21] the "have regard to" formulation, while suggesting that the chief constable must treat the plan as a key consideration when making decisions and developing practice, does not entirely remove his or her discretion to depart from the plan. Indeed, the Home Office Circular on policing plans issued to accompany the 1994 Act goes as far as to authorise the chief to deviate from the plan where it is deemed necessary in his or her "operational judgement".[22] Yet, even allowing for this concession, chief constabulary independence is inevitably compromised. Just as the lack of any clear conceptual boundary between policy and operations worked in favour of the chief constable in the original extension of the independence doctrine to the senior rank,[23] the same absence of demarcation lines left the extended jurisdiction of the office vulnerable to subsequent encroachment. Chief constabulary independence was never in any meaningful sense confined to operational matters. Accordingly, even if the policing plan were to focus on policy matters, which itself could only ever be a matter of degree because of the very same fundamental conceptual blurring, it would still overlap some of the domain claimed by the chief under the extended independence doctrine.

This conclusion is reinforced, but, paradoxically, also mitigated, if we consider the rules about the making of the plan. The chief constable is closely involved at a number of stages. He or she must be consulted by the police authority prior to the annual determination of local policing objectives,[24]

---

[18] See subsections (a)(iii) and (b)(iii) above.
[19] See subsections (a)(vii), (b)(vi) and (b)(vii) above, and chapters seven and eight below.
[20] Police Act 1996, s.10(2).
[21] *ibid.*, s.6(2); and see subsection b(ii) above.
[22] Home Office Circular 27/94. This echoes the approach taken to the interpretation of the new provisions by the Government spokesperson in the House of Lords, Earl Ferrers, during the passage of the Bill; quoted in Newburn and Jones (1997) p. 39.
[23] See chapter one, section 2(b)(i) and chapter two, section 1(d).
[24] Police Act 1996 s.7(3)(a).

which are one of the key components of the plan.[25] The chief constable is also responsible for the initial draft of the plan,[26] and must be further consulted by the police authority before it issues a plan which differs from that draft.[27] The chief constable would hardly have been allowed such a prominent role in the development of the plan if it had concerned matters deemed to be beyond his or her traditional remit or concern— that is to say, beyond the purview of chief constabulary independence. By the same token, the closeness of the chief officer's continuing involvement means that he or she retains a significant input into, if not ultimate control over these matters. How this new accommodation of central and local government influence in policy-making has been, and is likely to be resolved in practice is addressed in the final section of the chapter.

(ii) Developments in the Courts

In the opening chapter we considered some of the ways, often unremarked, in which the overall framework of constitutional arrangements affects the legal regulation of policing. One of the most pressing and intriguing trends in public law in recent years has been the interaction between external and internal factors in constitutional development; in particular, the new opportunities and constraints provided by deep structural changes in the relationship of our polity to the international order. In the final chapter, we consider the broader implications of this shift for the regulation of policing, but for the moment we concentrate on only one aspect—namely the view taken by the senior judiciary, as primary interpreters of the constitution, of the implications of new international or supranational norms for traditional constitutional doctrines, principles and techniques. In particular, our judges have been obliged to give close consideration to the ways in which the new forces represented by E.U. law and the ECHR impact upon our domestic law, not only challenging the fundamental premise of parliamentary sovereignty but also influencing substantive doctrine in various fields. Where once our judges tended to take a conservative approach to new constitutional influences, the stirrings of a more receptive judicial culture have recently been evident. This emergent "common law constitutionalism"[28] is characterised by a willingness to conceive of the judicial role in less positivist and more

---

[25] *ibid.*, s.8(20(b).
[26] *ibid.*, s.8(3).
[27] *ibid.*, s.8(4).
[28] See Hunt (1997) esp. chap.1.

creative terms—as less about "discovering" the intention of the sovereign legislator and more about developing novel solutions to hard cases by utilising new international standards in conjunction with the old values of the common law.

Developments in judicial review

In the late 1990s, these new European influences on judicial attitudes began to provoke a modest reassessment of the constitutional protection of the decision-making autonomy of the chief constable. In *R.* v *Chief Constable of Sussex, ex parte International Trader's Ferry Limited*[29] the question of the susceptibility of the chief to judicial review[30] was revisited. The case arose out of a matter of national controversy—the export of livestock to Europe. From the beginning of 1995, ITF sought to export veal calves on a daily basis from the port of Shoreham in Sussex, but were met by extensive, and in some cases violent protests by those opposed to the trade. At the peak of the protests, 1,125 police officers were required to ensure the safe passage of lorries carrying the livestock to the port, although by mid-January, this figure had settled at around 315 to deal with 100–150 protesters each night. This level of policing was sustained until April, when the chief constable, claiming that it had become impossible to provide saturation policing of the port as well as supplying the resources necessary to provide an efficient and effective general policing service throughout the force area, sought to introduce a more selective pattern of cover. ITF applied successfully to the Divisional Court to quash the chief's decision, but this was overturned in the Court of Appeal and in the House of Lords.

There were two strands of argument running through the case. The less noteworthy concerned the standard test of chief constabulary decision-making in domestic law. In response to ITF's claim that in failing to sustain blanket coverage of the port the chief constable was in breach of his duty to keep the peace and uphold the law, or that inasmuch as he retained a discretion over the deployment of his resources he had exercised it unreasonably, all three courts gave the now stock answer that the chief was entitled to take account of his overall responsibilities for the policing of the area and the limited resources available to meet them in

---

[29] [1996] Q.B. 197 (Divisional Court); [1998] Q.B. 477 (Court of Appeal); [1999] A.C. 418 (House of Lords); for discussion of the Divisional Court and Court of Appeal decisions, see Barnard and Hare (1997); and of the House of Lords decision, see Bernard and Hare (2000).

[30] See chapter three, section 1.

deciding the appropriate type and level of response in a particular operational context.[31]

The more noteworthy strand concerned the implications for the chief constable's decision-making authority of the right of free movement of goods granted under E.U. law. ITF claimed that the chief constable's failure to guarantee safe transit of the livestock amounted to a quantitative restriction on exports, so frustrating one of the fundamental freedoms guaranteed by the Treaty of Rome.[32] The Divisional Court accepted the argument that this failure was unlawful and that the chief constable could not rely upon law and order considerations under the statutory public policy defence[33] to justify selective coverage since he had not demonstrated that the cost of providing the resources necessary to ensure against civil disturbance and enable the lorries to get through to Shoreham on a regular basis was excessive. The Court of Appeal and the House of Lords took a different view. They were satisfied that the provision of assistance by the chief constable was proportionate to what was required, bearing in mind the dangers of violent disturbance, the finite resources available to the chief, the need to maintain a reasonable coverage in other parts of the force area, and the continuing availability of alternative ports through which ITF could trade.

Yet, despite the result, the case at least hinted at the prospect that appeal to European principles could provide a more rigorous form of judicial review. In the Divisional Court, the assumption had been made that the chief constable as an "emanation of the state"[34] had the full resources of the state at his disposal, so ignoring the constitutional division of functions described in the tripartite relationship, and in particular the budgetary control exercised by the police authority and the Home Secretary. The higher courts, crucially in the instant case, relieved the chief constable of this unrealistic burden, but still asked awkward questions. Where a fundamental freedom or entitlement under European law was at issue, the chief constable would have to show that the protection of a legitimate public policy interest, in this case the maintenance of civil order and an adequate policing balance in circumstances of finite resources, is proportionate in the sense that it should not restrict the fundamental freedom in question more than is necessary to protect the

---

[31] *ibid.*, See, in particular, the discussion of the *ex parte Levy* and the *ex parte CEGB* cases.
[32] Art.29 (ex art.34) EC Treaty.
[33] Art.30 (ex art 36) EC. Treaty.
[34] At p. 215; see also *Johnston* v. *Chief Constable of the RUC* [1986] ECR 1651; *Foster* v. *British Gas* [1990] E.C.R. I-3133.

legitimate public policy interest. In practice, the effect of the proportionality test[35] will often be the same as the traditional domestic test of *Wednesbury* unreasonableness,[36] particularly if—as it was by the House of Lords in the present case—the importance of allowing the domestic authority a "margin of appreciation"[37] to decide the most appropriate local application of European principles is acknowledged. This is not, however, to deny the conceptual distinction between the two tests[38] and, as the provisional conclusion reached in the Divisional Court indicates, the potential for more intensive scrutiny in the European test.

Liability in tort

An ultimately more successful, albeit less direct challenge to police decision-making authority took place in *Osman* v. *United Kingdom*.[39] As noted in the opening chapter, we are not generally concerned in this study with the legal powers, duties, rights and responsibilities of individual police officers, and since it is with individual liability that the law of tort is primarily concerned, we have little to say about its various forms. An exception is made, however, as regards the prominent line of cases, culminating in *Osman*, concerning the liability of the police in respect of their failure to prevent injury to third parties, typically through ineffective investigation of a crime or inadequate response to an emergency situation. These cases are relevant to the discussion of the legal responsibility of the chief constable for two related reasons. First, this area of tort

---

[35] See *e.g.*, Craig and De Burca (1998) chap. 8.

[36] *Associated Provincial Picture House Ltd* v. *Wednesbury Corporation* [1948] 1 KB 223.

[37] This phrase, which was used both in the Court of Appeal and in the House of Lords, is most commonly associated with the latitude allowed to national authorities under the case law of the European Convention of Human Rights to interpret the Convention in the light of local knowledge and circumstances (see *e.g.*, Jones (1995)). In the context of E.U. administrative law, the phrase appears functionally equivalent to "margin of discretion", commonly used by the European Court of Justice to describe the latitude allowed to national authorities to decide the appropriate application of E.U. norms in matters which overlap areas of Member State competence, such as the maintenance of public order and the safeguarding of internal security; see esp., *Commission of the European Communities* v. *French Republic* [1997] E.C.R. I-6959. The charitable reading of this transfer of concepts between different legal contexts is that it reflects the attempt to provide common principles to manage the relationship between national and supranational or international authorities in our changing constitutional order. The uncharitable interpretation is that it risks confusing two quite different legal contexts and that it is but the most recent manifestation of the long-standing difficulties experienced by the national judiciary in coming to terms with the complexities of European public law.

[38] See *e.g.*, *R.* v. *Secretary of State for the Home Department, ex parte Brind* [1991] 1 A.C. 696.

[39] [1998] 5 B.H.R.C. 293.

law has known its own conceptual wrangling over the policy/operations divide, and it is instructive to analyse how the distinction as here elaborated maps onto the specific context of policing. Secondly, and more importantly, such cases often turn as much if not more on general decisions about the allocation of resources as on individual neglect or incompetence. Legal intervention, then, might provide an oblique method of confining the discretion of senior decision-makers, in particular the chief constable.

A convenient starting point is the landmark case of *Anns* v. *Merton LBC*,[40] where the distinction between policy and operational decisions was first drawn in tort law. Under the *Anns* scheme, policy decisions on the part of a public authority were given special protection, and an allegedly negligent policy decision would not be actionable unless the decision-maker had also acted *ultra vires* in arriving at the decision. Operational decisions, on the hand, attracted no special protection. They could be challenged according to ordinary principles of tort law. Evidently, therefore, the significance of the policy/operations distinction in the public law framework of the tripartite relationship is stood on its head in the private law of tort. Within the conventional public law understanding of tripartitism, it is the operational prerogative of the police that is protected and it is the domain of policy decisions over which the other tripartite partners claim authority or influence. Conversely, within the context of tort law—including the law of police negligence—it is policy decisions that are offered special protection and operational decisions that are more susceptible to external intervention, in this case judicial intervention.

Many tort cases appear to fit easily within the *Anns* scheme. In *Anns* itself, a clear line could be drawn between a policy decision on the part of a local authority only to inspect every third building site, and the operational decision by an inspector to check a particular site only superficially because the inspector trusted the builder. Equally, in *Rigby* v. *Chief Constable of Northamptonshire*,[41] a line could be drawn between the financial policy decision not to acquire a particular type of CS-gas canister whose use did not create a fire risk, and the operational decision to use the canister of the type which did create a fire risk on a particular occasion despite the absence of a fire-engine in the vicinity.

Yet from the outset, the operational/policy distinction in tort was

---

[40] [1978] A.C. 728.
[41] [1985] 1 W.L.R. 1242.

plagued with difficulties.[42] In the first place, it was not clear that the distinction as drawn was consistent with the purpose, or purposes, which supposedly underlay it. These have to do with the legitimacy of judicial second-guessing of large policy questions about the weighing of values and the allocation of resources, the waste of scarce time and resources in litigation, the encouragement of negative litigation-avoidance strategies on the part of the managers of public bodies to the detriment of their positive duty to intervene in the public interest, and the irrelevance of legal sanctions of this sort to organisational decision-makers who are already infused with a sense of public duty.[43] Insofar as these purposes are legitimate considerations—and it is arguable that all apart from the first are naive in the trust they place in public bodies and in their underestimation of the force of the legal sanction—it is difficult to see why they should apply only (and always) to policy decisions and never to operational decisions. This difficulty is associated with the general problem of drawing a clear conceptual line between policy and operations; of isolating either a domain of policy without operational implications or a domain of operations uninformed by policy considerations.[44] These conceptual problems are generic and unavoidable, whether the context is provided by the private law of tort or by the public law of police governance. Inevitably, therefore, tort law merely replicates rather than resolves the problems thrown up in the public law context.

Recently, the domestic courts have become more aware of the problems associated with the *Anns* distinction and have become less inclined to apply it. This is unevenly evident in general tort jurisprudence,[45] but more

---

[42] See, e.g. Cane (1996) pp. 250–255.

[43] Steele and Cowan (1994) pp. 8–10.

[44] See chapter one, section 2(B)(i).

[45] From the late 1980s the distinction appeared to play a diminished role, and in some cases it was dismissed as unworkable or irrelevant; for example, in *Rowling* v. *Takaro Properties* [1988] A.C.; *Lohnro* v. *Tebbit* [1992]4 All.E.R. 280; *Stovin* v. *Wise* [1996] A.C. 923. However, it was recently referred to more approvingly in the House of Lords in *Barrett* v. *Enfield Borough Council* [1999] 3 W.L.R 79, especially by Lord Slynn of Hadley (95–97); see, *e.g.*, Hoyano (1999) pp. 922–923; Bayley and Bowman (2000); Mullender (2000). The fullest recent analysis of the liability in tort of public authorities remains *X* v. *Bedfordshire County Council* [1995] 2 A.C. 633, in which Lord Browne-Wilkinson argued that for a duty of care to be established; (i) the defendant ought to have foreseen that the plaintiff might suffer injury or damage if the defendant acted negligently; (ii) a sufficient relationship of proximity between the plaintiff and the defendant was required, and; (iii) it would be just and reasonable to impose such a duty on the defendant. In turn, the "just and reasonable" test contained three elements. In the first place, the imposition of the duty of care would have to be compatible with the statute in question. Secondly, in order to be actionable statutory "discretions", as opposed to other types of decisions, would have to be exercised unreasonably in the administrative law *Wednesbury* sense. Thirdly, the question of

pronounced in police negligence cases. In *Hill* v. *Chief Constable of West Yorkshire*,[46] the House of Lords did not rely upon the policy/operations distinction, and in *Osman* v. *Ferguson*,[47] McCowan L.J. in the Court of Appeal went further and rejected the distinction as "utterly artificial".[48] In putting the distinction to one side, however, the courts in *Hill* and *Osman* did not seek to replace it with a new distinction more adequate to the underlying purposes of the old distinction, still less did they reject or qualify the underlying purposes. On the contrary, *Hill* and *Osman* were instrumental in developing a general public policy immunity for the police from negligence actions in respect of their activities in the investigation and suppression of crime.

Hill was an action raised by the mother of the last victim of Peter Sutcliffe[49] claiming that the West Yorkshire police had been negligent in not apprehending Sutcliffe at an earlier point and thus failing to prevent the murder of her daughter. In rejecting the claim, the House of Lords relied not only on the absence of the requisite proximity, holding that the police owed no duty of care to the general public to identify or apprehend an unknown criminal, but also upon a general public policy immunity justified on the grounds of legitimacy,[50] waste of resources, defensiveness and public duty discussed above.

Osman took the reasoning in Hill a stage further. That case arose from an incident in which Mr Osman was murdered and his son severely injured after a shooting incident. Their assailant, Paget-Lewis, had been a secondary schoolteacher of the son, and had formed an unhealthy attachment to him. There was a history of slander, threats and violence directed by Paget-Lewis towards the boy and his family, activities which caused Paget-Lewis to be suspended from his teaching post and which attracted the attention of the police for almost a year prior to the critical incident. Indeed, at one point Paget-Lewis confessed to a police officer that he might do something criminally insane if his situation did not

---

breach of duty should raise no non-justiciable issues (see Cane (1996) pp. 241–250; Craig and Fairgrieve (1999); Bailey and Bowman (2000)). The various elements of the just and reasonable test appear to engage with the same range of underlying purposes as the policy/operations distinction, suggesting that even if the popularity of the terminology fluctuates the issues to which it is addressed are stubbornly resilient.

[46] [1989] 1 A.C. 53.

[47] [1993] 4 All E.R. 344.

[48] At 353.

[49] Known as the Yorkshire Ripper.

[50] Interestingly, for the House of Lords one consideration bearing upon the appropriateness of judicial inquiry was the availability of other, arguably more appropriate forms of inquiry through the other two parties to the tripartite relationship who are legally and politically responsible for securing police effectiveness and efficiency, *per* Lord Templeman, at 65.

improve. Despite the failure of the police to act on their specific knowledge to apprehend, interview, search or charge Paget-Lewis before March 1988, and despite the particular risk incurred by the Osman family, which arguably placed them in a special relationship of close proximity to the police, the Court of Appeal dismissed the claim of negligence by Mrs Osman against the Metropolitan Commissioner. For the reasons cited in the *Hill* case, the Court of Appeal asserted, the police could rely on a public policy immunity in the investigation of crime. It made no difference that in *Osman*, unlike *Hill* where the plaintiff's complaint concerned the general management of a wide-ranging investigation, the identity of the suspect and the victim and the likely nature of the crime were all known to the police. It made no difference, that is to say, that the investigation in *Osman* was much more advanced and much more focused than in *Hill*; that inasmuch as the distinction retains meaning, the facts in *Osman* were much closer to the operational end of the policy/operational spectrum than in *Hill*. The public policy immunity as regards the investigation and suppression of crime was deemed wide enough to embrace different levels and scales of decision-making, from major investigations to specific inquiries.

What is more, in the wake of *Osman* the courts were inclined to extend the scope of the immunity still further, to cover any scenario where public policy arguments about defensive policing and the diversion of scarce resources might apply. In *Ancell* v. *McDermott*,[51] the plaintiff's car had skidded on diesel, resulting in the death of Mrs Ancell and the injury of her husband. Two police cars had noticed the spillage before the accident, but had done nothing to make the road safe. Lack of proximity was again at the core of the Court of Appeal's decision against the plaintiff, but Beldam LJ made a point of applying the *Hill* immunity to the instant case,[52] even though the circumstances were far removed from the investigation or suppression of crime.[53]

The European twist to this tale was more decisive than in the judicial review line of cases. The decision in *Osman* was appealed successfully to the European Court of Human Rights.[54] The Strasbourg-based court held that the application of the exclusionary rule formulated in *Hill* to the circum-

---

[51] [1993] 4 All E.R.355.

[52] At 366.

[53] A later Scottish case arrived at the opposite conclusion on similar facts, but where the source of the hazard was a collapsed bridge rather than the spillage of diesel; *Gibson* v. *Orr* [1999] S.C. 420. For criticism of the domestic line of cases stemming from *Hill*, see Steele and Cowan (1994); Brodie (1995).

[54] [1998] 5 B.H.R.C. 293; see Hoyano (1999); Craig and Fairgrieve (1999)

stances of the instant case constituted a disproportionate restriction on the applicant's right of access to a court to have his civil rights and obligations determined, and so was in breach of Article 6.1 of the ECHR. The court conceded that the public policy underlying exclusion served a legitimate aim, "being directed to the maintenance of the effectiveness of the police service and hence to the prevention of disorder or crime", but determined that this could not justify conferring a "blanket immunity" on the police for their acts and omissions during the investigation and suppression of crime. In particular, the immunity could not, as it did here where the action was struck out before proof in the domestic court, deny the appellant's right to have a determination on the merits of the claim against the police in deserving cases.[55] Public policy considerations in favour of immunity were persuasive but not decisive, and it must be open to the domestic court to have regard to other public interest considerations which pull in the opposite direction in the circumstances of a particular case.

The import of this decision should not be exaggerated. It is not clear how comprehensively it challenges the public policy immunity,[56] nor how vigorously it may be resisted by a domestic judiciary whose initial reception has in some instances been distinctly lukewarm.[57] The most persuasive reading of the decision, and the one which is beginning to find favour with the U.K. authorities, is that it requires a more explicit weighing of the merits in cases which are closer to the operational end of the spectrum, where there is a catalogue of acts or omissions which are arguably negligent,[58] but that in broader policy cases such as *Hill* the immunity will be allowed to stand. For those who are generally sceptical of the force of the public policy considerations in favour of immunity—regardless of where the facts of the case are placed on the

---

[55] The Court was influenced by the fact that the applicants, unlike the plaintiff in *Hill*, had already complied with the proximity test, "a threshold requirement which was in itself sufficiently rigid to narrow considerably the number of negligence cases against the police which could proceed to trial".

[56] See Hoyano (1999) esp. pp. 934–935.

[57] In particular, Lord Browne-Wilkinson in *Barrett* v. *Enfield London Borough Council* [1999] 3 W.L.R. 79, at 84–86. See also the strong extra-curricular criticism voiced by Lord Hoffman; Hoffman (1999).

[58] Even before the European Court decided in *Osman*, there were indications of a more restrictive approach to the public policy immunity in some cases, such as *Swinney* v. *Chief Constable of Northumbria* [1997] Q.B. 464 in which the Court of Appeal held that there was no immunity in a case of police failure to protect the identity of an informant. For post-*Osman* development along similar lines, see *Brindle* v. *Metropolitan Police Commissioner*, March 29, 1999; *Swinney* v. *Chief Constable of Northumbria Police (No.2)*, 11 Admin.L.R. 811; *Costello* v. *Chief Constable of Northumbria* [1999] 1 All E.R. 550; *Kinsella* v. *Chief Constable of Nottinghamshire, The Times*, August 24, 1999; *Gibson* v. *Orr* [1999] S.C. 420.

policy/operations spectrum, and who see tort law as a legitimate tool for interrogating the broad discretion of senior management, the decision is of modest value. Yet it retains a toehold for tort law in this area, one which is internationally supervised. And with the full implementation of the Human Rights Act 1998,[59] the domestic courts will be bound to give effect to Convention rights wherever possible,[60] taking account of judgments of the European Court of Human Rights.[61] *Osman* v. *United Kingdom*, therefore, may provide a springboard for a domestic private law jurisprudence which does not easily defer to the organisational power of the police and is more sceptical of their claims to exceptional status.

In conclusion, neither *ITF* nor *Osman* announces a major breakthrough in judicial control over the chief constable. Yet both open up important avenues of challenge to the independent authority of the position; one suggesting that the chief is bound to have regard to fundamental freedoms under E.U. law, the other restricting the ambit, if not challenging the principle of a blanket police immunity in tort law. Perhaps more importantly, as their source is external, these developments are in some measure[62] protected against domestic legislative or judicial backlash and offer tangible support to those seeking to develop a more radically interventionist common law constitutionalism. The new emphasis upon fundamental rights and upon proportionality considerations cuts across both E.U. law and Convention law and is gradually becoming domiciled within British public law more generally.[63] This offers the interesting prospect of more exacting judicial scrutiny of public authority in general, and of police authority in particular, at precisely the point that statutory developments such as those contained in the Police Act 1996 are beginning to provide more effective cues for such scrutiny.[64]

---

[59] As of October 2, 2000.

[60] That is to say, unless primary legislation of the U.K. Parliament requires them to reach a different conclusion; Human Rights Act 1998, ss.3 and 6.

[61] Ibid., ss.2(1)(a).

[62] Although both residual judicial hostility (n. 57) and, in the case of the Human Rights Act, legislative override (n. 59) may curtail this ambition. It should also be noted that developments within E.U. law and convention law will not necessarily be mutually coherent or supportive in any particular case and this too will limit their cumulative impact. For example, from one perspective the ITF case itself presents a conflict between the E.U. right of free movement and the convention right of public assembly protest, with the former prevailing; see Baranrd and Hare (2000).

[63] See *e.g.* Hunt (1997).

[64] For instance, it is not difficult to imagine a more fully developed domestic doctrine of proportionality being used to challenge the grounds for or extent of the chief constable's departure from a local police plan in view of his obligation to have regard to this plan under s.10(2) of the 1996 Act.

3. The New Framework Assessed

(A) THE EARLY IMPACT

April 1999 marked the end of the first four year term of office of the independent members of the new police authorities under the new statutory regime. How had the new regime bedded down? Only limited evidence is available, most notably Jones and Newburn's study of the first two years.[65] On the basis of this, we can draw only tentative conclusions about the early effectiveness and longer-term prospects of the strategy which underpinned the White Paper. To recall our earlier discussion,[66] this strategy involved matching governance roles more closely to authority and expertise, ensuring transparent accountability and encouraging co-operation; all conceived in strongly instrumental terms, with a view to delivering more effective and efficient policing services.

According to Jones and Newburn, the restructuring of the tripartite relationship and of its constituent roles has "not been nearly as far-reaching as first anticipated,"[67] although there are signs that the pace of change is quickening. The Home Office may have acquired new powers over the setting and monitoring of objectives, but this has tended to consolidate their existing capacity rather than break new ground. This was partly because the early national objectives and performance indicators tended to be general and uncontroversial, although, as we have seen,[68] a more detailed and politically responsive approach to objective-setting seems to be gaining ground. Furthermore, these objectives cannot be viewed in isolation. They are the centrepiece of an expanding "suite of indicators"[69] developed and monitored by the Inspectorate, the Audit Commission[70] and ACPO, and now reinforced by New Labour's Best

---

[65] Jones and Newburn (1997). See also Weatheritt (1996), Baker (1996), Loveday (1998), Johnston (1999) chap.5.

[66] See section 1 above.

[67] Jones and Newburn (1997) p. 209.

[68] See section 2(A)(i) above.

[69] Home Office (1999a) para. 6.15.

[70] The Audit Commission's powers over policing and other local authority services, including the power to carry out studies to make recommendations to improve the economy, efficiency and effectiveness of a service (ss.33–35) and to require the publication of information relating to standards of performance (ss.44–46) were consolidated in the Audit Commission Act 1998. It has since been amended and supplemented to take account of the role of the Audit Commission under the new Best Value regime; see Local Government Act 1999, ss.10,13,22.

Value initiative[71] and local crime reduction strategies.[72] Slowly but surely, this national policy community organised around the Home Office is ensuring that the centre's commitment to a performance culture is internalised by all local police forces.

Despite significant changes in their make-up and powers, police authorities have also been slow to develop a new role. Insofar as the new independent members have made a difference, this has been somewhat double-edged. The clerks of the new authorities are generally of the view that the independent members, over half of whom come from management, business, commerce and the professions,[73] have given the police authorities a more "business like" complexion.[74] On the one hand, this has led to a more focused and more rigorous approach—a more "professional" attitude—to the supervisory work of the authority. On the other hand, it may have contributed to the depoliticization of police authorities. Although there continues to be a marked contrast between some authorities where party politics loom large and others where they do not, the overall tendency has been towards a less prominent political agenda. Equally, however, there are indications that the new authorities have also been slow to forge a political role in the broader sense, in terms of the development of a strongly independent normative perspective on the best policing strategy for their force.

The best evidence of this is the distribution of influence in the making of local police plans, the main statutory plank of the new strategic role of the police authorities. Jones and Newburn divide the new police authorities into three categories in terms of their involvement in the drafting process.[75] First, there are "rubber stampers", a small group with minimal involvement in the policing plan. Secondly, and by far the largest group, there are "redrafters", who are involved in the consultation process at an earlier stage and at a deeper level. Thirdly, there are "junior partners", the authorities with greatest involvement in the planning process. Unlike the others, they tend to have some input into the initial

---

[71] Local Government Act 1999, Part I.

[72] Crime and Disorder Act 1998, ss.5–6.

[73] Of the 213 new independent members in the 1995–99 cycle, 86(40 per cent) came from management, business and commerce, while 45(21 per cent) came from the professions. The next largest occupational group was academics, teachers and lectures with 24(11 per cent). Only 19 of the 41 authorities had ethnic minority members; see Howe (1999). The report of the Stephen Lawrence Inquiry noted the low level of ethnic minority representation and recommended improvement; MacPherson (1999) Recommendation 7; Home Office (1999c) p. 7.

[74] Jones and Newburn (1997) pp. 75–79, 203–205.

[75] *ibid.*, pp. 79–89.

draft, although they remain in a subordinate position to the chief constable. Even at its highest, therefore, police authority involvement in the planning process is not that of the dominant, or even equal partner. This conclusion is reinforced by a content analysis of the early plans. For instance, in 1996/97 by far the largest single subject matter of local objectives contained in local plans concerned internal managerial and organisational objectives,[76] an emphasis which clearly reflects internal police concerns and which diverts the attention of police authorities from larger strategic issues.

It might be argued that this is a fair reflection of the statutory position. After all, the chiefs have the power of planning initiative, and, on a purely formal reading police authorities cannot reasonably expect to be more than redrafters.[77] Yet a more dynamic reading would suggest that as the police authorities have the last word in approving the plan, they possess the leverage to enter the planning process from the outset as full partners.[78] Moreover, as regards the local objectives—and now also the Best Value local performance plan, even in formal terms the police authorities have the power of initiative, and so there is no reason in strict law why they should not take the lead in formulating these central components of the local plan. The explanation for the relatively passive performance of the police authorities, therefore, must lie elsewhere. In part, it may simply be that the police authorities are taking time to find their feet, and there is some evidence that they are gradually beginning to assert a greater strategic authority.[79] In part, however, the problems are more structural, and less easily corrigible. Even with the influence of the new independents, there are still indications of a "compliance culture"[80] within police authorities—a reluctance or inability to challenge the authority of chief constables and their senior officers. Compliance does not necessarily indicate full satisfaction. It is also in some measure a function of the continuing lack of an independent knowledge-base for police authorities. Faced with the vastly increased audit information generated to promote the new performance culture, most police authorities have

---

[76] *ibid.*, p. 59. 54 such objectives were listed, compared to 38 for crime prevention/reduction—the next largest category.

[77] Police Act 1996, s.8.

[78] By comparison, the fact that the Home Secretary enjoys a power of veto rather than a power of initiative over the choice of the chief constable does not prevent him from being involved at the initial stage in drawing up a shortlist; Police Act 1996, s.11(1).

[79] Jones and Newburn (1997), p. 209, Howe (1999).

[80] A term used by one of Jones and Newburn's police authority clerk respondents; (1997) p. 208.

neither the expertise nor the secretarial support[81] to assimilate this, still less—despite some evidence of a greater willingness to involve local community representatives as consultative partners in the planning process[82]—to generate their own data as a counterweight to that controlled and produced by the police and other agencies.[83]

The other side of this coin is the enhanced managerial control of the chief constables. Whereas the police authorities have benefited least in the short term from the redistribution of authority under the new legislation, the chief constables arguably have benefited most.[84] The more detailed financial and managerial powers available to chief constables under the new legal framework, together with their own concern to cope with the new audit environment, has led them, with at least some success, "to assimilate the annual planning process within a wider strategic planning system which is police driven and police controlled."[85] Furthermore, there is little early evidence that fixed-term contracts for senior officers—the other side of the new calculative equation—will offer an effective mechanism for police authorities to claw back power from the chiefs.[86]

It is clear that in practice, as well as in design, performance audit is a central feature of the new tripartitism. Yet as the means selected by the White Paper to ensure the transparent accountability of the new arrangements, performance audit has limitations as well as strengths. Its strengths lie in the commitment to measure what can sensibly and relevantly be measured in police work, from detection rates to response times and levels of public satisfaction. Yet there are also significant limitations of a methodological, political and democratic sort which are more apparent as the performance culture becomes more deeply embedded.[87]

Methodologically, there are problems associated with the selectivity of what is measured; with the difficulty of measuring the more qualitative aspects of police work and the consequent danger of their neglect;

---

[81] While there is provision for some civilian employees to continue to work directly for the police authority, this requires the consent of the chief constable, or, in its absence, the authorisation of the Home Secretary; Police Act 1996, s.15(3).

[82] Police Act 1996 s.7(3)(b); Jones and Newburn (1997) pp. 87–89.

[83] Jones and Newburn (1997) pp. 215–217.

[84] ibid., pp. 205–208.

[85] Loveday, (1998) p. 146. Loveday relies on HMIC Reports from the early years of the new legislation in drawing this conclusion.

[86] This is largely because in the early years many existing ACPO officers were not placed on fixed-term contracts, and even where contracts were used they tended to be linked to retirement dates; see Jones and Newburn (1997), pp. 90–91, 217; Baker (1996).

[87] See generally, Power (1997).

relatedly, with the trade-off between crude but easily verifiable standards and those which are more sensitive to the "interlinked complexity of tasks,"[88] but also more difficult to measure adequately and reliably; and with the costing of discrete outputs, without which the measurement of *efficiency* cannot be integrated with the measurement of *effectiveness* and the financial implications of strategic alternatives cannot be accurately projected.

Politically, with its neutral and technocratic discourse, performance audit may obscure, but certainly does not avoid large political questions about policing priorities. On the one hand, the hegemony of management-speak threatens to forestall candid and wide-ranging discussion of these large political questions; on the other, however, the fundamental inescapability of these questions gives rise to tensions which threaten the internal logic of the audit process. As we observed,[89] the new framework creates both vertical lines of accountability to a national political constituency and horizontal lines of accountability to the local community, reflecting the perennial tension between locally and nationally articulated aspirations in the political contest over policing.[90] In this system of dual accountability, recently reinforced by the Best Value initiative, something has to give and the integrity of either or both audit chains may be compromised. This compromise is recognised in the use of the "have regard to" formulation to qualify the responsibilities both of police authorities[91] and of chief constables[92] to comply with the vertical chain of responsibility. It is also reflected in the continuing ambivalence towards performance audit on the part not only of police authorities and chief constables,[93] but also of the rank and file of the police organisation who must address these various accountability demands.[94] In turn, this raises concerns about the propensity of police organisations to exploit the methodological limitations of audit and the low visibility of operational practice, and so to resort to "mock"[95] compliance with some aspects of the new regime.

These methodological and political problems also underwrite the

---

[88] Jones and Newburn (1997) p. 211.

[89] See section 1 above.

[90] See chapter one, section 2(B)(iii).

[91] Police Act 1996 s.6(2).

[92] Police Act 1996 s.10(2).

[93] Reflected, for instance, in the lack of enthusiasm from either police or police authorities to produce plans which are output-costed; Jones and Newburn (1997) p. 207.

[94] See *e.g.*, Waddington (1999) pp. 234–243.

[95] Gouldner (1954).

democratic problems associated with performance audit. Audit has a strong self-reinforcing dynamic. Audit is intrinsically self-critical and infinitely self-improving—since "efficiency is a direction and not a terminus we can never arrive at the ideal "lean, fit" efficient organization."[96] This attitude feeds on and is reinforced by the underlying methodological and political difficulties, as the technical shortcomings of audit are tackled with new and ever more sophisticated standards, indicators and planning systems, and as unyielding questions of political choice and conflict continue to insinuate themselves within the audit process. Yet the increased flow and greater sophistication of information which this ceaseless dynamic brings threatens to make the accountability of the new approach less rather than more transparent. Police authorities, we have already noted, lack the capacity to assimilate fully the new burden of audit information, and this is even more the case for the general public as the ultimate democratic constituency.[97] The danger is that audit information will be viewed by the consumer and by the voter as too plentiful, too unwieldy, too inconsistent, too arcane and too easily manipulated by politicians to provide a tool for democratic enlightenment and empowerment. Relatedly, the problem of information overkill and crosscutting lines of accountability means that the culture of avoidance which plagued the previous system of accountability and which was criticised in the White Paper is not necessarily overcome. The precise allocation of responsibility between local and central state remain uncertain and contestable, and the weight and complexity of the information produced in the audit cycle allows continued scope for defensive rationalisation.

Finally, the White Paper strategy of encouraging co-operation and defusing conflict also seems delicately poised. Co-operation amongst the tripartite parties is encouraged through the new planning process, reinforced by the new joint local authority and police obligation to develop a local crime reduction strategy. Further, it has been suggested that there is some early evidence of improved working relations between the chief constable and the local police authority in particular, building upon their strategic co-operation during the tensions which attended the passage of the 1994 Act.[98] Yet there remains significant scope for conflict between the tripartite parties. Any possibility that the reconstituted police authorities would be politically neutered, and would readily defer to the policy prerogative of central government and the managerial prerogative of the

---

[96] McLauchlin and Murji (1997) p. 100.
[97] Jones and Newburn (1997) pp. 215–216.
[98] *ibid.*, (1997) p. 214.

chief constable, did not survive those amendments to the 1994 Bill which reasserted the autonomy of the local bodies from the Home Office. But while the political identity of the police authorities may have been preserved, their aspirations risked being frustrated. As we have seen, the involvement of the police authorities in the planning process did not yet guarantee them a top-seat in police policy-making, whereas the removal of their detailed managerial powers deprived them of the indirect and incremental levers of influence which had for long provided them with a guaranteed role identity and, for some, the means to a broader strategic involvement.

It would be wrong, however, to view the new regime as a zero-sum game in which the police authorities were the only potential losers. Despite early evidence that their position had been strengthened under the new system, chief constables too could not be entirely sanguine about the longer term prognosis. The relentless march of the new managerialism threatened increasingly intrusive forms of challenge to areas of their domain previously considered sacrosanct. Equally, central government and its collaborators in the audit process could not be convinced about the success of their new technology of control. After all, audit promised government at a distance. The auditor's leash might be made of powerful and sophisticated materials but it was still a *long* leash, allowing a great deal of practical autonomy to the locals and the professionals in the day-to-day running of policing. In these circumstances, much trust had to be invested in the new system, and while the growth and refinement of audit shows a continuing willingness to make that investment it also betrays a resilient anxiety about the adequacy of its methodologies.

It would seem, therefore, that none of the tripartite parties are entirely confident of their position under the new regime, and, in consequence, that none are entirely comfortable about the basis and terms of their relations with the others. Against that background, the temptation to deploy what powers are possessed in an instrumental fashion, as a way of asserting an authority more commensurate with aspirations, remains strong. In such a climate, there are no guarantees that a culture of co-operation will take root.

(B) Prospects: The Partner Model Prefigured?

Even by its own standards, therefore, the White Paper model is inadequately realised in the new legislative framework, and these inadequacies threaten perverse consequences. In the name of a more appropriate division of labour within tripartitism, some old anomalies remain and some new frustrations are born. In the name of transparency, new forms of opaqueness are nurtured. In the name of co-operation, new opportunities for conflict arise.

Yet this is by no means intended as a damning indictment of the new approach. In the first place, the scheme is still bedding down and the perverse consequences anticipated above may be avoided or substantially mitigated. In the second place, the aspirations of the White Paper—role optimisation, transparency and co-operation—are intrinsically sound, and, as noted at the beginning of the chapter, identify and seek to correct fundamental weaknesses in the traditional model of tripartitism. Thirdly, a less ambivalent approach to the virtues of local democracy, of which there are already signs as the new model matures, would address some of its problems and cover some of its risks.

The White Paper blueprint tends to treat democracy in instrumental terms, as a means to more efficient and effective policing, rather than in its classical sense as an ideal in itself; as reflecting the worth and enhancing the dignity or development of the individual, or as constitutive of the virtue or well-being of the political order as a whole.[99] Yet in some later refinements and developments—the last-minute pre-legislative pardon for the democratic tradition in the composition of the local police authority is the most obvious example[1]—the new approach of the last decade appears to take democracy more seriously. As it now stands, however, the model threatens to fall between two stools. On the one hand, it pays enough regard to democratic values to disturb the narrow instrumental reckoning of the White Paper, most obviously in setting aside the White Paper's initial fears that a democratic majority and a strong independent element would produce a police authority insufficiently receptive to the new national planning framework. On the other hand, the model does not go far enough in recognising the intrinsic value of democracy, and in so doing it also, paradoxically, fails to exploit a broader instrumental calculus. That is to say, it fails to contemplate that a more robust assertion of democratic values in the local sphere (where they are presently most deficient), far from jeopardising police effectiveness and

---

[99] Although democracy has for long been a highly contested and polysemic concept, defying any simple distinction between classical and modern versions; Jones, Newburn and Smith (1994) p. 38. See also Arblaster (1994) chaps. 1–4; Held (1996).

[1] Others already discussed in this chapter include the involvement of local authorities in crime reduction strategies under the Crime and Disorder Act 1998 and the introduction of a police authority for the Metropolitan Police under the Greater London Authority Act 1999.

efficiency might instead provide a sounder and more ambitious instrumental basis for their achievement.

More specifically, a less ambivalent embrace of local democracy promises to strengthen the model's core commitment to role optimisation, transparency and co-operation and so marginalise the danger of perverse consequences. In this vein, we may contemplate enhancement of the local democratic element in terms of composition, resources and powers. As regards composition, the locally elected constituency on the police authority would be bolstered by the replacement of the magistrates' constituency- a pointless anachronism—with more locally elected members,[2] and by greater efforts to broaden the social and cultural mix of the independent element.[3] At a lower level, the profile of local consultative committees, already raised by their inclusion as consultative parties in the development of local policing objectives, could be further highlighted by their formal involvement in local policing plans and, perhaps, by their inclusion in a new district level of joint planning. As regards resources, given the reduced influence of police authorities over civilian staff, and indeed over resources generally, it has been argued that minimum levels of secretarial support for police authorities ought to be centrally determined and guaranteed.[4] This would improve the capacity of police authorities to fulfil their expanding statutory responsibilities, particularly in producing, assimilating and analysing information within the planning process. The newly elevated local consultative committees could also be important allies in developing an informational capacity independent of the police.

As regards legal powers, uncertainty over ownership of the police plan could be resolved by removing the chief constable initiative and providing for joint production of the draft, as well as retaining the police authority's status as final author. Furthermore, more could be done to reduce the long shadow cast by the doctrine of constabulary independence—and by its close ally—the idea of operational autonomy.[5] As we have seen, the new regime seeks to "side-step"[6] the difficulties caused by the uncertain boundaries of the independence doctrine by focusing instead on the seamless inclusiveness of the planning process within a regulatory framework which clarifies the previously underspecified[7]

---

[2] Jones and Newburn (1997) p. 220.
[3] See MacPherson (1999) Recommendation 7; Home Office (1999c) p. 7.
[4] Jones and Newburn (1997) pp. 220–221.
[5] See chapter 2, section 1(D).
[6] Reiner (1993) p. 19.
[7] See chapter two, section 2.

broad governance roles of the tripartite parties. Yet while the new planning environment ensures a prominent role for the police authority at the policy end of the continuum, it does nothing to rein in the authority of the chief constable at the operational end of the continuum. While it is quite proper that the constabulary should retain its independence in matters of law enforcement,[8] this does not justify, as the present legislation invites,[9] the refusal of operational information after the event to the police authority. If police authorities are to meet their policy responsibility in the production and monitoring of police plans effectively, they require a more robust power to make the chief constable retrospectively answerable, one which penetrates the notoriously expansive shield of operational autonomy.[10]

If the present model were to be refined along these lines, it would, in the first place, allow the police authority to match the other tripartite parties in meeting its role aspirations. The local community would be allowed a voice in police policy-making similar in strength to that enjoyed in other areas, while the continuing requirement of independent members—broadly recruited—would assuage concerns about crude majoritarianism and unduly narrow forms of interest representation and ideological commitment.[11] Moreover, although the challenge of rendering the new information-intensive planning and audit process transparent should not be underestimated, the improved resources and powers of the local police authority would enhance its capacity to make an informed contribution and to provide an effective monitor.

For these improved capacities of the police authority to reap dividends in terms of police effectiveness and efficiency, however, progress towards the White Paper's third objective of improved co-operation between the tripartite parties would also be required. In a co-operative climate, an enhanced police authority may complement professional expertise by bringing a different and less insular perspective to the negotiation of police policy, but also one more sensitive to local circumstances than a national policy agenda; may communicate public concern about the legitimacy and efficacy of operational practice; may increase public confidence and co-operation by certifying the amenability of the police to

---

[8] See chapter two, section 1(D).

[9] Police Act 1996, s.22(5).

[10] This suggestion has already been made in the context of police reform in Northern Ireland under the Belfast Agreement; see Patten (1999) paras. 6.19–622; see chapter six, section 2(B), chapter ten, section 3(C).

[11] See chapter two, section 1(D).

external scrutiny and influence; and may, given its more informed perspective and its own increased accountability for policing output, make more realistic and sympathetic, and therefore more effective demands of rank and file officers.[12] In other words, an enhanced police authority operating within a co-operative framework promises extended policy insight, more sensitive representation of local interests and concerns, a more legitimate foundation for the police mandate, and improved prospects of overcoming the recalcitrance of junior ranks—all of which conduce to greater effectiveness and efficiency. In an unco-operative climate, on the other hand, a more potent police authority may generate precisely the opposite effect. It may induce a professional siege mentality, leading to a strategic stand-off which blocks mutual learning and threatens to trigger a confrontational spiral with police policy makers and encourage defensive accounting within the ranks.

Clearly, co-operation is complexly dependent upon cultural histories, contemporary politics and personal relations, and cannot simply be engineered through legislation. But insofar as law remains a significant variable, the shift towards a partner model[13] of accountability hinted at in the 1994 restructuring—and guaranteed additional impetus by the refinements suggested above—enhances the prospects of a more harmonious model of governance. The proposed elevation of the role of the police authority within the planning process, the expanded right of information, the enhanced secretariat and the improved capacity to draw upon the consultative committees, like some of the reforms already in place, invest directly in the *relational* dimension of the role. That is to say, they promise improved status and influence to the police authority to the extent that it channels its energies in a co-operative manner. Reciprocally, the involvement of the chief constable in the local planning process also promises role enhancement and extended influence as a reward for developing a more co-operative approach, as indeed the introduction of a statutory level of district planning would within the lower police managerial echelons.

Some of the legislative instruments towards a viable partner model of police governance, therefore, are already in place, while the implementation of others would involve a modest additional commitment to local democracy. That such a commitment to democratic principle is necessary makes the model in question all the more worthy of pursuit.

---

[12] See chapter one, section 2(B)(v).
[13] Morgan (1986).

Chapter Five

Variations in Tripartitism: The Case of Scotland

The governance of the police of Scotland and Northern Ireland, which we consider over the next two chapters, provide two important and long-standing variations on the theme of tripartitism.[1] The constitutional arrangement for the policing of Northern Ireland, as we shall see, are inextricably bound up with the highly distinctive and fundamentally divided social and political structure of a contested territory, so much so that it is remarkable how many similarities to the system in England and Wales they retain. If anything, in Scotland the opposite holds. As part of the same state as England since 1707—a constitutional landmark which pre-dated the origins of the "new police" by around a century in both jurisdictions—Scotland would appear to have had limited scope from the outset for developing a policing sector along different lines. Nevertheless, as many commentators have remarked,[2] within the common constitutional framework of 1707 Scotland maintained a relatively autonomous social and political system, notably through the preservation of indigenous Scottish traditions in key areas such as law, religion and education and through the development of a substantial framework of devolved administrative authority in the nineteenth and twentieth centuries. This tradition of difference is at least in some respects attributable to the constitutional origins of Britain as a "union state",[3] a joining together of distinct polities with interests and cultures of their own already well developed.

---

[1] For more recent variations within the new national policing arrangements, see chapter seven.

[2] See *e.g.*, Midwinter, Keating and Mitchell (1991); Nairn (1997); Kellas (1989); Paterson (1994).

[3] Rokkan and Urwin (1982) p. 11; Keating (1998); Walker (2000a).

In what follows, we investigate to what extent, and for what reasons, the tradition of difference within the union state extends to the police. We also examine how current changes in the constitutional relationship between Scotland and the rest of the United Kingdom are affecting the distinctiveness of Scottish policing.

1. Historical Context [4]

In view of the "remarkably early growth"[5] of Scottish policing, it is regrettable that its history is under-researched in comparison to the policing of the rest of the British Isles.[6] The establishment in the towns of "new police" forces of professional officers with a clear public mandate took place through a series of private acts of Parliament at the turn of the nineteenth century. Aberdeen led the way in 1795, followed by Glasgow in 1800, Edinburgh in 1805, and, in rapid progression, a cluster of smaller urban centres, until in 1833 the first public Act enabling the establishment of police forces in all royal burghs or burghs of baronny was passed.[7] Equally, in rural Scotland, as many as a dozen counties had, through their Commissioners of Supply, established police forces prior to the enactment of general enabling legislation in 1839.[8]

The dearth of serious historical investigation and analysis hinders attempts to account for this early development, but, drawing upon Carson's work,[9] at least two explanations may be suggested. First, the relevant legislation could be enacted so early because it still chimed quite closely with the old police idea. The police provided for under the early urban statutes were not merely specialists in order maintenance and crime prevention, but continued to provide a broader measure of public welfare in matters such as road maintenance, lighting and public health. This does not imply, as some have suggested,[10] that the early Scottish forces may be dismissed as an inconsequential legacy of the old police; in particular, their full-time,

---

[4] For a fuller development of the arguments set out in this section, see Walker (1999b).

[5] Carson (1984) p. 207.

[6] See Emsley (1996) p. 25. Apart from Carson's work (1984;1985), there are very few historical analyses. Brief overviews are provided by Gordon (1980) and Murdoch (1985), while Smout (1970) is valuable for its contextualization of policing within a broader social history.

[7] Burghs and Police (Scotland) Act 1833.

[8] County Police Act 1839.

[9] Carson (1984);(1985).

[10] See *e.g.*, Hart, (1981) pp. 158–69

professional status sets them apart from their predecessors. It does, however, demonstrate the lack of any clear historical rupture between old and new in the development of Scottish policing,[11] and explains how a broader conception of the police task—one which has remained under serious contemplation in the modern age—remained prominent within Scottish policing discourse and practice well into the nineteenth century.

Inasmuch as the early Acts were genuine harbingers of the new police, a second strand of explanation has to do with the pattern of economic development peculiar to Scotland. The major agricultural and industrial developments which ushered in the age of capital took place rather later in Scotland than in England, but accelerated more rapidly. As a result, the effects of economic transformation in terms of social dislocation and altered routines of daily life, and in terms of new insecurities attendant upon these changes, "were experienced much more acutely north of the border."[12] Rural depopulation was triggered by the actions of Scottish landlords, unhampered (unlike their English counterparts) by the need to proceed through costly and difficult acts of enclosure in developing large-scale commercialised agriculture and thereby dispossessing large numbers of small tenants. The absence under the Scottish poor laws of a safety net for the able-bodied pauper together with the thickening flow of immigration from Ireland in the first half of the nineteenth century converged with these changes in the rural economy to provide mid-century Scotland with a large migrant population. In turn, this created a sizeable pool of cheap labour to service the new industries of the rapidly expanding lowland towns. For a number of reasons, then, the socio-economic condition of Scotland in the early-to-mid nineteenth century was conducive to the emergence of an organised police. The migrant population produced high levels of vagrancy in the countryside and new towns. The new and densely populated urban communities posed new problems of order. So, too, did discipline in the new industrial workplace and the traumas of rural dispossession, for which the imposition of military force provided a crude and increasingly unacceptable solution.

As it did in England and Wales, the development of nineteenth century policing also reflected the struggle between different groups over control of the state. The new police clearly served the "specific order" requirements of both the traditional landed classes and the new industrial *bourgeoisie*, but the institutional politics of the age nevertheless reflected

---

[11] Although recent histories of the English police have also questioned the received wisdom of a sharp break between old and new systems. See *e.g.*, Emsley (1983; 1991).

[12] Carson (1984) p. 218.

the shifting balance of political power between these groups. For much of the nineteenth century, despite the democratic reforms of 1832, the landed interest continued to dominate the national level of politics, and so bourgeois strategies for gaining political influence tended to be locally concentrated. Even here, though, it proved difficult to remove the traditional unelected power base of the landowners in the magistracy or the town councils, or in the counties as Commissioners of Supply. The institution of local police forces—particularly through private legislation in the towns—promised an alternative source of municipal power for the new bourgeois and professional interests who sought to control such forces, and provided a particular incentive to define the new police mandate as widely as possible. After 1833 when generic local government began to develop its own limited democratic franchise on the basis of property ownership,[13] the *bourgeoisie* began to strengthen its grip on local political power, and this encouraged the gradual integration of policing into the general system of local administration.

In the century from 1850 until the post-war years, the Scottish police built upon these local foundations, gradually developing a more centralised and harmonised administrative structure. Again, the general trend was similar to that in England and Wales, although differences of detail left an important legacy. In the towns, the facility to establish a police force was extended to progressively smaller conurbations between 1847 and 1862, while in the counties comprehensive policing coverage was secured in 1857 when the maintenance of a force became compulsory.[14] The same legislation saw the Scottish establishment of the office of Inspector of Constabulary, whose power to withhold government grant on grounds of inefficiency and whose influential role in the framing of detailed regulations on conditions of service allowed the embryo of a central model of good police administration to develop. One of the new measures of efficiency concerned force size, and so 1857 also triggered the gradual consolidation of forces into larger and larger units. From over ninety forces in mid-century, the Scottish police organisation was reduced through progressive rationalisations to sixty-four forces in 1900 , forty-nine at the end of the Second World War, twenty-two in 1968, and, finally, to the present figure of eight following the introduction of regional government in 1975.

Meanwhile, the rationalisation of local government eliminated differences between town and county more rapidly than in England and

---

[13] Royal Burghs Municipal Reform Act 1833; see Carson (1984) pp. 220–222.
[14] Police (Scotland) Act 1857.

Wales, producing a uniform framework which contained elements of both urban and rural systems of governance in the other jurisdiction. The general system of policing established in 1833 was made compulsory in the towns in 1892[15] and became the direct responsibility of the Town Council itself in 1900.[16] In the counties, too, the Commissioners of Supply were eventually replaced by the county council as police authority in 1929.[17] Unlike their Southern neighbours, therefore, prior to the Royal Commission, Scotland already boasted a uniform system of tripartite police governance. The local authority itself was the police authority, and as such the business of the police authority was carried out by a committee which, like the watch committee in England and Wales, was composed entirely of elected members. Unlike the watch committee system, however, and like the English county system, powers of appointment, dismissal, promotion and discipline in Scotland were uniformly vested in the chief constable.

2. The Present Arrangements

(A) PERIPHERAL CONSTITUTIONAL VISION

In the period since the 1962 Royal Commission and its implementing legislation north of the border—the Police (Scotland) Act 1967, Scottish policing has been further affected by the U.K.-wide trend towards centralisation and uniformity. Paradoxically, however, the political dynamics of this trend have also served to underline the distinctiveness of the Scottish system. What is more, a strong case can be made

---

[15] Burgh Police (Scotland) Act 1892.

[16] Town Councils (Scotland) Act 1900.

[17] Local Government (Scotland) Act 1929. This followed an intermediate phase under the Local Government (Scotland) Act 1889 when, as in the English and Welsh counties prior to 1964, the administration of the police was in the hands of a Standing Joint Committee. This comprised one half county councillors, the other half supplied by Commissioners of Supply in Scotland and justices of the peace in England and Wales. As the Willink Commission itself commented (Royal Commission on the Police (1962) para. 47), the early history of the Scottish police, like that of England and Wales, therefore contained elements of control by the lower judiciary alongside an emerging democratic influence. And while, unlike England and Wales, the judicial element was not directly evident in Scotland as the tripartite framework matured in the twentieth century it remains indirectly relevant even today. The Police (Scotland) Act 1967 obliges the chief constable to comply with all lawful instructions from the local sheriff principal (s.17(3)), and prior to local government reorganisation in 1973 a similar authority was vested in local magistrates.

that this distinctiveness has increasingly been a function of constitutional neglect, threatening to undermine the legitimacy and effectiveness of the governance framework.

The Royal Commission itself sought to change the Scottish tripartite system no more radically than it did the system in England and Wales, with the consequence that the two systems remained very similar in type. The Royal Commission successfully recommended harmonisation of practice in some areas, as in the adoption in England and Wales of the Scottish precedent of empowering the police authority to call for reports on policing matters from the chief constable.[18] Elsewhere, the Commission was prepared to let historical differences lie, as in its recommendation that Scottish police authorities should remain wholly composed of elected councillors.[19] In other respects, however, differences remained or opened up because the legislature was not prepared to take the Commission's advice on questions of harmonisation or centralisation. Its recommendation that Scotland, while retaining fully-elected police authorities, should adopt the legislative practice of England and Wales of identifying a committee of the council or, in joint police areas, a joint committee of the constituent councils, rather than the council itself as police authority was not adopted.[20] Neither was the Royal Commission's suggestion to appoint a common Chief Inspector of Constabulary for Great Britain endorsed by legislation.[21] And while its proposal to make the Home Secretary legally responsible for efficient policing[22] met only a half-hearted and ambiguous response in England and Wales, it was entirely absent from the Scottish scheme—as indeed, again unlike England and Wales, was any residual general responsibility on the part of the police authority to secure the maintenance of an adequate and efficient force. As we shall see, these differences, albeit minor, were harbingers of a broader failure of contemporary Scottish legislation to specify broad strategic roles for the tripartite parties. At the time, however, they appeared to be no more than minor variations on a common theme.

In the years that followed, a wider gap between the two systems gradually opened up. The Royal Commission's strictures against small police forces, followed by Scottish local government reorganisation in 1975,[23] and its matching, with two exceptions, of police forces to the new

---

[18] Paras. 162–164.
[19] ibid., para. 216.
[20] ibid., paras. 213–217. See Police (Scotland) Act 1967, s.2.
[21] ibid., paras. 237–252.
[22] ibid., paras 159 and 230.
[23] Local Government (Scotland) Act 1973.

regional boundaries, produced an unusually uneven pattern of forces. On the one hand, Strathclyde serviced almost half the population of Scotland. On the other, the remaining seven forces included many of the smallest in the U.K. The need for a reasonably uniform and a reasonably local framework of police accountability appeared to play second fiddle to the political imperatives of local government reform.

Of course, although the resulting structure was less lopsided, in England and Wales, too, there has been a progressive delocalization of the police and, more pronouncedly than in Scotland, a loss of direct accountability through the introduction of joint boards. As we saw earlier,[24] however, in the wake of serious inner city disorders in 1984, some effort was made to refill the local accountability gap through the introduction of a statutory requirement for local consultative committees to complement the work of the police authorities. Despite representations from many interest groups, particularly ethnic minority groups,[25] the Scottish Office decided that the state of police/public relations did not demand a like response in Scotland. A similarly conservative approach is evident in the repeated refusal of the Scottish Office to follow the English lead in introducing an independent element of accountability within the police complaints system.[26]

Two possible explanations offer themselves for the lowly position of Scottish police governance on the reform agenda, one cultural[27] and the other structural. In chapter three we drew upon the well-documented argument that in the last 30 years the social legitimacy of the British police has declined.[28] The police are no longer such credible occupants of the "sacred" zone at the "awe-inspiring center"[29] of our social order as they were in the early post-war years when they were more generally and more readily viewed as disciplined bureaucratic professionals; faithful to the rule of law and operationally impartial; committed to preventive policing and the minimal application of force; wedded to a service ethos; properly accountable; and effective in preventing and clearing up crime.

---

[24] See chapter three, section 3 above.

[25] The author was given access to the responses to the consultation procedure initiated by the Scottish Office in 1983 when deliberating whether to introduce statutory consultative committees on the English model.

[26] See Uildriks and Mastrigt, (1991) pp. 40–42; Walker (2000c); see further section 3 below.

[27] For fuller discussion, see Walker (1999b) pp. 100–104.

[28] See e.g., Reiner (1992a); (1992b); (1994); (1995).

[29] Shils (1982) p. 131.

The Scottish police have been by no means immune from the general decline in police legitimacy. They, too, have been implicated in the more explicit politicization of the debate over police powers, most notably in the vigorous campaign to introduce a legal status of pre-arrest detention under the Criminal Justice (Scotland) Act 1980.[30] The miners strike of 1984–85, included the Scottish coalfields and involved the police in a number of public order flashpoints. The decline of local beat policing and the marginalisation of the broader service role has been just as pronounced in Scotland as elsewhere.[31] So, too, until the mid 1980s, was the increase in crime levels and the decrease in clear-up rates;[32] and this decline together with the imposition of new financial disciplines on the public sector generally has led, as in England and Wales, to a rationalisation and reduction of the public police role in crime-fighting and increasing scope for private or collaborative initiatives[33]—developments which further challenge the claim of the police to be the central agency in crime control.[34]

On the other hand, the decline in the legitimacy of Scottish policing may be less pronounced, more nuanced, and more easily reversible than in England and Wales. Many of the specific causes of decline are less emphatic in the Scottish setting. The major corruption scandals of the past thirty years have been concentrated south of the border, and in the Metropolitan Police in particular. The main incidents of police subversion of the rule of law in pursuit of convictions in Irish terrorist cases and other major crimes have occurred in England.[35] The periodic urban disorders since the summer of 1981, while not excluding Scotland, have mainly focused upon English cities and towns, and have often been sparked by confrontation between the police and young Afro-Caribbean or Asian populations. The politicization of policing has been less overt

---

[30] See Baldwin and Kinsey (1982) chap. 6.

[31] *ibid.*, chap. 2.

[32] See Chambers and Tombs (1983).

[33] See Fyfe and Bannister (1999).

[34] Evidence from crime surveys seems to bear out a general reduction in support for policing and declining levels of satisfaction with police presence in the neighbourhood, with the outcome of police-public encounters, and with the propensity of the police to disobey rules (Allen and Payne, 1991, chaps 2–3). These figures and trends are broadly comparable with similar data for England and Wales, as is the concentration of greatest dissatisfaction and of abrasive police contacts amongst the young (Anderson, Kinsey, Loader and Smith, 1994; Loader, 1996) and socially and economically vulnerable groups (Kinsey, 1992).

[35] Although the introduction of a Scottish Criminal Cases Review Commission in 1999, constructed along similar lines to the Criminal Cases Review Commission established in 1995 for England, Wales and Northern Ireland, reflects growing public concern in this area.

and less abrasive in Scotland. After the miners' strike, for example, a number of Scottish chief constables spoke openly of the need to restore good relations with the mining communities and to reaffirm their reputation for impartiality; and, tellingly, there have been no disputes between forces and local police authorities over police accountability of the intensity experienced in England. Furthermore recent crime surveys in Scotland suggest a growing divergence from England and Wales as regards levels of victimisation and the reporting of crime.[36] These findings imply that Scotland differs subtly from England on both sides of the police legitimacy equation. The underlying crime rate is lower, suggesting that a higher level of credibility continues to attach to the police claim to pre-eminence and reasonable effectiveness in crime control. Reporting levels are also healthier, which implies both a better informed and more responsive police, and a police which continues to inspire sufficient confidence amongst most sections of the population to provide the natural repository of crime complaints. Taken together, these factors suggest a different cultural climate within which political consideration is given to reform proposals—one which, depending upon perspective, has encouraged either a prudent conservatism or a complacent inattentiveness to the demands of police governance.

The other, perhaps more significant explanation for the low profile of police reform has to do with the peripheral nature of the Scottish political system. The marginal status of the Scottish Office within the Whitehall executive and the absence of an independent law-making process for Scotland meant that prior to devolution Scottish legislation had to fight an unequal battle for its place within the U.K. Government's legislative programme.[37] As a result Scottish legislation was often delayed, or included within a wider statute primarily concerned with England and Wales and not fully appreciative of the peculiarities of the Scottish position.[38]

The structural marginalization of police governance issues in Scotland was never more apparent than in the lead up to the Police and Magistrates' Courts Act 1994 which bequeathed the present system of police governance.[39] From the outset, the coverage extended to Scotland within

---

[36] See Anderson and Leitch (1994), MVA Consultancy (1997); Hale and Uglow (1999).
[37] See e.g., Finnie (1991).
[38] This was acknowledged in the latter days of the Conservative Government and some limited reforms were passed to improve the flow of Scottish legislation; see Her Majesty's Government (1993). For a critique of these measures, see Himsworth (1996b).
[39] See Walker (1995); Fortson and Walker (1995) pp. 55–56.

the crowded policy-making agenda of the early 1990s was marginal. Although the Sheehy Inquiry[40] extended to Scotland, the White Paper on *Police Reform*,[41] so central to the reform agenda south of the border,[42] did not. The first indication that some of its proposals would nonetheless extend to Scotland was provided shortly after its publication by the Secretary of State for Scotland in a brief statement to the House of Commons.[43] Unlike the White Paper, however, there was no attempt to justify particular proposals or to assemble a general philosophy underpinning the overall package.

If the Government's distracted attitude to Scotland until that point could be attributed largely to cultural factors—the absence of institutionalised conflict within the Scottish tripartitism encouraging a low-key approach to the preparation and presentation of reform, then it was destined for a rude awakening. Vehement opposition to the measure was voiced by two powerful Scottish interest groups—local authorities and the police themselves—who were concerned with its centralising potential. While this led to a measure of successful opposition to the Bill in Parliament,[44] it also underlined the difficulty in the contemporary constitutional framework of conducting a meaningful Scottish debate about a legislative project pitched mainly at an English and Welsh audience, even in the face of now palpable public concern north of the border. Exacerbating the lack of any initial attempt to justify the Scottish reform agenda, the major debates on the floor of each House were typically only residually concerned with the Scottish dimension. Just as predictably, the Standing Committee in the Commons, the forum best equipped to delve into detail, was weighted heavily towards English and Welsh business, numbering only four Scottish M.Ps amongst its twenty nine members and devoting only two of its seventeen sittings to the Scottish provisions. Further, little or no attempt was made to co-ordinate police reform with other policy initiatives in Scotland, most pertinently the wider reorganisation of Scottish local government under the Local Government etc. (Scotland) Act 1994. As we shall see, this systematic structural marginalisation was not without consequence for the measure that eventually emerged as law.

---

[40] Home Office (1993a).
[41] Home Office (1993b).
[42] See chapter four, section 1.
[43] HC Debs, 9 July 1993, cls. 306–307, *per* Ian Lang MP.
[44] In particular, the original clause 45, which would have empowered the Secretary of State for Scotland to require police forces, on the grounds of efficiency, to participate in a campaign or operation which others had already adopted, thereby apparently sanctioning direct operational control by central government, was eventually withdrawn at committee stage in the Lords.

(b) Scottish Tripartitism Amended[45]

Just as for England and Wales,[46] as it concerns Scotland the 1994 Act[47] applies a new "calculative and contractual" approach to the tripartite model. However, the piecemeal application of the White Paper north of the border means that the new approach is applied less comprehensively and less consistently.

There is considerable common ground in the measures expanding the authority of central government and of their appointees, the Inspectorate of Constabulary, over local forces and police authorities. As in England and Wales, central government, in the form of the Secretary of State for Scotland, is empowered to give directions to police authorities to remedy inefficient or ineffective policing where certified by the Inspectorate.[48] There are also common provisions, both general and specific, as to the power of the central purse north and south of the border. Generally, central government in Scotland can now impose a cash limit on the overall 51 per cent police grant payable to police authorities and decide how to allocate this between the eight forces.[49] Specifically, it is now able to make separate provision for expenditure to safeguard national security.[50] Another significant area of common expansion of central influence concerns amalgamation schemes. Where no satisfactory scheme has been submitted by the police authorities themselves,[51] central government can now impose such schemes in the interests of efficiency or effectiveness without resort to a local inquiry, although procedural requirements to give notice and consider objections remain.[52]

An associated tenet of the calculative and contractual approach is that the chief constable and his force, as operational experts, should be allowed greater day-to-day autonomy and control of the necessary resources to perform their functions. There are provisions for Scotland, paralleling those for England and Wales, removing the power of the

---

[45] For extended analysis, see Walker (1995); Fortson and Walker (1995) pp. 53–81.

[46] See chapter four, section 2.

[47] Part II of which amends the Police (Scotland) Act 1967, which, in the absence of a consolidating measure, remains the governing statute in Scotland.

[48] Police and Magistrates' Courts Act 1994, s54. inserting s.26A of the Police (Scotland) Act 1967.

[49] Police (Scotland) Act 1967, s.32.

[50] Police and Magistrates' Courts Act 1994, s.56, inserting s.32A of the Police (Scotland) Act 1967.

[51] Police (Scotland) Act 1967, s.19.

[52] Local Government etc. (Scotland) Act 1994, s.35, replacing s.20 of the Police (Scotland) Act 1967.

police authority and Secretary of State to decide upon the size[53] and rank profile[54] of the force, and also transferring the power to direct and control civilian employees from police authorities to chief constables.[55]

Also common to both jurisdictions are changes in conditions of service and organisational structure which emphasise the importance within the new model of control both *of* and *through* police management. The Sheehy based reforms introduce fixed term appointments of between four and seven years for chief constables and their assistants[56]—providing new leverage for central government and police authorities, both of whom were already involved in senior appointments, resignations and dismissals[57]—and reduce the number of ranks from nine to seven by abolishing deputy chief constables and chief superintendents.[58] The Scottish provisions, like those for England and Wales, seek more generally to narrow the gap between the employment conditions of police officers and those of other public and private sector employees. Officers may now be investigated and sanctioned in respect not only of their conduct, as under the previous system, but also their efficiency and general competence,[59] and may now appeal to a new independent police appeals tribunal, rather than, as before, to the Secretary of State.[60]

In other respects, however, the Scottish provisions depart significantly from the English and Welsh. Police authorities, substantially changed in composition in England and Wales to reduce local and enhance central influence, continue to be the local authorities themselves in Scotland. A second major centralising initiative absent from the Scottish provisions is the power of central government to establish national policing objectives and related performance targets. On the other hand, some measures enhancing the influence of the centre are peculiar to Scotland. The Secretary of State may prescribe matters to be included in the annual reports of chief constables,[61] a power which arguably detracts from the annual

---

[53] Police and Magistrates' Courts Act 1994 Act, s.47(1), replacing s.3 of the Police (Scotland) Act 1967.

[54] 1994 Act, s.47(2)(b), removing s.7(2) of the 1967 Act.

[55] 1994 Act, s.49, replacing s.9 of the 1967 Act.

[56] And, in time, perhaps also superintendents; 1994 Act, s.53(1)(b), inserting s.26(5A) of the 1967 Act.

[57] 1967 Act, ss.4,5 and 31.

[58] 1994 Act s.47(1), amending s.7(1) of the 1967 Act, and 1994 Act s.48, replacing ss.5 and 5A of the 1967 Act. In practice, however, several Scottish forces continue to use the term deputy chief constable.

[59] 1994 Act s.52(2), amending s.26(2) of the 1967 Act.

[60] 1994 Act, s.55, replacing s.30 of the 1967 Act.

[61] 1994 Act, s.51, amending s.15(1) of the 1967 Act.

report as a vehicle for the chief constable's own public reflections on the performance of his force. A new power is vested in the Inspectorate to direct a chief constable to reconsider complaints by members of the public against the police,[62] a form of review unnecessary in England and Wales due to the existence of an independent Police Complaints Authority. Two other provisions furnish central government in Scotland with powers they held already in England and Wales. The investigative authority of the Scottish Inspectorate is extended to cover all matters concerning or relating to the operation of a police force, or of police forces generally.[63] Also, the powers of the Secretary of State for Scotland to provide common services and to require local forces to use particular facilities and services are broadened and specified in greater detail.[64]

There is further divergence between the two jurisdictions in the functions added to or subtracted from police authorities. Unlike the English and Welsh authorities, the Scottish police authorities retain the power to provide resources such as vehicles, equipment, land and buildings.[65] However, the difference may be more formal than real, since Scottish authorities are newly empowered to delegate managerial responsibility for their functions to the chief constable.[66] Conversely, the English and Welsh police authorities possess two functions for which there is no Scottish equivalent. Where English law extends the general responsibility of the police authority to secure the maintenance of an efficient force to include effectiveness, the Scottish legislation remains entirely silent on this matter. Secondly, and very significantly, the absence of a statutory planning framework, so prominent in the English legislation, extends in Scotland to police authorities as well as central government. There is no trace of the English provision for the collaborative production with the chief constable of local policing objectives or a local policing plan.

(C) CENTRALISING DRIFT

Despite the absence of two of the major centralising planks of the new English and Welsh system—central influence over the composition of police authorities and the introduction of a national planning framework,

---

[62] 1994 Act s.61, inserting s.40A of the 1967 Act.
[63] 1994 Act s.57(3), replacing s.33(3) of the 1967 Act.
[64] 1994 Act s.59, replacing s.36 of the 1967 Act.
[65] 1967 Act, s.2.
[66] 1994 Act, s.64, inserting s.2A–B of the Local Government (Scotland) Act 1973. This provision has indeed led to a measure of delegated budgeting. See Scottish Office (1995).

it is arguable that the unsystematic nature of the Scottish reforms encourages a centralising trend which is just as marked, and within a less transparent and defensible overall framework. In the first place, as the Secretary of State acknowledged when giving notice of the Scottish provisions to the House of Commons, a planning framework may not be explicitly provided for, but the measures allowing central direction of police authorities to ensure efficiency and effectiveness and imposing new reporting obligations on chief constables presuppose—and so encourage—the development of just such a central steering mechanism. With its ballast of wide ranging legal powers and well developed administrative controls, the Scottish Inspectorate has not been deterred by a lack of explicit legislative authority from developing—in conjunction with the Accounts Commission[67] and the Association of Chief Police Officers for Scotland—a detailed and influential performance management framework.[68] On the contrary, the absence of an explicit planning framework makes the policy process less visible and leaves the Inspectorate—and its central government employers—unencumbered by formal procedural rules, so allowing central policy formation and monitoring to take place in a less accountable and more flexible manner.

In the second place, as already intimated, the unheralded and haphazard introduction of the Scottish measures suggested little co-ordination with other reform measures, and allowed little scrutiny of these wider ramifications. The simultaneous reintroduction of unitary local authorities in 1995 prompted a further attenuation of the link between force and community, already stretched by the local government reforms of 1975. The regions were now abandoned but the eight regional forces were maintained; in consequence, the preservation of democratic accountability to the 32 new unitary authorities required the creation of joint boards for all but two of the forces[69]—a consideration which particularly affects the Strathclyde force, now extending over twelve separate local authority areas. If we remind ourselves of the evidence that joint boards tend to be

---

[67] The Accounts Commission, which has functions similar to the Audit Commission in England and Wales, was created by the Local Government (Scotland) Act 1973. It was given extended powers to ensure economy, efficiency and effectiveness in the use of local authority resources, including police resources, under the Local Government Act 1988; see 1973 Act , s.97A; see also Local Government etc. (Scotland) Act 1994, inserting s.122A of the 1973 Act. As well as the development of performance indicators, the Accounts Commission has also carried out a number of studies of particular areas of police practice under its general terms of reference. See generally, Himsworth (1995) chap. 7.

[68] See, e.g., Her Majesty's Chief Inspector of Constabulary for Scotland (1999), chap. 2.

[69] Local Government etc. (Scotland) Act 1994, s.34.

more fragmentary and less vigilant supervisors of policing than unitary authorities,[70] there would appear to be a danger that just when they face their strongest challenge from encroaching central influence, Scottish police authorities will lack the cohesion necessary to rise to the defence of their position as major players in the tripartite system.

A third and final connection between policy drift and centralising drift relates to the effect of the legislation upon the internal coherence of the tripartite system. As we discussed in chapter four, while considerable reservations have been expressed at the centralising trend of the new provisions in England and Wales, they do at least address some of the complaints of functional mismatch levelled at the Royal Commission settlement. Operational support functions are transferred to the chief constable, while the police authority assumes a modest policy role. In Scotland, by comparison, the incoherent entanglement of functions largely remains. The chief constable is granted operational support powers over manpower, but not—in formal legal terms at least—over resources. Conversely, the police authority is deprived of most of its operational support powers, but, despite remaining partial paymaster, is also still denied an explicit role in policy formation. So, to, are more local communities, which continue to lack the formal consultative standing of their southern counterparts. The local government element is thus restricted to an even narrower base from which to exercise influence, which threatens to emphasise its negative role at the expense of the positive contribution it could otherwise make to the new system of policy planning and monitoring. Only central government has a role which clearly suits its institutional capabilities, although even here, as we have seen, much is left unstated.

The net result of this undesigned and hastily compromised package has been a drift towards "a kind of constitutional no man's land.".[71] It is a destination which, arguably, none of the parties to the tripartite relationship in Scotland finds particularly satisfactory,[72] but one which, in the absence of more precisely demarcated and appropriately allocated functions, favours by default the brute political and economic power of central government.

---

[70] See *e.g.*, Loveday (1991); see also chapter four.

[71] Walker (1995) p. 204.

[72] For instance, the continuing tension and confusion of functions may have contributed to the controversy surrounding the resignation of Dr Ian Oliver, chief constable of Grampian Police, in April 1998. The police authority and the Secretary of State appeared dissatisfied, *inter alia*, with the force's efficiency in responding to the murder of a child in the summer of 1997, and with the chief constable's continuing insistence that his personal

3. Refocusing the Constitutional Debate

Ironically, then, the contemporary institutional distinctiveness of Scottish policing and its governance is in some measure a function of its secondary status and marginal treatment within the British political system; that is to say, it is a distinctiveness borne of dependence and neglect rather than independence and close attention. Since the election of New Labour, however, the constitutional context has altered radically. Following the emphatic endorsement of devolution proposals[73] by referendum, the Scotland Act 1998 was passed. As of May 1999, it delivered a new Scottish Parliament with law-making powers and a Scottish Executive and First Minister drawn from and responsible to that Parliament.[74] Under its abortive predecessor scheme of 1978, in a revealing statement of the constitutional *zeitgeist*, responsibility for law enforcement would have remained at Westminster on the basis that "key law and order functions are basic to sovereignty".[75] In contrast, the 1998 Act transfers the majority of policing functions to the new Edinburgh Parliament and Executive, the main exceptions being immigration control, national security and emergency powers.[76] This fundamental constitutional development raises two important and connected questions about the future of police governance in Scotland. First, should we expect devolution to correct the peripheral constitutional vision documented above and to refocus the debate over Scottish police governance? Secondly, should we expect an end to the centralising drift and the blurring of accountability lines which has accompanied this lack of focus?

Some of the early signs suggested that the policing debate would remain at the margins. The Scottish Office made an anticipatory move

---

conduct and force procedure and practice during and after the investigation of the murder had been professionally adequate. In turn, the chief constable was critical of the police authority and the Scottish Office ministers on account of their public denunciation of his conduct and that of his force, and on account of their aggressive, and, in his view, incorrect exploitation of the procedures under the 1967 Act concerning the resignation or dismissal of the chief constable (see White, 1998). On the one hand, one might sympathise with the frustrations of the police authority and the Scottish Office in the absence of a clear mandate to influence the review of law enforcement policy within the local force. On the other hand, one might sympathise with the chief constable that these frustrations were vented through a personal attack on his position.

[73] Her Majesty's Government (1997).

[74] See *e.g.*, Walker (1998a); Himsworth and Munro (1999).

[75] 59 HC Debs. Vol. 903, col. 737, January 15, 1976, *per* Ronald King Murray (then Lord Advocate).

[76] Scotland Act 1998, Sched.2, Part II, Head B, paras B6, B8 and B11.

166

to establish a review of the organisation of Scottish policing in 1998, with particular reference to the adequacy of the lop-sided eight force structure.[77] From the outset, however, the planned review met with substantial criticism from police and local authorities alike.[78] It was perceived to be driven by narrow financial considerations, rather than by a broader concern for the quality and effectiveness of governance arrangements. Procedurally, too, it was taken to task for its narrowness of approach. Its critics were concerned, *inter alia*, that its timetable was too cramped, that, unlike the contemporaneous Patten Inquiry in Northern Ireland[79] it lacked independent standing, and that it sought to pre-empt the authority of the new Parliament to decide for itself the question of review and its parameters. As it eventually proceeded, the review did take account of some of these concerns.[80] It broadened its remit, with less emphasis on financial considerations, and was co-ordinated through a steering group including police and local authority representatives. Nevertheless, the whole exercise provided an indication that the culture of pragmatism and minimalism which had been encouraged by the constitutional marginalisation of the Scottish political system would not easily change, even in the face of radical constitutional reform.

Other indications, too, suggest the persistence of a minimalist approach to the governance framework. Although in practice a centrally-driven planning framework continues to thrive and to accommodate important policy developments such as the Action Plan for Scotland which followed the Sir William Macpherson's Stephen Lawrence Inquiry,[81] there has been no sign that the absence of formal legislative acknowledgement of the planning regime under the Scottish provisions of the 1994 Act will be rectified. The minimalist Scottish approach has also been conspicuous with regard to more recent legislative initiatives. For example, while both Best Value and community safety partnership

---

[77] Speech by Donald Dewar to Scottish Police Federation, 22nd April 1998.

[78] See Association of Chief Police Officers in Scotland (1998)

[79] Patten Commission (1999); see further chapter six.

[80] Her Majesty's Chief Inspector of Constabulary for Scotland (1999) Introductory Remarks; Scottish Executive (2000).

[81] Scottish Executive (1999). For example, while the absence of a statutory framework meant that the Scottish Executive, unlike the Home Secretary in England and Wales, could not formally adopt Recommendation One of the Macpherson Report and establish as a ministerial priority that all police services should increase trust and confidence in policing amongst minority ethnic communities, the Executive determined that they would instead "let Chief Constables know that they supported the basic principle" and would direct the Inspectorate to measure force compliance with the priority at future inspections.

initiatives have been taken in Scotland,[82] they have lacked the statutory backing found in England and Wales.[83]

If these various developments serve to reinforce the power and limited accountability of the centre, as the new devolved institutions bed down the first buds of a more focused and transparent approach may be emerging. Criminal justice, by any reckoning, is one of the most politically significant of the devolved functions, and one of the few where policy options are not heavily circumscribed by the existence of an overriding competence at the European Union level.[84] It provides, therefore, an obvious and attractive area for policy development for the Scottish Executive. Under the new arrangements, the Ministry of Justice is now responsible for the majority of devolved criminal justice functions including policing, taking the place of the Secretary of State and the Scottish Office as the central player in the tripartite system. In its new role, it has already taken a number of steps to develop the regulatory framework of policing. These include the introduction of legislation to supervise intrusive surveillance by the police[85] and—prompted by the Macpherson Report,[86] reconsideration of the possibility of an independent police complaints system for Scotland.[87]

Yet we cannot assume that the more focused approach to police governance which is gradually taking shape will necessarily lead to a system which is more accountable and transparent and less subject to central executive discretion. Even as it creates new regulatory systems for particular aspects of policing, the Scottish government may also, through the attitude it strikes towards the general tripartite governance framework and its reform, use its new constitutional authority to retain or enhance its overall position of dominant influence. In this regard, the early indications are mixed. The review of police organisation discussed above appeared to rule out the possibility of a single national force in advance,

---

[82] Her Majesty's Chief Inspector of Constabulary for Scotland (1999) chap. 2 paras. 5 and 17.

[83] Local Government Act 1999 Part I; Crime and Disorder Act 1998, ss.5–6.

[84] See chapter eight.

[85] Regulation of Investigatory Powers (Scotland) Bill 2000.

[86] Macpherson (1999) Recommendation 58; Scottish Executive (1999) para.58

[87] Scottish Executive Press Release, 19 August 1999. The Minister for Justice, Jim Wallace, chairs a Steering Group to oversee the implementation of the Action Plan for Scotland, and this Group will consider the case for an independent system. The Minister for Justice later instructed a thematic review by the Inspectorate of the investigation of police complaints in Scotland; see Her Majesty's Inspectorate of Constabulary for Scotland (2000). Despite the lukewarm reception of the Inspectorate to the idea of independent investigation (Walker 2000c), legislation along these lines remains a likely prospect.

although it was prepared to consider various formulae for reducing the number of forces. On reflection, however, the steering group recommended in its Interim Report of May 2000 that the current eight-force structure be retained.[87a]

A more telling institutional trend has been the development of multi-tier policing. Alongside the territorial forces, themselves increasingly committed to devolved budgeting and command, there is an expanding range of organisations involved in the policing of Scotland at Scottish, United Kingdom and even European level. The European level we discuss in a later chapter.[88] The British level includes the National Criminal Intelligence Service (NCIS), the Police Act 1997 endorsing an earlier decision in favour of Scottish participation.[89] We should also note the Scottish interest in other United Kingdom wide organisations with an expanding policing role, particularly the Security Service[90] and HM Customs and Excise. At the Scottish level, alongside expanding training and technological facilities, we find the Scottish Crime Squad,[91] the Scottish equivalent of the old regional crime squads in England and Wales. The Scottish profile of this institution was heightened by the decision not to include it alongside the regional crime squads within the new National Crime Squad, established as a sister organisation to NCIS under the 1997 Act.[92] Significantly, the new Scottish Executive has encouraged the multi-tier approach, quickly adding to the Scottish organisational level by establishing a Scottish Drug Enforcement Agency, its remit including intelligence-gathering and operational responsibilities for drug-related and other organised crime and the co-ordination of police involvement in wider drugs policies.[93]

The implications for police governance of the multi-tiered approach as it is developing in Scotland remains unclear. On the one hand, a multi-tiered complex compounds the problems of transparency, co-ordination and accountability associated with the governance of any modern policing system. From a pessimistic viewpoint, the establishment of a new constitutional level of government in Scotland threatens to

---

[87a] Although it also recommended that priority be given to developing more common police services and collaboration between forces; Scottish Executive (2000), esp. paras 34–37.

[88] See chapter eight.

[89] See chapter seven.

[90] *ibid.*

[91] Maintained under a collaboration agreement by virtue of s.12 of the 1967 Act.

[92] See chapter seven.

[93] Scottish Executive Press release, 14 December 1999. The new agency became operational in June 2000.

exacerbate matters. It encourages the development of the sub-state Scottish level itself as a key organisational site alongside the supranational, state and local levels, the additional tier making Scotland's arrangements more intricate than that for many other multi-layered polities. At the same time—to return to the debilitating constitutional legacy—the historical absence of a mature and effective Scottish policy-making framework has obstructed efforts to establish coherence between the tiers, or even to establish accountability for ensuring coherence. For example, the decision in 1996 to locate the United Kingdom based Scottish NCIS and Customs and Excise alongside the Scottish-based, but functionally connected Scottish Crime Squad in the same purpose-built accommodation near Glasgow raised—but failed to answer—acute questions about their interrelationship, and the adequacy of the accountability mechanisms for tracing this.

On the other hand, the new constitutional settlement also offers a clear opportunity for improving accountability over the multi-tier complex which it has helped to encourage. Under a voting system sufficiently proportional to produce a coalition government at the first election[94] and to make majority Government unlikely in the foreseeable future, the new Scottish Parliament is in a more powerful position than its Westminster equivalent to act as a counterweight to the Executive. Also, as for the Executive itself, so also for the Parliament, criminal justice and policing offer an important and, in jurisdictional terms, relatively unencumbered area of policy development and oversight. If the long centralising drift of Scottish policing is to be effectively checked and if its governance arrangements are to be made properly accountable and coherent with other institutional levels, much, then, depends upon how well the new Parliament takes its opportunity to assert a measure of independent constitutional authority.[95]

---

[94] A Labour/Liberal Democrat Coalition, elected in May 1999.

[95] The Scottish Parliament has established a Justice and Home Affairs Committee to shadow the work of the Ministry of Justice. The Parliament's committees have potentially greater influence than their Westminster counterparts, with authority not merely to scrutinise and investigate the work of the Executive but also to participate in the preparation of legislation. The higher profile for the Scottish Parliament and its committees reflect not just the relative weakness of minority governments but also the determination of those involved in the campaign for a Scottish Parliament, particularly the Scottish Constitutional Convention, that the imbalance of power between legislature and executive typical of parliamentary systems of Government be redressed; see *e.g.*, Scottish Constitutional Convention (1995).

Chapter Six

Variations in Tripartitism: The Case of Northern Ireland

In the opening chapter we introduced two constitutional paradoxes of policing—the paradox of the police function and the paradox of police governance. These paradoxes tax all attempts to devise fair, effective and consensual constitutional frameworks for policing in the United Kingdom, or indeed any other polity. However, their relevance is most immediate, the difficulties they raise most pressing and least tractable, in the context of Northern Ireland. Since the partition of Ireland in 1920, Northern Ireland has been a divided society[1]—a contested "statelet". The cleavage between unionists—who want partition to continue and for Northern Ireland to remain part of the British state—and nationalists—who want the North to be constitutionally united with the Irish state, affects every sphere of public life and civil society. The police inevitably provide a focal point for the struggle—often violent—between the two communities and their conflicting aspirations. As the guardians of specific order, the police have since Northern Ireland's difficult birth been deeply implicated in the fundamental contest over political identity. They have been custodians of the constitutional *status quo* and have been perceived as such by both communities. Relatedly, they have also been viewed as partisan in their pursuit of general order, as favouring the day-to-day security interests of the (mainly Protestant) unionist community over those of the (mainly Catholic) nationalist community. The nationalist community, it follows, has traditionally suffered the negative consequences of the paradox of the police function. The police have been perceived by the nationalist community less as a guardian of their security interests and more as a threat to these interests, and as a potent

---

[1] See *e.g.* Hillyard (1997).

symbol and resolute defender of a political order implacably opposed to their effective representation. And in that implacable opposition also lies the paradox of police governance. The British state, authorised to regulate policing in Northern Ireland, has, from the perspective of the nationalist community, been the source of the problem, the jealous guardian of its own security interests and so constitutionally incapable of providing a regulatory solution that respects nationalist interests and aspirations.

Below, we sketch the general contours of the historical policing settlement in Northern Ireland, tracing how the tripartite model came to be adapted by the British state to the special circumstances of Northern Ireland. We also discuss the profoundly significant constitutional developments presently taking place and the centrality of policing reform to these developments. The current peace process offers the best chance yet to resolve the fundamental contest of political identity, and, as we shall see, the debate over the constitutional refashioning of the police is an integral part of that process.

1. Policing a Contested Polity

(A) THE LEGACY OF PARTITION

Northern nationalists have never been policed by services they consider to be impartial and legitimate.[2] The New Police took formal shape in Ireland before it did so in any other part of the British Isles.[3] The Union settlement of 1800, when Ireland became formally part of the United Kingdom, merely consolidated a long historical process of the imposition of political control by England, the coercive cornerstones of which were police and military power. From 1836 onwards, policing was organised through the Royal Irish Constabulary, a centralised, politically-directed entity organised along the same lines as many British colonial forces.

In many respects, the Royal Ulster Constabulary (RUC), established in 1922,[4] adopted the same model within the more limited jurisdiction of the partitioned North, now with its own devolved legislature and

---

[2] McGarry and O'Leary (1999) p. 41.
[3] Provision was made for a professional police force for Dublin in 1786, and for the Irish counties a year later.
[4] The Constabulary Act (Northern Ireland) 1922.

executive. From the outset, the RUC was concerned with twin threats to the specific order of the North—internally from its large nationalist minority and externally from the hostile Irish state to the south. It was effectively a national force. The RUC's chief officer—accorded the military title of Inspector-General—was directly answerable to the Minister of Home Affairs within the unionist-controlled parliamentary executive at Stormont Castle, Belfast, to which the British government had delegated jurisdiction over internal security.[5] The financing of the force and, at the outset, the appointment and dismissal of all personnel, was also under Stormont control. The sense of the police as a force of occupation was underlined by the fact that initially there were more than four times as many police officers *per capita* in Northern Ireland as there were in England or Scotland.[6] The bottle-green uniforms, the wearing of weapons and the designation of police stations as "barracks" added to the quasi-military flavour,[7] as did the acquisition of draconian powers to intern without trial, to arrest without warrant and to issue curfews.[8] In other respects, however, the RUC resembled the forces of the British mainland. Like them, it consisted of a body of constables, each enjoying all the common law powers and privileges and subject to all the common law duties associated with the office, and under the general direction and control of a chief officer.

The outbreak of a new wave of violence in the late 1960s reinforced the image of the RUC as a partisan force, but also triggered reforms which sought to introduce more elements of the regular British policing template. The personnel of the RUC had always been predominantly Protestant, and Catholic membership dwindled over the years.[9] In addition, the RUC was backed by the Ulster Special Constabulary (USC), an exclusively Protestant force of full-time and part-time officers,[10] deployed to assist in the repression of IRA action. During periods of relative calm, when the counterinsurgency role of the police was marginalised, relations between the RUC and the nationalist community could be relatively civil. However the combined and cumulative effect of partisan central control, protestant rank and file and emergency powers ensured

---

[5] Government of Ireland Act 1920, s4(1) gave the Stormont Parliament a general power to make laws "for the peace, order and good government of Northern Ireland".

[6] Weitzer (1995) p. 34.

[7] Walsh (1998) p. 3.

[8] See the Civil Authorities (Special Powers) Act 1922 and its successors.

[9] Catholic representation peaked at 21 per cent in 1923, fell to 10 per cent by the outbreak of the troubles in 1969, and then to a low of 6 per cent in the 1980s.

[10] Known respectively as the A Specials and the B Specials.

a strong undercurrent of antagonism and an abiding perception within the nationalist community that the partiality of the RUC was not confined to the "high politics"[11] of state security but extended across the entire spectrum of policing.[12] Police bias against a nationalist community that was not only denied its preferred political identity but also found itself systematically discriminated against socially, economically and in the internal representative politics of the North,[13] was undoubtedly a significant catalyst for the heightened conflict of the last 30 years. Clashes between the police and civil rights marchers led to the introduction of British troops into the province in 1969, a move intended both to control mounting nationalist protests and—tellingly of the reputation of the RUC—to provide a more impartial security presence in nationalist areas.

In parallel with military intervention, a series of political reforms took place, culminating in the suspension of the devolved system of government at Stormont in 1972. Policing was high on the reform agenda. A number of official inquiries criticised the police role in the Troubles,[14] and following the report of a committee chaired by Lord Hunt,[15] the Police Act (Northern Ireland) 1970 was passed. Its central initiative was the introduction of a version of tripartitism. A police authority was established, breaking the direct link between the police chief - now to be renamed the chief constable—and the Minister of Home Affairs (or, after Stormont was prorogued, the Secretary of State for Northern Ireland). The Police Authority for Northern Ireland (PANI) had substantially the same powers and responsibilities as its mainland counterparts. Unlike them, however, and against the advice of Hunt, it contained no elected element, since, according to the British Government, an elected body would simply have mirrored the existing communal divide. Instead, PANI would be appointed by central government, with the proviso that it should be "representative" of the population as a whole, including district councils and other public bodies, the legal profession, trade unions, agriculture, industry and commerce, and voluntary organisations concerned with the welfare of young persons.[16] Over the

---

[11] Brodeur (1983).

[12] For example, a National Council for Civil Liberties Inquiry in 1936 found that the RUC failed to act impartially, showing favouritism towards Orange mobs and tolerating attacks on Catholics. See McGarry and O'Leary (1999) p. 29.

[13] See McCrudden (1990) pp. 330–337.

[14] Most notably, the Reports of the Cameron Commission (1969) and the Scarman Inquiry (1972).

[15] Hunt (1969).

[16] Police Act (Northern Ireland) 1970, s.1.

same period, a number of other reforms were introduced with a view to stressing the civil rather than the paramilitary dimension of policing the North. The routine arming of the police was ended—if only briefly, and the special powers legislation was repealed in 1973. The USC was disbanded, to be replaced by two supposedly less sectarian corps—a new RUC reserve force and a locally-recruited Ulster Defence Regiment under the general authority of the British Army in Northern Ireland. A Community Relations Branch was also introduced and a more liberal training ethos fostered.[17]

Undoubtedly, these reforms had some positive impact upon the quality and impartiality of policing in Northern Ireland. The termination of direct rule and the introduction of PANI ended the Ulster Unionist party's direct control over security policy. Senior police officers became more conscious of the need for neutrality between the contending communities, and the RUC became demonstrably more even-handed in its policing of public disorder and in its actions against paramilitary groups—so much so that it increasingly attracted the animosity of activist Unionist Groups, most prominently the Orange Order.[18]

However, the underlying structure of domination and inequality and the associated culture of mistrust within the nationalist community remained. Without a political solution which took nationalist political aspirations seriously the structural position of the RUC as the defenders of the specific order of the statelet remained unaltered. The absence of a political solution also generated unprecedented civil and political violence from the early 1970s onwards, with RUC members deemed legitimate targets within the Republican movement, which also began to build upon an earlier tradition of community self-policing and to claim the mantle of legitimate policing authority in nationalist areas.[19] In the deteriorating security environment, the flashpoints between police and nationalist community in violent and public-disorder situations were many. The police were re-armed, their stations re-militarised, and their numbers grew exponentially. They acquired a fresh catalogue of emergency powers, and the new reserve forces proved just as unpopular as their predecessors.[20] Further, as both the internal and the international

---

[17] McGarry and O'Leary (1999) p. 33.

[18] *ibid*. pp. 33–34.

[19] See *e.g.* Connolly (1997) chap. 4.

[20] The new RUC Reserve Force was retained, but the Ulster Defence Regiment was eventually absorbed into the Royal Irish Rangers, which in due course became the Royal Irish Regiment

acceptability of the army presence quickly foundered, from 1976 onwards a policy of "police primacy" was pursued.[21] This placed the police rather than the army in the front-line of combating the Republican challenge, and while this approach was one of supposed "normalisation" of crime and security policy in the province, it inevitably cut against the parallel attempt to cultivate a practice and image of professional neutrality. The various controversies and scandals that the RUC became embroiled in from the early 1980s onwards, ranging from its "supergrass" strategy to its alleged "shoot to kill" policy, can be seen as inextricably linked to the decision to present them as the "ordinary", but senior, custodians of a quite extraordinary security regime.

The marginal role of PANI since its introduction of 1970 can be seen as eloquent testimony to the impossibility of devising acceptable governance arrangements for policing a violently divided society. If the use of appointment rather than election signalled the ambivalence of the Government towards the idea of popular accountability, the independence of PANI was further compromised by the broader institutional architecture. As the Patten Commission put it, this involved a set of "one-to-one relationships: one police force, one police authority and one Secretary of State".[22] There was no local dimension, nothing to divide the attention of successive Secretaries of State. This maximised their influence over both the force and the appointed PANI, and made it possible to by-pass PANI with impunity in matters of security-related policing, The one-to-one relationship also accentuated the association between PANI and the constabulary itself. Like its mainland counterparts, PANI had various administrative support functions to perform for the force, and the fact that these were provided not on a local basis but for the whole of the contested polity tended to reinforce the perception of the two bodies as "executive collaborators".[23]

The structural weakness of PANI's position was reinforced by the attitudes and approaches of various key players in the North's policing politics. PANI acquired a reputation for a low public profile and for deference towards the professional police perspective. It did not meet publicly, and until recently even the names of its members were not publicly known.[24] This was largely on account of the fear of paramili-

---

[21] See *e.g.,* Oliver (1997) chapter 12, Ellison and Smyth (1996) pp. 175–176.

[22] Patten (1999) para.5.6.

[23] *ibid.*, para 5.13. Indeed, according to its own survey data, less than half (41 per cent) of all respondents were aware that the RUC and the Police Authority were independent organisations; Police Authority for Northern Ireland (1998) p.27.

[24] Even in 2000, the identity of some members remained secret.

tary violence, two of its members having been murdered and a third
forced to resign after being targeted by the IRA. Its deference was manifest in a failure to investigate some of the weightiest charges against the
RUC, including the deployment of supergrasses, illegal interrogation
methods and undercover units, and the use of plastic bullets. This
silence over particular blackspots was matched by an equally eloquent
articulation of general support for and loyalty to the RUC, leading
some commentators to claim that "[r]ather than representing the community to the police, it has appeared more interested in representing
the police to the community".[25] The long years of appointments by
predominantly Conservative Secretaries of State, the refusal of the
Northern Ireland Committee of the Irish Congress of Trade Unions
and the SDLP to participate, and the failure by the Secretary of State
to extend any like invitation to more militant nationalist opinion all
contributed to the pattern of deferential support, as did the perception
within PANI of the damaging effect upon the morale and legitimacy of
a force under constant threat of violence if they were to strike an
attitude of public criticism.

Latterly, PANI did take more active steps to find a distinctive public
voice, including a comprehensive survey of community views and a radical set of proposals for increasing its own powers.[26] Yet their reputation
proved very difficult to shed, not least because the police themselves did
not take PANI particularly serious as an accountee. On those occasions
where they were in disagreement with PANI, they would, like some of
their mainland counterparts,[27] be prepared to insist upon an expansive
definition of "operational independence" and a restrictive reading of
their reporting responsibilities in order to deflect criticism and suppress
inquiry.[28] More generally, there was little attempt by the police to grant
public recognition of PANI as a valued partner in governance.[29] In turn,
this reinforced the perception of the nationalist community that PANI

---

[25] McGarry and O'Leary (1999) p. 100.

[26] Police Authority for Northern Ireland (1998); see also Oliver (1997) chap. 13.

[27] See chapters two, three and four.

[28] See also Connolly, Law and Topping (1996). They point out that, as on the mainland,
the most significant strategic power of the police authority in the complex and ambiguous
legal edifice of tripartitism has been resource allocation, but that since PANI has no independent local source of funding and must make out a case to the Secretary of State and the
Northern Ireland Office, in practice the operation of this strategic power merely tempts
the Chief Constable to view the Police Authority as "at best, a cipher for the NIO, and at
worst, irrelevant"(p. 238).

[29] McGarry and O'Leary (1999) p. 102.

could not be taken seriously as an institution capable of holding the RUC to critical account.

A downward spiral of limited effectiveness and doubtful legitimacy has also affected the various Community-Police Liaison Committees set up since the 1980s[30] in the train of the Scarman-inspired initiative to introduce a new, local tier of accountability in England and Wales. One detailed study reveals how these groups have tended to mirror the very deficiencies in PANI for which they were established to compensate.[31] Their meetings have tended to take place in private and to avoid controversial issues. Their composition has been unrepresentative in terms of both class and political identity, and they have been boycotted both by the SDLP and by Sinn Fein.

(B) CURRENT ARRANGEMENTS

The last decade has witnessed a seismic shift in the politics of the North. The fundamental disagreement between unionists and nationalists has begun to be addressed within a political climate and constitutional machinery no longer predestined to produced zero-sum results. The Downing Street Declaration between Irish and British Governments in 1995 consolidated the paramilitary cease-fire of the previous year, and although this original peace did not hold the process of dialogue continued. This led, finally, to the Belfast Agreement,[32] concluded at Stormont on Good Friday 1998. The Good Friday Agreement is "compelling",[33] if complex constitutional architecture, of which more shortly.

First, though, we should note that as the political landscape gradually changed, policing underwent its own linked transformation. As in earlier phases, the trend was one of adapting developments in mainland policing to the quite different circumstances of a contested polity. The new managerialism which had so influenced British policing from the early 1980s onwards found a powerful echo across the Irish Sea. In part, this was merely a geographical extension of a philosophy of public administration developed by the Conservative Government and largely endorsed by its New Labour successor. A year after the publication of the water-

---

[30] In accordance with the legal requirement on the Police Authority to consult the community on policing matters under Art. 82 of the Police and Criminal Evidence (Northern Ireland) Order 1989. See now Police (Northern Ireland) Act, 1998, s.7.

[31] Weitzer (1995) pp. 229–243

[32] Her Majesty's Government (1998).

[33] McGarry and O'Leary (1999), p. 2.

shed White Paper *Police Reform*[34] in England and Wales in 1993, the Northern Ireland Office produced a consultation paper along similar lines,[35] followed by a more detailed White Paper in 1996[36] and an independent review of the procedures for dealing with citizens complaints against the RUC.[37] These formed the basis of New Labour's Police (Northern Ireland) Act 1998, which came into force on 1st April 1999 and which provides the current, if transitional, constitutional foundation for policing in the province.

This political initiative was supported and complemented by professional developments in the RUC. It, too, enthusiastically seized the managerialist baton as a "vision of normality"[38] for an improving security environment. The RUC emphasised the importance of "policing in partnership", stressed the need to focus on ordinary crime and road traffic, and anticipated the introduction of the new managerialist legislation by introducing its own public planning mechanism in March 1998.

Like the equivalent legislative initiatives on the mainland, the 1998 Act seeks to revise the tripartite framework so as to match the governance roles of the parties more closely to their authority and expertise, to increase transparency and to encourage more effective co-operation. There remain, however, a number of distinctive features within the Northern Ireland model.

The Secretary of State sets the overall objectives for the force after consultation with the other tripartite parties and other appropriate persons .[39] He or she has a general duty to exercise his or her powers in a manner calculated to promote the effectiveness and efficiency of the police[40] and more specific powers to require the dismissal of senior officers on the grounds of effectiveness or efficiency[41]; to issue codes of practice to PANI[42]; to require the use by police of specified facilities, equipment and services[43]; to appoints Inspectors of Constabulary[44]

---

[34] Home Office (1993b).

[35] Northern Ireland Office (1994)

[36] Northern Ireland Office (1996).

[37] Carried out by Dr Maurice Hayes, previously Northern Ireland Ombudsman and soon to be a member of the Patten Commission. See Hayes (1997).

[38] Mulcahy (1999) esp. pp. 288–291. See also Ellison and Smyth (1996) p. 185 *et seq.*

[39] Police (Northern Ireland) Act 1998, s.14.

[40] *ibid.*, s.36.

[41] *ibid.*, s.21(3)(b).

[42] *ibid.*, s.38.

[43] *ibid.*, s.40.

[44] *ibid.*, s.41.

and arrange for publication of their reports[45]; to establish a research facility[46]; to fund advisory and support organisations, facilities and services[47]; to establish inquiries; to require reports from PANI[48] and the chief constable[49]; and to make regulations for the administration[50] and discipline[51] of the force.

Alongside this familiar catalogue, the Secretary of State also has important legal resources not found in any of the other tripartite frameworks. Unlike them, the financing of the police and PANI is provided entirely through central grant, with no local element.[52] The Secretary of State also has two significant new sources of authority. He or she is obliged to issue a statement of the principles on which the policing of Northern Ireland is to be conducted[53]—one of which must be impartiality,[54] and this statement is to provide a common framework for all the tripartite parties.[55] The Secretary of State also acquires a catch-all power to issue general guidance to individual police officers concerning the exercise of their functions.[56]

PANI continues to be appointed by the Secretary of State, who must consult district councils and other appropriate bodies before doing so, and must publish the names of the bodies consulted.[57] PANI also has a general duty to secure the maintenance of the police force[58] and its effectiveness and efficiency,[59] and specific powers over the appointment and dismissal of senior officers[60]; the engagement of its own administrative

---

[45] Police (Northern Ireland Act) 1998 s.42.

[46] *ibid.*, s.45.

[47] *ibid.*, s.46.

[48] *ibid.*, s.47.

[49] *ibid.*, s.49.

[50] *ibid.*, s.25.

[51] *ibid.*, s.64.

[52] *ibid.*, s.9.

[53] *ibid.*, s.37(1).

[54] *ibid.*, s.37(2).

[55] *ibid.*, s.37(1).

[56] After consulting PANI, the chief constable and the Police Association; *ibid.*, s.39. The Police Association is the equivalent of the Police Federation, representing members of the RUC in matters affecting their welfare and efficiency; *ibid.*, s.32.

[57] *ibid.*, s.1 and Sched.1.

[58] *ibid.*, s.2(1).

[59] *ibid.*, s.2(3). The separation of "maintenance" from "effectiveness and efficiency"—combined as a single obligation under the equivalent English and Welsh legislation (Police Act, 1996, s.6(1))—appears to be for symbolic purposes. The difference in wording has no discernible practical effect, but it does emphasises the point, in deference to loyalist sensibilities, that the RUC in its current form should for the time being continue to be the only force maintained by PANI; see Walsh (1998) p. 8.

[60] *ibid.*, s.21.

staff[61]; the maintenance of accounts[62]; charging for special services[63]; the receipt of an annual general report and other policing report from the chief constable[64]; consultation of the public about policing[65] and encouragement of their co-operation with the police in preventing crime.[66] Within the strategic planning framework, PANI acquires the power, after consultation with the chief constable and local public groups, to determine annual objectives and performance targets, provided these are consistent with the overall objectives specified by the Secretary of State.[67] These various objectives and performance targets form part and parcel of the annual policing plan which is also the final responsibility of PANI,[68] although the power of initiative rests with the chief constable.[69]

As in the other modified tripartite arrangements, the chief constable of the RUC now acquires from PANI detailed management powers in respect of the provision and maintenance of buildings and equipment[70] and the employment and direction of civilian staff[71]—including, uniquely in the United Kingdom context, the power of direction and control of the police authority's own administrative staff.[72] The chief constable also continues to be responsible for the appointment and promotion of all officers below the senior ranks.[73] His or her general power of direction and control of the force[74] is qualified by his or her duty to "have regard to" not only the police authority's annual policing plan,[75] as in England and Wales,[76] but also the Secretary of State's statement of principles.[77]

---

[61] *ibid.*, s.3.

[62] *ibid.*, s.12.

[63] *ibid.*, s.11.

[64] *ibid.*, s.48.

[65] *ibid.*, s.7(1)(a).

[66] *ibid.*, s.7(1)(b).

[67] *ibid.*, s.15.

[68] *ibid.*, s.17(1).

[69] *ibid.*, s.17(3).

[70] These powers are deemed to be exercised by the chief constable on behalf of PANI; *ibid.*, s.5(2).

[71] Again, these powers are deemed to be exercised by the chief constable on behalf of PANI; *ibid.* s.3(5)(a).

[72] *ibid.*, s.3(5)(b). Note, however, that under s3(6), this does not extend to such members of PANI's own administrative staff as it shall determine with the approval of the Secretary of State.

[73] *ibid.*, s.22.

[74] *ibid.*, s.19(1).

[75] *ibid.*, s.19(2)(a)

[76] Police Act 1996 s.10(2).

[77] Police (Northern Ireland) Act 1998 s.37.

Two further new provisions, enacted in the cause of greater transparency, arguably contribute further to the qualification of chief constabulary independence, although other assessments are possible. In the first place, the 1998 Act, again for the first time in a U.K. police statute, provides a statutory definition of the general functions of the police, although these are couched in familiar, general and uncontroversial terms.[78] Secondly, and more significantly, the Act adds a further tier to the strategic planning structure patented in England and Wales. The chief constable is required, after consultation with the Secretary of State and PANI, to issue a strategic policing plan setting out the proposed arrangements for policing Northern Ireland for a period of between three and five years[79]—the same time-frame as for the Secretary of State's statement of overall objectives. On the one hand, this requires the chief constable to show his or her long-term strategic hand in a more publicly accountable fashion than in the past. On the other, however, the chief constable is under no statutory obligation to have regard to this strategic plan, and even in formulating it, he or she is not constrained by, but, instead, need only "give particulars of"[80] the broader catalogue of government and PANI objectives and performance targets. Moreover, the strategic plan can be viewed as an opportunity as much as a constraint, allowing the chief constable an influential voice at the formative stage of policy planning.

Even in its own terms, the Act promises to be at best a qualified success. The strategic role of PANI is only half-heartedly delivered, and is potentially significantly weakened by the introduction of the long-term strategic plan. Indeed, as one commentator has noted, a more appropriate functional division of labour would have reversed the new allocation, making the strategic plan the responsibility of PANI and the annual plan that of the chief constable.[81] Further, so intricate and cluttered is the new audit framework that it is likely to be self-defeating in terms of its avowed aim of transparency. Granted, these new arrangements might augment the culture of close co-operation between the tripartite parties, but in the contested polity of Northern Ireland and against a backdrop of deep-rooted nationalist fears of unionist hegemony, even that is a distinctly

---

[78] Namely: (1) to protect life and property; (2) to preserve order; (3) to prevent the commission of offences; (4) where an offence has been committed, to take measures to bring the offender to justice. Police (Northern Ireland) Act 1998, s.18.

[79] *ibid.*, s.16.

[80] *ibid.*, s.16(2).

[81] Walsh (1998) p. 22. The Patten Commission adopts a similar attitude; see section 2(B) below.

mixed blessing. In essence, the new legislation, in failing to address the method of composition of the police authority, does not tackle the underlying problem of ensuring democratic answerability to, and building trust within and between all communities of the divided society. In the circumstances, the smoother running of the tripartite machinery risks being dismissed by some sections of the community as at best an irrelevance, and at worst an indication of the unbroken and unmitigated partiality of policing and its governance.

2. Policing and the Peace Process

(A) THE BELFAST AGREEMENT

Possibly the most remarkable feature of the Police (Northern Ireland) Act 1998 is that it was passed at all. As its managerialist approach was being honed another, more radical and controversial debate on the prospects for a new and more broadly legitimate policing system for the North was gaining momentum.[82] Indeed, as the Belfast Agreement neared its tense conclusion, precisely because policing was such a hotly contested subject between the parties the decision was taken to postpone its consideration and to refer it instead to an Independent Commission chaired by the former British Conservative Cabinet Minister and Governor of Hong Kong, Chris Patten. Undaunted by these developments, however, the British Government persevered through the later parliamentary stages of the more narrowly conceived measure which was to become the 1998 Act. Even the Patten Commission confessed itself "mystified"[83] that this had been allowed to happen. But perhaps it is not such a great mystery. For the Government, as noted earlier, the 1998 Act put in place its preferred template of public administration, one on which arguably quite different democratic and constitutional visions of policing could be constructed. Also, for the more conservatively-minded within the province, including influential opinion associated with the RUC itself,[84] the busy managerialist agenda of the 1998 Act supplied a pre-emptive argument against the more radical measures they feared

---

[82] Some of the possible models for reform are laid out in a New Labour discussion paper, see Northern Ireland Office (1998). For an overview of proposals from various points across the political spectrum, see Oliver (1997) chap. 13.

[83] Patten (1999) para.5.11.

[84] See Mulcahy (1999).

from the Patten Commission. As we shall see, the Government's approach appears to have had at least some success, the Patten Report duly accepting many of the 1998 provisions as building-blocks for its own recommendations.

Let us now attempt to locate the Patten Commission in the broader context of the Belfast Agreement, much of which is now reduced to legislative form in the Northern Ireland Act 1998. A number of more detailed analyses of the agreement are available,[85] but its basic structure consists of three Strands and an array of interlocking institutional machinery and underlying principles and commitments. Strand One is concerned with the internal politics of the North, instituting a proportionally elected Parliament with parallel consent voting procedures and a power-sharing executive headed by a First Minister and a Deputy First Minister who are themselves elected by parallel consent and who must operate in tandem. Strand Two links the North to the South, through the North-South Ministerial Council, a policy-making and consultative forum shadowing the competences devolved to the new Northern Ireland Parliament. Strand Three links the British and Irish governments through the British-Irish Intergovernmental Conference and also joins these two sovereign governments, the devolved governments of Northern Ireland, Scotland and Wales and the Crown dependencies of the Channel Island and the Isle of Man in a joint ministerial forum known as the British-Irish Council. The underlying principles endorsed by both governments in the Agreement include a commitment to national self-determination on the basis of the consent of the two parts of Ireland, the introduction of strong institutional mechanisms for the protection of human rights and the eradication of discrimination, and recognition of the right to choose the citizenship(s) of one's choice. And alongside police reform, there is a parallel commitment to reform of the wider criminal justice system in Northern Ireland.[86]

Underscoring the entire edifice and linking each of its elements, the Agreement seeks to extend equal respect to the two communities of the North. It combines both internal and external projects for accommodating the diverse traditions and divergent aspirations of unionists and

---

[85] See e.g. Hadfield (1998), O'Leary (1998), Brazier (1999), Munro (1999) chap. 2, Boyle and Hadden (1999).

[86] This was preceded by a review, which under the terms of the Belfast Agreement (para.9.5), was to be carried out by the British Government, albeit with an independent element, rather than by an entirely independent body as in the case of the Patten Commission. The review body's findings were published in March 2000; Criminal Justice Review Group (2000). See also Walker and Telford (2000).

nationalists. Internally, the main strategy for pursuing the ideal of equal respect has been described as one of "consociationalism"—an internal association of equal communities based upon executive power-sharing, minority veto rights, proportionality of representation in public life and community self-government.[87] Externally, the Agreement also contains, at least tentatively, elements of co-sovereignty—or condominium. Its elaborately ambitious institutional structure ensures that the government of the North can no longer be an exclusively British affair.

(b) The Patten Commission

Policing reform is mainly, though not exclusively,[88] located within the internal project of constitutional transformation. The Agreement talks of "a new beginning to policing in Northern Ireland", of a police that is "effective and efficient, fair and impartial, free from partisan political control; accountable, both under the law for its actions and to the community it serves; representative of the society it polices, . . . conforms with human rights norms . . . [and] . . . capable of maintaining law and order". The new structures and arrangements, the Agreement continues, "should be capable of delivering a police service, in constructive and inclusive partnerships with the community at all levels, and with the maximum delegation of authority and responsibility, consistent with the foregoing principles" Only thus, it asserts, will the police service "win public confidence and acceptance".[89] How then, has the Patten Commission, given flesh to the Belfast Agreement's bold aspirations?

The Patten report—and, indeed, the subsequent Police (Northern Ireland) Bill which seeks, however imperfectly, to implement its findings[90]—is based, at least implicitly, upon a subtle and insightful

---

[87] O'Leary (1998), applying Lijphart (1977).

[88] If and when policing is devolved under the Northern Ireland Act 1998, the North-South Ministerial Council will acquire a parallel role in that area. Prior to that, the British-Irish Intergovernmental Conference guarantees the Irish state access to policy discussion on non-devolved matters, with special emphasis given to the areas of "rights, justice, prisons and policing"; Her Majesty's Government (1998) para. 5.2.6.

[89] *ibid.*, para.9. These themes are expanded upon in the Terms of Reference for the Commission on Policing for Northern Ireland in Annex A of the Agreement.

[90] Police (Northern Ireland) Bill 2000. This was presented to the House of Commons on 16th May, and all references below are to the Bill as initially published. The Second Reading Debate took place on June 6, HC Debs. cols. 177–260. Sinn Fein had argued that there were at least 44 differences between the Patten report and the Bill as eventually published (*The Guardian*, May 25, 2000). Some of these discrepancies are due to the fact that

understanding of the relationship between policing and politics. On the one hand, Patten clearly accepts, as indeed its terms of reference assume, that the legitimacy of policing within a polity is inextricably bound up with the legitimacy of the polity itself.[91] Where the specific order of the state embodies and is perceived as embodying one of two sets of contending values and interests within a society, as in the case of Northern Ireland, then we cannot expect the police, as defenders of that specific order, to attract acceptance across that society as a whole. For so long as they are seen by a dominant unionist community as "custodians of nationhood", the police will likewise be viewed by the nationalist community as "symbols of oppression".[92] Fundamental reform of the state and the specific order it represents is thus prerequisite to building a broad base of police legitimacy. However, while the Patten report accepts that fundamental political reform may be a necessary condition for the cross-community legitimacy of policing, it clearly does not view political reform as sufficient in itself. There are two reasons for this. The first reason, again, concerns the inextricability of policing from broader political processes, while the second, in contrast, has to do with the relative autonomy of policing from politics.

In the first place, policing is so bound up with the nature of the polity that we cannot simply consign it to the status of a derivative variable, its well-being symptomatic of the health of the body politic generally. Rather, policing is a primary political variable, a defining characteristic *of* the polity. As the fundamental guarantor of the power of the polity, policing is part of what shapes the relationship to that polity of communities with divergent political aspirations. Policing "goes right to the heart of the sense of security and identity of both communities" [93] in the north, and in so doing helps to constitute these communities *qua* political communities.[94] A reconfiguration of policing may address the political aspirations of these communities in an equally direct and immediate fashion. Just as policing is an integral part of the problem of polity legitimacy, so it must also be an integral part of any solution.

---

several of Patten's recommendations do not require legislation, and are separately provided for under an implementation plan published on June 6th (Northern Ireland Office (2000)). Other discrepancies remain, however, and at the Second Reading Debate the Secretary of State conceded that the Bill as presented would require "fine tuning"; col. 178, *per* Peter Mandelson.

[91] See further, chapters one, eight and ten.
[92] Patten (1999) para.1.3 and chap. 3.
[93] *ibid.,* (1999) para. 1.3.
[94] Mulcahy (1999) p. 292.

In the second place, the Patten report is emphatic that many of the problems it identifies and the solutions it proposes are relevant not only to a divided Northern Ireland. Rather, "(t)hey touch on the efficiency, acceptability and accountability of the police service in Northern Ireland in any imaginable circumstance,"[95] and, by extension, they are relevant to the governance of policing any modern democratic society.[96] Policing may be a defining feature of a polity, and so undeniably influenced by that context, but it may also be viewed as a distinctive and universal social practice, raising similar difficulties and facing similar normative choices regardless of political circumstance.[97]

The report's insistence that its proposals do not attempt to pander to particular sectional interests and aspirations[98] reflects both its acceptance of the constitutive role of policing in legitimating the polity and its insistence upon the relative autonomy of policing values from their broader political context. An approach which treated reform suggestions as axiomatic just because they emanated from powerful community interests would strike the wrong note in a political environment where the identification of policing with the highly partial foundations of the polity has left such a bitter legacy. Further, the notion that policing has its own distinctive normative register made it *possible*—not merely desirable—to conduct the debate in a language disengaged from sectional interests. To be sure, there are points where Patten does resort to a transparent balancing of sectional interests. For instance, the deeply controversial suggestion that the RUC be renamed the Police Service of Northern Ireland is a clear compromise between the unionist wish to retain the original name and the nationalist aspiration to disband the traditional force altogether.[99] For the most part, however, Patten succeeds in transcending such obvious sectional conflicts of interest.

---

[95] *ibid.*, para. 1.2.

[96] *ibid.*, para. 1.5.

[97] One indication of the Patten Commission's commitment to this approach is the fact that the ideas on two-tier accountability it proposes (see below) bear a family resemblance to the "dual policing" proposals for the new South Africa developed a number of years ago by one of the Commissioners, the Canadian academic Clifford Shearing; Brogden and Shearing (1993).

[98] Patten (1999) para.1.10.

[99] In fact, the Patten report suggested that the force be renamed the Northern Ireland Police Service (para. 17.6), but the British Government subsequently preferred a slightly modified version, perhaps to avoid an unfortunate acronym! See HC Debs, 19 Jan 2000, Col. 848, *per* Peter Mandelson. Subsequently, considerable pressure was exerted by unionists to retain the RUC name, and this was reflected in the more equivocal stance adopted in the Police (Northern Ireland) Bill, clause 69(3) of which requires the Secretary of State in due course to determine the name of the reformed police service.

The report covers every aspect of policing in the North, including human rights; neighbourhood policing; demilitarisation; public order; management and organisation; size, composition and recruitment; training, education and development; culture, ethos and symbols; and co-operation with other forces. In all of these areas, there are important recommendations which seek to develop the conception of a service which accords equal respect to both communities. For example, a new oath of office should include a commitment to accord equal respect to all individuals and to their traditions and beliefs.[1] Community representatives in all areas should be consulted over local priorities by neighbourhood policing teams.[2] All police suspects, regardless of affiliation or crime category, should forthwith be detained in custody suites in police stations and existing military holding centres should be closed.[3] There should be joint planning of public order events by police and community representatives, with organisers also providing their own marshals.[4] The new Sheehy-style administrative dismissal procedures for ineffective or incompetent officers introduced under the 1998 Act[5] should be used against officers not committed to the new policing style.[6] In the context of a force reducing in size to reflect the improved security situation, the Full Time Reserve—associated throughout its various incarnations with security-related work—should be disbanded[7]; at the same time, the overwhelmingly protestant Part Time Reserve should be enlarged in a recruitment drive concentrating on Catholic/nationalist areas.[8] Within the regular force, too, where Catholic representation is a mere 7.5 per cent,[9] steps should be taken to ensure that equal numbers of Protestants and Catholics henceforth be recruited.[10] In Patten's inclusionary vision,

---

[1] Patten (1999) para. 4.7.

[2] *ibid.*, para. 7.14.

[3] *ibid.*, para. 8.15.

[4] *ibid.*, para. 9.9. Accepting this recommendation in principle, the Government undertook to have discussions with the Parades Commission to determine whether legislation would be required; Northern Ireland Office (2000) p. 37.

[5] Police (Northern Ireland) Act 1998, s.25.

[6] Patten (1999), para. 10.15. Revised Conduct Regulations providing for administrative dismissal were due to be introduced by October 2000; Northern Ireland Office (2000) p. 43.

[7] *ibid.*, para.12.17. The Government subsequently intimated that progress on this proposal was dependent upon the security situation; Northern Ireland Office (2000) p. 55.

[8] *ibid.*, para.12.18; Police (Northern Ireland) Bill 2000 clause 35. The Government subsequently ruled out the possibility of former terrorists joining the part-time reserve; Northern Ireland Office (2000) p. 55.

[9] Although cultural Catholics make up 43 per cent of the population of the North.

[10] Patten (1999) para. 15.10; Police (Northern Ireland) Bill clause 43.

moreover, even membership of organisations perceived to be sectarian, such as the Orange Order or the Ancient Order of Hibernian, should be no bar to recruitment, provided it is publicly declared.[11] A training and education strategy linked to the aims of the Report should be developed.[12] The new service should adopt a new badge and symbols entirely free from any association with either the British or Irish states.[13] Co-operation between the new service and the Garda Siochana in the South should be enhanced through agreement of protocols, policy conferences, personnel exchanges, headquarters and border liaison officers, training co-operation, joint disaster planning, improved communications, joint database development and even joint investigative teams for major incidents.[14]

For all the significance of these proposals, however, the provisions on accountability and governance provide the self-proclaimed centrepiece of the Report and its commitment to equal respect.[15] In the vision of Patten, the deficiencies in the existing tripartite structure are tackled by the dual strategy of rebalancing its component parts and introducing or improving other and complementary accountability mechanisms. An entirely new Policing Board is proposed, rather like the new Police Authority in England and Wales, although with explicitly consociational overtones. It is patently more democratic and more proportionately representative of the two communities than the Police Authority of Northern Ireland which it replaces. Of its 19 members, 10 are to be drawn from the non-ministerial membership of the New Northern Ireland Assembly, which is selected on the basis of the proportional d'Hondt system. The remaining nine are to represent a range of different interests and functions, appointed in the first instance by Secretary of State, and, after devolution, jointly by the First Minister and the Deputy First Minister.[16]

The new body also has a broader range of powers and responsibilities than its predecessor, wresting authority from both chief constable and central government. It should continue to have the powers of

---

[11] *ibid.*, para. 15.15–15.16; Police (Northern Ireland) Bill 2000 clause 47.

[12] *ibid.*, para. 16.4; Northern Ireland Office (2000) p. 73.

[13] *ibid.*, para. 17.6. The Government gave qualified acceptance to this proposal, holding that the new arrangements, including arrangements for flying flags, need not necessarily "be entirely free of association with both traditions providing this is consistent with the principles of the Good Friday Agreement"; Northern Ireland Office (2000) p. 83; Police (Northern Ireland) Bill clause 50.

[14] *ibid.*, ch. 19; Police (Northern Ireland) Bill 2000 clause 52.

[15] *ibid.*, para. 1.12–1.16.

[16] *ibid.*, para. 6.11–6.13; Police (Northern Ireland) Bill 2000 clause 1.

appointment and dismissal of senior officers of its predecessor.[17] Within a strategic planning framework less convoluted than established under the 1998 Act,[18] the Policing Board retains the power to approve the annual plan,[19] but it rather than the chief constable, should also be responsible for the development of objectives and priorities over a three to five year time-scale,[20] though still taking account of longer-term objectives and principles set by the Secretary of State or successor.[21] The Policing Board should also have explicit responsibility for negotiating the annual polic-ing budget with the Northern Ireland Office or its devolved successor, for allocating that budget to the chief constable, and for holding the chief constable to account for the efficient and effective use of resources.[22] As well as monitoring police performance, recruitment trends and training needs, the Board should also co-ordinate with other agencies involved in public safety, in a manner similar to the crime reduction partnerships under the Crime and Disorder Act 1998.[23] The Board might also pro-vide a suitable regulatory body for the private security industry.[24]

One of the potentially most significant new powers of the Board lies in the previously sacrosanct operational sphere of the chief constable. In a bold move, Patten seeks to cut through the conceptual minefield of the policy/operational distinction.[25] The Report argues that while the chief constable should continue to be free from external direction in the con-duct of an operation, he or she should not be exempt from inquiry or review after the event by the Board. "Operational responsibility" is thus deemed a more appropriate term than "operational independence", cap-turing the twin features of prospective control by the police and retro-spective answerability to the Board.[26] Consequently, the Board's right to be informed by the chief constable should be greater than that of its pre-

---

[17] Patten (1999) para.6.9; Police (Northern Ireland) Bill 2000 clause 33.

[18] ibid., para.6.16.

[19] Police (Northern Ireland) Bill clause 24.

[20] ibid., clause 23.

[21] ibid., clause 22.

[22] Patten (1999) paras.6.17 and 6.46–6.47; Northern Ireland Office (2000) p. 19; Police (Northern Ireland) Bill 2000, clause 2(2)(c). See also the Best Value provisions under clauses 26–29.

[23] ibid., para. 6.10. Police (Northern Ireland) Bill clause 2(4)(c).

[24] ibid., para.6.10.

[25] See further chapter two, section 1(D),chapter four and chapter 10(3)(C).

[26] ibid., para. 6.19–6.21. While accepting this recommendation in principle, the Gov-ernment was of the view that its implementation did not require legislative recognition of the general concept of "operational responsibility." Rather, it could be achieved through extending the right of the Board to receive information from the chief constable; North-ern Ireland Office (2000) p. 13.

decessor. Each month the Board should meet in public to receive a report from the chief constable.[27] Restrictions upon answerability should be minimal, applying only where serious matters such as national security or the prejudice of a forthcoming trial are at stake.[28] Answerability should be further enhanced by investing the Policing Board with the power to initiate an inquiry following receipt of a report, which inquiry might be conducted or aided by other institutions such as the new Police Ombudsman, the Inspectorate of Constabulary or the Audit Office.[29] While this constitutes a new challenge to the authority of the chief constable from the Police Authority, Patten seeks to balance this by protecting the police from direct governmental influence, recommending that the recent threat of central government guidance under section 39 of the 1998 Act be removed.[30]

The Report is equally radical in promoting a stronger local tier of accountability than presently provided by the Community and Police Liaison Committees to complement the Policing Board and to reflect a more decentralised organisational structure. For each new policing district Patten recommended the creation of a District Police Partnership Board (DPPB), although the Government subsequently preferred the term District Policing Partnership (DPP).[31] As a committee of the District Council, the DPPB would comprise a majority of elected members with the remainder appointed by the Council with the agreement of the Policing Board.[32] Community concerns could be articulated and local performance held to account at monthly meetings between DPPB and the District Commander.[33] The DPPB would be linked both horizontally to the District Council, from which it receives 25 per cent funding

---

[27] ibid., para.6.36; Northern Ireland Office (2000) p. 16.

[28] ibid., para.6.22. The Government accepted this proposal as regards both reports and subsequent Board inquiries, conceding that these extended to operational decisions, but stressed the need for restrictions on disclosure in order to protect national security, sensitive personal information, statutory investigations and court proceedings. More controversially, given its possible encroachment on the duty to report on operational decisions, Government also sought to restrict disclosure where it "would be likely to prejudice the prevention or detection of crime, the apprehension or prosecution of offenders or the administration of justice." Police (Northern Ireland) Bill 2000, clause 55; Northern Ireland Office (2000) p. 13

[29] ibid., para.6.23; Police (Northern Ireland) Bill clause 56; Northern Ireland Office (2000) p. 13. See n. 127.

[30] ibid., para.6.18; Police (Northern Ireland) Bill Sched.7.

[31] ibid., para.6.26; Northern Ireland Office (2000) p. 14; Police (Northern Ireland) Bill 2000 clause 13.

[32] ibid., para.6.26; Sched.3.

[33] ibid., para.6.29–6.30; Northern Ireland Office (2000) p. 15; Police (Northern Ireland) Bill clause 15.

and to which it submits an annual report, and vertically to the Policing Board, with which there is regular contact and from which it receives 75 per cent funding.[34] Patten also recommended that District Councils should have the power to provide the equivalent of a 3p in the pound rate towards improved policing, which would allow the DPPB to purchase additional local policing services from the public or private sector.[35]

Other accountability recommendations sound at the individual rather than the community level. Patten offers a strong endorsement of the new Police Ombudsman set up under the 1998 Act, recommending that it should be generously staffed to accommodate a proactive as well as reactive role in the investigation of complaints, and also a general entitlement to comment on police policies and practices which are perceived to give rise to difficulties.[36] Patten also recommends the institution of a commissioner for covert law enforcement in Northern Ireland[37] to cover those areas of covert practice not already regulated under existing U.K. legislation.[38] Finally, at the apex of this new pyramid, should stand a new complaints tribunal, comprising senior members of the legal professional and able to investigate all cases referred to it, including those involving covert operations.[39]

3. Conclusion

Predictably, the Patten Report did not enjoy a quiet reception. Unionists were concerned with its radical departure from the existing institutional framework, while nationalists, although initially more welcoming, remain unconvinced—particularly in the face of the subsequent implementing Bill—that its proposals were radical enough to constitute a clean break from the sectarian past.[40] Nonetheless, the British government quickly accepted Patten in principle,[41] and were not deflected by broader

---

[34] Patten (1999) para.6.32; Northern Ireland Office (2000) p. 15.

[35] *ibid.*, para.6.33. Northern Ireland Office (2000) p. 15.

[36] *ibid.*, para.6.39–6.42; Northern Ireland Office (2000) p. 18; Police (Northern Ireland) Bill 2000, clauses 58–61.

[37] *ibid.*, para.6.43–6.44; Northern Ireland Office (2000) pp. 18–19.; Regulation of Investigatory Powers Bill 2000 Part II.

[38] See chapter seven.

[39] Patten (1999) para.6.45; Regulation of Investigative Powers Bill 2000 Part IV.

[40] Of the main political parties, only the SDLP called for Patten to be implemented in its entirety. See *Statewatch*, vol. 9 no 6, November–December 1999, pp. 20–23.

[41] HC Debs. 19 January 2000, Cols. 845–848, *per* Peter Mandelson.

difficulties in the Peace Process from proceeding to introduce legislation. Does it, therefore, point the way to a more legitimate framework for policing in the North? The answer to this depends upon how problems of substance and process associated with Patten and the wider Peace Process are faced.

First, let us deal with an important question of substance. In accepting the Report in principle, the British Government was nevertheless luke-warm about much of the detail surrounding the proposal to create District Police Partnership Boards. Quite apart from deciding that they should simply be known as District Police Partnerships, the Government also stressed that their powers should be consultative rather than executive; that they should be regulated by a Code of Practice issued by the Police Board; and that, at least in the first instance, they should not, as Patten had sug-gested, be empowered to purchase additional policing services locally.[42] This recommendation had precipitated unionist fear and indignation at the prospect of the involvement of those with a paramilitary background in the provision of local policing, and the Government was clearly wary that this could prove a fundamental stumbling-block. Beneath this con-cern to be politically prudent, and also not to pre-empt the findings of the wider review of criminal justice which was covering the overlapping ques-tion of community safety,[43] there lay a genuine problem of institutional design for a contested polity. Within a philosophy of policing committed to equal respect of two communities in a divided society there is a tension between two of its constituent values, between the consociational precept of community autonomy on the one hand and cross-community impar-tiality on the other. Strong cultural and geographical divisions indicate the attractiveness of community autonomy as a way of avoiding or mitigating the difficulties of centralist solutions. These difficulties include not only the majoritarian abuses of the past, but also the potential for decisional gridlock and policy stagnation in the type of consociationalist parallel consent provisions found in the Belfast Agreement and designed precisely to overcome such majoritarian abuses. However, in a policy area such

---

[42] *ibid.* Col. 846; see also Northern Ireland Office (2000) pp. 14–17; Police Northern Ireland Bill 2000 clauses 13–18.

[43] Criminal Justice Review Group (2000) chap. 11. When published in March 2000, the review recommended a considerable degree of integration of policing and community safety at the local level, including the renaming of DPPS as Community Safety and Polic-ing Partnerships (CSPP) (para.11.61), with district councils permitted to fund the "com-munity safety initiatives" of the CSSPs to the value of a rate of 3p in the pound (para.11.75). After this fairly warm endorsement, it became more difficult for the Govern-ment to cite the criminal justice review as a reason to proceed cautiously in this area.

as policing, where cultural communities cannot be hermetically sealed off from one another and where choices, say between victims and offenders, often involve winners and losers across the divide,[44] community autonomy may compromise impartiality and merely displace the problem of majoritarian abuse to the local level. While the society remains deeply divided this tension between community autonomy and impartiality will be recurrent and unavoidable.[45]

A second obstacle arises from the relationship between the politics of constitutional reform and the enduring paradox of police governance. The British state is a party whose interests are directly affected by policing change in the North, but it also remains the primary agent of constitutional change in Northern Ireland, including policing change. On the one hand, it is reluctant to sanction reform of policing unless and until it is satisfied that such reform will not compromise its capacity to defend its own interests from the "security threat" offered by rival interests. On the other hand, since policing is perceived to be part of the constitutional problem and part of the constitutional solution by these rival interests, then unless and until the British state sanctions policing reform, or at least appears genuinely committed to reform, these rival interests will be reluctant to remove the security threat.

The Belfast Agreement and the Patten Commission seek to avoid an *impasse* between these positions through a number of linked strategies, each of which puts some distance between the British Government and the reform process while permitting the Government an important continuing influence. The Patten Commission itself was established as an "independent" non-governmental Commission, albeit appointed by the British Government. Under the Belfast Agreement, implementation of its proposals would follow discussion with the political parties and with the Irish Government, although the final power of initiative remains with the British Government.[46] The Belfast Agreement also contains a commitment, after consultation with the Irish Government, to devolve responsibility for policing to the new Northern Ireland Assembly,[47] a

---

[44] In this sense, policing is a less appropriate subject for consociational arrangements than social policy areas such as housing, education and social security, where separate service provision is possible without the same direct inter-community implications.

[45] One of the inherent obstacles to successful consociationalist settlements, highlighted by the issue of community self-policing, is a political culture, such as Northern Ireland, in which the opposing elites and the organisations they control are even more hostile than the general population; see *e.g.*, Evans and O'Leary (2000); Bellamy (2000) p. 209.

[46] Her Majesty's Government (1998), para. 9.6.

[47] Para. 9.7; para.11.

commitment upgraded by the Patten Commission so that it be honoured "as soon as possible".[48] On the other hand, matters involving national security are conspicuously excluded from this commitment, and, indeed, are constitutionally incapable of devolution under the present scheme.[49] Next, to offset the continuing fear of devolution as a way of consolidating rather than diluting the authority of the state—understandable enough given the experience of the unionist bias of the devolved Minister of Home Affairs before 1969—the Patten Report also contains a commitment that the balancing power of the Policing Board should in no way be diminished when the central government role in the tripartite arrangement finally passes to the new Northern Ireland Executive.[50] Finally, as an independent monitor of the progress towards reform and, indeed, as "an important impetus in the process of transformation",[51] Patten recommends the appointment of an independent oversight commissioner for a period of five years. However, although this commissioner will possess the not inconsiderable power to publicise failures or delays, he or she will not be able to compel change against the wishes of the Government.

These proposals, inevitably, retain the British state as the constitutional authority of last resort in matters of policing. Whether, as a counterweight, the proposals are also sufficiently open to external oversight and to nationalist aspirations to sustain the confidence of all parties and maintain the momentum of the reform process in the longer-term remains to be seen. Like the problem of community autonomy, the problem of constitutional process is rendered more acute by the depth of the divide between the two communities. To the extent that oppositional group consciousness persists, the more difficult it is to satisfy both communities as to the integrity of the constitutional reform process and the good faith of the other side.

As ever, then, it would appear that policing in Northern Ireland remains both effect and cause—both consequence of and catalyst for larger political forces and events. The aspiration of a broadly legitimate police service may become a casualty of sustained civil hostility and of a faltering Peace Process. Alternatively, progress towards realising this aspiration may provide the impetus for the Peace Process to find or regain its stride. The persistence of a divided society makes it more difficult to

---

[48] Patten (1999), para.6.15. See also, Northern Ireland Act 1998, Sched.3, para.11
[49] Patten(1999), para 6.15; Northern Ireland Act 1998, Sched.2, para.17.
[50] Patten (1999) para.6.15.
[51] *ibid.*, para. 19.4–19.5.

reform policing, yet the reform of policing remains prerequisite to overcoming social and political division. The difficulties posed by this double-edged, paradoxical characteristic of policing of course remain formidable, but the very fact that they are so keenly appreciated in the governing political texts of the Belfast Agreement and Patten allows us to be cautiously optimistic about future prospects.

PART III

NEW DIMENSIONS OF POLICING

Chapter Seven

The National Dimension

1. Nationalising Trends

So far we have had much to say about the way in which the state has gradually increased its influence over the New Police since its inception. To be sure, this has been by no means an uninterrupted progress. Constitutional developments in Scotland and Ireland in particular have promised some increase in policing diversity. And as we shall see in subsequent chapters, there are other factors at work which are conducive towards a more plural policing order. Yet it is undeniably the case that the state has become an ever more prominent actor in the provision and regulation of policing.

Partly this has been about unification and standardisation, an ever-decreasing number of forces conforming to an increasingly detailed and *dirigiste* organisational template—a process culminating in the new managerialism of the 1990s.[1] Partly, it has been about national networking, with ACPO, the Inspectorate, the Audit Commission, local authorities, police authorities and the business community coming together in a national policy community around the Home Office, sometimes collaborating informally and sometimes in more formal structures such as the tripartite framework itself, or in the National Crime Prevention Agency—established in 1995 to advise the new Ministerial Group on Crime Prevention.[2] Partly, it has been about institutional expansion within the centre. Alongside its policy-making, co-ordination and standard-setting roles within the tripartite system, the Home Office has

---

[1] See chapters three and four.

[2] The culmination of a number of national crime prevention initiatives which began with the establishment of the Home Office Crime Prevention Unit in 1983. For discussion, see Morgan and Newburn (1997) pp. 57–65; Crawford (1997) chap.2;(1998b) chap.2.

gradually developed various expert facilities. In recent years, for example, new internal units and initiatives have been developed such as the National Directorate of Police Training and the associated National Crime Faculty, the National Strategy for Police Information Systems and the Police Information Technology Organisation.[3]

Partly, too, it has been about the development of national operational policing units. Ever since Dr Goodhart's memorandum of dissent to the 1962 Royal Commission recommending the establishment of a nationally controlled police force administered on a regional basis,[4] the development of a more centralised institutional architecture has never been far from the political agenda. Given the degree of anxiety about state authoritarianism which such proposals provoke,[5] it is ironic that those specialist national police forces which already exist attract such little public attention.[6] Ironic, but perhaps not particularly surprising, given the low legal and organisational profile of non-Home Office police forces.[7] They include, most prominently, the British Transport Police,[8] but other significant examples are the Ministry of Defence Police[9] and the Atomic Energy Authority Constabulary.[10] Each of these organisations has a significant legal ancestry,[11] but each is also now the subject of a modern statute which extends its jurisdiction and powers.[12] In all cases, the main channel of accountability is to the primary user. There is no equivalent to the tripartite system of governance and accountability to the general public is negligible, despite the fact that much of their activity takes place on public space and involves ordinary citizens.[13]

Our main focus of attention in this chapter, however, is a newer set of

---

[3] Placed on a statutory footing by virtue of the Police Act, 1997, Sched.8. For details of recent developments in these agencies, see Home Office (1999) chap.6

[4] Royal Commission on the Police (1962), pp. 157–179.

[5] See chapter one, section 2(B)(iii).

[6] See Johnston (1993), pp. 787–788.

[7] Wright (1979).

[8] See Appleby (1995); Jones and Newburn (1998) pp. 125–128.

[9] See Johnston (1992a); Jones and Newburn (1998) pp. 128–130.

[10] See Johnston (1994); Jones and Newburn (1998) pp. 130–131.

[11] In particular the British Transport Police, whose origins are in the various railway companies which established the rail network in the 1820s.

[12] Respectively, British Transport Commission Act 1949; Ministry of Defence Police Act 1987; Atomic Energy Authority (Special Constables) Act 1976.

[13] Attempts by MPs to raise questions in Parliament about the conduct or policy of these forces are invariably frustrated; see Johnston (1993) p. 783. S.78 of the Police Act 1996, however, enables a series of voluntary agreements between the Police Complaints Authority and the non-Home Office forces applying the statutory police complaints procedures to the officers of these forces, with provision for the Home Secretary to compel application of these procedures in the absence of agreement.

national operational initiatives which have enjoyed far greater political visibility and public controversy, and which, by and large, have been made the subject of more sophisticated governance regimes. The three developments we discuss—the formation of the National Criminal Intelligence Service (NCIS) and of the National Crime Squad (NCS) and the addition of policing functions to the remit of the Security Service—are united by an underlying policy thrust to tackle serious and organised crime on a national basis, using systematic intelligence-led policing. On the one hand, they may in some measure be viewed as the outgrowth of local and regional efforts to concentrate police resources on particular types of criminal activity. On the other hand, they provide the state-level response to the new international agenda to combat serious crime, which is the topic of the next chapter. Let us now examine the background, mandate and structure, and governance arrangements of each of these three initiatives in turn, drawing out the similarities and differences both *inter se* and between them and the tripartite model for local forces discussed earlier.

2. Three National Initiatives

(A) THE NATIONAL CRIMINAL INTELLIGENCE SERVICE

(i) Background

NCIS had been in existence in a non-statutory form since April 1992, but was not formally recognised until the Police Act 1997[14] NCIS pulled together a wide range of supra-force intelligence functions, many with an international flavour. These included existing national units, notably the National Drugs Intelligence Unit (NDIU),[15] the National Football Intelligence Unit[16] and the National Central Bureau of Interpol, as well as existing international liaison officers. The new umbrella organisation also housed new initiatives in areas such as organised crime and financial

---

[14] Part I.

[15] Established in 1985 following a recommendation in ACPO's Broome Report (Association of Chief Police Officers, 1985). Another ACPO policy document, known as the Baumber Report, had been instrumental in the establishment of regional criminal intelligence offices ten years previously (Association of Chief Police Officers, 1975). See also Dorn, Murji and South (1992).

[16] Established in 1989.

intelligence and placed previously local efforts to combat paedophilia, kidnapping, product contamination, fine art fraud and counterfeit currency on a national footing. Alongside this domestic agenda, the establishment of NDIU, and later of NCIS itself, also anticipated requirements at the European level to have in place national satellites as part of the Trevi and Europol organisations respectively.[17] From the outset, NCIS was organised both territorially, in regional offices,[18] and functionally, in different specialisms at its London headquarters. Prior to the 1997 Act, NCIS operated on the margins of the conventional tripartite structure, situated within and resourced by the Home Office and accountable to the Home Secretary. The Act itself followed a government decision in 1995[19] to recognise a growing tide of elite opinion in favour of a statutory national intelligence and investigative capacity,[20] the latter to be supplied by the new National Crime Squad. Controversy surrounding an inquiry into missing notebooks containing material obtained by NCIS officers through telephone-tapping meant that the legislation was delayed until the Spring of 1997—at the very tail-end of 18 years of Conservative administration.

(ii) Mandate and Structure

In line with its original informal remit, the statutory functions of NCIS as of April 1, 1998 have been: (i) to gather, store and analyse information in order to provide criminal intelligence; (ii) to provide criminal intelligence to local forces, RUC, NCS and other law enforcement agencies; and (iii) to act in support of these forces and agencies as they carry out their criminal intelligence activities.[21] Clearly, then, NCIS is not intended as a law enforcement or investigative agency, but as performing a supply and support role in relation to agencies which do have enforcement and investigative functions.

Some lines, however, are less strictly drawn. The "other law enforcement agencies" that NCIS is required to support include not only for-

---

[17] See Walker (1993a); (1994c). See further chapter eight.

[18] Although the Scottish regional office did not open until 1997. See chapter five above.

[19] As with so many criminal justice initiatives over the last 20 years, it was first announced by the then Home Secretary, Michael Howard, at the annual Conservative Party conference. The decision was confirmed and developed in a White Paper published the following March; Home Office (1996) chap.3.

[20] See, *e.g.,* the Report of the influential House of Commons Home Affairs Committee; Home Affairs Committee (1995a).

[21] Police Act, 1997 s.2(2).

eign and international agencies with a criminal intelligence remit[22] and domestic government departments,[23] but also a residual category[24] which would embrace both specialist statutory law enforcers such as Customs and Excise and non-statutory investigators such as the Royal Society for the Prevention of Cruelty to Animals.[25] Another hazy line, which drew criticism during the passage of the Bill, concerns the purposes for which NCIS may exercise its intelligence role. Unlike NCS, the remit of NCIS is not limited to serious crime, and this despite the fact that the Europol Convention restricts the international communication of intelligence from national bodies to the category of serious crime. If this overreach may be justified by reference to the broader scope attributable to NCIS's additional role in respect of local crime, it is more difficult to defend the failure of the text to exclude purposes other than the prevention or detection of crime. Arguably, this leaves it open to NCIS to gather intelligence for broader security purposes, such as the monitoring of social and political dissent.[26]

The current organisational structure of NCIS is an elaboration of the pre-statutory pattern. Its U.K. division oversees operational units in six regional offices, [27] where the emphasis is on the gathering and development of intelligence. In the London headquarters of NCIS, the U.K. Division also houses a Strategic and Specialist Intelligence Branch which includes an organised crimes unit, a drugs unit, an economic crimes unit and a residual specialist crimes unit.[28] The primary tasks of the other main section, the International Division, are: to manage the networks of European Drugs Liaison Officers and Europol Liaison Officers stationed abroad; to host foreign liaison officers stationed in Britain in an International Liaison Unit; and to house the U.K. National Central Bureau of Interpol—the oldest surviving international criminal intelligence agency.[29] There are two additional support sections—the Resource Division and the Intelligence Development Division. The latter includes a Special Projects Branch, which embraces an operations support unit dealing with police requests for warrants to

---

[22] *ibid.*, s.2(3)(d).
[23] *ibid.*, s.2(3)(a).
[24] *ibid.*, s.2(3)(c).
[25] Uglow and Telford (1997) p. 12.
[26] *ibid.*, p. 13.
[27] In London, Birmingham, Bristol, Manchester, Wakefield and Paisley.
[28] Which comprise sections dealing with kidnap and extortion demands, the suppression of counterfeit currency, football hooliganism and paedophile activity.
[29] See chapter eight.

intercept communications[30] and a special liaison unit which provides an interface between police and the security and intelligence services in tackling organised crime.[31]

This complex organisational structure is staffed by various categories of personnel. First, there are permanent police members, namely the Director-General,[32] who must be of chief constable or equivalent rank or eligible for appointment at such rank[33], and his assistants, who, equally, must be of assistant chief constable or equivalent rank or be eligible for appointment at such rank.[34] Secondly, and by far the largest group, there are police officers on temporary secondment from other forces.[35] Thirdly, there are non-police members, either direct employees of the Authority[36] or seconded from other organisations, such as customs and excise officers.[37] Finally, there are other civilian staff who are not members of NCIS but who may be employed by the NCIS Service Authority[38] to enable it to discharge its functions.[39]

(iii) Governance Arrangements.

The governance arrangements for NCIS offer further evidence of the contemporary pre-eminence in matters of police governance of the traditional tripartite model in a newer managerialist variant. The NCIS Service Authority is the body charged with maintaining NCIS.[40] Its membership, which numbers 19[41] unless the Home Secretary otherwise provides,[42] includes 10 core members who are also members of the NCS Service Authority.[43] The common membership, and the requirement to

---

[30] The existing arrangements are established in the Interception of Communications Act 1985, but following a 1999 consultation paper (Home Office, 1999d), this is due to be replaced by a new statutory regime; see Regulation of Investigatory Powers Bill 2000, Part I.

[31] See further, section 2(c) below.

[32] Currently John Abbott.

[33] Police Act 1997 s.6(3).

[34] *ibid.,* ss.9(2)(a) and 9(3).

[35] *ibid.,* s.9(2)(b).

[36] *ibid.,,* s.9(1)(c).

[37] This continues the pattern of police-customs collaboration established by NCIS's predecessor organisation, NDIU. See generally, Dorn, Murji and South (1992) chap.9.

[38] See subsection (iii) below.

[39] Police Act 1997 s. 13(1).

[40] *ibid.,* s.2(1).

[41] *ibid.,* s.1(2).

[42] *ibid.,* s.1(3).

[43] *ibid.,* Sched.1, Pt.1, para.1(1).

have a common chair,[44] are intended to facilitate co-ordination of the activities of the two national organisations. The composition of the Service Authority acknowledges the interest of all three tripartite parties and also the wider territorial and functional constituencies that NCIS represents and serves. Four of the core membership are appointed by the Home Secretary, including three independent (*i.e.*, not Crown servants) members (one of whom must be the chair and one (non-voting) Crown servant to represent the Home Office constituency.[45] A further four of the core membership are appointed by local authority members of local police authorities in England and Wales from among their number,[46] and two by chief constables in England and Wales from among their number.[47] Of the non-core membership, there are an additional two (non-voting) members from the Crown servant constituency;[48] a further four from the local police authority constituency, including one apiece from the Scottish and Northern Ireland police authorities; [49] a further two from the police constituency, again one apiece from Scotland[50] and Northern Ireland;[51] and one customs officer appointed by the Commissioners of Customs and Excise.[52]

In three basic respects, the tripartite model as applied to NCIS is more centralist than it is in the case of local police forces. In the first place, the Home Secretary retains direct control over certain appointments to the Service Authority, including the chair. Attempts similar to those which marked the passage of the Police and Magistrates" Courts Act 1994[53] were made to water down the Home Secretary's control, but the relative remoteness of the national body from the local authority base of opposition and the rhetorical urgency of its claim to champion the fight against international and organised crime[54] meant that challenges to

---

[44] *ibid.*, Sched.1, Pt.1, para.2(3).

[45] *ibid.*, Sched.1, Pt.1, para.6.

[46] *ibid.*, Sched.1, Pt.1, para.4, as amended by Greater London Authority Act 1999 Sched. 27. Prior to the 1999 Act, the Home Secretary, as the then Metropolitan police authority, could appoint a nominee to represent him in that capacity, while the local authority core membership was only three. Now that the latter has been increased to four, one must be a member of the new, local authority-based Metropolitan police authority, thus retaining the dedicated London member.

[47] *ibid.*, Sched.1, Pt.1, para.3; one of these officers must be London-based.

[48] *ibid.*, Sched.1, Pt.11, para.7(f).

[49] *ibid.*, Sched.1, Pt.11, para. 7(c)-(e).

[50] *ibid.*, Sched.1, Pt.11, para.7(a).

[51] *ibid.*, Sched.1, Pt.11, para.7(b).

[52] *ibid.*, Sched.1, Pt.11, para.7(g).

[53] See chapter four, section 1.

[54] See chapter eight.

central power during the legislative process were less successful on this occasion.[55]

Secondly, and more fundamentally, viewed through the lens of tripartitism there is a marked structural imbalance in the NCIS governance arrangements. As we have seen, only in Scotland, where the local authority *is* the police authority,[56] does the local authority remain a distinctive entity within the tripartite relationship. In the other versions of contemporary tripartitism considered so far, whereas the other two broad constituencies traditionally represented within tripartitism—police and central government—retain a separate legal identity, local government either fails entirely to be represented within the police authority, as in Northern Ireland,[57] or is only partly represented by the police authority, as in England and Wales.[58] The local police authorities have no direct and autonomous role. The Service Authority for NCIS constitutes a different variation on the theme of structural imbalance. It represents all three major constituencies—police, local government and central government. It therefore provides a kind of corporate microcosm of the tripartite system, yet performs the legal role of the third party in a reworked tripartite relationship alongside central government and police. This dilution of local government authority is mitigated to some extent by special voting rules which privilege police authority members of the Service Authority in certain decision-making contexts.[59] Against this formal compensation, however, we must weigh the fact that police authority and other non-police members of the Service Authority are less likely than their counterparts in local police authorities to assert themselves before the professional expertise of senior and specialist police officers on such specialist matters as intelligence-led policing, international mutual assistance and trans-border organised crime, particularly as some of these professional experts will be their direct colleagues on the Service Authority.[60]

The third centralising factor is more subtle, and may only be appreciated upon an examination of the substance of the tripartite relationship as it applies to NCIS. As noted, the Service Authority fills the institutional space in the tripartite relationship vacated by the local police

---

[55] See Uglow and Telford (1997) p. 10.
[56] Police (Scotland) Act 1967, s.2(1); See further chapter five.
[57] See chapter six.
[58] Police Act, 1996, s.4. See also chapter four, section 2(B)(i).
[59] Police Act 1997, Sched.2 para.13 (discipline); Sched.3, para.1 (budget).
[60] See Johnston (1999) chap.6.

authority, but, that apart, the 1994 (now 1996) model is adhered to very closely in the 1997 Act, to the extent that the language used by the legislative draftsman is in many cases identical. Likewise, in the discussion that follows, we adhere very closely to the order of exposition and analysis applied to the 1994 model in chapter four.[61]

To begin with, central government has most of the same formal powers it acquired within the framework of local police governance. A generic provision requires the Home Secretary to exercise his powers so as to promote the efficiency and the effectiveness of NCIS.[62] In his strategic role, the Home Secretary may by order, and after consulting representatives of the other two traditional tripartite parties and the Directors-General and Service Authorities of NCIS and NCS,[63] determine objectives for NCIS.[64] In the 1999 programme,[65] one objective, which is a reworking of the initial mandate set in 1998,[66] required NCIS to provide high quality and relevant criminal intelligence leading to (i) the dismantling or disruption of criminal enterprises engaged in serious and organised crime, and (ii) the arrest and prosecution of criminals whose activities take place in or impact on the United Kingdom. A second, and entirely new objective was to provide high quality and relevant criminal intelligence and information to law enforcement agencies, having regard to the Government's ten-year anti-drugs strategy.[67] The Home Secretary may also direct the NCIS Service Authority to establish performance targets aimed at achieving these objectives.[68]

Just as he has within the local accountability framework, the Home Secretary also has direct influence over and oversight of the other two tripartite parties. He may cause an inquiry to be held by a third party into the workings of NCIS and may require its findings to be published.[69] He may require reports on relevant subjects from both the NCIS Service Authority[70] and the Director General,[71] and may require from the latter

---

[61] See chapter four, section 2.
[62] Police Act 1997 s.25.
[63] ibid., s.26(2).
[64] ibid., s.26(1).
[65] The NCIS (Secretary of State's Objectives) Order 1999; S.I. 1999/822.
[66] S.I. 1998/110.
[67] See Her Majesty's Government (1999). This also provides the framework for one of the new local police objectives (see chapter four, section 2(A)(i)) and for one of the new NCS objectives (see subsection (B)(iii) below).
[68] Police Act 1997 s.27.
[69] ibid., s.34.
[70] ibid., s.31.
[71] ibid., s.32.

a periodical return of criminal statistics.[72] Additionally, the Home Secretary is a recipient of an annual report by the Service Authority,[73] which must include an assessment of the extent to which the Authority's service plan for that year has been carried out,[74] and he must also receive a copy of the Director General's annual report to the Service Authority.[75] Other more directive forms of communication include the power of the Home Secretary to issue codes of practice to the Service Authority,[76] and his linked capacities to instruct Inspectors of Constabulary[77] to carry out inspections of NCIS,[78] to require and receive a copy of a dialogue between the Service Authority and the Director General in response to an Inspectorate report, [79] and to compel the Service Authority to take remedial measures in the event of a finding of inefficiency or ineffectiveness.[80] A final direct power over the Director General concerns tenure of employment. The approval of the Home Secretary is required before the appointment of the Director General[81] and the Home Secretary may require the NCIS Service Authority to exercise its power to call upon the Director General or any other NCIS member directly appointed by the Service Authority to retire in the interests of efficiency,[82] provided representations are sought, and, where necessary, an inquiry is held, before any such decision is ratified.[83]

The budgetary powers of the Home Secretary are rather different than in the local governance arrangements, reflecting the different sources of NCIS revenue.[84] Whereas local policing is financed through a mix of direct and indirect central expenditure and local authority taxation, in the case of NCIS, after initial financing by the Home Secre-

---

[72] Police Act 1997, s.33.

[73] *ibid.*, s.5(3)(a).

[74] *ibid.*, s.5(2).

[75] *ibid.*, s.32(4).

[76] *ibid.*, s.28.

[77] The powers of the Inspectorate are duly extended to cover NCIS and NCS in Sched.9, para.76 of the 1997 Act, amending s.54(2) of the Police Act 1996.

[78] Police Act 1997, s.30(1).

[79] *ibid.*, Sched.9, para.77, adding s.55(7) to the Police Act 1996.

[80] *ibid.*, s.30(2).

[81] *ibid.*, s.6(2). Unlike the local tripartite system, the same power of veto over appointment does not extend to the deputy or assistants of the chief officer. However, as is the case with the local chief constable (Police Act 1996, s.12(4)–(5)), the Director General is obliged to designate one member of NCIS as his deputy and that person's authority cannot continue beyond a period of three months without the consent of the Home Secretary (Police Act 1997 s.8).

[82] *ibid.*, s.29(1).

[83] *ibid.*, s.29(2)–(5).

[84] See Uglow and Telford (1997) pp. 14–16.

tary,[85] it derives the majority of its income directly from police authorities, with some contribution made by the Secretaries of State for Northern Ireland[86] and Scotland[87] to reflect the organisation's United Kingdom-wide remit. The money is raised from local police authorities and the Metropolitan police authority through levies issued by the NCIS Service Authority,[88] the total amount of which is initially determined by a quorum of the Service Authority which includes a majority of police authority members.[89] This determination should take account of the Director General's expenditure plans, any income which may be derived from direct charging of police forces, the Service Authority's financial reserves, current and projected levels of borrowing, and the views of all other members of the Service Authority.[90] To this point, the budget-setting procedure is sensitive to the views of its local financial base, but thereafter the authority of the centre is asserted, just as it is in the context of local police spending. The total amount levied must be approved[91] and may be varied[92] by the Home Secretary, having consulted with representatives of police authorities and chief officers generally.[93] The Home Secretary is also empowered to make an order regarding the calculation and collection of levies,[94] including the terms of its apportionment among local police authorities.[95]

Finally, the existing powers of the Home Secretary to make detailed regulations about policing standards and provide for common services[96] are augmented to take account of NCIS. The Home Secretary may make regulations relating to the conduct of members of NCIS and the maintenance of discipline,[97] and also as to standards of equipment.[98] The

---

[85] Police Act 1997, s.18.

[86] *ibid.*, s.132.

[87] HL Deb., Vol. 575, No.11, col.791, *per* Baroness Blatch.

[88] Police Act 1997, s.17(1), as amended by Sched. 29 of the Greater London Authority Act 1999.

[89] *ibid.*, Sched.3, para.1(1)–(3). The only other members of the Service Authority entitled to take part in this decision are Home Secretary-appointed independent members.

[90] *ibid.*, Sched.3, para.4.

[91] *ibid.*, Sched.3, para.2.

[92] *ibid.*, Sched.3, para.3.

[93] *ibid.*, Sched.3, para.2(3). It was intended by the government that this decision should be made by the tripartite group as part of a broader consideration of police spending and the contribution of central government; Leigh (1997) p. 18.

[94] *ibid.*, s.17(2).

[95] *ibid.*, s.17(3).

[96] See chapter four, section 2(A)(vi)–(vii) above.

[97] Police Act 1997 s.37(1).

[98] *ibid.*, s.35.

Home Secretary may also make regulations which require NCIS, in co-operation with local police forces or NCS, to use specified facilities or services, provided he believes this would be efficient or effective.[99] More-over, the Home Secretary has default powers to require collaboration[1] or mutual aid[2] between NCIS and local police forces or NCS where no prior initiative has been taken by the relevant chief officers and police authorities and been agreed between them.

As already noted, the NCIS Service Authority follows closely in the legislative footsteps of the local police authorities under the 1996 Act. Its overriding duty is to secure that NCIS is efficient and effective.[3] In so endeavouring, the Service Authority, after consulting the Director General and other interested parties,[4] shall determine annual objectives for NCIS,[5] which may reflect the prior objectives set by the Home Secretary[6] or identify other priorities, but which in any event must be framed so as to be consistent with the national objectives.[7] The bare bones of these responsibilities are filled out by the requirement to issue an annual service plan[8]—the equivalent of the local policing plan under the 1996 Act.[9] Like the 1996 prototype, the service plan must include a statement of the Service Authority's priorities for the year and of the financial resources expected to be available and their proposed alloca-tion.[10] It must also give particulars of Home Secretary and Service Authority objectives, and any related performance targets, whether

---

[99] *ibid.*, s.36(1). Before doing so, the Home Secretary should consult the chief officers or their representatives and the police authorities or their representatives for the areas or func-tions affected. officer (s.36(2)).

[1] *ibid.*, s.22(7).

[2] *ibid.*, s.23(3).

[3] *ibid.*, s.3(1). Conceivably, the difference in formulation from the equivalent duty under the 1996 Act (s.6(1) on local police authorities, their being required to *secure the mainte-nance* of an efficient and effective force, may be not insignificant. On one reading, the ear-lier formulation is concerned with providing the material preconditions of efficiency and effectiveness (and thus is consistent with the police authority's traditional role as resource provider), while the later formulation is concerned with identifying and applying the very standards of efficiency and effectiveness. On another view, the difference in language is trivial, and probably non-justiciable (Leigh (1997) p. 10), particularly given the trend in both the 1996 and 1997 Acts to give police authorities an active role in policy formulation which clearly goes beyond their traditional brief as resource provider.

[4] *i.e.*, representatives of local police authorities in the U.K., the NCS Service Authority and the Commissioners of Customs and Excise; Police Act, 1997, s.3(4).

[5] *ibid.*, s.3(2).

[6] *ibid.*, s.26.

[7] *ibid.*, s.3(3).

[8] *ibid.*, s.4(1).

[9] Police Act 1996 s.8.

[10] Police Act, 1997 s.4(2).

ministerially determined[11] or separately established by the Service Authority.[12] The Director General, like the chief constable under local arrangements, takes the drafting initiative,[13] but the final version is decided by the Service Authority, although the Director General must be consulted before it is issued if it differs from the draft.[14] As with the 1996 Act,[15] there is an explicit linkage requiring the Service Authority to "have regard to"[16] these various strategy documents and directives. While this is no less an ambiguous formulation in the present context, the power of the Home Secretary to direct the Service Authority to take remedial measures in response to an adverse report by the Inspectorate as to the efficiency or effectiveness of NCIS[17] may be a more effective, if less direct, means to police the Service Authority's compliance with the strategic documentation.

The Service Authority also has significant powers of influence over and oversight of the force. Like local police authorities,[18] the Service Authority has the power to appoint the Director General, [19] subject to the consent of the Home Secretary,[20] and also to appoint his assistants.[21] Appointments below that level should be made by the Director General,[22] except where otherwise agreed with the Authority, or, in the absence of such agreement, as determined by the Home Secretary.[23] The Director General[24] and those other officers directly appointed by the Service Authority[25] may also be called upon by the Authority to retire in the interests of efficiency and effectiveness, subject to representations by the officer concerned and the approval of the Home Secretary. The Service Authority is also entitled to receive an annual report and other relevant reports from the Director General, subject to the proviso, adjudicated by

---

[11] *ibid.*, s.27.
[12] *ibid.*, s.4(2)(a)–(c).
[13] *ibid.*, s.4(3).
[14] *ibid.*, s.4(4).
[15] Police Act 1996 s.6(2).
[16] Police Act 1997 s.2(4).
[17] *ibid.*, s.30.
[18] Police Act 1996 ss.11–12.
[19] Police Act 1997 s.6(1). The appointment must be made by a panel which excludes members of the Authority who are serving police officers (s.6(4)).
[20] *ibid.*, s.6(2).
[21] *ibid.*, s.9(9)(a).
[22] *ibid.*, ss.9(8) and 44.
[23] *ibid.*, s.9(9)(b).
[24] *ibid.*, s.7.
[25] *ibid.*, s.9(10).

the Home Secretary, that such reports are necessary and not prejudicial to the public interest.[26]

We have already explained how the budgetary arrangements favour the Home Secretary, although the main immediate source of the finance is local. However, the administration of the budget, as well as its draft specification, is the responsibility of the Service Authority, which must maintain a service fund.[27] Apart from the basic levies, the Service Authority may accept gifts or loans,[28] and may charge for services,[29] including special services provided on request by the Director General.[30] Like the post-1994 local police authorities, the Service Authority has no discrete statutory control over specific budgetary heads such as establishment, buildings and equipment. Its administrative control of the overall budget and its authorship of the service plan,[31] however, should guarantee it some measure of general control over spending, although the Director General also has considerable influence on account of his entitlement to be consulted about his spending estimates prior to the provisional fixing of the budget by the Service Authority,[32] his power to submit a draft service plan[33] and his control of the day-to-day running of the service.

Unlike local police authorities,[34] there is no presumption that the civilian officers and employees of the Service Authority should be under the direction and control of the chief officer,[35] although this may be provided for.[36] Like local police authorities,[37] the Service Authority may appoint non-employees to carry out certain duties on its behalf.[38] Finally, the relationship between the NCIS tripartite parties in respect of mutual aid[39] and collaboration[40] closely resembles the local policing model.[41]

---

[26] *ibid.*, s.11.
[27] *ibid.*, s.16.
[28] *ibid.*, s.20.
[29] *ibid.*, s.19.
[30] Provide these are consistent with the functions of NCIS and do not prejudice its efficiency or effectiveness, *ibid.*, s.24.
[31] *ibid.*, s.4(1).
[32] *ibid.*, Sched.3 para.1(4)(a).
[33] *ibid.*, s.4(3).
[34] Police Act 1996 s.15(2).
[35] Police Act 1997, s.13(1).
[36] *ibid.*, s.13(2).
[37] Police Act 1996, s.17.
[38] Police Act 1997, s.15.
[39] *ibid.*, s.23.
[40] *ibid.*, s.22.
[41] Police Act 1996, ss.24 (mutual aid) and 23 (collaboration).

Apart from the Home Secretary's longstop powers, collaboration can be initiated by either the Service Authority or the Director General, although the consent of the Service Authority is required for the latter. In contrast to the local arrangements for mutual aid, there is no formal provision for agreement between the Service Authority and local police authorities to cover the costs incurred in supplying or receiving mutual aid, although the balance of mutual aid costs might be taken into account by the Service Authority when issuing its annual levy to a police authority under section 17 of the 1997 Act.[42]

Turning finally to the professional police party—the Director General—we observe a similar profile to that of the local chief constable. The Director General is responsible for the direction and control of the service[43]—the contemporary statutory version of chief officer independence.[44] His specific powers include appointment of all or most members of NCIS below assistant chief constable rank,[45] and he is also a key figure in disciplining junior officers.[46] He may take the initiative along with other chief officers in mutual aid[47] or collaboration agreements.[48] Against that, the Director General has less formal control of civilian staff than local chief constables. Additionally, like his local colleagues, he has extensive reporting obligations to the other two tripartite parties and his statutory independence is explicitly qualified by a duty to "have regard to" the service plan[49]—a document over which he has much influence but no final control.

On the face of it, therefore, the NCIS Service Authority has marginally more formal authority than the local police authority, and the Director General marginally less than the local chief constable. That apart, the basic content of the tripartite relationship with regard to NCIS is very similar to the local policing model. Yet this very similarity of form yields a telling difference of substance. It is difficult to avoid the conclusion that the consequence of translating the local tripartite model more or less wholesale to the context of a national policing facility is significantly to enhance the authority of the third party to the relationship— the Home Office. It this translation—or mistranslation—effect, which

---

[42] Uglow and Telford (1997) p. 23.
[43] Police Act 1997, s.10(1).
[44] Police Act 1996, s.10(1). see also chapter four section 2(c)(i).
[45] Police Act 1997, ss.9(8)–(9) and 44.
[46] *ibid.*, s.37(2)(a).
[47] *ibid.*, s.23(1).
[48] *ibid.*, s.22(1).
[49] *ibid.*, s.10(2).

accounts for the third centralising dynamic within the NCIS framework of governance alongside the imbalance of influence in the composition of the Service Authority and the structural marginalisation of the local dimension. As we saw earlier,[50] the managerialist model articulated within the 1994 Act was designed as a means of retaining central "steering" control over a service of significant and unavoidable local diversity, one in which, moreover, greater professional autonomy in policy implementation was being simultaneously encouraged. Translated into the context of a single national service, the managerialism of national objectives, performance indicators and service plans looks less like an understandably robust form of "rule at distance" and more like a belt-and-braces system of proximate control. For a national service, the national managerial framework cannot serve as a template within which local variations may develop, and threatens instead to be an orthodoxy to which the exclusively targeted Service Authority and service is bound to conform. Unlike the equivalent local policing framework, the whole of the centralised audit and inspection effort is aimed solely and unreservedly at this unitary structure. It cannot be treated as an abstraction which misses some of the particular picture for the sake of the general, so justifying significant qualification or elaboration at the point of application.[51] In other words, to return to a debate addressed earlier in this section, the Service Authority has very little option but to comply closely with the dictates of the national managers, notwithstanding the weasel statutory words used to convey this.[52]

(b) The National Crime Squad

The National Crime Squad can be dealt with much more briefly that NCIS, not because it is any less significant a development—arguably it has even greater potential to redraw the map of British policing, but because in its basic governance arrangements it is modelled almost exactly on NCIS.

---

[50] See chapter four, section 1.

[51] In the linear relationship between the three tripartite parties and the control this gives to the centre, there are clear similarities with the statutory arrangements in Northern Ireland, particularly after the Police (Northern Ireland) Act 1998; see chapter six, section 1.

[52] i.e., the "have regard to" formulation in Police Act 1997, s.2(4).

(i) Background

Unlike the statutory NCIS, the statutory NCS had no direct non-statutory predecessor, but like NCIS, it builds upon earlier and less centralised initiatives in the same field. One of the earliest collaborative agreements under the general police governance legislation provided for a network of Regional Crime Squads to deal with drugs[53] and other serious crime which transcended force boundaries or where force resources were insufficient. Established in 1965, each squad was headed by a regional co-ordinator and answerable to a management committee. Responsible for key personnel, financial and organisational decisions, the management committee comprised the chief constables of the region and a representative of the Inspectorate. Standing above the regional framework was a national co-ordinator based in the Home Office and appointed by a national Standing Committee on Regional Crime Squads.[54] The national co-ordinator could advise and assist the regional offices but had no ultimate executive or operational responsibility. Running parallel to this managerial line of accountability was a fainter line of political accountability, with a joint committee of local police authority representatives providing oversight and resources in each region.

The number of officers committed to the RCS system grew significantly over the decades,[55] the regions were reduced from nine to six in the 1990s,[56] and, as noted earlier, elite opinion began to favour a greater degree of national co-ordination. The prospect of a nationally organised force with full operational capacity and executive powers to deal with serious crime, however, presented a more direct challenge to the localist traditions of British policing than did a specialist intelligence-gathering unit such as NCIS. It is no surprise, therefore, that government trod more carefully before announcing a national initiative. It delayed until NCIS had established an initial national foothold and when it finally took the crucial step it insisted that the new body would remain a secondary focus for policing which, in the absence of an exclusive jurisdiction over certain crimes, would not develop into a "British 'FBI' ".[57]

---

[53] The Regional Crime Squads developed dedicated Drugs Units following a recommendation from ACPO's Broome Report in 1985; Association of Chief Police Officers (1985).

[54] Made up of chief officers.

[55] From 839 in 1973 to over 1200 immediately prior to the inception of NCS.

[56] Excluding the Scottish Crime Squad, which is very similar in form but which remained apart from the proto-national structure of Regional Crime Squads, as it would from NCS. See further chapter five, section 3, and subsection (b)(ii) below.

[57] Home Office (1996) para 3.34.

(ii) Mandate and Structure

The statutory functions of NCS suggest greater or lesser degrees of autonomy from other local or central law enforcement agencies. Most autonomously, the primary function of NCS is to prevent and detect serious crime which is of relevance to more than one police area in England and Wales.[58] It may also co-operate with other police forces in the U.K. (including Scottish and Irish forces)in the prevention and detection of serious crime.[59] At the other end of the spectrum, it may also act at the request and in support of NCIS,[60] other police forces in England and Wales,[61] or other law enforcement agencies[62]—including government departments, international police agencies and other non-statutory investigators[63]—in the prevention and detection of serious crime. NCS also has the capacity to institute criminal proceedings.[64] Clearly, then, the first priority of NCS is serious crime in England and Wales, but its activities can extend to the rest of the United Kingdom and beyond on a partnership or support basis.

As of 1st April 1998, NCS absorbed the existing Regional Crime Squads into a national structure, still with regional groups but under the direction and control[65] of a Director General [66] Like his NCIS equivalent, the Director General of NCS has various categories of staff under him, including permanent police members at ACC level,[67] temporary police staff,[68] and civilians—both full members[69] and other officers or employees.[70]

(iii) Governance Arrangements

We identified three reasons why adapting the tripartite system to NCIS has had centralising consequences, and a similar analysis applies to the

---

[58] Police Act 1997, s.48(2).
[59] *ibid.*, s.48(3)(d).
[60] *ibid.*, s.48(3)(b).
[61] *ibid.*, s.48(3)(a).
[62] *ibid.*, s.48(3)(e).
[63] *ibid.*, s.48(4).
[64] *ibid.*, s.48(3)(c).
[65] *ibid.*, s.56(1). The first Director General was Roy Penrose; see Hook (1998).
[66] *ibid.*, ss.52 and 55(1)(a).
[67] *ibid.*, s.55(2)(a).
[68] *ibid.*, s.55(2)(b).
[69] *ibid.*, s.55(1)(c).
[70] *ibid.*, s.58.

governance arrangements put in place for NCS. Despite attempts to dilute the Home Secretary's influence during the passage of the Bill,[71] his direct control over the appointment of independent members and the chair from within the core membership[72] of ten which the NCS Service Authority shares with the NCIS Service Authority [73] entails that central influence is more direct than in the case of local policing. On the other hand, the composition of the non-core membership avoids much of the structural imbalance which affects the NCIS Service Authority. Alongside its core membership the NCS Service Authority has an additional seven members[74] (unless the Home Secretary otherwise provides),[75] six of whom are appointed by local authority members of local police authorities in England and Wales from among their number[76] and the other by ACPO ranks in England and Wales from among their number.[77] The difference in composition reflects not only the absence of any Scottish or Northern Irish representation—due to NCS's lack of direct jurisdiction beyond England and Wales—but also a heavier weighting of local authority members. As in the new local police authorities for England and Wales,[78] the local authority members have majority membership—nine out of seventeen—in recognition of the local and regional roots of the crime squad idea. Thus while professional representation within the core means that the NCS Service Authority, like the NCIS Service Authority, reflects the interests of all three tripartite parties to some extent, the more favourable representation of local authorities means that it speaks much more strongly for local interests.

The final centralising tendency noted in the governance arrangements for NCIS applies equally to NCS. As the following summary of the powers and responsibilities of the NCS tripartite parties shows, managerialist methods are grafted onto a national accountability structure and policing sector in fashion almost identical to the governance of NCIS, and with the same implications for close central direction.

Central government has the now familiar array of strategic, oversight,

---

[71] See *e.g.*, HC Debs, Standing Committee F, February 25 1997.

[72] Police Act 1997, Sched.1, Pt.1 para.2.

[73] *ibid.*, Sched.1, Pt.1

[74] *ibid.*, s.47(2).

[75] *ibid.*, s.47(3) and Sched.1, Pt.III, para.10.

[76] *ibid.*, Sched.1, Pt.III, para.9(b). Local police authority members should ensure that, so far as practicable, the members of the Service Authority they appoint reflect the balance of parties prevailing among local authority members of police authorities as a whole.

[77] *ibid.*, Sched.1, pt.III, para.9(a).

[78] Police Act 1996 s.4; see further chapter four, section 3(B)(i) above.

instructional, personnel, budgetary, regulatory and co-ordination powers, all of which must be exercised so as to promote the effectiveness and efficiency of NCS.[79] Strategically, the Home Secretary may determine objectives for NCS after consulting relevant parties.[80] In the 1999 programme,[81] one objective, which is a reworking of the initial mandate set in 1998,[82] required NCS—in partnership, where appropriate, with other law enforcement agencies—to improve the quality of operations leading to the arrest or prosecution of individuals, or the dismantling or disruption of criminal enterprises engaged in serious and organised crime within or which impacts on the United Kingdom. A second and entirely new objective required NCS, having regard to the Government's ten-year anti-drugs strategy,[83] and in partnership, where appropriate, with other law enforcement agencies, to suppress the availability of controlled drugs in the United Kingdom: (i) by reducing the unlawful manufacture and distribution of controlled drugs within the United Kingdom; (ii) by reducing the quantity of such drugs entering the United Kingdom unlawfully, and (iii) by the arrest and prosecution of individuals leading to the dismantling or disruption of criminal enterprises engaged in serious or organised crime connected with drug trafficking. The Home Secretary may also direct the NCS Service Authority to establish performance targets aimed at achieving these objectives.[84]

As regards oversight and instruction of the other tripartite parties, the Home Secretary may: require an inquiry into NCS by a third party;[85] require reports from the NCS Service Authority[86] and the Director General[87]; issue codes of practice to the Service Authority[88]; instruct the Inspectorate to carry out an inspection of NCS,[89] require subsequent dialogue between the Service Authority and the Director General,[90] and

---

[79] Police Act 1997 s.70.

[80] *ibid.*, s.71.

[81] The National Crime Squad (Secretary of State's Objectives) Order 1999 S.I.1999/821.

[82] S.I. 1998 no.109.

[83] See Her Majesty's Government (1999).This also provides the framework for one of the new local police objectives (see chapter four, section 2(A)(i) above) and for one of the new NCIS objectives (see subsection (A)(iii) above).

[84] Police Act 1997 s.72.

[85] *ibid.*, s.79.

[86] *ibid.*, s.76. The Home Secretary is also a recipient of the NCIS Service Authority's statutory annual report; *ibid.*, s.51(3)(a).

[87] *ibid.*, s.77. The Home Secretary may also require a periodic return of statistics from the Director General; *ibid.*, s.78.

[88] *ibid.*, s.73.

[89] *ibid.*, s.75(1).

[90] *ibid.*, Sched.9, para.77, adding s.55(7) to the Police Act 1996.

compel the Service Authority to take measures to remedy any inefficiency or ineffectiveness.[91] Underpinning many of these capacities, the Home Secretary must approve the appointment of the Director General[92] and may require the Service Authority to compel the Director General or any other NCS member directly appointed by the Service Authority to retire in the interests of efficiency.[93]

As in the case of NCIS, initial funding for NCS is provided by the Home Secretary,[94] but thereafter the Service Authority[95] is responsible for setting a budget financed through a levy on local police authorities,[96] the total amount of which may be varied by the Home Secretary after consulting with representatives of police authorities and chief officers generally.[97] Once again, the Home Secretary is empowered to make an order regarding the calculation and collection of levies,[98] including the terms of apportionment among local police authorities.[99] The prospect of a measure of central financial control, indeed, supplied one of the most significant incentives for government to put the system of crime squads on a statutory footing. The budget of the regional crime squads had been at the mercy of regional committees of police authorities, and a combination of "free rider" anxieties and the ideological reluctance of the town hall to embrace national or proto-national policing institutions meant that only modest resources were available in some areas.[1]

Finally, the Home Secretary acquires additional powers of detailed regulation and co-ordination. He may make regulations relating to the conduct and discipline of NCS members,[2] and also as to standards of equipment.[3] He may make regulations requiring NCS to use specified facilities in common with local police forces in England and Wales where he believes this to be efficient or effective.[4] For the purposes of

---

[91] Police Act 1997 s.75(2).

[92] ibid., s.52(2).

[93] ibid., s.74.

[94] ibid., s.63

[95] Constituted for these purposes only by independent members and police authority members, with a majority of police authority members; ibid., Sched.5 para.1(1)–(2).

[96] ibid., s.62(1). Unlike NCIS, there is no residual funding from Northern Ireland or Scotland.

[97] ibid., Sched. 5 para.2. See further n.93 above in section 2(A)(iii).

[98] ibid., s.62(2).

[99] ibid., s.62(3)(a).

[1] Although other areas, such as the south east, were traditionally well funded; Uglow and Telford (1997) p. 50.

[2] Police Act 1997 s.81.

[3] ibid., s.80.

[4] ibid., Sched.9, para.78, inserting s.57(3A) of the Police Act 1996.

collaboration[5] and mutual aid,[6] NCS is treated like a local police authority, the Home Secretary possessing equivalent default powers to require co-operation where no prior initiative has been taken or agreed between the relevant chief officers and police authorities.

Like its NCIS equivalent, the overriding obligation of the NCS Service Authority is to secure that NCS is efficient and effective.[7] The Service Authority also has the same strategic powers in pursuit of that obligation, including the power, after due consultation,[8] to set objectives[9] which should not be inconsistent with the Home Secretary's national objectives;[10] and, elaborating on these objectives, the power to issue a service plan,[11] the draft of which is prepared by the Director General.[12] In discharging its functions, the Service Authority must "have regard to"[13] this strategic documentation.[14]

The NCS Service Authority also has identical powers to the NCIS Service Authority as regards appointment[15] and dismissal[16] of the Director General and his assistants; receipt of reports from the Director General;[17] setting and administration of the budget,[18] raising money from gifts, loans[19] and charges for services[20] as well as local levies;[21] employment of civilian employees[22] and appointment of non-employees as officers;[23] and initiation of collaboration agreements with local police authorities in England and Wales[24] or the NCIS Service Authority.[25] The NCS Service Authority also shares with local police authorities, but not with the

---

[5] *ibid.*, Sched.9, para.73, inserting s.23(8) of the Police Act 1996.
[6] *ibid.*, Sched.9, para.74, amending s.24(5) of the Police Act 1996.
[7] *ibid.*, s.49(1).
[8] With the Director General of NCS, the NCIS Service Authority and representatives of the interests of local police authorities in England and Wales; *ibid.*, s.49(4).
[9] *ibid.*, s.49(2).
[10] *ibid.*, s.49(3).
[11] *ibid.*, s.50(1).
[12] *ibid.*, s.50(3).
[13] *ibid.*, s.48(5).
[14] An obligation underlined by the Home Secretary's powers under s.75(2).
[15] Police Act 1997 ss.52(2) and 55(9).
[16] *ibid.*, ss.53 and 55(10).
[17] *ibid.*, s.57.
[18] *ibid.*, ss.61–62.
[19] *ibid.*, ss.65 and 69.
[20] *ibid.*, s.62.
[21] *ibid.*, s.62(1).
[22] *ibid.*, s.60.
[23] *ibid.*, ss.58–59.
[24] *ibid.*, Sched.9, para 73, inserting s.23(8) of the Police Act 1996.
[25] *ibid.*, s.22(4)

NCIS Service Authority, the capacity to reach agreements with other police authorities to cover the costs incurred in supplying or receiving mutual aid. [26]

Equally, the position of the Director General of NCS is equivalent to that of his NCIS colleague. Responsible for the direction and control of the service,[27] he appoints non-ACPO ranks and exercises a disciplinary authority over them.[28] The Director General may also take the initiative along with other chief officers in collaboration[29] or mutual aid agreements.[30] On the other hand, although the Director General must be consulted over national[31] and local[32] objectives and drafts the service plan,[33] he has no ultimate authority over any of these strategy documents. Furthermore, the Director General must "have regard to"[34] the service plan in performing his duties and, as we have seen, is obliged to report extensively to the other two tripartite parties.

(c) THE SECURITY SERVICE

Over the last ten years the British security and intelligence services have come "in from the cold"[35] in more ways than one. In 1989 the Security Service,[36] and in 1994[37] the Secret Intelligence Service (SIS)[38] and Government Communications Headquarters (GCHQ)[39] were given statutory baptisms, some ninety years after a security facility was first developed by the War Office in the Liberal administration of Asquith. [40] Statutory recognition coincided with a significant shift in the remit of the secret services generally, and in particular the Security Service—the agency concerned with internal security. Whereas during the Cold War it was primarily concerned with counter-subversion

---

[26] *ibid.*, Sched.9, para.74, inserting s.24(5) of the Police Act 1996.
[27] *ibid.*, s.56(1).
[28] *ibid.*, s.81(2)(a).
[29] *ibid.*, Sched.9, para.73, inserting s.23(8) of the Police Act 1996.
[30] *ibid.*, Sched.9, para.74, inserting s.24(5) of the Police Act 1996.
[31] *ibid.*, s.71(2)(b).
[32] *ibid.*, s.49(4)(a).
[33] *ibid.*, s.50(3).
[34] *ibid.*, s.56(2).
[35] The title of a comprehensive study by Lustgarten and Leigh (1994).
[36] The Security Service Act 1989.
[37] The Intelligence Services Act 1994; see Wadham (1994).
[38] Responsible for external security.
[39] Responsible for the Government listening centres at Cheltenham and elsewhere.
[40] In 1909; see *e.g.*, Bradley and Ewing (1997) chap.24.

and counter-espionage, from the late 1970s onwards, and increasingly during the 1980s and 1990s, its resources were redirected into international and Irish terrorism, culminating in October 1992 in the transfer from the Special Branch to the Security Service of responsibility for leading the intelligence effort against Irish republican terrorism on the British mainland. A combination of the Service's post-Cold War excess capacity—reinforced from the mid 1990s by the move towards political reconciliation in Ireland and the prospect of reduction of the terrorist threat, its experience of collaborating with the police against terrorism, and the determination of Government to mount a multi-strategic offensive against organised crime, produced a climate of policy which favoured the progressive encroachment of the Security Service upon the traditional domain of policing.[41]

Following earlier statutory acknowledgement that the brief of SIS and GCHQ should extend to activity in support of the prevention or detection of serious crime,[42] the Security Service Act 1996 went a step further and exhorted active collaboration by the Security Service with the police service. This "short and startling"[43] measure provided that alongside its existing duties, first, to protect national security, in particular against threats from espionage, terrorism and sabotage, from the activities of foreign powers and from actions intended to overthrow or undermine parliamentary democracy by political, industrial or violent means,[44] and, secondly, to safeguard the economic well-being of the United Kingdom against external threats,[45] the Security Service now also acquired formal authority to act in support of the activities of police forces and other law enforcement agencies in the prevention and detection of serious crime.[46] It further provided that the Director General of the Security Service should make arrangements with the Director General of NCIS for co-ordinating Security Service and police activity.[47]

Jurisdiction over a category of activity as open-textured as "serious crime" clearly announces a significant involvement by the Security Ser-

---

[41] See *e.g.,* Intelligence and Security Committee (1995); Home Office (1996) esp. para.3.33.

[42] Intelligence Services Act 1994 ss. 1 and 3.

[43] O'Higgins (1996).

[44] Security Service Act 1989 s.1(2).

[45] *ibid.,* s.1(3).

[46] Security Service Act 1996, s.1(1), inserting s.1(4) of the Security Service Act 1989.

[47] Security Service Act 1996, s.1(2), as amended by Police Act 1997, s.12, inserting s.2(20)(c) of the Security Service Act 1989. On the police side, this liaison function is located within the Special Projects Branch of the Intelligence Development Division of NCIS; see subsection (A)(ii) above.

vice in law enforcement.[48] Yet while an extensive new field of collaboration has been opened up, beyond the formal liaison arrangement with NCIS this has not been recognised within the relevant governance regimes. Different cultures and regulatory frameworks are juxtaposed, courting confusion, conflict, undesirable cross-influence and evasion of responsibility. An organisation with a broad national security remit is required to work with one mandated to develop intelligence to the more limited end of disrupting or dismantling criminal enterprises and apprehending the entrepreneurs. Equally, an organisation with a weak and low-profile complaints and scrutiny framework,[49] must now stand alongside one boasting a statutory complaints procedure and the comparatively robust standards of accountability associated with tripartitism.

3. Conclusion

What do these three recent national initiatives in operational policing tell us about the overall trend towards national policing and about the appropriateness and adequacy of the governance arrangements which attend these? Clearly there is a powerful incrementalist dynamic at work, not dissimilar to that which is observable in the European

---

[48] Further evidence of the enhanced involvement of the Security Service in policing activities is provided by s.2 of the Security Service Act 1996, which amends s.3 of the Intelligence Services Act to provide that the Security Service, alone of the three secret services, may be granted a warrant by the Home Secretary authorising intrusive action on property *within* the British Islands (i.e. U.K., Channel Islands and Isle of Man) provided it is granted in pursuit of its new duties as regards the prevention and detection of serious crime, and that it relates to certain restricted categories of serious crime.

[49] The introduction of a statutory regime has improved this framework, but it is still open to criticism for its narrow concerns, limited access to information, weak sanctions, restricted capacity to make candid public reports, and questionable independence; see Wadham (1994). The main elements are, first, the Security Service Tribunal (Security Service Act 1989, s.5) and Security Service Commissioner,(*ibid.,* s.4) which handle and monitor complaints about the Security Service, including in the case of the Commissioner monitoring the exercise by the Home Secretary of the power to issue warrants interfering with property, trespassing on land or interfering with wireless telegraphy (*ibid.,* s.3); secondly, the Intelligence and Security Committee, (Intelligence Services Act 1994, s.10) a committee of Parliamentarians—but appointed by the Prime Minister rather than Parliament—charged with oversight of the three services; and, thirdly, non-statutory executive oversight, including review of priorities and performance by a senior Whitehall Committee (SO(SSPP)) and ministerial oversight of funding arrangements. Following the publication of a consultation paper (Home Office 1999d), some aspects of the investigatory powers of the security services and some aspects of their governance system are due to be modified; Regulation of Investigatory Powers Bill 2000.

domain.[50] In a political climate still significantly resistant to the idea of a national police force with full operational capacity and a broad remit, a gradualist approach was always most likely. NCS, the more radical option, was only pursued once the building block of NCIS was firmly in place, allowing the idea of an operational force against organised crime to be portrayed as the natural complement to and progression from a national intelligence capacity. Similarly, it became easier to bring the Security Service in from the cold and add it to the national policing strength once an intermediary such as NCIS was available, as NCIS itself is a hybrid combining the intelligence-led strategies familiar within the secret services with the focus on "normal" crime familiar within traditional police forces.

Further, taken together these initiatives impact on many of the different dimensions of nationalisation discussed at the beginning of the chapter. The development of new national operational units alongside the existing local forces, paradoxically, has also been an exercise in standardisation, with the new managerialist version of tripartitism translated with little variation from local to national context. The new initiatives have also reinforced the corporatist dimension of police governance. Their emergence, NCIS in particular, reflects and reinforces the synergy between two prominent members of the national police community—government and ACPO. The form taken by the new initiatives, too, encourages a dense network of consultation and interaction within the policy community. In some respects, this is about ensuring close co-ordination between NCIS and NCS. Common core membership of the Service Authorities[51] and mutual consultation over the setting of local[52] and national[53] objectives and service plans,[54] and also about the general state of each service,[55] bear testimony to this strategy of co-ordination. More generally, particular institutions within the governance framework already presuppose, and so nurture, a national policy community in which central and local interests are interlocked, as in the tripartite composition of the Service Authorities.[56]

If the nationalising trend is unmistakable and multi-dimensional, it is also increasingly formal. Many have complained about "nationalisation

---

[50] See chapter eight, section 4(a).
[51] Police Act 1997, Sched.1, pt. I, para.1.
[52] *ibid.*, ss.3(4)(c) and 49(40)(b).
[53] *ibid.*, ss.26(2)(e)–(f) and 71(2)(e)–(f).
[54] *ibid.*, ss.4(5)(d)–(e) and 50(5)(d)–(e).
[55] *ibid.*, ss.41 and 85.
[56] *ibid.*, Sched. 1.

by stealth"[57] in recent years. Might, then, the governance arrangements for NCIS and NCS, and the parallel formalization of the security and intelligence services, act as a corrective to this, imposing a considered and transparent institutional design and accountability framework on the key national institutions? In principle, this is a sound proposition. In the particular context in question, however, two caveats have to be entered. First, in a political environment conducive to rapid institutional growth, formalization can be as much an invitation to further expansion as a means of reining in existing institutions. Once granted a certain formal identity and capacity, organisations such as NCIS, NCS and the security and intelligence services have a secure platform from which they may be minded to and capable of expanding their horizons.[58] Secondly, while the constitutional framework may have become generally more alert to police institutional development, it may still suffer from regulatory lag in the sense that it applies an inappropriate and outmoded style of governance. Arguably, as the tortuous efforts to fashion the new Service Authorities indicates, tripartitism is the square peg which is basically suited to a primarily local system of policing, but which does not fit the round hole of national institutions. Just as those who are wary of international policing risk falling into the national sovereignty trap by their reluctance to consider new supranational forms of regulation,[59] arguably those who are wary of national policing risk falling into the localism trap in their reluctance to look beyond the local paradigm of governance to embrace new regulatory mechanisms custom built for national institutions.[60]

---

[57] See *e.g.,* Reiner (1991) chap.1

[58] See also chapter eight, section 4(A) below for a similar discussion of institutional development in Europe.

[59] See chapter eight, section 4(B) below.

[60] The obvious national candidate for an enhanced role in the governance of national policing institutions is the Westminster Parliament itself, in particular its Home Affairs committee which already has an impressive reputation for general security of the Home Office (Reiner and Spencer (1993) p. 185). Reform of Parliament has figured from the outset in New Labour's constitutional reform agenda, although early indications of concrete developments have been modest (Hazell, 1999). In this regard, the devolved assemblies, in particular the Scottish Parliament which has been designed to avoid the excesses of executive domination evident at Whitehall, might serve as an example and an inspiration (see chapter 5, section 3). Such a development would accord with the dynamics of "eclectic governance", discussed in chapter ten, section 3(c).

Chapter Eight

The European Dimension

As we saw in the last chapter, in terms of their origins, domain of activity and institutional relationships, the new national policing institutions face in two different directions. They are linked with developments in local crime patterns and security concerns, local communities and local systems of police organisation, but also with developments in transnational crime patterns and security concerns, transnational communities and transnational systems of police organisation. In the present chapter, we examine the constitutional architecture of transnational policing, concentrating on its most significant and mature component—the European dimension. We begin by assessing the background arguments and pressures for and against the development of transnational policing. We then examine the institutional record, concentrating on the contemporary development of Europol as part of the Third Pillar of the European Union (E.U.). In the second half of the chapter we join the first two strands, suggesting that the distinctive system of governance of European policing is attributable to the interaction of the various background factors with the unique character of the E.U. political order, and that this volatile mix suggests a uncertain future for transnational police regulation.

1. The Boundaries of State Policing

The very idea of European policing—indeed, of any form of transnational policing—might appear incongruous from the state-centred perspective from which the history of policing is typically viewed. Traditionally, the integrity of the state and the viability of the modern police as a specialist institution have been regarded as closely

227

intertwined, even symbiotically linked.[1] This connection is attributable, most fundamentally, to the pattern of coercive authority as it unfolded in the developing European state system after the Peace of Westphalia in 1648. As we have seen,[2] theories of the state, ranging widely from the sixteenth century analyses of the absolutist state by Thomas Hobbes and Jean Bodin to the current century of political sociology originating with Max Weber, have agreed that a key defining feature of statehood is ultimate control over the legitimate use of force, which is exercised to provide and preserve security against internal and external threats.[3] Correspondingly, theories of modern policing have stressed the importance of the specialist organisational form of the police as the vehicle through which the state asserts its title to the internal dimension of security.[4]

A second, and related, reason for the close fit between policing and the modern state has to do with broader matters of governance. As the etymology of the term "police" as a descriptor of a broader range of government administration suggests,[5] the growth of policing has also been closely linked to the unprecedented claim of the modern state from the eighteenth century onwards to provide a *general* programme of detailed regulation of the population with a view to promoting tranquillity and security—or "general order",[6] expediting trade and communication, and enhancing health and prosperity.[7] The role of the police in this wider governance project is performed at two levels; at the foundational level, drawing on the authority of its latent coercive power to guarantee the daily routines of general order which are prerequisite to the pursuit of the more specific goods (trade, communication, *etc.*); and also, to varying degrees and with variable levels of support at different times and places,[8] at the policy generation and implementation levels, involving active co-ordination with, direction of and support or substitution for other agencies in the supply of the more specific state-guaranteed goods.

---

[1] The argument that follows in developed in Loader and Walker (2001, forthcoming).
[2] See chapter one, section 1.
[3] See, *e.g.* Weber (1948); Giddens (1985).
[4] See, *e.g.* Bittner (1971); Reiner (1994); (1997).
[5] See, *e.g.* Pasquino (1991).
[6] Marenin (1992) p. 258.
[7] See, *e.g.* Foucault (1991); Garland (1997a).
[8] For example, community policing, problem-oriented policing and, multi-agency policing are but three modern labels which seek to describe and develop a more expansive version of the police project, actively engaged in public policy-making.

A third link between police and state is symbolic rather than instrumental. Because policing has been pivotal to the security of the state and integral to its project of governance, control over policing institutions has become central to the political and constitutional integrity of the state—a jealously guarded incident of its sovereign authority. In earlier chapters we noted the ideological connection between policing and sovereignty in the context of the challenge to the authority of the United Kingdom in Scotland and, more especially, in Northern Ireland. Yet what is true of the re-configuration of authority *within* a state, as in the Scottish case, or of disputed authority *between* states, as in the Irish case, is also true of the general dispersal of authority *away* from the state to the transnational domain.

A related symbolic link is cultural in kind. The development of the political form of the modern state since the eighteenth century has not just been about the harnessing of coercive power, the sponsorship of a more ambitious conception of governance and the delineation of sovereign authority. In many instances, the modern form of the state, additionally, has provided a framework to nurture and sustain the collective identity of the nation. The development of policing, therefore, has also become interwoven with this wider project—the police officer or police institution often providing an important aspect of the iconography of the *nation* state.[9]

If, in the ways set out above, "police organisations around the world have had nation states as their nesting sites",[10] this suggests limited scope for transnational policing to flourish. Yet from the outset, modern policing as it has developed within the nourishing capsule of the nation state has been accompanied by a range of policing practices which cut across national boundaries. This ever-expanding transnational field has both professional and political roots.

Professionally, police officers and police institutions have always cultivated international contacts, however informally.[11] Partly, this has to do with the practicalities of law enforcement. Just as the mobility of populations and the reach of criminal acts, strategies and networks across state boundaries inevitably encourages the exchange of criminal intelligence, there is a corresponding supply of operational mutual assistance. The willingness of police officers to co-operate is underscored by cultural factors. While the traditional focus of policing on the neighbourhood community and the sense of loyalty to the "local patch" might in certain

---

[9] See, *e.g.*, Walker (1996a); (1996c); Loader (1997a); Emsley (1999).
[10] Sheptycki. (1998a) p. 498.
[11] See, *e.g.*, Nadelman (1993) chap. 1.

circumstances discourage the generation of the mutual trust, interest and understanding required to forge transnational links,[12] policing also has a social meaning which transcends state boundaries and which encourages transnational solidarity. In every culture policework is "dirty work"[13]— an activity which many citizens find socially necessary but unpalatable, and so consign to the margins of their consciousness. Further, the impersonal authority of the state borne by police officers builds an imbalance of power into every operational encounter, so exacerbating the social distance between them and the public.[14] For these reasons police officers tend to turn inwards to their own professional corps and are well equipped to empathise with the experiences of other officers, regardless of national context.

For more positive reasons, too, police officers may be receptive to the overtures of foreign colleagues. A strong sense of vocation and a keen perception of the centrality of their function to the maintenance of the fragile bonds of social order[15] are traits which encourage mutual respect and reliance amongst police officers and which facilitate understanding across frontiers of the burdens of professional responsibility. It is, moreover, not insignificant that since, as we shall see, transnational police officers and institutions by and large lack operational capacity, their efforts, accentuating a trend also evident within states, are increasingly focused upon IT-based "knowledge work."[16] They are primarily concerned with the "collection, collation and dissemination"[17] within "informated space"[18] of knowledge about specific cases or general patterns of insecurity or of security risk, and this shared technocratic imperative provides an additional basis for bonding across national borders.[19]

Politically, transnational links are encouraged for a number of reasons. Just as police officers find pragmatic grounds for informal co-operation, sovereign states find pragmatic grounds for formal co-operation in bilateral and multilateral arrangements to allow informational exchange, operational support or liaison between their separate police organisations and mutual assistance between their discrete criminal justice systems.

---

[12] See, *e.g.,* Walker (1993a).

[13] Harris (1973) p. 3.

[14] See, *e.g.,* Reiner (1992) pp. 115–117.

[15] *ibid.,* pp. 111–114

[16] Ericson, (1994) pp. 149–176.

[17] Sheptycki, (1998b) p. 71, n.2.

[18] *ibid.,* p. 60.

[19] Although Sheptycki (198b, pp. 66–70) notes that even within this specialist context there is scope for the development of a number of different policing styles and attitudes.

Even in those areas, such as terrorism and other forms of political crime, where a direct threat to the "specific order"[20] of the state is posed and where the state is most jealous of its policing prerogative, the international context in which many such crimes are planned and perpetrated encourages co-operation. This is facilitated by the fact that the framework of criminal law which defines the boundaries of order—both general and specific—shows a remarkable similarity from one state to the next, providing a common normative register in terms of which co-operation may proceed.[21]

Co-operation may also be encouraged for strategic reasons. The development of an international agenda on law enforcement presents new opportunities for national governments engaged in "law and order" politics. In matters of internal security the flip-side of the robust assertion of state sovereignty tends to be an uncomfortably intense public concentration on national governments as exclusively or predominantly responsible for the success of criminal justice policy.[22] The opening up of a transnational policy arena may displace a measure of political responsibility upwards to the wider policy community. It may, moreover, provide leverage to home affairs departments engaged in the domestic politics of competitive resource allocation to seek the deployment of extra resources towards the new international security agenda.

Increasingly, however, the politics of transnational police co-operation are not only about the assertion of state sovereignty. They also reflect the gradual emergence of a new global order in which the nation state is no longer the unrivalled unit of political authority, but is challenged by new transnational or supranational regulatory regimes such as the United Nations, the North American Free Trade Association (NAFTA),[23] and the European Union (E.U.). These new entities claim authority of a type traditionally associated with state sovereignty and may even seek to wear the label of sovereignty. This shift has been most profound, and with the most significant consequences for policing, in the context of the E.U. As we shall see in the final section of the chapter, however, it is important

---

[20] Marenin (1982) p. 258.

[21] It is this common register which has made possible the proliferation of extradition and mutual legal assistance treaties in and beyond the E.U. in recent years, a development which complements the growth in police co-operation. For a recent overview, see Cullen and Gilmore (1998).

[22] See, *e.g.* Garland (1996); (1997b).

[23] On policing and security developments associated with the development of NAFTA, which in its present form embraces United States, Canada and Mexico, see for example Taylor (1992); Andreas (1996).

to view the E.U. as but one instance of a global trend towards the relocation of political authority in multiple levels of governance and in non-state sites, in which altered framework policing and its regulation is no longer securely domiciled within the nation state.[24]

2. Institutional Development

How has the opposition between the statist tradition in policing and the growing social forces in favour of police connections between and beyond nation states been resolved in practice? In addressing this question, we examine the continuities and discontinuities between early initiatives and the emerging formal regime of E.U. police co-operation.

(A) EARLY FORMS

The earliest concerted attempt to institutionalise transnational policing involved a series of initiatives amongst European states in the late nineteenth century to secure co-operation in the fight against terrorism, revealing a common concern to address the danger posed to national security by nationalist and socialist revolutionary movements.[25] In contrast, with the exception of mutual extradition treaties and cross-border controls, for which the regulatory authority of government was indispensable, early forms of co-operation with regard to "ordinary crime" tended to involve professionals—lawyers, academics and police officers—rather than politicians. The predominance of professionals was reflected in the organisation of the first permanent international agency—the International Criminal Police Commission (ICPC)—established in Vienna in 1923. Both the ICPC and its post-Second World War successor, the French-based International Criminal Police Office (ICPO)—or Interpol, as it soon became known—supplied a communication network for the participating national police organisations, as well as providing a "policeman's club"[26] in which senior officers could cultivate social and professional contacts with international colleagues. Formal international legal agreements prepared between state authorities were conspicuous by their absence from the foundations of these organisations, and, with the

---

[24] See, e.g., Walker (1999a); Loader (2000); Loader and Walker (2000a, forthcoming).
[25] Fijnaut (1991) p. 104.
[26] Anderson (1989) p. 43.

notable exception of the Nazi take-over of the ICPC in 1938, the involvement of governments in these organisations remained "minor or low-key".[27]

Today, Interpol has expanded its activities significantly. Its membership, originally nineteen, has grown tenfold. Through its network of National Central Bureaux (NCBs) located in each participating state,[28] it has exploited new forms of information technology to expedite and broaden its flow of communications between national forces. It has attempted to rationalise and augment its activities in the crucial European field within a separate organisational unit.[29] Yet these advances have been made with little formalisation of the position of Interpol in international law. Although successive Headquarters Agreements with the French Government in 1972 and 1982 endowed Interpol with independent legal status and underlined its recognition in practice as an international organisation by bodies such as the UN and the Council of Europe (CoE),[30] it still lacks a proper Treaty basis.[31]

Such has been the overall expansion of the network of transnational policing in the last 30 years that Interpol is no longer the main player. Its influence has been lessened by two developments in particular. First, there is the marked internationalisation of United States law enforcement. The United States was slow to become involved in matters of law enforcement, partly for reasons of geography and partly because of the fragmented nature of its national law enforcement effort and the attendant difficulties of identifying the most appropriate and legitimate representative of federal law enforcement interests. However, particularly since the explosion of international drug-trafficking in the 1960s and 70s and President Nixon's declaration of a "war on drugs", there has been a sharp increase in activity, only a modest proportion of which is realised in greater American involvement in Interpol.[32] Instead, internationalisation of American criminal justice policy is most marked in the increased concentration of resources upon international work in existing federal law enforcement agencies dealing with drugs, internal revenue, organised

---

[27] *ibid.*, p 37.

[28] The U.K. NCB is situated in the National Criminal Intelligence Service (NCIS).

[29] See, *e.g.*, Anderson, den Boer, Cullen, Gilmore, Raab and Walker,(1995) pp. 49–53.

[30] See *e.g.*, Anderson (1989), pp. 57–73.

[31] This has been recognised by Interpol's senior management, which has indicated support for the negotiation of a new convention; see, *e.g.*, Anderson, den Boer, Cullen, Gilmore, Raab and Walker (1995) p. 251.

[32] Although between 1967 and 1991, the U.S. national central bureau of Interpol increased its staff from 6 to 110; Nadelman, (1993) p. 3.

crime, immigration, *etc.*, including the widespread placement of liaison officers, training units and other support agencies in embassies and law enforcement institutions abroad.[33]

Unlike the American intervention, the second major development is not dominated by bilateral arrangements, but involves multilateral, and increasingly, supranational initiatives. It has taken place within the European field, particularly within the E.U., undoubtedly the most ambitious experiment the modern world has seen in polity-building beyond the state. Yet the beginnings were inauspicious. While the Pompidou Group pioneered policy-level collaboration in the area of drug-trafficking, the Trevi organisation provide the first major initiative in the policing field in 1975, a full eighteen years after the signing of the Treaty of Rome, the foundational document of the supranational organisation which was eventually to become the European Union.[34] Although, like Interpol, Trevi lacked a formal treaty basis, it provided a forum for member states to develop common measures with regard to counter-terrorism, and later, with regard also to drugs, organised crime, police training and technology and a range of other matters. The intensification of Trevi's activities coincided with the development of the European Commission's Single Market Programme after 1985. Whereas previously, Trevi had been isolated from the mainstream of Community policy-making, now its priorities were integral to the doctrine of compensatory measures through which the Co-ordinator's Group on the Free Movement of Persons responded to the "security deficit" of open internal frontiers.[35]

A second important step towards a European law enforcement capacity, the Schengen system, is even more closely associated with the Single Market initiative. The initial Schengen Agreement of 1985 embraced a core of five member states who wished to take the initiative in abolishing border controls and so accelerate the completion of the internal market. A more detailed Implementation Agreement of 1990 established a number of associated law enforcement measures including the computerised Schengen Information System (SIS) and police co-operation not only as regards the exchange of information and intelligence, but also in more concrete operations such as "hot pursuit", cross-border observation and controlled delivery of illegal drugs. After various false dawns, the Strasbourg-centred organisation eventually became operational in March 1995, although even then a zone

[33] See, *e.g.*, Nadelman, (1993), chaps 2–3, Anderson, (1989), chap. 2.
[34] Treaty on European Union (TEU) [1993] O.J. C224.
[35] See *e.g.*, Anderson, den Boer, Cullen, Gilmore, Raab and Walker (1995) chap. 4.

234

entirely free of permanent border controls was not immediately achieved amongst the seven fully participating members. Despite these problems, Schengen's sphere of influence grows ever wider. All except the United Kingdom and Ireland of the fifteen members of the E.U. have now joined and are at various stages of the implementation process,[36] while the two non-E.U. members of the Nordic Passport Union—Norway and Iceland—have been granted associate status. Further, as explained below, recent developments in the E.U. Treaty architecture have reversed the long-standing assumption that the gradual extension of the frontier-free regime of the internal market would lead to the eclipse of Schengen by the E.U. acting as a whole

Unlike Interpol and Trevi, Schengen does possess a formal legislative basis in international law. However, like the other two bodies, it has attracted sustained criticism for its weak legislative and judicial accountability.[37] Its Executive Committee, comprising one government minister from each Schengen state, has key responsibility for implementing the Convention, but its decision-making is largely in private, and there is no provision for systematic national parliamentary scrutiny of measures prior to their adoption. What is more, many of the decisions of the Executive Committee and many of the activities of Schengen agencies, in particular SIS, bear directly on individual rights and freedoms, but there is no central judicial authority to ensure consistent interpretation and application of Convention provisions.

(B) THE THIRD PILLAR AND EUROPOL

(i) The Maastricht Treaty Framework

While Trevi and Schengen represent noteworthy advances in the development of a European law enforcement capacity, in terms of breadth of jurisdiction, institutional authority and scope for further development,[38] the European Police Office (Europol) constitutes the most ambitious plan yet conceived in this field. Its foundations are laid in the Maastricht Treaty on European Union of 1992, which included policing within a

---

[36] The target date for the final wave of implementation—by the Nordic members (Sweden, Denmark and Finland)—October 2000.

[37] See, *e.g.* House of Lords (1998) Part 4B.

[38] Although at its present stage of development it lacks the operational powers of Schengen; but see section four below.

new Third Pillar[39] of E.U. competence over Justice and Home Affairs (JHA).[40] Whereas Trevi, to which the Third Pillar is the institutional successor, was an intergovernmental arrangement in the shadow of the "official" Europe, and Schengen was the separate international organisation of an inner core, the Third Pillar was built into the stonework of the new E.U.

Under the Third Pillar, there is an elaborate administrative structure—originally spanning five organisational levels. Beneath two familiar Community executive organs—the Council of E.U. Justice and Interior Ministers and the Committee of Permanent Representatives (Coreper)—lies the Article 36 (previously K4)[41] Committee, which comprises permanent representatives of the justice and interior ministries of the member states. In turn, the Article 36 committee has generated a number of sub-groups which constitute the lower levels of the hierarchy. Initially, there were three steering groups, one dealing with police and customs co-operation and the others with immigration and asylum and with judicial co-operation in criminal and civil matters respectively. This fourth tier of decision-making was abolished under the Luxembourg Presidency of the E.U. in the second half of 1997, but the various specialist Working Groups which had been formed under each of these functional heads, remain, and indeed have expanded in number. In the area of police co-operation these include permanent groups on Europol, police co-operation (more generally), police technology, terrorism and drugs.[42]

The Third Pillar structure has spawned various initiatives, ranging from the adoption of high-profile Conventions to new networks of exchange of information and ideas on practical issues. The focal initiative in policing, however, has remained Europol, the development of which was in fact one of the few clearly stated *specific* objectives of the Third Pillar.[43] Yet the history of the birth of Europol offers an instructive example of the halting progress of co-operation under the Third

---

[39] The informal term for JHA co-operation coined during the negotiation of the Maastricht Treaty, with the Second Pillar representing common foreign and security policy and the First Pillar representing the traditional economic core of the single market, *etc.*, regulated through the classical system of E.C. law in accordance with the principles of sovereignty and direct effect.

[40] See, *e.g.*, Peers (2000) chap. 9.

[41] This reflected the authorising provision under the original Treaty of Maastricht. Article 36 refers to the authorising provision under the revised Title VI introduced by the Treaty of Amsterdam O.J. C 340 1997.

[42] For a full list, see European Parliament (2000) Vol. 2 p. 133.

[43] See, *e.g.*, Monar (1998).

Pillar generally. Maastricht projected Europol as a system of exchange of information and experience for the purposes of preventing and combating terrorism, drug trafficking and other serious crimes within the E.U., and as a means of providing co-operation in aid of criminal investigations and analyses more generally.[44] Some, including Chancellor Kohl of Germany,[45] envisaged the new organisation as providing the template for an American-style FBI, with a key operational role in particular investigations. However, in the first generation of the Third Pillar and Europol at least, a more limited remit was endorsed. Europol's basic structural design would consist of a central organisation in a network of relationships with a "national unit"[46] in each member state—in the case of the United Kingdom the National Criminal Intelligence Service (NCIS).[47] The central organisation would supply the national units with criminal intelligence and analysis and would receive from them information on themes and issues connected with certain forms of transnational crime.

If the ambitions of some parties concerning the depth of the new policing capacity were frustrated, so, too, their expectations as to the speed of progress were disappointed. Again, the German Government was prominent in advocating the early negotiation and establishment of Europol, but it was soon evident that agreement would be achieved only in modest increments. Indeed, the early negotiating objective was a limited one, to set up the Europol Drugs Unit (EDU) as a precursor to a fully-fledged Europol. But even here the timetable slipped. Originally intended to be established by the end of 1992, the EDU did not become operational at The Hague until November 1993, and it was not until 1995 that it was granted formal recognition under the Third Pillar as a joint action.[48] By that time, the remit of the fledging organisation had been extended beyond drug-trafficking and associated criminal organisations and money laundering activities to cover nuclear crime, illegal immigration networks and international vehicle crime, and it was further extended in December 1996 to cover traffic in human beings for sexual and other purposes.[49] Despite the extension of the breadth of the EDU's

---

[44] The following Treaty references and unless otherwise specified those for the remainder of this subsection, are to the now repealed Title VI of the Treaty of Maastricht; Art. K.1(9) and Declaration on Police Co-operation, TEU.

[45] A variety of different positions were advanced by the negotiating parties prior to the agreement on police co-operation in the Treaty of Maastricht, and, subsequently, in the Europol Convention; see Bigo (1996) pp. 224–243.

[46] Europol Convention ([1995] O.J. C316) Art. 4.

[47] See chapter seven

[48] [1995] O.J. L62/1, (March 20).

[49] [1996] O.J. L342/4.

competence, the depth of it powers over these matters remained strictly limited. While it provided a focus for liaison officers from each state to exchange information and provide mutual support for police investigations with a transnational element in the various jurisdictions, there was no power to hold personal data centrally and to allow the EDU as an *independent* entity to communicate criminal data with third states and organisations.

The full Europol Convention, which conferred these additional powers, and which also supplied a mechanism for the wide-ranging extension of the criminal jurisdiction of Europol beyond the EDU core provided these crimes involved an "organised criminal structure",[50] was not ultimately signed until July 1995, following protracted debate over the mandate and powers of a mature Europol and over the adequacy of its data protection systems and its framework of legal and political accountability. Even then, there were a number of obstacles to overcome before the process of ratification and implementation could be completed. Given its Eurosceptic stance, the United Kingdom had opposed any role for the European Court of Justice—the EU's "Supreme Court"—throughout the negotiation of the Convention, and when a solution was eventually found in a protocol of July 1996, it effectively took the form of an agreement to differ.[51] The United Kingdom would not itself recognise the jurisdiction of the Court, but acknowledged the right of the other fourteen member states to accept its jurisdiction over a limited range of questions. However, important questions about the legal capacity and immunities of Europol officials and about the powers of the central data protection agency—the Joint Supervisory Board—remained unresolved, delaying the formal implementation of the Convention until October 1998, and even then preventing its operationalization until July 1999.

The structural arrangements under the Third Pillar which govern the establishment, operation and accountability of Europol and other forms of police co-operation were a peculiar hybrid, particularly in their initial Maastricht shape. They are not, and have never been pure intergovernmental co-operation in the mode of Trevi, since E.U. institutions have always been involved at a number of points. Neither, however, are they part of European Community law in the same way as the First Pillar. The new co-operative structures notwithstanding,[52] the member states retain

---

[50] Europol Convention Art. 2(1).

[51] Protocol on the interpretation, by way of preliminary rulings, by the Court of Justice of the European Communities of the Europol Convention; O.J. C299/1.

[52] Art. K2(2) TEU; and see now, new Art.33 TEU.

ultimate control over decision-making with regard to the maintenance of law and order and the safeguarding of internal security, and so also, in theory at least, ultimate accountability for those matters should continue to be owed to member state institutions.[53] Relatedly, the E.U. continues to lack direct legislative competence in JHA matters. More generally, the balance of influence between E.U. institutions and member states in the policy process continues to favour the latter. Thus, under Maastricht, the major E.U. institutions (Commission, Parliament and Court of Justice) other than the most state-dominated (the Council of Ministers), were less central to the Third Pillar than to the traditional First Pillar, where the Union has full legislative, executive and judicial authority.

In the absence of direct legislative competence, the Council under Maastricht nevertheless has various types of decision-making authority, namely joint positions, joint actions and conventions.[54] While the development of specific instruments was an important advance upon the "soft" law of Trevi, doubts remained over their efficacy. Joint positions and joint actions borrowed the terminology of the Second Pillar, but were less obviously suited to a jurisdiction which by its nature favours "legislative action rather than external posture".[55] Further, they were subject to the requirement of Council unanimity, thereby ensuring that progress could only be made at the pace of the most reluctant member state. Third Pillar conventions occupy the firmer legal ground of classical public international law, but, under Maastricht, they required not only unanimity within the Council but also ratification by all Member States in accordance with their domestic constitutional requirements.

A similarly mixed picture emerges from an examination of the relevant institutional competences. The Commission was " fully associated with"[56] the work of the Third Pillar. Yet in contrast to its role under the First Pillar, the Commission did not enjoy exclusive powers to propose the adoption of legislative measures. Indeed, as regards the key areas of judicial co-operation in criminal matters, customs co-operation and police co-operation, it had no right of initiative whatsoever.[57] The European Parliament was consulted on "principal aspects of [JHA] activities",[58] yet, while it could also ask questions of the Council and

---

[53] See section four below.

[54] Art. K3(2) TEU.

[55] Monar (1998) p. 330.

[56] Art. K.4(2) TEU.

[57] Art. K.3(2) TEU; in the other Third Pillar areas, it shared the power of initiative with the member states.

[58] Art. K.6 TEU.

make recommendations to it, the Parliament lacked the significant role in the law-making process and in the monitoring of executive power which it had gradually acquired under the First Pillar. Accordingly, while the Parliament, particularly through its Committee on Civil Liberties and Internal Affairs, sought from the outset an active role in consultation and oversight, it was often frustrated in its efforts. Indeed, it was particularly critical of the failure of member states to consult it on the Europol Convention,[59] and its similar disappointment over lack of input into the important Action Plan on Organized Crime of 1997[60] indicates the absence of any clear trend of improvement.[61] As for the Court of Justice, its initial jurisdiction under the Third Pillar "to interpret . . . the provisions [of conventions] and to rule on any disputes regarding their application"[62] was not compulsory, as it was under the First Pillar. Rather, as the example of the Europol Convention indicates, it depended on the terms of the Convention in question. Accordingly, the authority of the court was likely to remain limited and uneven.

While it marked a qualitative shift from the informality of the pre-Maastricht era, the first generation of Third Pillar activity in general and police co-operation in particular has tended to attract two kinds of criticism. On the one hand, the Third Pillar has been criticised as being unduly authoritarian in its policy orientation.[63] On this view, it has demonstrated an excessive concern with repressive instruments of security and order, an emphasis supported by the marginalization of those European institutions most concerned with democratic accountability and the protection of individual rights, namely the Parliament and the ECJ. On the other hand, it has been criticised as ineffectual; as an unduly complex and cumbersome framework whose early record suggests that it will be unable to deliver a significant policy programme. Early progress on the conclusion and ratification of conventions—the highest legal instrument under the Third Pillar—was slow and uneven; as regards other less formal decision-making mechanisms, although joint actions became increasingly popular, joint positions were almost entirely neglected, and there developed a tendency to fall back instead upon

---

[59] See Anderson, den Boer, Cullen, Gilmore, Raab and Walker (1995) pp. 255–258.
[60] [1997] O.J. C251.
[61] European Parliament (1997).
[62] Art. K.3(2) TEU.
[63] See, *e.g.*, the consistent critique offered by the Statewatch organisation, both in its bi-monthly Bulletin and various other publications, and in its campaigning activities.

familiar non-binding measures of intergovernmental action such as resolutions, statements and conclusions.[64]

(ii) "Maastricht II"—The Amsterdam Treaty

These criticisms gathered momentum during the period leading up to
the 1996 Intergovernmental Conference to discuss reform of the treaty
framework, with all the E.U. institutions, including the normally sceptical Council, admitting that there was a case for greater involvement of
E.C. institutions to improve effectiveness and accountability.[65] The concerns were reflected in the Reflection Group report, and ultimately, in
the draft Treaty of Amsterdam itself.

Signed in October 1997, and implemented in May 1999, this latest
adornment to the architecture of the E.U. substantially alters the context
within which the emerging system of police co-operation will henceforth be shaped. It introduces a new Treaty chapter on the so-called
"area of freedom, security and justice". The new chapter contains both
a new First Pillar title on visas, asylum, immigration and other matters
related to free movements of persons, most of which competences have
been transferred from the Maastricht Third Pillar, and a revised and trun-
cated Third Pillar restricted to police and customs co-operation and judicial co-operation in criminal matters.

This new dual structure within justice and home affairs might seem to
distance policing yet further from the mainstream of E.U. governance. As
one of the few non-transferred matters, it does not share the majority-
voting procedures, the exclusive policy-making role of the Commission
and the system of parliamentary and judicial supervision associated with
the First Pillar. Yet within the limits set by the retention of the multi-
pillar structure, there is some recognition of a more extensive and more
integrated European policing capacity. Reflecting the aspirations agreed
in the E.U.'s Action Plan on Organised Crime of April 1997, police co-
operation is extended to cover some aspects of "operational co-operation
between the competent authorities, including the police, customs and
other specialised law enforcement services of the Member States."[66] In
consequence, Europol is allocated a range of new functions, including
the authority to establish joint operational teams to support national

---

[64] See, *e.g.*, Meyring (1997).
[65] See, *e.g.* De Burca (1996); Walker (1998d).
[66] Art. 30(1)(a) TEU.

investigations,[67] the power to ask the competent authorities of the Member States to conduct and co-ordinate investigations in specific cases, and the capacity to develop specific expertise which may be put at the disposal of member states to assist them in investigating organised crime.[68]

Moreover, this extended police jurisdiction applies within an institutional context less distinct than previously from that of the First Pillar. The decision-making authority of the Council is reinforced, with "framework decisions for the purpose of approximation of the laws and regulations of the Member States"[69] joining Third Pillar conventions as available legislative mechanisms, and other non-legislative "decisions"[70] (which replace joint actions) joining common positions as the proper vehicle for decisions which are less general or less formal. The utility of this new decision-making regime is underlined by a modest departure from the unanimity principle which previously applied without exception in the Third Pillar. The double-lock on conventions is relaxed slightly to allow their entry into force once adopted by at least half of the member states,[71] while measures implementing both conventions and non-legislative decisions may now be passed by special majority.[72] The consultative role of the European Parliament in policy-making is clarified and strengthened by a requirement that they be allowed at least three months by the Council to deliver opinions on draft onventions and decisions.[73] The Commission acquires the same authority as the member states to propose initiatives to the Council.[74]

The Court of Justice is also the recipient of new powers, as general provision is made for it decide Third Pillar cases. However, the jurisdiction of the court is only compulsory: (i) in actions brought by the Commission or a member state to review the legality of Council decisions and framework decisions; (ii) in actions between member states in dispute over the interpretation and application of any of the forms of Council decision; and (iii) in actions between member states and the Commission where there is a dispute over the meaning and application of Conventions.[75] Significantly, in a qualification strongly advocated by the United

---

[67] Art. 30(2)(a) TEU.
[68] Art. 30(2(b) TEU.
[69] Art. 34(2)(b) TEU.
[70] Art. 34(2)(c) TEU.
[71] Art. 34(2)(d) TEU.
[72] Art. 34(2)(c)–(d) TEU
[73] Art. 39(1) TEU.
[74] Art. 34(2) TEU.
[75] Art. 35(6)–(7) TEU.

Kingdom at the IGC, jurisdiction is not compulsory instead requiring a general declaration by the member state in the vital area of preliminary rulings on issues arising in domestic court proceedings concerning the validity and interpretation of the various decisions and implementing measures.[76] Not only does this deprive the Court of Justice of a key mechanism to ensure Union-wide uniformity of interpretation of Third Pillar law, but in those states which have chosen not to opt-in, including the United Kingdom, it also closes off the only avenue available to individuals to challenge actions under the Third Pillar. Even in Member States in which the preliminary ruling jurisdiction is accepted, the court is explicitly prohibited from adjudicating on the validity or proportionality of the operations of domestic police forces and other law enforcement agencies, or of the exercise by member states of their responsibilities with regard to the preservation of law and order and internal security.[77] A broad reading of this provision could leave the court with little scope for intervention, since the thrust of police co-operation under the Third Pillar is precisely to safeguard the internal security of the member states. For example, it is unclear to what extent, if at all, the court could act to protect an individual aggrieved by the operational actions of "joint teams" of Europol representatives, or by investigations of domestic police agencies requested by Europol.[78]

Finally, the principle of uniformity of treatment of justice and home affairs matter established at Maastricht, and already compromised by the transfer of some functions to the First Pillar, is further undermined by the incorporation of the Schengen system into the new dual justice and home affairs structure. This reaffirmation and "communitization" of Schengen flows from the decision at Amsterdam to allow Britain and Ireland to retain their border controls within the E.U.[79] while allowing the other member states to proceed at their own pace, and with the full authority of the E.U., to manage the security implications of the abolition of such controls.[80] As the competences of Schengen cut across the new division within the justice and home affairs structure, one consequence of the new flexibility is to provide Britain and Ireland with an

---

[76] Art. 35(1)–(2) TEU.

[77] Art. 35(5) TEU.

[78] Monar (1998) p. 332.

[79] Protocol on the application of certain aspects of Article 7a of the Treaty establishing the European Community to the United Kingdom and to Ireland (Protocol B3); Protocol on the Position of the United Kingdom and Ireland (Protocol B4).

[80] Protocol integrating the Schengen Acquis into the framework of the European Union (Protocol B2).

"opt out" in respect of Schengen-associated policing measures.[81] As we shall see,[82] this and other elements of "variable geometry" within the field of European police regulation demonstrate that the present structure—with Europol at its apex—offers no more than a provisional design for the new European policing order, and reinforces doubts about the susceptibility of the emergent system to adequate regulatory control.

3. Tensions within the Emergent Order

In accounting for the unprecedented yet uneven progress towards a "state-like" policing capacity within the E.U. we are faced with a paradox. Some of the relevant explanatory factors refer to the growth of transnational policing *between* states while others, in contrast, refer to the resilience of the notion of policing as a domestic function *of* the state. This paradox derives from the ambiguous political status of the E.U. Insofar as it retains the attributes of a classical international organisation, the well-worn pragmatic explanations for transnational co-operation— or "intergovernmentalism"—are appropriate. Yet insofar as it has acquired some of the characteristics of a state, the arguments which link policing to the state become relevant. In turn, this explanatory duality is reflected in the peculiarly hybrid quality of Third Pillar institutions in general and the policing provisions in particular. As we have seen, more pronouncedly than any of the other aspects of the political architecture of the E.U., the Third Pillar sends conflicting messages about its political pedigree. The Third Pillar, unlike its predecessor Trevi, is part of the institutional machinery of the E.U., but stands at some remove from the First Pillar. The more integrationist constitutional organs of the new European order—Parliament, Commission and Court of Justice have a role to play in the Third Pillar, but less significant than in other areas. The Third Pillar confers institutional autonomy and some operational powers upon E.U. policing, but in contrast to other areas of European policy reserves supreme law-making and executive authority to the member states.

What, then, are the conflicting factors which have left European policing under the Third Pillar delicately poised between classic intergovernmentalism and supranational polity-building? On the side of

---

[81] See House of Lords (1998).
[82] See section 4 below; see also Den Boer (1999); (2000).

intergovernmentalism, there have been numerous incentives for the sovereign states to engage in pragmatic co-operation, including the common threat of international terrorism in the 1970s, the subsequent growth of "clandestine markets"[83] in drugs and other forms of organised crime, the development of international computerised financial transactions and associated crimes, and increasing concern in all Western European countries about patterns of immigration.[84] Further, as stubbornly high official crime rates and the findings of successive victimisation studies render increasingly implausible the myth of the capacity of the bounded state to provide "sovereign crime control",[85] the fostering of a new international agenda against matters which appear to challenge the social, economic and political order of the state as profoundly as terrorism, drug-trafficking, money laundering and organised crime is of strategic value to beleaguered national authorities in reallocating part of the political burden of crime control beyond the state. As noted earlier, the construction of a new site for crime control projects, unsullied by association with past failures and disappointments at national level, also provides a basis from which fresh support and new resources for the security project can be mobilised.

At the professional level, too, the Third Pillar has been welcomed and supported by the transnational police community. In one sense, the new structure might seem to challenge rather than enhance practitioner autonomy and influence. After all, the Third Pillar announces a formalisation of law enforcement co-operation, which implies *subordination* of the work of the operational professional to a framework of legal and political control. In practice, however, the ideological context, organisational structure and policy innovation of the Third Pillar encourage the thickening of transnational professional networks. Ideologically, as we shall see, a number of the main political discourses associated with European police co-operation provide a favourable context for the linkage of a wide range of issues in and around policing—drugs, organised crime terrorism, smuggling, immigration, asylum—which previously had been treated separately. Organisationally, this is acknowledged in the wide-ranging structure of the Third Pillar which broadens and strengthens professional connections, especially at the lower levels of the bureaucratic machinery. Indeed, as the Third Pillar has matured, the influence of police and other law enforcement

---

[83] Sheptycki (1998b) p. 93.
[84] See, *e.g.*, Guyomarch (1997) pp. 123–50, 137–41.
[85] Garland (1996) p. 445.

practitioners has become more pronounced, with Britain setting an early example, since followed by other member states, in including operational officers in their working group delegation. The abolition of steering groups—the original fourth tier of the Third Pillar bureaucracy—in 1997 has further heightened the profile of the practitioner-influenced working groups, as did the parallel decision to develop new "horizontal" working groups on Organised Crime and Drugs, with competence across the entire range of Third Pillar activities.[86] At the policy level, the establishment of Europol as a dedicated organisational unit with an expanding remit provides for the first time a permanent international facility within which a solidary professional culture can develop.

What of the supranational influences underpinning the Third Pillar? There are three main public political discourses in terms of which arguments for and against police co-operation in the context of an increasingly integrationist E.U. tend to be framed.[87] These discourses are important not only as evidence of the ideas that genuinely structure and motivate this debate, but also because they tend to dominate the agenda, and so provide the ideological context in which, regardless of their underlying motives, interested parties must conduct their argument if they wish to exert influence. What is more, each of the three discourses draws upon one of the one of the main rationales linking police to state—security, governance and symbolic association, in so doing adapting the rationale in question to the quasi-state context of the E.U. polity

To begin with, there is the discourse of *internal security*, which, naturally enough, connects with the security rationale linking police and polity. The fashioning of a new Treaty objective "to develop the Union as an area of freedom, justice and security",[88] and the provision of a separate Treaty chapter to that effect, together with a similar commitment to external security through a common foreign and security policy, is indicative of a wider project which focuses on the E.U. as a self-contained "security community".[89] This project is premised upon the identification of a range of common interests amongst the states and populations of Western Europe, the perception of a series of threats to these common interests, and the selection as appropriate of a "security-orientated" response to these threats.

---

[86] (1998) *Statewatch European Monitor*, Vol. 1 No.1 pp. 28–29.
[87] For earlier versions of the following analysis, see Walker (1996c); (1998c); (2000d).
[88] New Art. 2, Treaty on European Union.
[89] See, *e.g.*, Adler and Barnett (1998).

There are powerful political and economic strands within this ideological matrix. The stable prosperity of the E.U. in the more fluid post–Cold War world order stands in stark contrast with the insecurity and poverty of the polities and economies to the south and east. In particular, the "arc of instability"[90] along the Eastern flank of Europe during the 1990s, from Russia through Ukraine, the Balkans and Turkey into the south and eastern Mediterranean, has begun to provide the "dangerous other" of E.U. politics. While one policy response is incrementally inclusionary—there are at present a dozen candidate states of central and eastern Europe who are on track to join the 15 of the E.U. in the early years of the next century and others in more distant ante-rooms—a parallel response views exclusion and resistance to migratory pressures as prerequisite to the maintenance of Western Europe's political pedigree and economic advantage.[91]

The use of a discourse centred on the idea of insecurity, with its connotations of crisis and the need for "extraordinary means"[92] to counter threats, has undoubtedly provided the political elites of Western Europe with a usefully reductionist method of viewing complex multi-faceted problems. The power of the security metaphor has also encouraged the treatment of a range of relatively discrete issues, each with a security dimension, as one, indivisible problem. Thus the core economic and political anxieties associated with the prospect of sharing the privileged European space with outsiders become connected to more specific concerns about the development of criminal organisational links across the inner and outer borders of the E.U. In this vein, Bigo has argued that the elaboration of an "internal security ideology" around the institutional complex of the Third Pillar has allowed a number of issues, ranging from immigration and asylum to terrorism,[93] organised crime and public

---

[90] Michael Emerson, former E.U. ambassador to Moscow, quoted in *The Economist*, 7th November 1998, p50.

[91] See, *e.g.*, Anderson, den Boer, Cullen, Gilmore, Raab and Walker (1995) chap. 5.

[92] Waever (1996) p. 106.

[93] Because terrorism represents the most direct challenge to state security, states have traditionally been particularly reluctant to concede any control over policy in this area when developing international links. This is the main reason why terrorism was not included in the initial list of crimes falling within the remit of Europol, although the Europol Convention did provide that terrorism should be included no later than two years after the entry into force of the convention (Art. 2(2)). In the event, it was incorporated well within that time-limit. On the initiative of Spain, the decision was taken at the British JHA Council meeting of 19th March 1998 to extend the remit of Europol to cover terrorism as of January 1, 1999—a mere three months after the entry into force of the Convention. Since the Convention was signed, Europol's remit has been further extended beyond EDU's brief to cover counterfeit currency and—following the Tampere Summit in October 1999—money-laundering as a general offence.

order[94] to be located along a single "security continuum"[95] and treated to a one-dimensional response. On this analysis, the mind-set and rhetoric of some of the politicians, civil servants and practitioners associated with the Third Pillar implies that it is the "security" of the Western European "way of life" itself which is at stake across the range of JHA policies, from reinforcing the hard outer shell of the E.U.'s external frontiers to conducting systematic internal identity checks and developing an autonomous policing capacity.

A second public discourse closely associated with the development of E.U. policing, and which resonates with the governance rationale for linking police and polity, is the discourse of *functional spillover*. Since its inception, a key argument associated with the extension of the European project into new domains has been that the optimisation of a programme of intervention in one sector requires adjustments in related policy sectors.[96] The development of an efficient and effective common market— the founding mandate of the E.U.—was deemed to require spillover policies as diverse as anti-discrimination measures to ensure a level playing-field within the labour market and common welfare and environmental protection measures to ensure some equivalence of "externalities" across business enterprises located in different states. The argument about the need for security measures, including common policing measures, to compensate for the opening of internal frontiers, can be viewed as but one more instance of the functionalist theme.

If we look beyond the particular policy framework of the E.U., we may observe how the logic of functionalism, and, more broadly, the logic of a multi-purpose programme of governance within a polity, is generally conducive to enhanced police co-operation. As we saw in chapter one, given their flexible capacity to provide an authoritative solution and their round-the-clock accessibility, the police tend to exercise a "'stand-in' authority"[97] in all polities, plugging the gap wherever the normal authoritative solution or practice has failed. Or in functionalist language, wherever a polity develops a broad competence to govern, there is inevitable spillover into the policing domain from a wide range of other policy sectors and "governed" social activities. Whether, to take some examples from current debates and events, the argument is that the

---

[94] Public order is a growing area of Third Pillar co-operation, as reflected in the Joint Action on Public Order and Internal Security of May 26, 1997 (8012/97 ENFOPOL 111).

[95] Bigo (1994) p. 164.

[96] See, *e.g.*, Lindberg (1963).

[97] Cohen (1985) p. 37.

growth of business enterprise across Western, and, increasingly, Eastern Europe leads to a corresponding increase in crime connections; or that the development of international leisure has produced the international football hooligan and the international paedophile ring; or that the information revolution has led to increased use of computers in the commission of international crimes; there is a persuasive case to be made for policing measures to compensate for dysfunctions in other sectors.

For present purpose, the political efficacy of these arguments is more significant than their intrinsic validity. Indeed, as indicated by the expansion of the scope for police co-operation amongst all 15 E.U. members in the new Treaty of Amsterdam alongside its explicit acknowledgement of the right of the United Kingdom and Ireland to retain border checks, the removal of which was the classical functionalist justification for a Third Pillar, such reasoning may not bear close scrutiny.[98] Yet a functionalist rhetoric of governance remains influential because it appeals to a technocratic vision of policing,[99] and a similar "Eurocrat" vision of European public policy in general,[1] as the performance of a range of necessary but neutral tasks, and so justifiably insulated from partisan politics.

The third and most general public political discourse affecting the development of European police co-operation, which corresponds to the general symbolic rationale linking police and polity, is the discourse of *European integration* itself. Unlike the other two discourses, it does not operate in a manner generally favourable to the expansion of an E.U. policing capacity. The discourse of European integration is directly and unequivocally concerned with the growth of the European polity as an equal player with, and perhaps as a rival to the state, and inasmuch as policing is seen as one of the crucial building-blocks of statehood, the continuing emphasis upon state sovereignty as the bottom line of political commitment within the international order has acted as a brake upon the development of a European police capacity. Indeed, the resurgence of nationalist sentiment against a strong E.U. in the early 1990s, which coincided with the ratification difficulties of the Maastricht Treaty, has provided an important subtext to the erratic progress of the Europol Convention. And, tellingly, in the pre-Amsterdam negotiations, despite broader disagreement about the future of justice and home affairs, there was a considerable degree of consensus, strongly supported by a British Conservative government explicitly concerned

---

[98] See, *e.g.* Anderson, den Boer, Cullen, Gilmore, Raab and Walker (1995) chap. 1.

[99] See, *e.g.*, Sheptycki (1995).

[1] See, *e.g.*, Weiler (1991).

with the integrity of the link between policing and sovereign statehood,[2] that, while pragmatic considerations favoured an extension of police co-operation, it should remain firmly grounded in the predominantly intergovernmental soil of the Third Pillar.

Yet the discourse of European integration can also work in favour of European policing. The balance between pro-E.U. and pro-state sentiment is complex and unstable. The general Euroscepticism of the second half of the 1990s may be a prelude to a renewed federalist drive associated with the deepening of economic integration and the launch of the European single currency in 1999. Euroscepticism is also in part a reaction against an earlier period in which the European project was buoyant, and where European policing prospered in a favourable macro-political climate. Thus it is no mere coincidence that the crucial Third Pillar initiatives were planned at the high tide of European institutional self-confidence in the integration process, following the Commission's audacious success in marketing the 1992 project. In particular, German Chancellor Kohl's original proposal for a European Police Office (Europol) in 1991 was in tune with the political mood, typifying the ambitions of the increasingly dominant and most commitedly integrationist E.U. Member State at a point when a significant deepening of the integration project appeared politically viable.[3] It was intended, and partly succeeded, as a symbol of integrationist virility, precisely *because* it was so audacious, promising to transfer authority in an area which was one of the most traditional and closely-guarded preserves of the state. Nothing rules out the occurrence of a similar conjunction of circumstances in the future, and with similar consequences for the JHA agenda.

There is a second, and more subtle sense in which policing connects favourably with a macro-political integrationist discourse. Just as from the nineteenth century policing has been symbolically connected not only to the political project of state-building but also to the linked cultural project of nation-building, so as we enter the twenty-first century, policing at the E.U. level may be connected not only to the political project of "suprastate" building but also to the linked cultural project of building a European identity and a cohesive European civil society. This project has assumed a greater urgency in recent years because of the questionable legitimacy of the move towards a more integrated Europe, and also because the ambitious programme of E.U. expansion has had to

---

[2] See Her Majesty's Government (1996) para. 49; See further, Monar (1998) p. 322.
[3] See, *e.g.*, Cullen (1992).

confront head-on the challenge of the significant resurgence of the politics of national identity in the fragmented post-Communist Eastern Europe.[4] Yet in the absence of the vivid, readily accessible and well grounded mythology and symbolism from which a common identity is typically constructed at national level, the development of a European identity is a pioneering and precarious exercise. Lacking more positive material and given the economic and political background, Europe as a symbolic construct tends, at least in some of its manifestations,[5] to accentuate certain tones found in all identity politics, namely exclusion and otherness.[6] In turn, this resonates with the anxieties and distinctions of European security politics, in which, as we have seen, European policing is deeply implicated. In other words, the idea of a security community also has a cultural dimension; it provides one way of defining European identity beyond the level of the nation state, and insofar as this cultural project is important to the development and legitimation of the European polity—however ambitiously defined—this provides a further, if indirect, support for the growth of European policing.

4. Prospects for European Police Governance

The emergence and regulation of a significant European policing capacity, therefore, has been determined by a wide range of factors. Pragmatic, strategic and professional arguments in favour of classical state-centred international co-operation have combined, and in some cases vied, with the internal security, functional and integrationist discourses of a very new form of polity to leave European policing uneasily poised between intergovernmentalism and supranationalism. We noted earlier[7] that the balance struck in its original Maastricht manifestation led to the dual critique of the operation of the Third Pillar as, one the one hand, narrow-minded and deficient in accountability and, on the other, cumbersome, bureaucratic and lacking in momentum.

---

[4] See, *e.g.*, Brubaker (1996).

[5] There are alternative influences at work within the identity politics of the E.U. For instance, the JHA has become increasingly concerned with the parallel development of a more inclusionary politics through its various initiatives to combat racism and xenophobia, culminating in the incorporation of this as an additional objective under the Amsterdam Third Pillar; see Art. 29 TEU. However, in terms of priorities set and resources deployed, this remains very much a secondary theme.

[6] See, *e.g.* Cable (1994).

[7] Section 2(B)(i) above.

The narrowness of perspective and deficiency of accountability is relatively easily understood in terms of the forces driving co-operation. Neither the discourse of functional spillover, with its privileging of technocratic expertise and its denial of grand politics, nor the discourse of internal security, with its emphasis upon the uncompromising pursuit of a single objective, is particularly receptive to an expansive debate about the purposes of the Third Pillar or an elaborate framework of external accountability, with detailed overview of tasks and consultation of a wide range of opinions. Furthermore, the transnational bureaucracies and practitioner networks and the national criminal justice policy communities whose interests are favoured by the hybrid arrangements are disinclined to upset the prevailing balance of power by exposing the decision-making processes within European policing to external scrutiny and influence.[8] On the other hand, the initial lack of momentum within the Third Pillar was at least in some part due to the reluctance to accept majoritarian decision-making, which in turn is directly attributable to the pre-occupation of member states with the retention of sovereignty in JHA matters.

The amendments introduced by the Treaty of Amsterdam go some way towards introducing majoritarian decision-making,[9] and so we may expect that the Third Pillar's reputation for lacking dynamism and an effective cutting-edge, which in any case it was already beginning to lose,[10] will be short-lived. On one reading of the situation, it might seem simply a matter of time before the accountability side of the balance sheet matches up to the effectiveness side. On this view, the sheer pace of change within the European Polity in general and JHA in particular over the past decade has caused certain transitional problems, but once a mature form of co-operation is in place and the institutional structure has bedded down, these difficulties will be overcome. In particular, it might be argued, the continuing concern with national sovereignty should ensure that, in the long run, any concessions in terms of authority to the European centre are matched by a more intense invigilation of the exercise of that authority.

---

[8] The continuing reluctance of Third Pillar politicians and administrators to permit a high level of external scrutiny of their activities, despite consistent criticism of their weak accountability, can be seen in the failure to consult the European Parliament and other interested bodies as to the content of the strategically important Action Plan to Combat Organised Crime: European Parliament, (1997).

[9] See section 2(B)(i) above.

[10] To take a simple indicator, the number of meetings, informal decisions and more formal measures passed under the Third Pillar has increased year by year since its introduction.

But such an assessment and projection is unduly complacent. As is argued below, the continuing significance of the factors underpinning the changes of the last decade, in particular the influential priorities of the international professional community and the commitments, rhetoric and strategy associated with the contest over sovereignty suggest that we cannot easily assume that an adequate system of governance will develop alongside the international dimension of policing.

(A) THE PREVALENCE OF THE PROFESSIONAL AGENDA

As we have seen, international police co-operation was initially driven by a professional "old boys network",[11] and, due to the pragmatism inherent in functionalist and internal security discourses and the opportunity for close and continuous operational liaison provided by the Third Pillar structure, the new, and apparently formalised European framework helps to sustain such an approach. Moreover, against the view that the formal structure of authority and control is bound to prevail in the long run, a number of more detailed arguments can be made.

To begin with, we should consider the dynamics of law-making in international policing. In our discussion of the history of domestic policing, we noted the prevalence and significance of "incompletely theorised agreements".[12] Similarly, there appears to be a general tendency in international policing, not restricted to the particular circumstances of recent Europolitics, towards the symbolic affirmation of consensus, leading to the conclusion of agreements prematurely and on terms, "watered down to carry as little legal obligation as possible"[13] The Schengen Implementation Agreement, the Ministerial Agreement founding the EDU, the Europol Convention, and the new operational powers of the Amsterdam Treaty, were all endorsed before important matters of principle had been resolved and at a point when considerable delay could be anticipated prior to implementation. The main attraction of premature and diluted agreements in the European context is that they strike a compromise between pro-integrationist and anti-integrationist tendencies; a documented instance of progress to add to the integrationist vision, but balanced against the guarantee to the defenders of state sovereignty that no formal measures be taken on the

---

[11] Anderson, den Boer, Cullen, Gilmore, Raab and Walker (1995) pp. 74–76.
[12] See chapters two and three.
[13] See Turnbull-Henson (1987).

basis of the agreement pending resolution of outstanding matters of principle.[14] Yet as the busy preparatory schedules undertaken by the various new European police organisations prior to their official commencement date indicate, the public affirmation of an international commitment to action, however premature, in fact conveys an informal sense of permission to those committed to enhanced co-operation to proceed in anticipation of a final resolution of outstanding disputes. In this vein, for example, the extension of police co-operation under the Treaty of Amsterdam was repeatedly invoked as a legitimising device for the preparation of new co-operative initiatives in the early post-Treaty period, even while the ratification process remained incomplete and the process of formal development of new measures and arrangements under the new institutional context had yet to commence.[15]

The problem of regulatory "lag" is compounded by the tendency of the practitioner community not merely to anticipate the implementation of new rules, but also to move beyond these regulatory thresholds in a series of incremental shifts of practice and strategy. The cumulative effect may be for a professionally-driven agenda to cross important policy thresholds without rounded public debate or candid acknowledgement of the consequences. For example, notwithstanding the determination in the original Europol Convention that Europol should be without executive powers (arrest, search, questioning, etc.) or operational competence, but should instead provide a service function in matters of information exchange and intelligence analysis to national operational units, the Director of the EDU (and future Director of Europol), Jurgen Storbeck,[16] was soon advocating the practical inevitability and desirability of an extension of his unit's remit. In suggesting the establishment of *ad hoc* Europol task forces to direct operations in particular states, Storbeck contended that since Europol in its intelligence co-ordination role would acquire a unique overview of certain transnational crime patterns and incidents, it would be better placed than any national policing units to respond operationally. As we have seen, Storbeck's arguments, complemented by those advanced in the Action Plan against Organised Crime, appear to have borne fruit in the Amsterdam Treaty, where the idea of task forces is endorsed and

---

[14] As with the unresolved status of the European Court of Justice under the original Europol Convention.

[15] See, *e.g.*, the Austrian Presidency Work Programme for the K4 Committee (July–December 1998), discussed in *Statewatch European Monitor*, (1998) vol. 1 no.1 p. 8.

[16] Storbeck (1996).

additional authority is given to Europol to direct national authorities towards specific investigations.[17]

Post-Amsterdam trends provide further confirmation of a gradualist agenda. The landmark Tampere summit of October 1999 focused exclusively on the development of the new "area of freedom, justice and security. It built upon the implementation of the Amsterdam provisions to call for the prompt setting up of joint investigative teams, the establishment of a European Police Chiefs Operational Task Force, the receipt by Europol of operational data from member states, co-ordination between Europol and a new co-operative unit named EUROJUST (composed of prosecutors and magistrates from each member state), and the founding of a European police college.[18] In a related development, the long-delayed Third Pillar Convention on Mutual Assistance in Criminal Matters was signed in May 2000,[19] having been extended beyond its initial pre-Amsterdam brief to give flesh to some of the new policing competences established at Amsterdam, including the establishment of joint investigative teams[20] and the creation of frameworks of mutual assistance for the investigation of suspects,[21] controlled deliveries[22] and covert investigations.[23]

Superficially, these developments may be attributed to the so-called "law of inevitable increment", whereby "whatever powers the police have they will exceed by a given margin".[24] To the extent that, despite the scepticism of the author who coined this phrase, the proposition may contain a kernel of truth, it does so in recognition of an important structural tendency in policework. Where the police operate, as the prototype European police do, within a multi-functional polity, the scope to define issues in security terms and intervene on that basis is such that they will inevitably contest any restrictions upon the "normal" allocation of police powers.

Furthermore, a police organisation in such a situation is well placed to achieve the momentum to avoid, or even overcome, such restrictions. In legal terms, as the debate over European police powers has indicated, the key measure of policing control over a particular jurisdiction is generally

---

[17] See section 2(B)(ii) above.
[18] Council of the European Union 13370/99; see, e.g., *Statewatch European Monitor* (2000) vol. 2 no.1 pp. 2–13.
[19] O.J. 2000 C 197/01 (May 29).
[20] Art. 13.
[21] Art. 9.
[22] Art. 12.
[23] Art. 14.
[24] Reiner (1992a) p. 217.

taken to be possession of executive powers. However, in broader socio-logical terms, this is only one, somewhat narrow, dimension of control. The possession of an intelligence capacity, granted at Maastricht, and the ability to take operational initiatives, conceded at Amsterdam, are surely equally important indicators. Arguably, therefore, there has already been a qualitative shift in European policing in a manner which bypasses conventional legal understanding. And given that significant slippage from a service to a directive role has already taken place, it may well be that a similar incrementalist logic will be used by the professional community in the future to argue that, alongside intelligence and operational co-ordination, Europol should be granted the third and final dimension of control over national units, namely executive powers.

(B) THE NATIONAL SOVEREIGNTY TRAP

Even if we allow for the considerable informal power of the professional community to influence or adapt the formal agenda, the masters of the formal agenda still possess the regulatory potential to impose a more effective system of accountability. Yet, while the Member States were prepared to sharpen the decision-making tools of JHA at Amsterdam, only minor concessions were made in terms of democratic accountability to those institutions best placed to exercise an external overview of these functions—namely the European Parliament and the Court of Justice, and there is no indication in the post-Amsterdam era of any significant shift in this position. But why should this be so, given that the more Eurosceptic member states, whose unanimous consent is required before there is any amendment to the fundamental framework of police and criminal justice co-operation, have particular reason to be wary of the empire-building of powerful and Third Pillar institutions, and to require full compensation in terms of effective oversight?

The answer to this conundrum lies in the fact that from a traditional state-sovereigntist perspective, the proper lines of accountability are through national channels, which means domestic parliaments and domestic courts. On this view, which retains some influence in British Government circles even under the more *communautaire* regime of New Labour,[25] the strengthening of *any* European institution, even those which are designed to reduce the deficit in accountability and democ-

---

[25] See *e.g.*, House of Lords (1998) pp. 40–42.

racy, may be perceived in narrow zero-sum terms as contributing to the erosion of national self-determination, and for that reason resisted. There is, therefore, a refusal, or at least a reluctance, to contemplate that the locus of power has already shifted so much to the European centre that the accountability system must adapt accordingly, even if that entails empowering particular European institutions, or developing a dual framework of governance linking national and supranational institutions.[26]

It should, moreover, be recognised that the significance of sovereigntist discourse is not only as a political dogma which in its myopic inflexibility risks becoming self-defeating. It may also provide a convenient cover for a more basic aversion to external accountability, which, as we have already seen, is all too prevalent in this area. Thus, the logic of the sovereigntist position would seem to imply that at least the national channel of accountability should be fully exploited. Yet the powers of national parliaments to hold their respective executives to account for their part in the formation and implementation of JHA policy are distinctly uneven, and often the most vociferous champions of national sovereignty are least willing to accept a strong national role.[27] The United Kingdom has been a particular culprit, and was just as reluctant to allow effective Westminster scrutiny of the negotiation of the Europol Convention[28] as the Commission was to involve the European Parliament. Indeed, the House of Lords Select Committee on the European Union, widely acknowledged as a vigilant and effective defender of parliamentary oversight of the executive in respect of E.U. policy and legislation, has on numerous occasions challenged the Home Office to be more co-operative in allowing oversight of the Third Pillar,[29] as has its counterpart in the House of Commons, the European Scrutiny Committee. The parliamentary committees have urged that as a consistent practice as wide a range of documents as possible be deposited with them; that they be deposited early, and in successive drafts where there have been significant changes; and that Government policy in general should be concerned with allowing Parliament and other interested parties more effective consultation and influence over JHA policy.[30] However, despite much dialogue and some

---

[26] See *e.g.* Kerse (2000) pp. 99–100, discussing the implications of the Treaty of Amsterdam's Protocol on the Role of National Parliaments in the European Union (D13).

[27] House of Lords (1997).

[28] See *e.g.* House of Lords (1995)

[29] See *e.g.* House of Lords (1995); (1997); (1998); see also Kerse (2000).

[30] See *e.g.* House of Lords (1997) pp. 40–42

success,[31] and despite creeping acknowledgement within the E.U. Treaty framework itself of the important role of national Parliaments in ensuring accountability,[32] there remains a gap between Westminster aspirations and the practice of the Home Office.

(c) Variable Geometry

A final difficulty associated with governance of the new international policing system, again closely connected to the sovereignty debate, is the degree of flexibility and pluralism which is beginning to influence the design of the E.U. in general and the Third Pillar in particular. If a key promise of European police co-operation was the eclipse of the tradition of fragmented organisation and rival facilities and the imposition of a stable hierarchy of transnational policing mechanisms—with the Third Pillar and Europol clearly first and foremost, then this neatly ordered solution has become blurred and is in danger of being supplanted even before its full implementation. The Treaty of Amsterdam has built on a number of recent developments, such as the European Monetary Union opt-outs, the individual Europe Agreements with candidate states and the opt-out of the previous British Government from the Social Protocol, to endorse a general principle of flexible integration, whereby different states can integrate at different rates in different combinations in different policy spheres.

The reasons for this are many and varied,[33] but the most important is that in the current finely-balanced political debate over the future allocation of sovereignty in the E.U., flexible integration as a broad strategy appeals to both pro-integration and anti-integration forces. For those in favour of greater integration, flexibility avoids institutional stagnation, in which the overall European project proceeds at the pace of the most reluctant Member State. For those who defend national sovereignty, particularly in the context of an ever expanding E.U., flexibility promises a more loosely structured set of arrangements. On the latter view, if states are allowed to co-operate on an *a la carte* basis, not only will this arrange-

---

[31] For example, the most recent Scrutiny Reserve Resolutions (House of Commons, November 17, 1998, House of Lords, December 6, 1999) extend from the First to the Third Pillar the formal Scrutiny Reserve preventing a Minister giving agreement to a proposal still under domestic parliamentary scrutiny; see Kerse (2000) pp. 84–85.

[32] See Treaty of Amsterdam, Protocol on the role of national parliaments in the European Union (D13); see also Kerse (2000) pp. 99–100.

[33] See Walker (1998b) pp. 369–374; and, more generally, De Burca and Scott (2000).

ment be more respectful of divergent national interests, but it will also begin to dilute the significance of the Union as a distinctive and cohesive entity with particular interests and a common set of institutions.

Whichever view is more plausible, a situation is clearly emerging where the debate over European sovereignty can no longer be perceived in traditional vein as the relationship between two fixed entities—the E.U. and the member states. The E.U. increasingly means different things in different sectors, while the member states, together with a number of non-member states, now find themselves in variable relationships with the institutions of the E.U.

The move towards flexible integration in a post-sovereign Europe applies as much, and perhaps more—given its long history of influence by the shifting sands of state expediency—to policing and JHA matters as it does to any other area of E.U. activity. This is demonstrated by the opt-out on the jurisdiction of the Court of Justice negotiated by the U.K. under the Europol Convention. It is also indicated by the general willingness of the IGC negotiators, recorded in the Florence summit of June 1996, to accept the idea of flexible integration more readily in the context of the Second and Third Pillars than in the traditional sphere of the First Pillar, where the perceived need to preserve the essentials of the single internal market reduces the scope for differentiation. In turn, this willingness was reflected in the final form of the Amsterdam Treaty, which as well as providing a general permission for particular states to forge ahead with advanced forms of co-operation,[34] allows the full incorporation of a non-E.U. structure, Schengen, together with a range of more detailed opt-outs and opt-ins.[35] Arrangements such as these, moreover, cannot be dismissed as merely theoretical possibilities. For instance, in May 2000, the United Kingdom concluded an agreement with the other member states to apply some aspects of the Schengen Agreement, including those relating to the strategically important Schengen Information System, but not others. The upshot, then, is a structure of Byzantine complexity, with the prospect of the JHA Council, which is supposed to provide some overall level of policy coherence at the political level, in the area of freedom, security and justice, wearing as many as ten different hats and boasting ten different memberships depending upon subject-matter.[36]

---

[34] Art. 11 EC Treaty (First Pillar); Art. 40 TEU (Third Pillar); Arts. 43–44 (general principles).

[35] See, *e.g.*, Monar (1998); Walker (1998b) pp. 368–369.

[36] See *Statewatch* (1998) vol. 8 no.5 pp28–29.

The prevalence of a flexible and diversified approach in policing and Third Pillar matters is also apparent at a more detailed level from the spate of security agreements and liaisons recently negotiated between the E.U. and other states. Prominent examples include an agreement between Europol and third party states concerning exchange of data, a developing dialogue on police co-operation between the U.K. and the main non-European player in transnational co-operation—the U.S., and the launch of a strategy to exploit a new provision of the Amsterdam Treaty[37] to allow the 11 candidate states of Central and Eastern Europe to join in Third Pillar co-operation with the existing 15. These, however, are only the tip of a large and expanding iceberg.[38]

While it seems highly likely that these trends towards the diversification and fragmentation of political authority will continue, and indeed accelerate, it is very difficult to predict what their implications will be for the long-term future of police co-operation in and beyond Europe. As is developed in the concluding chapter, it is likely that, increasingly, we will have to try to understand trends in police co-operation not simply in relation to the shifting balance of sovereign authority, but against a background of increasing challenges to the very idea of sovereign authority. What is imperative, however, is that the subtle dangers of variable geometry be appreciated and that, even in the unpromising circumstances of renewed fragmentation, the steady and consistent political will necessary to craft new regulatory tools which are adequate to this complexity be mobilised and sustained. Otherwise, the growing intransparency and diversity of transnational policing arrangements will exacerbate the problems of informalism and attenuated accountability which have plagued the history of transnational policing.

---

[37] Art. 38, TEU, the application of which in this context is discussed in the 1998 Austrian Presidency Work Programme for the K4 Committee, *Statewatch European Monitor*, (1998) vol. 1, no.1, p. 8.
[38] See Walker (1998c).

Chapter Nine

Policing Beyond "the Police"

In the opening chapter we noted that until very recently students of policing worked on the often unstated, perhaps even unconsidered, assumption that nothing properly counts as policing unless it is done by officers in blue serge uniforms.[1] That limited focus is also a feature of the constitutional treatment of policing. Its main concern, too, has traditionally been with the public constabularies, in particular Home Office police forces, with a largely permissive attitude taken to other forms and manifestations of policing. Arguably, this permissive legacy has allowed a serious regulatory deficit to accumulate, since, as contemplated below, policing beyond the police may need just as vigilant regulatory attention as the traditional public police. Yet only very recently have the broad governance implications of the spread and diversification of policing beyond the paradigm case begun to be taken seriously by the shapers of our constitutional order.

1. The Policing Continuum

Let us begin by analysing the nature and extent of the "non-police" policing domain, and by considering why it cannot be left beyond the regulatory pale.

The diversification of policing takes a number of forms, the classification and quantification of which are matters of some debate and controversy. And like all difficult questions of classification, at root lies a contested definition. The definition of policing is a conceptual minefield, which we have managed to avoid thus far in the book. It is impossible, however, to arrive at a defensible classification of non-police

---

[1] Chapter one, section 2(B)(ii).

policing without a clear sense of the boundaries of the policing idea, and, relatedly, of the dimensions along which variation is possible within these boundaries.

As regards the boundary question, Jones and Newburn offer the following useful definition: "(T)hose organised forms of order maintenance, peacekeeping, rule or law enforcement, crime investigation and prevention and other forms of investigation and associated information-brokering—which may involve a conscious exercise of power—undertaken by individuals or organisations, where such activities are viewed by them and/or others as a central or key defining part of their purpose."[2] This is an expansive view, but an intelligent one. It rejects two alternative types of essentialist assumption at the heart of many debates about policing. It eschews functional essentialism—the idea that policing involves one central purpose, such as order maintenance or law enforcement.[3] It also has no truck with instrumental essentialism, recognising that policing need not necessarily involve any particular means or mode of activity—coercion and its threat being the most popular candidate within this approach.[4] Instead, the only limits are highly permissive. The specification of broad organisational and experiential/reputational boundaries recognises that policing must be distinguished from the vast spectrum of alternative formal and informal social control mechanisms known to modern society—with its unprecedented range of disciplinary techniques,[5] but also that the point of distinction lies far beyond the central constitutionally-paradigmatic case of the Home Office police forces. The conviction that policing must be "organised" refers to our sense that policing is a collectively planned and orchestrated activity rather than isolated or episodic. Perhaps even more importantly, the experiential/reputational qualification refers to the constitutive quality of the social *recognition* of a certain practice as policing. Of course, this social recognition will depend upon the practice in question performing some of the tasks and using some of the methods associated with functional and instrumental definitions of policing, but in the final analysis it is the sense made of the practice by the practitioners and their clients which is crucial.

---

[2] Jones and Newburn (1998) pp. 18–19. While I endorse much of their argument, I develop my case in support of this definition in a rather different fashion than Jones and Newburn themselves.

[3] See, *e.g.*, Reiner (1992a) chap. 4.

[4] See, *e.g.*, Bittner (1974).

[5] See, *e.g.*, Rose (1999).

In turn, such a capacious and inclusive definition can accommodate variation along a number of different axes. It lays the groundwork, therefore, for a second important insight within the authors" conceptual framework, namely their development of a "multi-dimensional"[6] conception of policing. Policing, according to Jones and Newburn, varies in terms; first, of its sectoral location; secondly, the type of space in which the practice is typically located; thirdly, the legal powers available to individual practitioners; fourthly, its functional range and remit; and, fifthly its geographical level of operation.[7] The fifth variable—geographical level, has been dealt with in our analysis of devolved, national and supranational policing in previous chapters, and so we will confine discussion to the first four variables.

The sectoral distinction, which divides policing bodies into public and private sectors depending upon the source of their funding and the status of their employees, is the focus of most single-dimensional taxonomies of policing. While such taxonomies are too fragile and rudimentary to bear the weight of explaining the range of significant diversity within such a complex activity, the sectoral distinction remains a familiar and important one, and a good starting-point for analysis. On the public side of the divide, the Home Office forces are joined by: (1) specialist national police forces with a narrower clientele than the general public, such as the British Transport Police, the Ministry of Defence Police and the Atomic Energy Authority Constabulary[8]; (2) investigative departments of other public organisations, including the Health and Safety Executive, the investigation department of the Benefits Agency and the Post Office Security and Investigation Service, and (3) municipal policing bodies established by local authorities. On the private side of the divide, the main type of policing is commercially sponsored, whether provided in-house by a commercial organisation or supplied on a contract basis by a specialist security organisation. Services include: the provision of physical and mechanical security; the provision of electronic security equipment; and staffed services, embracing the supply of personnel to guard persons or property, for investigative purposes, and for bailiffing and debt collection. Also, at the very margins of policing, there are various citizen-based forms of self-policing or "civil policing,"[9]

---

[6] *ibid.* p. 200. The authors draw heavily upon the work of Johntson (1992b) in developing their multi-dimensional perspective.

[7] *ibid.*, chap. 7.

[8] See, chap. 7, section 1 above.

[9] Johnston (1999) chap. 9.

including Neighbourhood Watch and the Special Constabulary, but also shading into vigilantism.

The post-war period has seen an expansion of all of these sectors, the reasons for which are many, varied and of contestable weight.[10] In some part, the growth of the non-Home Office Sector, in particular commercial and municipal policing, is a compensatory response to the fiscal crisis of the state—a general pressure on public expenditure from the 1970s onwards which, as we saw in chapter three, did not fully impact upon the policing sector for another decade, but which made it increasingly difficult to match supply of police resources to additional demand. In part also, it has too do with the growth of "mass private property"[11]— locations such as office plazas, shopping malls and sports complexes in which private ownership and responsibility are combined with relatively free public access and the security problems associated with such access. In turn, this is connected to a more general commodification of security—an increased awareness of and sensitivity to the intensity and diversity of social risks and a self-reinforcing (but arguably self-defeating)[12] shift from collective to individual or "club"[13] solutions. And undergirding these changes are fundamental transformations in the organisation of both political and economic spheres. The gradual de-centring of the sovereign state—one of the major transformations of the constitutional order which we have highlighted—and the post-Fordist shift away from large-scale, monolithic top-down organisations both pose broad ideological challenges to the central role of the conventional public police bureaucracy in the provision of security.

The most spectacular growth has been in the commercial sector. Measurement is notoriously difficult, but the most considered estimates[14] suggests as many as one-third of a million—more than double the public police figure—with guarding services and the supply of electronic security equipment accounting for the vast majority of that figure. It is noteworthy too, reinforcing the point that until very recently objective growth in the private security sector was not reflected in public or political awareness, that the greatest proportionate increases in the largest sub-sector—guarding persons and property—actually took place in the 1950s and 1960s, with electronic security equipment providing the main area of current growth.

---

[10] See, *e.g.* Jones and Newburn (1998) chap. 8.
[11] Shearing and Stenning (1987).
[12] See, *e.g.* Loader (1997b); (1997c).
[13] See, *e.g.* Hope (2000).
[14] Johnston (1999) chap. 8; Jones and Newburn (1998).

Since the 1980s, there have also been closely monitored developments in municipal policing, which fall into two categories.[15] On the one hand, there has been a growth in the direct employment by local authorities of bodies of people who have, within certain contexts and within limited jurisdictions, constabulary powers. An earlier tradition of parks police, charged with the enforcement of local bye-laws, has been revived, with London boroughs in the vanguard of this movement. The best known example is the Wandsworth Parks Constabulary, established in 1995. It includes within its remit foot and mobile patrol and CCTV-monitoring of open spaces, security patrol and order maintenance around public service buildings, and the guarding of cash in transit to or from council offices. The legal basis for the powers of these new forces is varied, ranging from local legislation to general legislation in the area of public health and local government.[16] The scope of these powers is also disputed, with the Home Office and the Metropolitan Police favouring a restrictive interpretation which would treat the municipal forces as pure creatures of statute, and so confined to the enforcement of bye-laws, and some of the municipal forces themselves advocating a broader view which would allow them full constabulary powers within their particular jurisdictional space.[17] A second category of municipal policing consists of uniformed personnel without formal police powers. There have been a number of high profile developments of this type, most recently the Sedgefield Community Force in Durham. Established in 1993, it was the first municipal force to be charged with patrolling residential areas, its remit one of prevention, public liaison and crime reporting.

A third area of growth which has attracted public and political attention is that of civil policing, in which local groups "below government"[18] take their own security initiatives. This may be done with official encouragement—in line with the "active citizenship" strategy favoured by incumbent governments since the 1980s, as registered in the growth of Neighbourhood Watch, the renewed prominence of the Special Constabulary and the institution of new reporting facilities such as the Crimestoppers phone line. Alternatively, civil policing may take the form of vigilantism—civil movements which lack official sanction, and which

---

[15] See, e.g. Johnston (1999) chap. 9.

[16] For example, Public Health (Amendment) Act 1907; Local Government and Housing Provisional Order Confirmation (Greater London Parks and Open Spaces) Act 1967; Local Government (Miscellaneous Provisions) Act 1982, s.40.

[17] For a fuller discussion, see Jones and Newburn (1998) pp. 228–239; see also Johnston (1993) pp. 776–777; (1999) pp. 142–143.

[18] Loader (2000).

may transgress the criminal law or even challenge the authority of the criminal justice system and the specific order of the state itself. Developments have taken place across a broad spectrum, ranging from the growth of self-help Guardian Angel street patrols and the rise in incidents of retributive justice pre-empting the official criminal justice process or compensating for its perceived adequacies, to the "communal vigilantism"[19] of Loyalist and Republican paramilitaries in Northern Ireland.

The limitations of the public/private sectoral distinction in the above analysis are readily apparent. Even in its own terms, the distinction does not describe clearly contrasting forms of economic organisation, but entities in which public and private elements are intertwined. Increasingly we see public policing bodies selling services to private bodies, from Home Office police forces charging for special services[20] and parks police providing security for privately run events, to the British Transport Police establishing police services agreements with private rail companies and the Post Office Investigations Department selling crime prevention advice to banks. Equally, private policing bodies may sell their services to public agencies, from the Ministry of Defence contracting private security companies to guard military bases to local authorities hiring private organisations to enforce parking regulations or to undertake covert surveillance and investigation of neighbour harassment problems on council estates.[21] In addition, the essential character of civil policing is hardly captured by economic criteria, and so the public/private distinction adds little to our understanding of this "sub-sector".

If we turn to the other facets of Jones and Newburn's multi-dimensional conception of policing, the significance of the public/private sector distinction is further diminished. Consideration of the spatial dimension indicates that public sector policing does not take place exclusively in public space, while private sector policing does not take place exclusively in private space. Clearly, much Home Office policing takes place in unambiguously private space, such as private residences, while the domain of many private patrol and investigation services is unambiguously public space. Moreover, both public and private sector policing increasingly operate in the hybrid domain of mass private property—often in conjunction, as in the case of shopping centre security.

---

[19] Johnston (1999) p.148.

[20] Police Act 1996, s.25.

[21] Jones and Newburn (1998), chap. 7, who draw many of their examples from their case study of the policing of Wandsworth Borough.

The legal dimension indicates more telling differences between public and private sectors. Whereas Home Office constables have extensive powers of arrest, detention, personal search and entry and search of premises, and other public bodies possess some of these powers, private policing bodies have no special legal status and so are limited to ordinary citizens' powers of arrest. Yet the importance of this formal distinction is not fully mirrored in practice. Just as non-Home Office bodies, such as the Parks Police, play on the combination of legal uncertainty, lack of public awareness and the symbolic authority of uniformed force to apply a generous working definition of their powers, so too private bodies stretch their legal powers by trading on public ignorance, deference and the imbalance of power in enforcement situations, and, often, also upon their ability to make supply of a valued service conditional upon the imposition of security checks.[22]

Finally, and perhaps most significantly, a functional analysis of policing suggests further similarities between public and private sectors. On the one hand, particular public sector police forces undoubtedly have a broader general remit than particular private forces, and within the public sector Home Office forces have a more open-ended mandate than other local or national forces. On the other hand, if the private sector is taken as a whole, it performs all the tasks and more of the local[23] territorial divisions of Home Office forces, including call response, investigation, patrol, traffic control, order maintenance and crime prevention.

What this multi-dimensional analysis ultimately suggests is not only that a large and expanding policing sector exists beyond the Home Office police, but also that the differences between sectors should not be overstated. Policing cannot for any serious purpose be divided into mutually exclusive categories, but instead must be mapped onto a finely graded continuum, with Home Office forces differing only *in degree* from their specialist, municipal, commercial and civil counterparts in terms of sectoral, spatial, legal and functional criteria. In particular, for governance purposes it is indisputable that many of the reasons for placing the Home Office police under constitutional authority also apply to other forms of policing. Like the Home Office police, other policing sectors have a broad capacity to define, secure and threaten general order. Like the Home Office police, they serve public customers, exercise

---

[22] See, *e.g.* Morgan and Newburn (1997) pp. 37–41.

[23] Although there is no private sector equivalent to the national police functions of Home Office forces, such as Special Branch and royal and diplomatic protection. See Jones and Newburn (1998), pp. 242–243.

dominion over public or hybrid space, possess effective authority in a wide range of dealings with the public, and carry out a broad range of security functions. Moreover, this similarity extends beyond objective practice to embrace public perceptions, the evidence suggesting that the public does not distinguish sharply, if at all, between the Home Office police and other policing bodies in terms of trust, expectations and deference to authority.[24]

2. Governing "the Beyond"

What, then, are the trends in constitutional recognition of this wider policing sector? In the last chapter we briefly considered the limited accountability arrangements for some of the specialist public police forces. At the other end of the spectrum, some forms of vigilantism are literally beyond regulation.[25] Here, we will concentrate on the two most significant non-Home Office sectors—commercial policing and munic-ipal policing, both of which have been the subject of recent regulatory initiatives.

(A) COMMERCIAL POLICING

For many years, Britain has possessed the unenviable distinction of being one of the few European countries in which private security is not sub-ject to statutory control. In recent times the problems associated with staff reliability and competence and with overall standards of service have been extensively documented. A degree of self-regulation exists within the industry, with a number of trade associations[26] instrumental in setting up inspection frameworks and registration and training schemes in vari-ous sectors. But these schemes exhibit the problems typically associated with self-regulatory regimes, such as fragmentation of regulatory effort and variability of standards and of enforcement, low public recognition and confidence, and, perhaps most crucially, lack of compulsion and the

---

[24] See, e.g. Morgan and Newburn (1997) pp. 37–41.

[25] Although forms of communal self-policing which arise in circumstances of deep divi-sion, as in Northern Ireland, must be taken account of, and perhaps even be incorporated into political and constitutional solutions; see chapter six above.

[26] The two largest are the British Security Industry Association and the International Professional Security Association.

consequential self-exclusion of those operators most in need of scrutiny. Over the years, a number of Private Members Bills unsuccessfully sought to introduce some measure of compulsory regulation, A political turning-point was, however, reached in 1995 when a Home Affairs Select Committee delivered an extensive critique of the private security industry and recommended that legislation should be introduced to license security providers and regulate standards and training in the area of the industry where contact with the public and involvement with local communities is greatest, namely the manned guarding sector.[27] The Conservative government accepted the need for reform in principle in 1996, and New Labour endorsed this view when it came to power the following year. Eventually, in March 1999 a White Paper fleshed out this commitment, but still with no timetable for implementation.[28]

The White Paper, which in keeping with the new constitutional framework leaves reform in Scotland and Northern Ireland to the devolved authorities in these jurisdictions, proposes the establishment of a new regulatory agency, the Private Security Industry Authority (PSIA). PSIA is to be answerable to the Home Secretary, who will appoint its part-time Board, comprising a chair with no interest in the security industry together with representatives of relevant constituencies including the security industry, police, local authorities, insurers, customers and members of the public. Addressing the two main areas of regulatory concern, PSIA will license individuals who provide security services in certain areas of the industry, and will also have a role in securing the maintenance and improvement of standards.

Individuals will require a license before establishing a private security firm, or becoming a manager or employee providing security services. The grant of a license by the PSIA will depend upon fitness for the role, based upon a full assessment of the applicant's criminal record, and additionally in the case of managers and directors, their record of bankruptcy and directorship disqualification. Enforcement will be carried out by a full-time inspectorate, and breach or evasion of the licensing conditions and procedures will carry a criminal penalty.

As regards maintenance and improvement of standards, the statutory framework will be less robust. Supervised by PSIA, an Inspected Companies scheme will be established under which companies can volunteer to be inspected to the standards set for their particular sector. Companies

---

[27] Home Affairs Committee (1995b).
[28] Home Office (1999b).

that attain the standard will be able to use a recognised quality mark, which PSIA will publicise. Additional inspectorates may be established, or existing self-regulatory inspectorates may be statutorily endorsed to administer the scheme. Drawing upon existing codes of practice and advised by specialist committees for each sector, PSIA will develop the relevant quality criteria, which will deal with matters such as training, equipment standards, operating criteria and administrative support. In time, PSIA may decide that a compulsory statutory framework of regulation is necessary for a particular sector and would then make recommendations to the Home Secretary to that effect.

The scope of the new scheme is greater than contemplated by the 1995 Select Committee, but in the first instance at least, it does not extend across the whole industry. The compulsory statutory licensing scheme, which will be phased in over the three year licensing cycle, will initially apply not only to the whole of the manned guarding sector—including "in-house" staff, door supervisors, cash-in-transit security, wheelclampers, security services in retail, public and semi-public areas and local or neighbourhood guarding or patrol service—but also to personnel involved in the installation, monitoring and maintenance of alarms and CCTV systems. In time, the legislation will be extended on a sector-by-sector basis to cover electronic tagging or monitoring systems, private investigators, security consultants, locksmiths, keyholders and contracted court enforcement officers. The endorsement of voluntary standards and the Inspected Companies scheme may be extended to a particular sector ahead of the compulsory licensing scheme for individuals, but the option of statutory regulation of standards will not be available in any particular sector unless and until the licensing scheme is in place.

The proposed scheme is a peculiar hybrid. It wears the clothes of statutory control but retains some of the unmistakable features of self-regulation. First, there is an expectation that at least some of the agencies and codes of practice from the existing self-regulatory regime will be retained and incorporated into the new regime. Secondly, in the area of performance standards, PSIA will endorse the continuation of a voluntary framework, at least in the early stages. Thirdly, and again at least in the early stages, some parts of the industry will remain entirely beyond the reach of the compulsory provisions of the legislation, and so still fundamentally dependent on self-regulation.

While there is much to be said for incrementalism as a way of gaining or retaining the support of the industry, a more cynical reading of official motives would suggest that it is the *only* workable option left to a government committed to introducing a system at no public cost, and entirely funded by the industry itself.[29] There are clear drawbacks, in that some of the problems of industry "regulatory capture", of avoidance and abuse, and of low levels of public trust and legitimacy associated with self-regulation will undoubtedly persist. There are also broader structural problems associated with private security *in general* that a system restricted to the regulation of the probity and standards of competence of particular providers cannot address. Commodified security may promote or exacerbate inequality of security provision, marginalizing and displacing crime and disorder problems to those citizens and communities who lack the economic capital to enter the private market. Relatedly, the absence of any direct control or oversight of private security by police or local authority means that, for all the particular regulatory checks that have been introduced, private security remains free from any general framework of accountability in the public interest.[30] But this is a complex issue with powerful political undercurrents, to which we return below.

(B) MUNICIPAL POLICING AND NEIGHBOURHOOD WARDENS

In recent years, the future direction of commercial policing and municipal policing has become bound up with the more general question of the demise of the police patrolling monopoly.[31] It is the growth of alternative patrols, stimulated by increasing public demand for a visible uniform presence and the flow of public police resources (only partially stemmed by successive policy initiatives in community policing and sector policing) away from the beat and towards specialist functions and emergency response, which has posed the greatest threat to the idea of the pre-eminence in core functions of a publicly provided and accountable service.

A number of options exist to address the governance problems associated with this shift. At one extreme lies the incorporationist option. Home Office police forces could seek to reassert a strong pre-eminence, perhaps by directly providing security services on a commercial basis or by establishing auxiliary patrol officers as a second tier of police officer. At the other extreme, lies the option of radical separation. On this view,

---

[29] Including license fees.
[30] See, *e.g.* Loader (1997b); (1997c).
[31] See Morgan and Newburn (1997) pp. 160–172.

the public police will best preserve their pre-eminence by doing more of the same, ideally with more resources, and any link with or concession to other forms of security should be avoided for fear that it might provide a pretext for cutting police resources, or that it might allow other security operators to trade on the good name of the police or to contaminate the police reputation by association.

For a number of years, the public policy debate, substantially influenced by the police themselves, appeared to be trapped on the horns of a dilemma shaped by these radical alternatives. On the one hand, there was some support from the higher echelons of the police service for the "Profitshire Constabulary"[32] model, with the police funding their own expansion into the private market.[33] The idea of auxiliary police officers, informed by the Dutch example of the *politeisurveillant*,[34] was also given serious consideration. However, in the face of significant police resistance, particularly from the lower ranks, two influential public reports in 1996 by the Audit Commission[35] and by the Committee on the Role and Responsibilities of the Police[36] drew back from recommending their introduction.

Gradually, a number of policy lines converged to open up an intermediate solution. Many existing schemes of neighbourhood patrol, including the Sedgefield Community Force, reported high levels of public satisfaction and a trend towards greater police acceptance.[37] In 1998 New Labour signalled its support for the concept of Neighbourhood Wardens by establishing a working group to examine their development, under the umbrella of the Social Exclusion Unit which reports directly to the Prime Minister. Wardens were defined as providing "some kind of official or semi-official presence in a residential area, with the primary aim of improving the quality of life".[38] The definition included neighbourhood patrol, whether employed directly by the local authority, social landlord or local community group or through contracting-out to private security, but also embraced a variety of concierge, caretaker and neighbourhood support worker roles. The sponsorship of such schemes as a relatively inexpensive adjunct to local policing also fitted the Government's broader legislative strategy for promoting partnership and

---

[32] Johnston (1992).
[33] Blair (1994).
[34] Morgan and Newburn (1997) p. 168.
[35] Audit Commission (1996) para.96.
[36] Independent Inquiry (1996) para. 4.24.
[37] Morgan and Newburn (1997) p. 162
[38] Home Office (2000a) para.2.3.

value-for-money in local crime prevention, pursued through the promulgation of crime and disorder strategies[39] and the introduction of the Best Value approach.[40] Yet the police professional attitude remained uncertain, the support of ACPO, who were represented on the working group, balanced by the continuing opposition of the Police Federation and the Superintendents" Association.[41] As ACPO's proposals for managing the relationship between police and Neighbourhood Wardens gradually found favour within the working group, however, this opposition began to subside and to be replaced by a strategy which sought to design the police into a central regulatory role.

It came as no surprise, therefore, when the working group's final report in 2000[42] supported the retention and further development of Neighbourhood Warden schemes, recommending the establishment of a new inter-departmental Neighbourhood Wardens Unit[43] to fund, promote, advise and monitor old and new Warden schemes within an informal framework. The governance model which it advocated was one of supervision by and co-operation with the police. A central plank of their approach was to endorse the fundamental principles articulated by ACPO's "Working the Beat" project group. These include: no additional powers for Wardens beyond those of the ordinary citizen; police retention of the exclusive right to non-consensual intervention; local authority and police to have joint accountability for the outcomes of warden schemes; clear line of accountability to the public provider either as employer, or by reference to the terms of a contract with a private security firm; private security probity and standards to be further assured by the proposed statutory scheme (discussed above), or, in the interim, through active monitoring by the police; relationship between police and local authority patrols to be grounded in crime and disorder partnerships under the 1998 Act; appearance of Wardens to be clearly distinct from police; standard operating procedures relating to recruitment, training and management to be developed for a range of different locations, circumstances, relationships and purposes; funding should not be from police budgets.

---

[39] Crime and Disorder Act 1998, ss.5–7.

[40] Local Government Act 1999, Part I.

[41] See *e.g.* Police Federation press release of July 16, 1998 viewing "with great concern" the anouncement by Ian Blair, chief constable of Surrey, that provate patrols be supervised by the police.

[42] Home Office (2000a) The final report substantially endorsed an earlier interim report of August 1999.

[43] Membership is to be shared between the Home Office and the Department of the Environment, Transport and the Regions.

To a significant extent, therefore, the working group report assuages police fears of encroachment and confusion of functions. At the same time, it allows the police and other public bodies a degree of supervisory and partnership influence and thereby establishes a link, however attenuated, in the chain of public accountability. It bears emphasising, however, that, in relation to the private sector, this element of public accountability will embrace only those few operators who have contracted responsibilities as Wardens, and so the proposals suggest no general solution to the public accountability of private policing. Unlike the general proposals for the private security industry, moreover, there is no suggestion of a statutory framework—however diluted—for Wardens. Instead, soft law will prevail. On one view, this is sensible regulatory restraint in the face of an emergent and only partly formed sector. On another view, it is precisely because the dynamic of growth we have charted in this chapter suggests there is potential for further development in non-police patrolling, with inevitable tensions, rivalries and blurred edges between these patrols and the public police, and with ensuing difficulties for any model of governance which is still premised upon the pre-eminence of the public police, that a *statutory* line in the sand should have been drawn.

PART IV

CONSTITUTIONAL FUTURES

Chapter Ten

Plural Policing and Constitutionalism Pluralism

By this point, hopefully, the initially sceptical reader will feel more persuaded of the various ways in which—to repeat the opening assertion of the book—policing is profoundly influenced by the constitutional order in which it is situated. The unitary form of the U.K. constitution has conditioned the terms on which it has been possible to accommodate new forms of policing within the devolved polities of Northern Ireland and Scotland and within the supranational polity of the European Union. Constitutional doctrine, too, has played a large part, most immediately in the form of the congeries of ideas around constabulary independence but also through more general patterns of public law doctrine. Fundamental constitutional principles, on the other hand, have been shy to assert themselves against the positivist and incrementalist grain of the British constitution, although the special transnational context of the Belfast Agreement and the Patten Commission provides a rare opportunity to lay new normative foundations.[1] Constitutional technique, finally, has been of broader significance. The New Public Management has been a pervasive influence across the various forms of tripartitism. The nurturing of a performance culture within the new national planning framework is the most obvious manifestation of this, but the shift in preference from public to private styles of service provision that NPM signifies also helps to explain the *laissez-faire* constitutional approach to the development of private policing.

In this concluding discussion, we stand back from the detail of the intervening pages and re-examine the broader framework set out in the opening chapter. How, 40 years after the landmark Willink Commission, 20

---

[1] See section 3 below.

years after Scarman, and 10 years after the managerialist agenda became constitutional orthodoxy, should we reassess the relationship between policing and the constitution? In the first place, what are the main regulatory problems associated with the new configuration of policing which has developed alongside the changing constitutional order? Secondly, how well-equipped is that changing constitutional order to address these problems? In addressing these questions, we do not seek simply to repeat our criticisms of the particular inadequacies of the emerging order. Neither, however, do we go to the other extreme, imagining utopian solutions to the problems identified. Rather, we attempt to lay the foundations for an ultimately more practical exercise in constitutional reform, one which examines the difficulties and opportunities generated by the underlying constitutional dynamic for the crafting of a more legitimate framework of police governance.

1. Plural Policing

Policing futurologists have become thick on the ground in recent years,[2] and this is no mere quirk of academic fashion. There is broad agreement that the age of the New Police as it was originally conceived in the early years of the 19th century is drawing to a close, and that a new and as yet inadequately comprehended "third wave"[3] of policing is taking shape. Prior to the New Police, the state was engaged in "steering" rather than "rowing" the vessels of organised security. It supervised and co-ordinated local policing systems, relying in particular on its centralised system of courts and its military capacity. However, the actual mechanics of policing, as indeed the bulk of the mechanics of governance more generally, were devolved to local power-centres within the feudal state. As industrialisation and urbanisation challenged the capacity of the old system of part-time, non-specialised police to maintain either specific or general order, the state sought to consolidate its pre-eminent title to legitimate violence by assuming direct responsibility for the provision of a uniform, full-time, specialised New Police. This Peelian strategy involved the state in both rowing and steering under a Keynesian conception of governance with its emphasis upon a sharp division

---

[2] See, *e.g.* Bayley (1995); Morgan and Newburn (1998); O'Malley (1998); Loader (2000); Bayley and Sharing (1996).

[3] Walker (1999a) pp. 77–79, drawing in particular upon Shearing (1996).

between government as provider of services and citizens and communities as their passive recipients.

Two centuries on, there are strong indications that the Peelian strategy is in secular decline. To be sure, the state retains traditional "rowing" functions through its control of local forces and has even acquired a more direct policing capacity through national policing initiatives.[4] Alongside this continuing evidence of "policing by government", however, there are growing indications of policing "through", "above", "beyond" and "below" central government[5] which we have mapped over the course of this book; through government, in the form of government agencies purchasing private policing services[6]; above government, in the form of Interpol, Europol and the growing internal security capacity of the European Union[7]; beyond government in the form of an expanding commercial sector[8]; below government, in the form of policing controlled by the devolved administrations of Scotland[9] and Northern Ireland,[10] and also, at a lower tier, municipal and civil policing more or less autonomous from the state.[11]

Superficially, the transfer of a significant amount of rowing from the central state to other constituencies and domains, whether this be the market place, the suprastate polity of the E.U., devolved government or the local community, might suggest a return to the Pre-Peelian model. Yet what is significantly different about the post-Peelian model compared to either of its predecessors is that it also begins to question the state's pre-eminence in the more basic steering task. While the state in principle continues to control the regulatory space within which the private security market operates, it has limited influence over demand, and so, ultimately, over supply. At the suprastate level, the continuing predominance of unanimity and supermajoritarian rules over matters bearing upon state sovereignty means that while, at least in strict constitutional terms,[12] an individual member state such as the United Kingdom retains considerable influence over the expansion of the E.U.

---

[4] See chapter seven
[5] Loader (2000).
[6] See chapter nine.
[7] See chapter eight.
[8] See chapter nine.
[9] See chapter five.
[10] See chapter six.
[11] See chapter nine.
[12] Although we should not underestimate the pressure towards expansion exerted by the professional community; see chapter eight, section 4(A).

policing jurisdiction, by the same procedural logic it can do little to *reduce* the considerable jurisdiction already granted. At the substate level, power devolved may in theory be power retained, but the trend in Scotland, and more emphatically in Northern Ireland, is towards a more complex constitutional configuration (of which more below) which challenges the continuing ultimate authority of Whitehall and Westminster. Finally, while some forms of civil policing remain closely monitored—even encouraged—by the state, others such as retributive vigilantism or community self-policing influenced by paramilitaries in Northern Ireland, escape state control.

The third wave of policing, therefore, is one of plural and diversified provision, networked across a number of institutional and regulatory sites. As Loader argues, plural policing raises more complex issues of police governance than we are accustomed to address under a one-dimensional statist perspective. No longer is it sufficient simply to ensure that the state police are democratically legitimate, effective and fair, although this remains an essential and pressing concern. Policing in other modes and domains must also be adequately "fenced in"[13] by regulatory controls. Furthermore, the different policing domains—state, substate, suprastate, commercial and civil—cannot be considered discretely. The adequacy of the governance arrangements for plural policing cannot be measured merely by aggregating the value of the various site-specific regulatory mechanisms. Rather, plural policing has to be assessed as a whole, in terms of its complexly interconnected practice and impact; and, correspondingly, the quality of its governance must depend in part upon the cohesion of the various regulatory sites and their capacity to complement one another.

Against this backdrop, the crucial constitutional question about the future of policing concerns the dynamics of multi-level, dispersed governance. To avoid conflicting agendas, the escape of "fugitive" power[14] or regulatory overkill there must be effective regulatory co-ordination between the different sites or nodes of authority, while to ensure that the overall pattern of policing and security is defined by reference to public interest considerations the source or sources of such regulatory co-ordination must be democratically accountable. But the very fact that the problem of governance now presents itself in this multi-level form means

---

[13] See Loader (2000).
[14] See, *e.g.* Morison (1998).

that the resource we have traditionally drawn upon in search of solutions to such problems—namely the state—is not the automatic candidate for the new regulatory role. The fact of multi-level governance implies that the regulatory monopoly of the state is already threatened. By the same token, therefore, we must doubt the capacity of the state to perform an effective role in co-ordinating the various sites of authority or guaranteeing their democratic accountability. But if the state is no longer the obvious choice, what, if anything, can take its place? Let us now turn to constitutional theory to see what answers it might suggest.

2. Constitutional Pluralism

Just as there is a contemporary trend towards the decoupling of state and policing, so there is a similar trend towards the decoupling of state and constitution. In a manner which parallels the discussion of the onset of plural policing, many commentators have observed how forces of globalization which "shift the spatial form of human organisation and activity to transcontinental or inter-regional patterns of activity, interaction and the exercise of power"[15] have begun to detach constitutionalism from its original statist moorings.[16] The international society of states emerged in a slow trajectory after the signing of the Treaty of Westphalia in 1648. Under the Westphalian model the world political order consisted of and was divided by sovereign states. State sovereignty in this context conveyed the double sense of *internal sovereignty*—the idea of the exclusive and unrivalled legal authority of the state within a particular territorial space, and *external sovereignty*—the idea of the state as the only significant legally recognised player on the stage of global decision-making. These two dimensions of sovereignty were supported by constitutional law and international law respectively. Constitutional law was the primary structure in the legal architecture of the Westphalian order, precisely because it presupposed, and so reinforced the hegemony of the state. International law occupied a secondary position to constitutional law, regulating relations between sovereign states but only in the voluntarist sense[17] of providing a juridical framework to contain and document agreements

---

[15] Held (1999) p. 92.

[16] See, *e.g.* Tully (1995); MacCormick (1999); Shaw (1999); Bankowski and Christodoulidis (1998).

[17] On voluntarism, or consensualism, as the dominant theory of international law, see Schachter (1991) chap.5.

between states as formally free and equal parties. That is to say, international law was not the ultimate regulator of states, but rather their regulatory tool.[18]

The gradual globalization of economic activity, of political institutions and agendas, of culture and communications media, of environmental problems and challenges and of security needs and capacities—many of which factors are also directly implicated in the move towards plural policing—has produced a more interconnected world which is gradually decentring national political communities and challenging the Westphalian order in which they were embedded. So, too, the two legal handmaidens of Westphalia—state constitutional law and international law—have become no longer sufficient to fill the regulatory space which has opened up in respect of the changing global order.

What new configuration of legal authority is emerging to fill the regulatory gap, and how effective is it likely to be in providing a framework of governance for our immediate object of concern—plural policing? The broader of these two questions has been approached from a number of different perspectives. At one extreme, state revivalists[19] refuse to acknowledge the permanence of the gap and decline to view the ebbing of state constitutionalism as anything other than a blip on a horizon still dominated by Westphalia. Constitutional fatalists are more realistic about the depth of the challenge of the state and fear that the "end of [state]constitutionalism"[20] as an adequate form of normative order for the public domain will not herald the emergence of a viable alternative. In contrast to this approach, a number of authors have begun to explore the idea of a "postnational constitutionalism"[21]—the notion that authoritative constitutional law need no longer be restricted to the state but can also be found at other levels and in other forms of political community—local, international, supranational and even non-territorial.[22] While this last body of work is interesting and richly suggestive in its consideration of new patterns of institutional normative order, it tends to neglect or to marginalise two related issues which are important to our understanding of post-Westphalian public law.

In the first place, and acknowledging the fears of the constitutional

---

[18] Thus under international law, the parties to a treaty may revoke or change it at any time, and may even disregard treaty provisions which establish a special procedure to be followed: see Vienna Convention on the Law of Treaties (1968).

[19] See, e.g. Hutchinson (1994); Milward (1992).

[20] See, e.g. Himsworth (1996).

[21] See, e.g. Curtin (1998); Shaw (1999).

[22] See, Tully (1995).

fatalists, the continued use by postnational constitutionalists of the language of constitutionalism to describe non-state frameworks of public authority risks underplaying the significance of detaching constitutional law from its ideological and intellectual roots in the state. If the basic themes of self-validating foundational legal authority, of exhaustive allocation of institutional competence and of the erection of (typically individual) rights and liberties as side-constraints upon the governmental order which characterise constitutions and constitutionalism have developed meaning and texture against the backdrop of the one-dimensional order of self-contained sovereign states, then we should not readily assume that the resultant constitutional discourse translates to the various new sites of public authority which make up the emergent multi-dimensional configuration of polities. Secondly, and of even more immediate significance for our purposes, postnational constitutionalism, with its emphasis upon the dispersal of authority to new sites, tends to beg the question of the continuing significance of the state within the new multi-dimensional order. If ultimate authority no longer rests with the state, how much influence does the state nevertheless retain? If it is no longer plausible to talk in the language of unassailable state sovereignty, then how do we best characterise the relationship between the regulatory authority of state and that of non-state sites?

I present here only in synoptic form a line of argument and a conceptual language which I have begun to develop elsewhere as a means of addressing these questions.[23] My approach conceives of the emerging post-Westphalian order as involving an interplay between state constitutional law on the one hand and non-state or cosmopolitan[24] *metaconstitutional* law on the other. Semantically, the prefix "meta" stands in relation to the activity denoted by the concept prefixed as "a higher science of the same nature but dealing with ulterior problems."[25] Metaconstitutionalism relates to constitutionalism, therefore, as metaphysics does to physics or as metaethics does to ethics. Metaconstitutional rules—or norms or axioms—are rules *about* the same subject matter as constitutional

---

[23] See, Walker (2000a); (2000b).

[24] Legal philosophy is already familiar with what might be labelled *state-centred*, or *domestic* metaconstitutionalism (see Kay (1981), Alexander (1998)) This refers to the internally generated and agreed rules and assumptions about what is to count as the constitution and as fundamental law within a state, whether, to take two examples, this metaconstitutional background is conceived of in terms of the Hartian rule of recognition or of the Kelsenian grundnorm. We are not here concerned with this local form of excavation but, instead, with a deep justificatory discourse articulated within a non-state or cosmopolitan context.

[25] *The Shorter Oxford English Dictionary.*

rules—the regulation of the public domain. Unlike constitutional law, however, metaconstitutional law is not nested in the state and does not look to the state as its fundamental source of validity. To the contrary, notwithstanding the often inconsistent and competing claims made on behalf of the state through its traditional constitutional discourse and representations of sovereignty,[26] metaconstitutional law tends to claim within its own terms a higher or deeper constitutional authority than state constitutional law. The nature of its claims are reflected in the way in which it characterises its relationship with state law. It may purport to authorise, instruct, influence, supplement or supplant state law, or any combination of these. Whatever the case, in no circumstances does it concede the normative superiority of state law. Metaconstitutionalism always conceives of its own authority as original and irreducible.

Metaconstitutional law comes in a wide variety of forms which cannot be easily distinguished or neatly classified. Nevertheless, we may identify five main types, which are ordered below in terms of their level of abstraction from the constitutional state.

First, there is legal discourse which seeks to reshape the traditional intra-constitutional law sphere of the structural relations between different groups within the state—whether defined by nation, ethnicity, territory, religion, language or other cleavage—in a manner which goes beyond those forms of legal "identity politics",[27] such as claims to mutual respect, to multicultural citizenship or to distinct political institutions, which can be accommodated within the existing framework of state authority. Instead, it questions the constitutional integrity of the state itself through secessionist or quasi-secessionist claims. For the most part this is a *counterfactual* legal discourse. Unlike the forms of metaconstitutionalism considered below, it is not located within an institutional site or sites which can make a plausible current claim to possess fundamental law-making authority. On the other hand, this form of metaconstitutionalism may be sustained and supported through its relationship to these other, more state-removed metaconstitutional sites which do possess plausible claims to fundamental legal authority.[28] Yet as long as the integrity and internal distribution of authority of the state which it challenges remains

---

[26] On sovereignty as a means of representing a unity of political power within a polity, see Lindahl (1998).

[27] See Tully (1995); (1999).

[28] Think, for example, of the way that minority national movements may be protected by international human rights regimes, or, in the context of the E.U., may be sustained and legitimated by the representational or resource-allocation possibilities of association with or membership of the supranational organisation; see, *e.g.* Keating (1998).

intact, then, *ex hypothesi*, secessionist or quasi-secessionist discourse can be no more than aspirational. That does not mean, however, that it is merely a form of constitutional law-in-waiting. It is *meta*constitutional in the sense that while its ultimate purpose may be the creation of a new state, and thus a new constitutional order, the process by which the transformation is sought addresses matters of fundamental political authority through arguments—historical, ethical or pragmatic[29]—which refuse to defer to the existing state constitutional order as a definitive authority, and in so doing necessarily poses a challenge to the *general* claim of constitutional law to ultimate authority.

This type of counterfactual metaconstitutionalism, more pertinently, may also have an indirect impact upon existing state constitutional law. In the development of state constitutional law, statecraft may demand or dialogic openness may encourage the taking into account of secessionist or quasi-secessionist discourse, and often with consequences which escape the intentions of the accommodators. The quickening narrative of constitutional reform in the multinational state of the United Kingdom is an apt example. Institutions developed to consolidate the British state, such as local referenda and devolved assemblies—including the devolution of policing in Scotland and Northern Ireland, also have a meaning and a role within alternative metaconstitutional discourses dedicated to national independence.

A second type of metaconstitutional discourse seeks to shape and instruct the traditional intra-state constitutional law sphere of the basic rights and duties of the individual vis-à-vis the state. The paradigm case here is "international" human rights law.[30] Mainly through Treaty law promulgated at both regional and local level, but backed by peremptory norms of international law (*ius cogens*) and the more general framework of international customary law, this area of law expanded exponentially in the wake of the Second World War. It is a movement which has challenged the premise of untrammelled state sovereignty preventing the traditional framework of international law from addressing individuals as well as states themselves as the subjects, rather than the mere objects, of its legal rules. As well as the development of a substantive state-transcendent human rights jurisprudence, including the landmark

---

[29] See, for example, the rich mix of arguments used on behalf of the secessionist case in the Quebec Secession Reference; *Reference by the Governor of Canada pursuant to s.53 of the Supreme Court Act, concerning the secession of Quebec from Canada* [1998] 2 SCR 217. See also Walters (1999) pp. 370–395.

[30] See, *e.g.* Steiner and Alston (1996).

Pinochet case,[31] this form of metaconstitutionalism has been increasingly secured by an infrastructure of non-state courts and tribunals within which such rights may be vindicated. The most prominent of these is undoubtedly the European Court of Human Rights, which, as we have seen,[32] is developing an increasingly influential presence role in domestic human rights matters, including rights which challenge and circumscribe police decisions and practices.[33]

A third type of metaconstitutional discourse shapes relations between states in ways which supplement and modify the internal constitutional structure of those states. The current metaconstitutional conversation between Britain and Ireland provides a good example.[34] Under the 1998 Belfast Agreement, as we have seen,[35] there are elements of condominium or joint sovereignty, including a permanent institutional complex embracing both east-west structures (British-Irish Council and British-Irish Intergovernmental Conference) and a North-South Ministerial Council with an interest in policing matters.

This type of arrangement shades into a fourth type of metaconstitutional authority, which in addressing relations between states develops an institutional structure with sufficient depth and scope of authority to constitute a non-state polity. Of course, the extent to which an institutional structure constitutes a separate polity is a matter of degree. Clearly the Good Friday structures, for now at least, fall short, but the GATT/WTO structure and the North American Free Trade Association, to take two of the most prominent examples, are less clear-cut cases, as also are some of the regional international organisations.[36] At the other end of the spectrum is the supranational legal framework of the E.U. Originally conceived of as a means to regulate certain fundamental economic relations between states and crafted with the orthodox tools of international law, the E.U. gradually developed its own claim to

---

[31] *R. v. Bow Street Metropolitan Stipendiary Magistrate, ex Parte Pinochet Ugarte (Amnesty International intervening (No.3)* (1999) 2 W.L.R. 827, in which the House of Lords, drawing upon both domestic law and customary international law, held that a former head of state enjoys no immunity in extradition or criminal proceedings brought in the UK in respect of the international crime of torture; see Fox (1999).

[32] See chapter four, section 2(C) above.

[33] Another key development in this regard is the new International Criminal Court; Rome Statute of the International Criminal Court, July 17, 1998, A/CONF. 183/9. 37 ILM 999; see Robertson (2000).

[34] Her Majesty's Government (1998); see also O'Leary (1998); Hadfield, (1998); Boyle and Hadden (1999).

[35] Her Majesty's Government (1998); see chapter six.

[36] See, *e.g.* Laffan (1992).

sovereign authority within a limited sphere. Indeed, as the E.U. has attracted a complexity of institutional structure, a range of legal competencies and an authoritative jurisprudence which begin to rival those of the state, then it has come to represent a particularly developed form of metaconstitutional law; such an organisation becomes, so to speak, a meta-state. As we have seen, the uniquely well-developed metaconstitutional site of the E.U. impacts upon policing in a number of ways, from the emerging institutional edifice of the Third Pillar and Europol[37] to free movement rules which threaten to circumscribe domestic police decisions and practices.[38]

Finally, and at the highest level of abstraction from state constitutional law, metaconstitutionalism embraces a further set of relations between polities—both states and non-state polities (including meta-states)—in the more complex multi-dimensional configuration of authority which characterises the post-Westphalian order. At this "meta-meta" level we are concerned, in the first place, with the relations between the E.U. and its member states, in particular with the judicial conversation between constitutional courts[39] and the political conversations in successive Treaty-amending Intergovernmental Conferences (IGCs)[40] and in the E.U. institutions through which these relations are negotiated. Then, at an even higher level of abstraction, the issues of flexibility and fragmentation within and around the E.U. come into view.[41] Here we are concerned with relations between different non-state polities; that is, between the E.U. meta-state and the other emergent polities of our fragmented order, whether located within the E.U. (*e.g.* the "Euro" zone), beyond the E.U. (*e.g.* Council of Europe, GATT/WTO), or, to take the most immediately relevant example of Schengen, overlapping E.U. and non-E.U. states.

This brief overview of the metaconstitutional perspective is, hopefully, sufficient to demonstrate its advantages as an explanatory tool. On the one hand, unlike state revivalism, it acknowledges the depth, scale and durability of the challenge to the authority of the constitutional state, as evident in the claims of normative authority emanating from the growing

---

[37] See chapter eight.
[38] See chapter four, section 2(C).
[39] The most significant recent contribution to this conversation was that of the German Constitutional Court in *Brunner* v. *The European Union Treaty* [1994] 1 C.M.L.R. 57: See also Everson, (1998); Stone Sweet (1998); De Witte, (1999).
[40] On the IGC negotiations prior to the Treaty of Amsterdam, see De Burca (1996); Walker (1996b).
[41] See chapter eight, section 4(C); See Walker (1998b); De Burca and Scott (2000).

range of metaconstitutional sites. On the other hand, it acknowledges more emphatically than the new postnational constitutionalism the abiding significance of the constitutional state, as the entity towards which much metaconstitutional regulatory discourse is ultimately directed and from which it is ultimately derived. Thirdly, it acknowledges both the similarities and the differences between the public law discourses of the state sphere and the non-state sphere. It moves beyond constitutional fatalism by indicating that there is an internal relationship between the two discourses; that metaconstitutionalism seeks to address at one or more removes the problems of public authority originating within and still much centred around state constitutionalism. Yet in its eschewal of the language of constitutionalism as a broad descriptor of public law discourse it recognises that the state-constitution coupling is deeply rooted and that the discourse of the non-state public law sphere is ultimately of a different order from the discourse of the state public law sphere.

If state constitutional and non-state metaconstitutional sites are different in kind yet complexly connected, how—to return to the heart of the matter—are their various regulatory outputs related? The basic answer offered is one of emergent pluralism. Within the developing multi-dimensional configuration the various constitutional and metaconstitutional sites make more or less plausible claims to autonomy for the different systems of law they purport to authorise, and there is no objective and incontestable way of adjudicating between their claims. That is to say, if we step outside the various legal sites and systems, we can no longer identify a "master discourse", whether state, state-counterfactual, suprastate or international, to which the others are prepared to defer. Instead, we must accept an irreducible plurality of claims to ultimate authority. In turn, this pluralist framework informs the spectrum of possible relations between different regulatory sites. At one end of the spectrum, the relation between sites may be authoritative; while pluralism implies that each site may not give up its *general* claim as an independent source of legal authority, various bridging mechanisms exist to ensure that the authoritative claims of one site may be accepted by another site in any *particular* regulatory context.[42] Alternatively, in those contexts where there is no agreed authoritative norm, or not yet, the relation between sites may be strategic, the legal resources of each site utilised by the representatives of these sites to bargain and compete in pursuit of

---

[42] For example, the preliminary reference procedure which allows matters of E.U. law arising in domestic courts to be decided by the European Court of Justice; Art. 23t E.C. Treaty.

site-specific goals. Finally, at the other end of the spectrum, where there is a more equal and non-strategic context of inter-site communication through which processes of mutual learning and mutual accommodation develop, relations between different sites may be dialogic. Of course, these three relational dynamic—authoritative, strategic and dialogic—need not be mutually exclusive. Indeed, typically, authoritative inter-site rules emerge through some combination of strategic and dialogic inter-action, while sites which are primarily authoritative or strategic may retain or develop space for genuine dialogue.

3. Governance Prospects

If, then, we bring plural policing and constitutional pluralism together as two aspects of a wider movement beyond the sovereign state, what are the prospects for a framework of police governance which is effectively co-ordinated and democratically accountable? There is, of course, no simple answer to a question with so many facets and involving so many contingencies. What we can do is to indicate some of the drawbacks and constraints, but also some of the benefits and opportunities associated with a more pluralist environment.

We have already alluded to some of the main drawbacks and constraints. The governance of a plural policing environment may require inter-site co-ordination, but, as we have seen, constitutional pluralism implies that there is no overarching authority to act as the co-ordinator —to guarantee consistency and to ensure against regulatory lacunae or excesses. The combination of a plural policing environment and constitutional pluralism also raises significant problems of democratic account-ability. Institutional complexity—an inevitable accompaniment of pluralism—in both the policing and the constitutional domain may erode accountability "by obscuring who is responsible for what and answerable to whom"[43] This is most marked in the context of European policing, but is also a potential problem in the increasingly crowded and elaborately interwoven institutional space around the new devolved policing arrangements in Ireland and Scotland. The multiplication of non-state forms of political community and policing also poses a more direct challenge to democratic accountability. For all its limitations, the political community of the state, particularly when combined with the

---

[43] Loader (2000).

cultural community of the nation,[44] provides a "community of attach-ment"[45]—of mutuality, reciprocity and common identity—within which it is possible to foster an effective democratic culture. For even the most long-standing and institutional elaborate non-state polities, such as the E.U., the generation of an effective *demos* is notoriously elusive.[46] Other less developed institutional sites, such as Schengen, or even, arguably, the E.U. policing project generally,[47] avoid or marginalise the daunting chal-lenge of democratic legitimacy by mobilising around other more sec-urity-orientated values. At the local end of the spectrum, private policing and some forms of civil policing, as products of the market and civil society respectively, are not easily accommodated and regulated within *any* polity, whatever its democratic credentials.

On the other hand, there are a number of opportunities associated with the changing policing and constitutional environment that are worth exploring in a little more depth. This excavation is organised around three connected themes.

(A) The Resilience of the State

To begin with, we should be careful not to overstate the extent to which the state has lost its capacity to steer the policing sector. The connection between policing—even its new plural mode—and the state, remains rel-atively robust.[48] A strong policing role continues to be important to the state's historical claim to non-negotiable coercive power in pursuit of general and specific order; to its need to provide a secure environment within which to deliver a broad range of governmental services; and even—given the intimate connection between policing and social atti-tudes towards fundamental matters such as life and death, order and chaos, and protection and vulnerability[49]—as a symbolic resource bear-ing upon the state's capacity to generate and sustain a strong sense of political community and collective identity.[50] For those reasons, the state has been more jealous of its pre-eminent policing role in the face of con-stitutional pluralism than it has of various of its other governmental func-

---

[44] See, *e.g.* Miller (1995) chap.2.
[45] See also Loader and Walker (2001, forthcoming); Miller (1995) chap.4.
[46] See, *e.g.* Weiler (1999) chap.8.
[47] See chapter eight, section 3.
[48] See Loader and Walker (2001, forthcoming).
[49] See, *e.g.* Walker (1996c); Loader (1997a).
[50] See chapter six above; see also Walker and Telford (2000).

tions. Even in the context of the E.U., where an alternative centre of authority is most fully established, policing and the Third Pillar are not part of the core. In the context of devolved power to Scotland and Ireland, important security functions are retained to the U.K. centre, as part and parcel of the remit of its expanded range of explicitly centralised policing institutions. If we add to this the fact that in the context of private and civil policing there is no *constitutional* impediment to the state's asserting or re-asserting control—although there are undoubtedly significant political and economic obstacles—then it seems clear that the state still has at least one hand on the tiller and retains some capacity to co-ordinate the governance of policing.

(B) COMPLEX ACCOUNTABILITY

Patently, however, if we are not to fall into the trap of the myopic state revivalist, we should not overstate the resilience and adaptability of the state or underestimate the remorselessness of the globalizing pressures pushing both plural policing and constitutional pluralism. To what extent, therefore, can we make a virtue out of necessity, and make a case for the effective *co-ordination* of the various strands of policing and police governance even in the absence of a fully effective *co-ordinator*?

We can begin by reminding ourselves that state control of policing is by no means an unqualified good. The two constitutional paradoxes of policing are essentially about the capacity of the state police to subvert the very values of general security they are charged to protect and about the propensity of some states, in the name of their own narrow security interests, to encourage this subversion or to fail to take the regulatory steps necessary to prevent it.[51] In contrast, the new metaconstitutional sites, with the partial exception of the E.U. with its growing police capacity, tend to be little affected these paradoxes. This may be because they have no policing capacity of their own (e.g. Council of Europe). Alternatively, it may be because such metaconstitutional sites, being themselves subject to some level of state control (albeit, at least in some contexts,[52] state control informed by constitutional norms, and so weighted towards the constraint of local or suprastate power rather than

---

[51] See chapter one, section 1.

[52] But not all, as the manner in which the British state chooses to limit the policing authority of the European Union is not subject to any domestic framework of constitutional norms. On the other hand, as regards the general grant of new policing competences to the E.U., the British state is externally constrained by the politics of European treaty-making, while,

the assertion of overweening central power),[53] they have only limited regulatory control over their own policing capacity (e.g. Scotland, Northern Ireland and the E.U.). What is more, at least some of these metaconstitutional sites may utilise their regulatory capacity to monitor or curtail the activities of the state police, in so doing breaking the circuit of self-interest that sustains the statist constitutional paradoxes.

The idea of "complex accountability" indicates the potential benefits involved in the reciprocal monitoring and mutual constraint of constitutional and metaconstitutional sites. Complex accountability involves the idea "that multiple forms of accountability of powerful government actors and organisations can compensate for the imperfections of single lines of accountability."[54] Just as the state may in some instances limit the policing power of metaconstitutional sites, the regulatory efforts of metaconstitutional sites in authorising, instructing, influencing, supplementing or supplanting state policing law adds additional independent layers to existing intra-state structures of complex accountability. The individual rights protection supplied by the Council of Europe's European Court and Convention of Human Rights, now firmly domesticated in the Human Rights Act 1998 falls within this category.[55] So too do the Third Pillar rules laying out the institutional requirements of the national satellites of Europol and the rules of engagement between national forces and Europol, and the Belfast Agreement rules establishing permanent Commissions to oversee standards of equality and human rights in the policing of the North.

(c) Eclectic Governance

The emerging multi-dimensional constitutional configuration provides an enabling context not only for the external imposition of new layers of accountability, but also for the active borrowing and reception of governance ideas, doctrines, institutions and mechanisms between sites. Of

---

as regards specific extensions or variations of the E.U.'s *existing* policing capacity, it is even more significantly constrained by the majoritarian voting rules applicable to Third Pillar legislation; see chapter eight, section 2.

[53] In the present British constitutional settlement, both aspects are clearly in evidence. On the one hand the imposition of a human rights framework on Scotland and Ireland constrains local police power over the citizen, while on the other retention of U.K. jurisdiction over national security represents a consolidation and reassertion of central authority.

[54] Saward (2000) pp. 41–42.

[55] See *Osman v. Ferguson* [1998] 5 B.H.R.C. 293, discussed in chapter four, section 2(C).

course, this already happened to some degree in the one-dimensional Westphalian order of states, and provided one of the traditional rationales for the disciplines of comparative public policy and comparative law.[56] Under a multi-dimensional framework, however, the connections between sites are much more intimate and much more systematic. That is to say, constitutional pluralism can provide a particularly receptive climate for mutual learning and reciprocal benefit across sites—an unprecedented opportunity for eclectic governance. In case this sounds naively utopian, it should be emphasised that mutual learning need not presuppose an entirely free and equal dialogue—an open seminar between interlocking constitutional sites where ideas are endorsed on the basis of merit and sound argument alone. If we recall our earlier discussion of the complex interpretation of authoritative, strategic and dialogic discourses, an eclectic approach is often underpinned by instrumental considerations; where, for example, a state pre-emptively takes on some of the counter-factual ideas of an oppositional site, or where an inter-state structure, such as the Belfast Agreement, is established as a compromise between competing national demands. Whatever the motivational backdrop, the multiplication and complex relation of different forms and levels of polities multiplies the possibilities of eclectic governance. To conclude, let us consider just a few examples of this as they bear upon some of the most abiding concerns of police governance, drawing from the report of the Patten Commission and subsequent developments in the politics of Northern Ireland, as the most recent, and arguably the most far-sighted, example of concerted constitutional debate on policing in the United Kingdom.[57]

Take, for instance, Patten's enthusiastic endorsement and extension of the Ombudsman institution in the policing context[58]—initially legislated for in the North the year prior to the publication of the Patten Report. The idea of a policing Ombudsman with a responsibility not only for reacting to specific complaints but also for initiating inquiries and for extrapolating from specific instances to general trends draws upon a number of sources. It builds upon a venerable Scandinavian institution, but one which was unknown in the U.K. until 1967, although it has since become an increasingly influential part of the British machinery of administrative justice.[59] It is also in line with a growing trend, evident in settings as diverse as Australia and Canada, to use the Ombudsman for

---

[56] But on the limitations of comparative law, see Legrand (1999).
[57] See chapter six.
[58] Patten (1999) para.6.41.
[59] See, *e.g.* Wade and Bradley (1997) chap.27.

criminal justice institutions.[60] Arguably, as an accountability mechanism which is external to the police but at the same time removed from direct political control, while also addressing many of the same questions as and working in close liaison with the Policing Board as the broader politically-constituted accountability body, the expanded Ombudsman idea offers the type of independent influence which is of particular value in the context of the politically divided North.

A second example concerns the need for a broad conception of policing and of policed communities to underpin the framework of governance. Patten shows a keen interest in taking and developing ideas and mechanisms introduced elsewhere in the U.K. over the course of the last decade, culminating in the Crime and Disorder Act 1998, in order to develop a more inclusionary conception of police policy and governance. Expanding upon earlier multi-agency and community safety initiatives on the mainland, Patten recommends that the focus of political accountability should, as in the new English and Welsh police authorities, be a body with a democratic majority and other diverse representation from civil society. The Policing Board—advisedly named on account of its ambitious remit—would co-ordinate its activities with other agencies whose work touches on public safety, and might even provide a future regulatory body for the private security industry. And although the subsequent Review of the Criminal Justice System in Northern Ireland stepped back from recommending that the Policing Board assume lead responsibility for co-ordinating community safety activity and the development of a community safety strategy, it endorsed—indeed extended—Patten's proposals[61] for a broader and more inclusive community safety approach at the local level,[62] where an accountability body composed on the same basis as the Policing Board would be established. As noted earlier, while the Government has subsequently adopted a cautious approach to the empowerment of District Policing Partnerships (DPPs), in particular refusing to offer immediate backing to the controversial recommendation of Patten and the Criminal Justice Review Group that district councils should be able to raise local rates to pay for additional policing or community safety services to be administered by the DPPs,[63] their broader community safety remit nevertheless remains intact and may in due course be developed further.

---

[60] See, *e.g.* Goldsmith (1991).
[61] Patten (1999) para.6.29.
[62] Criminal Justice Review Group (2000), para.11.53.
[63] Northern Ireland Office (2000), p. 15.

The Northern Ireland blueprint thus represents a more localised, and so potentially more diversely representative and participative variation of the mainland strategy.[64]

The importance of this set of proposals lies in their conscious acknowledgement of the new plural dimension of policing. The broad role and composition of the two accountability bodies suggests a dawning appreciation of the need to build into our governance structures what Loader has called "a politics of recognition" and a "politics of allocation."[65] These new "politics" register an awareness of the growing significance of the commercial and the non-state civic sector, and the need to include the voice and interests of constituencies involved in or affected by these new developments in the constitutional conversation over policing and the funding of policing priorities.

The two examples of eclectic governance considered above embody the potential for even more dynamic forms of institutional reflexivity. Just as policing in the North has drawn lessons from the use of Ombudsmen and more broadly-based accountability mechanisms elsewhere within the same multi-dimensional constitutional configuration, so too there is scope for reciprocal learning. As Patten itself implied, governance systems elsewhere, including the rest of the U.K., would arguably be enhanced by the adoption of the developed form of some of the initiatives which they themselves inspired. This applies even more forcibly to our third and final example, which allows us a final word on professional independence versus democratic accountability, the vexed question at the heart of police governance

As discussed in chapter six, the Patten Commission, with certain refinements to reinforce the role of the local democratic element in longer-term planning, adopted the strategic planning framework first introduced elsewhere in the U.K. in the Police and Magistrates' Courts Act 1994. In so doing, it recognised an opportunity to revisit the idea of the "operational independence" of the chief constable which has cast such a long shadow over the history of police governance in the United Kingdom.[66] It will be recalled that operational independence, and its even more inscrutable cousin constabulary independence, established a

---

[64] The idea of a multi-level accountability structure with broad representation and a broad community safety remit is also developed in Loader's model of "discursive policing" (1995, chap.7), which, in proposing the police commission as the institutional centre of the scheme, builds upon the earlier work of Jefferson and Grimshaw (1984). See also Loader (2000).

[65] Loader (2000).

[66] See generally chapters two, three and four.

conceptual fortress against some kinds of unwarranted political interference in policing. However, so indeterminate did these terms prove, that they could be—and often were—used to justify an open-ended discretion for the chief officer, extending far into areas which in any other aspect of public policy would be deemed the domain of general policy and thus appropriate for political influence. Furthermore, so deeply embedded did the idea of operational independence from political control become that it was used even to resist the retrospective answerabilty of the chief constable within his operational domain. A final perverse consequence of the open-texture and entrenched authority of these core terms was that they tended to dominate the available conceptual space, making it difficult to develop more precise and effective legal mechanisms at the boundaries between policy and operations. That is to say, the persistence of the old terminology militated against the development of the very additional legal mechanisms which its inadequacies demanded.

In this regard, the new strategic planning framework, whatever it lacked in democratic input and however anomalous its division of tasks, was a vital breakthrough. The immovable object of operational independence was buffeted by a sidewind carrying the irresistible force of the new managerialism. Suddenly, policy was a legitimate area of concern for the local democratic element, now enjoined to work in partnership with the other tripartite parties. Yet the juxtaposition of this new framework and the old concepts remains a somewhat uneasy one. The strategic planning framework has invaded the conceptual space configured by the old ideas, and no-one can be quite sure of the consequences. Patten recognised this, and, having democratised the planning framework, moved to confirm the restriction of chief constabulary independence to a more limited operational space. Within this space, moreover, the chief constable was to possess not "operational independence" but "operational responsibility."[67] In turn, this justified the imposition of a comprehensive duty to report to the Policing Board on operations after the event and a right on the part of the Board to initiate a follow-up inquiry, thereby both augmenting public transparency and providing the Board with additional information necessary for the effective performance of its planning function.[68]

---

[67] Patten (1999) para.6.21.
[68] *ibid.*, para.6.22–23.

If and when this conceptual innovation is introduced in the North,[69] and, in time perhaps, extended to the rest of the United Kingdom,[70] it will of course not put an end to boundary disputes and turf wars between the tripartite parties. As long as policing remains a bedrock function of the state and, indeed, as it becomes a more significant function of non-state polities, these "constitutional tensions"[71] between law enforcement and politics must be accommodated. Under the new dispensation, however, the disputed area between the tripartite parties would be more clearly visible, the general allocation of territory more appropriate to the talents of the parties, and the opportunities to work together and avoid boundary disputes greater.

In the new plural policing environment, the tripartite arrangement may no longer be the sole key to good police governance, yet it remains a vital cornerstone—a recurrent template and elaborately ramified theme within a more complex multi-dimensional regulatory map. The prospects for good police governance—the flourishing of tripartitism included—within this more complex space is intimately linked, in turn, to the development of more effective conversation and exchange both within and between constitutional and metaconstitutional sites. In the changing constitutional order the connections between effective and legitimate policing arrangements and the fundamental legal pattern of political authority may be undergoing a deep-seated transformation, but they remain as profoundly important as ever.

---

[69] As noted in chapter six, the Government has accepted the implications of the idea of operational responsibility for augmenting the right of the Policing Board to be informed without conceding the necessity of legislative endorsement of the central concept itself; Northern Ireland Office (2000) p. 13. Whether direct legislative endorsement would add much is a moot point, although it would offer more transparent, and perhaps more resilient, conceptual foundations for the detailed re-allocation of authority provided.

[70] For other possible democratic reforms of the system in England and Wales, see chapter four, section 3(b) above.

[71] Waddington (1999) p. 195.

Bibliography

Ackerman, B. (1991), *We The People: Foundations* (Cambridge Mass.: Harvard).

Adler, E. and Barnett, M. (1998), *Security Communities* (Cambridge: Cambridge University Press).

Alderson, J. (1984), *Policing Freedom* (Plymouth: Macdonald and Evans).

Alderson, J. (1984), *Human Rights and the Police* (Strasbourg: Council of Europe).

Alexander, L. (1998), "Introduction" in L. Alexander (ed), *Constitutionalism: Philosophical Foundations* (Cambridge: Cambridge University Press) pp. 1–15.

Allen, D.M. and Payne, D. (1991), "The Public and the Police in Scotland: Findings" from the 1988 British Crime Survey, (Edinburgh: Scottish Office).

Allen, T.R.S. (1993), *Law, Liberty and Justice: The Legal Foundations of British Constitutionalism* (Oxford: Clarendon Press).

Allen, T.R.S. (1997), "Parliamentary Sovereignty: Law, Politics and Revolution", 113 *Law Quarterly Review*, 443.

Anderson, M. (1989), *Policing the World* (Oxford: Oxford University Press).

Anderson, M. and den Boer, M. (eds), (1994), *Policing Across National Boundaries* (London: Pinter).

Anderson, M., den Boer, M., Cullen, P. , Gilmore, W.C., Raab, C. and Walker, N. (1995), *Policing the European Union; Theory, Law and Practice* (Oxford: Oxford University Press).

Anderson, S., Kinsey, R., Loader, I. and Smith, C. (1994), *Cautionary Tales: Young People, Crime and Policing in Edinburgh* (Avebury: Aldershot).

Anderson, S. and Leitch, S. (1994), *The Scottish Crime Survey 1993: First results; Crime and Criminal Justice Research Findings No. 1* (Scottish Office, Edinburgh).

Anderton, J. (1981), "Accountable to Whom?" 12 *Police*, no.6 (Feb).

Andreas, P. (1996), "US–Mexico: Open Markets, Closed Borders" *Foreign Policy*, 51.

Appleby, P. (1995), *A Force on the Move* (Malvern: Images Publishing).

Arblaster, A. (1994), *Democracy* (2nd ed., Buckingham: Open University Press).

Archibugi, D., Held, D., and Kohler. M. (eds), (1998), *Reimagining Political Community: Studies in Cosmopolitan Democracy* (Cambridge: Polity).

Association of Chief Police Officers (1975), *Report of the Sub-Committee on Criminal Intelligence* (ACPO).

Association of Chief Police Officers (1985), *Final Report on the Working Party on Drugs Related Crime* (ACPO).

Association of Chief Police Officers in Scotland (1998), *Review of the Structure of the Scottish Police Service* (18 September, ACPO(S)).

Atiyah. P. (1985), "Common Law and Statute Law" 48 *Modern Law Review* 1.

Audit Commission (1990a), *Footing the Bill: Financing Provincial Police Forces* (London: HMSO).

Audit Commission (1990b), *Effective Policing: Performance Review in Police Forces* (London: HMSO).

Audit Commission (1993), *Helping With Enquiries* (London: HMSO).

Audit Commission (1996), *Streetwise: Effective Police Patrol* (London: HMSO).

Baker, M. (1996), "On Whose Authority?" *Policing Today*, Vol. 2, September, pp. 10–13.

Baldwin, R. and Kinsey, R. (1982), *Police Powers and Politics* (Quartet, London).

Baldwin, R. (1987), "Why Accountability?" 27 *British Journal of Criminology* 1.

Baldwin, R. (1994), "Governing with Rules: The Developing Agenda" in G. Richardson and H. Genn (eds), *Administrative Law and Government Action: The Courts and Alternative Mechanisms of Review* (Oxford: Oxford University Press), pp. 158–188.

Bankowski, Z. and Christodoudilis, E. (1998), "The European Union as an Essentially Contested Project" 4 *European Law Journal* 337

Banton, M. (1974), "The Keepers of the Peace" *New Society*, December 5, p. 635.

Barendt, E. (1998), *An Introduction to Constitutional Law* (Oxford: Oxford University Press).

Barnard, C. and Hare, I. (1997), "The Right to Protest and the Right to Export: Police Discretion and the Free Movement of Goods" 60 *Modern Law Review* 394.

Barnard, C. and Hare, I. (2000), "Police Discretion and the Rule of Law: Economic Community Rights versus Civil Rights" 63 *Modern Law Review*.

Barzini, L. (1964), *The Italians* (New York: Atheneum).

Baxter, J. and Koffman, L. (1985), (eds), *Police: The Constitution and the Community* (Abington: Professional Books).

Bayley, D. (1983), "Accountability and Control of Police: Some Lessons for Britain", in T. Bennett (ed.), *The Future of Policing (Cropwood Papers 15)* (Cambridge, Institute of Criminology).

Bayley, D.H. (1985), *Patterns of Policing* (New Brunswick, NJ.: Rutgers University Press).

Bayley, D.H (1994), *Police for the Future* (New York and Oxford: Oxford University Press).

Bayley, D.H. and Shearing, C.D. (1996), "The Future of Policing" 30 *Law and Society Review* 585.

Bayley, S.H. and Bowman, M.J. (2000), "Public Authority Negligence Revisited" (2000) 59 *Cambridge Law Journal* 85.

Beaumont. P. (1997), "The European Community Cannot Accede to the European Convention on Human Rights" 1 *Edinburgh Law Review* 235.

Beaumont, P. and Walker. N, (1999), "The Euro and European Legal Order" in P. Beaumont and N. Walker (eds), *Legal Framework of the Single European Currency* (Oxford: Hart), pp. 169–194.

Becker, S. and Stephens. M. (eds), (1994), *Police Force, Police Service* (London: Macmillan).

Beetham. D. (1991), *The Legitimation of Power* (London: Macmillan).

Bellamy, R. (2000), "Dealing with Difference: Four Models of Pluralist Politics" 53 *Parliamentary Affairs* 198.

Bennett, T. (1983), (ed.), *The Future of Policing (Cropwood Papers 15)* (Cambridge: Institute of Criminology).

Bigo, D. (1994), "The European Internal Security Field: stakes and rivalries in the newly developing area of police intervention" in M. Anderson, and M. den Boer (eds) *Policing across National Boundaries* (London: Pinter), pp. 161–173.

Bigo, D. (1996), *Police en Reseaux: l'experience europeene* (Paris: Presses de Sciences Po).

Bittner, E. (1967), "The Police on Skid Row; a Study in Peace-keeping" 32 *American Sociological Review* 699.

Bittner, E. (1974), "Florence Nightingale in Pursuit of Willie Sutton: a Theory of the Police", in H. Jacob (ed.), *The Potential for Reform of Criminal Justice* (Beverly Hills, Cal.: Sage), pp. 17–44.

Blair, I. (1994), "Let the Police Fund Their Own Expansion" *The Times* October 1.

Boer, M. den (1994), "The Quest for European Policing: Rhetoric and Justification in a Disorderly Debate" in M. Anderson and M. den Boer (eds) *Policing across National Boundaries* (London: Pinter), 174–96.

Boer, M. den (1999), "An Area of Freedom, Security and Justice: Bossed Down by Compromise", in D. O'Keefe and P. Twomey (eds) *Legal Issues of the Amsterdam Treaty* (Oxford: Hart) pp. 303–326.

Boer, M. den (2000), "The Incorporation of Schengen into the TEU: A Bridge too Far?" in J. Mohar and W. Wessels (eds) *The Treaty of Amsterdam: Challenges and Opportunities for the European Union* (London: Cessels).

Boer, M. den and Walker, N. (1993), "European Policing after 1992" 31 *Journal of Common Market Studies* 3.

Boyle, K. and Hadden, T. (1999), "Northern Ireland" in *Constitutional Reform: The Labour Government's Constitutional Reform Agenda* (London and New York: Longman), pp. 282–306.

Boyne, G.A. (1999), "Introduction: Processes, Performance and Best Value in Local Government" 25 *Local Government Studies* 1.

Bradley. A.W. (1994), "The Sovereignty of Parliament—in Perpetuity?" in J. Jowell and D. Oliver (eds) *The Changing Constitution* (3rd ed., Oxford: Clarendon Press), pp. 79–108.

Bradley, D., Walker, N. and Wilkie, R. (1986), *Managing the Police. Law, Organisation and Democracy* (Brighton: Wheatsheaf).

Brazier, R. (1992), "The Non-Legal Constitution: Thoughts on Convention, Practice and Principle" 43 *Northern Ireland Legal Quarterly* 262.

Brazier, R. (1999), "The Constitution of the United Kingdom" (1999) 58 *Cambridge Law Journal* 96.

Bridges, L.C. (1999), "The Lawrence Inquiry: Incompetence, Corruption and Institutional Racism" 26 *Journal of Law and Society* 298.

Brodeur, J.P. , (ed.), (1983), "High Policing and Low Policing: Remarks About the Policing of Political Activities", 30 *Social Problems* 5.

Brodie, D, (1995), "Pursuing The Police" *Juridical Review* 292.

Brogden, M. (1977), "A Police Authority: The Denial of Conflict" *Sociological Review* 325.

Brogden, M. (1982), *The Police: Autonomy and Consent* (London and New York: Academic Press).

Brogden, M., Jefferson, T. and Walklate, S. (1988), *Introducing Policework* (London: Unwin Hyman).

Brogden, M. and Shearing, C. (1993), *Policing for a New South Africa* (London: Routledge).

Brubaker, R. (1996), *Nationalism Reframed; Nationhood and the National Question in the New Europe* (Cambridge: Cambridge University Press).

Bunyan, T. (1976), *The Political Police in Britain* (London: Quartet).

Burca. G. de (1996), "The Quest for Legitimacy in the European Union" 59 *Modern Law Review* 349.

Burca, G. de and Scott, J. (2000), *Constitutional Change in the European Union: From Uniformity to Flexibility?* (Oxford: Hart Publishing).

Butler, A.J.P. (1984), *Police Management* (London: Gower).

Butler, A.J.P. (1992a), "Developing Quality Assurance in Police Services" *Public Money and Management*, Jan.–March, pp. 23–27.

Butler, A.J.P. (1992b), *Police Management* (2nd ed., Aldershot: Dartmouth).

Cable, V. (1994), *The World's New Fissures* (London: Demos).

Cameron Commission (1969), *Disturbances in Northern Ireland: Report of the Commission appointed by the Governor of Northern Ireland*, Cmnd. 532.

Cane, P. (1996), *An Introduction to Administrative Law* (3rd ed., Oxford: Clarendon).

Carson, W.G. (1984), "Policing the Periphery: The Development of Scottish Policing 1795–1900: Part I" 17 *Aust. and NZ Journal of Criminology* 207.

Carson, W.G. (1985), "Policing the Periphery: The development of Scottish Policing 1795–1900: Part II—Policing and the production of social order" 18 *Aust. and NZ. Journal of Criminology* 3.

Chambers, G. and Tombs, J (1983), *The British Crime Survey Scotland* (HMSO: Edinburgh).

Charman, S. and Savage, S. (1998), "Singing From the Same Hymn Sheet: The Professionalisation of the Association of Chief Police Officers" 1 *International Journal of Police Science and Management* 6.

Cohen, S. (1985), *Visions of Social Control* (Cambridge: Polity).

Cohen, H. (1985), "Authority: The Limits of Discretion" in F.A. Elliston and M. Feldberg (eds) *Moral Issues in Police Work* (New Jersey: Rowman & Allanheld), pp. 27–42.

Connolly, J. (1997), *Beyond the Politics of "Law and Order": Towards Community Policing in Ireland* (Belfast: Centre for Research and Documentation).

Connolly, M., Law, J. and Topping, I. (1996), "Policing Structures and Public Accountability in Northern Ireland" 22 *Local Government Studies* 229.

Cotterrell, R. (1992), "Law's Community: Legal Theory and the Image of Legality" 19 *Journal of Law and Society* 405.

Cowell, D., Jones, T. and Young, J. (eds), (1982), *Policing the Riots* (London: Junction Books).

Craig, P. and de Burca, G. (1998), *EU Law: Text, Cases and Materials* (Oxford: Oxford University Press).

Craig, P. and Fairgrieve, D. (1999), "Barret, Negligence and Discretionary Powers" *Public Law* 626.

Crawford, A. (1997), *The Local Governance of Crime: Appeals to Community and Partnerships* (Oxford: Clarendon Press).

Crawford, A. (1998a), "Community Safety and the Quest for Community: Holding Back the Dynamics of Social Exclusion" 19 Policy Studies, 237.

Crawford, A. (1998b), *Crime Prevention and Community Safety: Politics, Policies and Practices* (London and New York: London).

Criminal Justice Review Group (2000), *Review of the Criminal Justice System in Northern Ireland* (Belfast: HMSO).

Cross, R. (1987), *Statutory Interpretation* (2nd ed., (eds J. Bell and G. Engle) London: Butterworths).

Crozier. M. (1964), *The Bureaucratic Phenomenon* (London: Tavistock).

Cullen, P. (1992), *The German Police and European Co-operation* (Edinburgh: European Police Co-operation Working Paper No.2).

Cullen, P. and Gilmore, W. (eds), (1998), *Crime sans frontieres: International and European Legal Approaches* (Edinburgh: Edinburgh University Press).

Curtin. D. M. (1997), *Postnational Democracy* (Universiteit: Utrecht).

Day, P. and Klein, R. (1987), *Accountabilities: Five Public Services* (London: Tavistock).

Department of the Environment, Transport and the Regions (1998a), *A Mayor and Assembly for London*, Cm. 3897.

Department of the Environment, Transport and the Regions (1998b), *Modernising Local Government: Improving Local Services through Best Value*, Cm. 4014.

De Smith, S., Woolf, L. and Jowell, J. (1995), *Judicial Review of Administrative Action* (5th ed., London: Sweet & Maxwell).

Dicey, A.V. (1959), *The Law of the Constitution* (10th ed. with intro. by E.C.S. Wade, London: MacMillan).

Dixon, B. and Stanko, E. (1995), "Sector Policing and Public Accountability" 5 *Policing and Society* 171.

Dixon, D. (1997), *Law in Policing: Legal Regulation and Police Practices* (Oxford: Oxford University Press).

Drewry, G. (1994), "Revolution in Whitehall: The Next Steps and Beyond" in J. Jowell and D. Oliver (eds) *The Changing Constitution* (3rd ed., Oxford: Clarendon Press), pp. 155–174.

Dorn, N., Murji, K. and South, N. (1992), *Traffickers: Drug Markets and Law Enforcement* (London and New York: Routledge).

Dryzek, J.S. (2000), Deliberative Democracy and Beyond: Liberals, Critics, Contestations (Oxford: Oxford University Press).

Dworkin, R. (1986), *Law's Empire* (London: Fontana).

Ellison, G. and Smyth, J. (1996), "Bad Apples or Rotten Barrel? Policing in Northern Ireland" in O. Marenin (ed) *Policing Change, Changing Police: International Perspectives* (Garland: New York), pp. 171–204.

Elliot, M. (1981), *The Role of Law In Central-Local Relations* (London: SSRC).

Emsley, C. (1983), *Policing and its Context 1750–1870* (Macmillan, London).

Emsley, C. (1996), "The Origins and Development of the Police" in E. McLaughlin and J. Muncie (eds) *Controlling Crime* (Sage, London), pp. 7–50.

Emsley, C. (1999), *Gendarmes and the State in Nineteenth Century Europe* (Oxford: Oxford University Press).

English, J. and Card, R. (1999), Butterworths Police Law (6th ed., London: Butterworths).

Ericson, R. (1994), *The Division of Expert Knowledge in Policing and Security* 45 British Journal of Sociology 149.

European Parliament (1997), Report on the Action Plan to Combat Organised Crime, Committee on Civil Liberties and Internal Affairs, Session Doc. A4–0333/97.

European Parliament (2000), The Impact of the Amsterdam Treaty on Justice and Home Affairs, Directorate General for Research Working Paper, LIBE 110 EN, Vols. I and II.

Evans, G. and O'Leary, B. (2000), "Northern Irish Voters and the British-Irish Agreement: Foundations of a Stable Consociational Settlement?" 71 *The Political Quarterly* 78.

Everson, M. (1998), "Beyond the *Bundesverfassungsgericht*: On the Necessary Cunning of Constitutional Reasoning" 4 *European Law Journal* 389.

Ewing, K.D. and Finnie. W. (1988), *Civil Liberties In Scotland: Cases and Materials* (2nd ed., Edinburgh: Greens).

Ewing, K.D. and Gearty, C.A. (1990), *Freedom under Thatcher: Civil Liberties In Modern Britain* (Oxford: Oxford University Press).

Ewing, K.D. and Gearty, C.A. (2000), *The Struggle for Civil Liberties:*

Political Freedom and the Rule of Law in Britain, 1914–1945 (Oxford: Oxford University Press).

Ferrajoli, L. (1996), "Beyond Sovereignty and Citizenship: A Global Constitutionalism" in R. Bellamy (ed) *Constitutionalism, Democracy and Sovereignty: American and European Perspectives* (Aldershot: Avebury).

Fijnaut, C. (1991), "Police Co-operation within Western Europe" in F. Heidensohn and M. Farrell (eds), *Crime in Europe* (London: Routledge), pp. 103–112.

Fine, B. and Millar, R. (eds) (1995), *Policing the Miners' Strike* (London: Lawrence & Wishart).

Finnie, W. (1991), "Public Order Law in Scotland and England 1980–1990" in Finnie, W., Himsworth, C.M.G. and Walker, N. (eds) *Edinburgh Essays in Public Law* (Edinburgh: Edinburgh University Press), pp. 251–277.

Fox, H. (1999), "The Pinochet Case No.3" 48 *International and Comparative Law Quarterly* 687.

Fortson, R. and Walker, N. (1995), *The Police and Magistrates' Courts Act 1994* (London: Sweet & Maxwell).

Foucault, M. (1991), "Governmentality" in G. Burchell, C. Gordon and P. Millar (eds) *The Foucault Effect* (Brighton: Harvester), pp. 87–104.

Friedrich, C.J. (1937), *Constitutional Government and Politics* (New York: Harper & Brothers).

Freeden, M, (1996), *Ideologies and Political Theory* (Oxford: Clarendon Press).

Freedland, M. (1999), "The Crown and the Changing Nature of Government" in M. Sunkin, M. and S. Payne (eds), *The Nature of the Crown: A Legal and Political Analysis* (Oxford: Oxford University Press), pp. 111–134.

Fyfe, N.R. and Bannister, J. (1999), "Privatization, Policing and Crime Control: Tracing the Contours of the Public-Private Divide" in P. Duff and N. Hutton (eds), *Criminal Justice in Scotland* (Aldershot: Dartmouth), pp. 335–354.

Galligan, D.J., (1996), *Due Process and Fair Procedures: A Study of Administrative Procedures* (Oxford: Clarendon).

Garland, D. (1985), *Punishment and Welfare: A History of Penal Strategies* (Aldershot: Gower).

Garland, D. (1996), "The Limits of the Sovereign State: Strategies of crime control in contemporary society" 36 *British Journal of Criminology* 445.

Garland, D. (1997a), "'Governmentality' and the problem of crime: Foucault, criminology, sociology" 1 *Theoretical Criminology* 173.

Garland, D. (1997b), "The Punitive Society: Penology, Criminology and the History of the Present" 1 *Edinburgh Law Review* 180.

Geary, R. (1985), *Policing Industrial Disputes* (Cambridge: Cambridge University Press).

Giddens, A. (1985), *The Nation State and Violence* (Cambridge: Polity Press).

Giddens, A. (1990), *The Consequences of Modernity* (Cambridge, Polity Press).

Giddens, A. (1991), *Modernity and Self-Identity: Self and Society in the late Modern Age* (Cambridge: Polity Press).

Gibbons, T. (1998), *Regulating the Media* (2nd ed., (London: Sweet & Maxwell).

Goldsmith, A. (1990), "Taking Police Culture Seriously: Police Discretion and the Limits of Law" 1 *Policing and Society* 2.

Goldsmith, A. (1991) (ed.), *Complaints Against the Police the Trend to External Review* (Oxford: Oxford University Press).

Goldstein, H. (1990), *Problem-Orientated Policing* (New York: McGraw Hill).

Gordon. P. (1980), *Policing Scotland* (SCCL: Glasgow).

Gouldner, A. (1954), *Patterns of Industrial Bureaucracy* (New York: Collier Macmillan).

Griffin, S. (1990), "Constitutionalism in the United States: From Theory to Practice" 10 *Oxford Journal of Legal Studies* 200.

Grimshaw, R. and Jefferson, T. (1987), *Interpreting Policework. Policy and Practice in forms of Beat Policing* (London: Allen & Unwin).

Guyomarch, A. (1997), "Co-operation in the Fields of Policing and Judicial Affairs", in S. Stavridis. S.E. Mossialos, R. Morgan and H. Machin (eds) *New Challenges to the European Union: Policies and Policy-Making* (Aldershot: Dartmouth), pp. 123–150.

Guyomarch, A. (1995), "Problems and Prospects for European Police Co-operation after Maastricht" 5 *Policing and Society* 249.

Hadfield, B. (1998), "The Belfast Agreement, Sovereignty and the State of the Union" *Public Law* pp. 599–616.

Hale, C. and Uglow, S. (1999), *The Police and Public in Scotland: An analysis of data from the British and Scottish Crime Surveys 1982–1996, Crime and Criminal Justice Research Findings No.33* (Edinburgh: Scottish Office Central Research Unit).

Harden, I. (1991), "The Constitution and its Discontents" 21 *British Journal of Political Science* 489.

Harden, I. (1992), *The Contracting State* (Milton Keynes: Open University Press).

Harden, I. and Lewis, N. (1986), *The Noble Lie: The British Constitution and the Rule of Law* (London: Hutchinson).

Harmsen, R. (1994), "A European Union of Variable Geometry: Problems and Perspectives" 45 *Northern Ireland Legal Quarterly* 109.

Harris, R. (1973), *The Police Academy: An Inside View* (Wiley: New York).

Hart, J. (1981), *The British Police* (London: Allen & Unwin).

Hartley, T. (1994), *The Foundations of European Community Law* (3rd ed., Oxford: Clarendon Press).

Hayes, M. (1997), "A Police Ombudsman for Northern Ireland? A Review of the Police Complaints System in Northern Ireland" (Belfast: HMSO).

Hazell, R. (1999), "Reinventing the Constitution: Can the State Survive?" *Public Law* 84.

Hazell, R. and O'Leary, B. (1999), "A Rolling Programme of Devolution: Slippery Slope or Safeguard of the Union?" in R. Hazell (ed) *Constitutional Futures: A History of the Next Ten Years* (Oxford: Oxford University Press), pp. 21–46.

Held, D. (1996), *Models of Democracy* (2nd ed., Cambridge: Polity).

Held, D. (1999), "The Transformation of Political Community: Rethinking Democracy in the Context of Globalization" in I. Shapiro and C. Hacker-Cordon (eds) *Democracy's Edges* (Cambridge: Cambridge University Press), pp. 84–111.

Held, D., McGrew, A., Goldblatt, D. and Perraton, J. (1999), *Global Transformations* (Cambridge, Polity).

Hillyard, P. (1997), "Policing Divided Societies: Trends and Prospects in Northern Ireland and Britain" in P. Francis, P. Davies and V. Jupp (eds), *Policing Futures: The Police, Law Enforcement and the Twenty-First Century* (Basingstoke: Macmillan), pp. 163–185.

Her Majesty's Chief Inspector of Constabulary (1998), Annual Report 1997–98 (1998 H.C. 1086) (London: HMSO).

Her Majesty's Chief Inspector of Constabulary for Scotland, Annual Report 1995–96, Cm.3313 (Edinburgh: HMSO).

Her Majesty's Chief Inspector of Constabulary for Scotland (1999), Annual Report 1998–99, Cm.4464 (Edinburgh: HMSO).

Her Majesty's Chief Inspector of Constabulary for Scotland (2000), *A Fair Cop? A Thematic Inspection into Police Complaints in Scotland* (Edinburgh: HMSO).

Her Majesty's Government (1993), *Scotland in Union: A Partnership for Good*, Cm.2225 (Edinburgh: HMSO).

Her Majesty's Government (1996), *A Partnership of Nations: The British approach to the European Union Intergovernmental Conference 1996* (London: HMSO).

Her Majesty's Government (1997), *Scotland's Parliament*, Cm.3658 (Edinburgh: HMSO).

Her Majesty's Government (1998), *Agreement Reached in the Multi-Party Negotiations*, Cm.3883 (Belfast: HMSO).

Her Majesty's Government (1999), *Tackling Drugs to Build a Better Britain: The Government's Ten-Year Strategy for Tackling Drugs Misuse*, Cm. 3945 (London: HMSO).

Himsworth, C.M.G. (1995), *Local Government Law in Scotland* (Edinburgh: T & T Clark).

Himsworth. C.M.G. (1996a), "In a State No Longer: The End of Constitutionalism?" *Public Law* 639.

Himsworth, C.M.G. (1996b) "The Scottish Grand Committee as an Instrument of Government" 1 *Edinburgh Law Review* 79.

Himsworth, C.M.G. and Munro, C.R. (1999), The Scotland Act 1998, Current Law Statutes (Edinburgh: Greens/Sweet & Maxwell).

Hoffman, Lord (1999), "Human Rights and the House of Lords" 62 *Modern Law Review* 159.

Hogg, P.W. (1992), *Constitutional Law of Canada* (3rd ed., Toronto: Carswell).

Holdaway, S. (1977), "Changes in Urban Policing" 28 *British Journal of Sociology* 119.

Holdaway, S. (ed), (1979), *The British Police* (London: Edward Arnold).

Holdaway, S. (1983), *Inside the British Police* (Oxford: Blackwell).

Holdaway, S. (1996), *The Racialisation of British Policing* (London: Macmillan).

Home Affairs Committee (1995a), Organized Crime: third Report 1994–95, HCP 1994–95 18–I (London: HMSO).

Home Affairs Committee (1995b), The Private Security Industry: first Report 1994–95 (London: HMSO).

Home Office (1993a), *Inquiry into Police Responsibilities and Rewards: Report*, Cm.2280, I-II (London: HMSO).

Home Office (1993b), *Police Reform: A Police Service for the Twenty-First Century*, Cm.2281 (London: HMSO).

Home Office (1995a), *Review of Core and Ancillary Tasks: Final Report* (London: HMSO).

Home Office (1995b), *The Role of HM Inspectorate of Constabulary for England and Wales* (London: HMSO).

Home Office (1996), *Protecting The Public: The Government's Strategy on Crime in England and Wales*, Cm.3190 (London: HMSO).

Home Office (1999a), Annual Report 1998–99 (London: HMSO).

Home Office (1999b), *Government's Proposals for Regulation of the Private Security Industry in England & Wales*, Cm.4254 (London: HMSO).

Home Office (1999c), *Stephen Lawrence Inquiry: Home Secretary's Action Plan* (London: HMSO).

Home Office (1999d), *Interception of Communications in the United Kingdom*, Cm.4368 (London: HMSO).

Home Office (2000a), *National Strategy for Neighbourhood Renewal: Neighbourhood Wardens Final Report of Policy Action Team 6* (London: Home Office).

Home Office (2000b), *Statutory Guidance on Setting Targets for Best Value Performance Indicators*, 29 February (London: Home Office) (http://www.homeoffice.gov.uk/ppd/pru/statgde.htm)

Hood, C. (1991), "A Public Management for All Seasons?" 69 *Public Administration* 3.

Hook, P. (1998), "A National Force for a National Problem" *Police*, April pp. 5–6.

Hope, T. (2000), "Inequality and the Clubbing of Private Security" in T. Hope and R. Sparks (eds) *Crime, Risk and Insecurity: Law and Order in Everyday Life and Political Discourse* (London: Routledge).

House of Lords, (1995), *Europol, Session 1994–95, 10th Report of Select Committee on the European Communities* (1995 H.L. 51) (London: HMSO).

House of Lords, (1997), *Enhancing Parliamentary Scrutiny of the Third Pillar, Session 1997–98, 6th Report of Select Committee on the European Communities* (1997 H.L. 25) (London: HMSO).

House of Lords (1998), *Incorporating the Schengen Acquis into the European Union, Session 1997–98, 31st Report of Select Committee on the European Communities* (1998 H.L. 139) (London: HMSO).

Howe, S. (1999), "Independent Thinking" *Police Review*, April 30, pp. 22–25.

Hoyano, L.C.H. (1999), "Policing Flawed Police Investigations: Unravelling the Blanket" 62 Modern Law Review 912.

Hughes, G., Mears, R. and Winch, C. (1997), "An Inspector Calls? Regulation and Accountability" in "Three Public Services" 25 *Policy and Politics* 299.

Hunt, Lord, *Report of the Advisory Committee on Police in Northern Ireland* Cmnd. 535 (1969) (London: HMSO).

Hunt, M. (1997), *Using Human Rights Law in English Courts* (Oxford: Hart).

Hutchinson, J. (1994), *Modern Nationalism* (London: Fontana).

Hutton, W. (1996), *The State We're In* (London: Vintage).

Ianni, E.R. and Ianni, F. (1983), "Street Cops and Management Cops: the Two Cultures of Policing", in M. Punch (ed.), *Control in the Police Organisation* (Cambridge, Mass: MIT Press).

Independent Inquiry (1996), *The Role and Responsibilities of the Police* (London: Police Foundation and Policy Studies Institute).

Intelligence and Security Committee (1995), *Report on Security Service Work against Organised Crime*, Cm.3605, (1995) (London: HMSO).

IPPR (1991), *The Constitution of the United Kingdom* (London: IPPR).

Jefferson, T. and Grimshaw, R. (1984), *Controlling the Constable: Police Accountability In England and Wales* (London: Muller).

Jefferson, T., McLaughlin, E. and Robertson, L. (1988), "Monitoring the Monitors: Accountability, Democracy and Police Watching in Britain" 12 *Contemporary Crises* 2.

Johnston, L. (1992a), "An Unseen Force: The Ministry of Defence Police in the U.K." 3 *Policing and Society* 23.

Johnston, L. (1992b), *The Rebirth of Private Policing* (London and New York: Routledge).

Johnston, L. (1993), "Privatization and Protection: Spatial and Sectoral Ideologies in British Policing and Crime Prevention" 56 *Modern Law Review* 771.

Johnston, L. (1994), "Policing Plutonium: Issues in the Provision of Policing Services and Security Systems at Nuclear Facilities and for Related Materials in Transit" 4 *Policing and Society* 53.

Johnston, L. (1995), "Policing Diversity: The Impact of Private Policing" in F. Leishman, B. Loveday and S. Savage (eds), *Core Issues In Policing* (London: Longman).

Johnston, L. (1996), "What is Vigilantism?" 36 *British Journal of Criminology* 220.

Johnston, L. (2000), *Policing Britain: Risk, Security and Governance* (Harlow: Longman).

Jones, T., Maclean, B. and Young, J. (1986), *The Islington Crime Survey: Crime, Victimization and Policing in Inner-City London* (Aldershot: Gower).

Jones, T., Newburn, T. and Smith, D.J. (1994), *Democracy and Policing* (London: PSI).

Jones, T. and Newburn, T. (1997), *Policing After The Act* (London: PSI).

Jones, T. and Newburn, T. (1998), *Private Security and Public Policing* (Oxford: Clarendon Press).

Jones, T.H. (1995), "The Devaluation of Human Rights under the European Convention" *Public Law* 230.

Jones, T.H. (1997), "Criminal Justice and Devolution" *Juridical Review* 201.

Journes. C. (1993), "The Structure of the French Police System: Is the French Police a National Force?" 21 *International Journal of the Sociology of Law* 281.

Jowell, S. and Oliver. D (1994) (eds), *The Changing Constitution* (3rd ed., Oxford: Clarendon Press).

Keating, M. (1998), "What's Wrong with Asymmetrical Government?" in H. Elcock and M. Keating (eds) *Remaking the Union: Devolution and British Politics in the 1990s* (London: Frank Cass), pp. 195–226.

Kay, R.S. (1981), "Preconstitutional Rules" 42 *Ohio State Law Journal* 187.

Kay. R.S. (1989), "Substance and Structure as Constitutional Protections: Centennial Comparisons" *Public Law* 428.

Keith, M. (1993), *Race, Riots and Policing: Lore and disorder in a multi-racist society* (London: UCL Press).

Kellas, J. (1989), *The Scottish Political System* (4th ed., Cambridge: Cambridge University Press).

Kettle, M. (1980), "The Policing of Politics and the Politics of Policing" in P. Hain (ed.) *Policing the Police*, vol. 2 (London: Calder).

Kerse, C.S. (2000), "Parliamentary Scrutiny of the Third Pillar" 6 *European Public Law* 81.

Kinsey, R. and Baldwin. R. (1982), *Police Powers and Politics* (London: Quartet).

Kinsey, R. (1984), *Merseyside Crime and Police Surveys: Final Report*.

Kinsey. R. (1992), *Policing the City* (Edinburgh: Scottish Office).

Kinsey, R., Lea. J. and Young. J. (1986), *Losing the Fight against Crime* (Oxford: Blackwell).

Klockars, C. (1985), *The Idea of Police* (Beverly Hills, Cal: Sage).

Laffan, B. (1992), *Integration and Co-operation in Europe* (London: Routledge).

Laws, J. (1995), "Law and Democracy" *Public Law* 72.

Laws, J. (1998), "The Limitations of Human Rights" *Public Law* p. 254.

Lea, J. and Young, J. (1982), "The Riots in Britain 1981: Urban Violence and Political Marginalisation", in D. Cowell, T. Jones and J. Young (eds), *Policing the Riots* (London: Junction).

Legrand, P. (1999), "Fragments on Law-as-Culture (Deventer: Tjeen Willink).

Leigh, I. (1997), The Police Act 1997, Current Law Statutes. London: Sweet & Maxwell.

Leishman, F., Cope, S and Starie, P (1995), "Reinventing and Restructuring: Towards 'New Policing Order'" in F. Leishman, B. Loveday and S. Savage (eds.), *Core Issues in Policing* (London: Longman), pp. 9–25.

Leishman. F., Loveday. B., and Savage. S. (eds) (1995), *Core Issues in Policing* (London: Longman).

Lidstone, K. and Palmer, C. (1995), *Bevan and Lidstone's The Investigation of Crime: A Guide to Police Powers* (2nd ed., London: Butterworths).

Lindahl, H. (1998), "The Purposiveness of Law: Two Concepts of Representation the European Union" in 17 *Law and Philosophy*, 481.

Lindberg, L.N. (1963), *The Political Dynamics of European Integration* (Stanford: Stanford University Press).

Loader, I. (1996), *Youth, Policing and Democracy* (London: Macmillan).

Loader, I. (1997a) "Policing and the Social: Questions of symbolic power" 48 *British Journal of Sociology* 1.

Loader, I. (1997b), "Private Security and The Demand for Protection in Contemporary Britain" (1997) 7 *Policing and Society* 143.

Loader, I. (1997c), "Thinking Normatively about Private Security" 24 *Journal of Law and Society* 377.

Loader, I. (2000), "Plural Policing and Democratic Governance", *Social and Legal Studies* (forthcoming).

Loader, I. and Walker, N. (2001), "Policing as a Public Good: Reconstituting the Connections between Policing and the State", *Theoretical Criminology* (forthcoming).

Loveday, B. (1985), *The Role and Effectiveness of the Merseyside Police Committee.*

Loveday, B. (1991), "The New Police Authorities in the Metropolitan Counties" 1 *Policing and Society* 193.

Loveday, B. (1995), "Contemporary Challenges to Police Management in England and Wales: Developing Strategies for Effective Service Delivery" 5 *Policing and Society* 281.

Loveday, B. (1998), "Waving Not Drowning: Chief Constables and the New Configuration of Accountability in the Provinces" 1 *International Journal of Police Science and Management* 133.

Loveland, I. (1999), "The Government of London" 70 *The Political Quarterly* 91.

Luhmann, N. (1993), *Das Recht der Gesellschaft* (Frankfurt: Suhrkamp).

Lustgarten, L. (1986), *The Governance of Police* (London: Sweet & Maxwell).

Lustgarten, L. (1987), "The Police and the Substantive Criminal Law" (1987) 27 *British Journal of Criminology* 23.

Lustgarten, L. and Leigh, I. (1994), *In From the Cold? National Security and Democratic Politics* (Oxford: Oxford University Press).

MacCormick, N. (1993), "Constitutionalism and Democracy" in R. Bellamy (ed.) *Theories and Concepts of Politics: An Introduction* (Manchester: Manchester University Press), pp. 124–147.

MacCormick, N. (1999), *Questioning Sovereignty* (Oxford: OUP).

MacPherson, Sir William (1999), *Steven Lawrence Inquiry*, Cm.4262 (1999).

McAuslan, P. and McEldowney, J.F. (1985), "Legitimacy and the Constitution: The dissonance between theory and practice" in P. McAuslan and S.F. McEldowney (eds) *Law, Legitimacy and the Constitution* (London: Sweet & Maxwell) pp. 1–38.

McBarnet. D. (1981), *Conviction* (London: Macmillan).

McCabe, S. and Wallington, P. (1988), *The Police, Public Order and Civil Liberties: Legacies of the Miners' Strike* (London: Routledge).

McCrudden, C. (1994), "Northern Ireland and the British Constitution" in J. Jowell and D. Oliver (eds) *The Changing Constitution* (3rd ed., Oxford: Clarendon Press), pp. 323–375.

McGarry, J. and O'Leary, B. (1999), *Policing Northern Ireland: Proposals for a New Start* (Belfast: Blackstaff).

McLaughlin, E. (1992), "The Democratic Deficit; European Unity and the Accountability of the British Police" 32 *British Journal of Criminology* 473.

McLaughlin, E. (1994), *Community Policing and Accountability* (Aldershot: Avebury).

McLaughlin, E. (1996), "Police, Policing and Policework" in McLaughlin E. and Muncie. J, *Controlling Crime* (Sage: London), pp. 51–106.

McLaughlin, E. and Murji, K. (1997), "The Future Lasts a Long Time: Public Policework and the Managerialist Paradox" in P. Francis, P. Davies and V. Jupp (eds) *Policing Futures: The Police, Law Enforcement and the Twenty-First Century* (Basingstoke: Macmillan), pp. 80–103.

Madison, J., Hamilton, A. and Jay, J, (1987), *The Federalist Papers* (I. Kramnick (ed)), (Harmondsworth: Penguin).

Mair, C. and Wilkie, R. (1997), "Policing Scotland: Past, Present and Future", *Policing Today*, Vol. 3.

Marenin, O. (1982), "Parking Tickets and Class Repression: The concept of policing in critical theories of criminal justice" 6 *Contemporary Crises* 241.

Marenin, O. (1996) (ed), *Policing Change, Changing Police: International Perspectives* (New York and London: Garland).

Marshall, G. (1965), *Police and Government* (London: Methuen).

Marshall, G. (1973), "The Government of the Police since 1963" in J. Alderson and P. Stead (eds) *The Police We Deserve* (London: Wolfe).

Marshall, G. (1978), "Police Accountability Revisited", in Butler, D. and Halsey, A.H. (eds) *Policy and Politics* (Macmillan, London).

Marshall, G. (1984), *Constitutional Conventions: The Rules and Forms of Political Accountability* (Oxford: Clarendon Press).

Marshall, G. and Loveday, B. (1994), "The Police: Independence and Accountability" in J. Jowell and D. Oliver (eds) *The Changing Constitution* (3rd ed., Oxford: Clarendon Press), pp. 295–322.

Mawby, R.I. (1990), *Comparative Policing Issues: The British and American system in international perspective* (London: Allen & Unwin).

Meyring, B. (1997), "Intergovernmentalism and Supranationality: Two Stereotypes for a Complex Reality" 22 *European Law Review* 221.

Midwinter, A., Keating, M. and Mitchell, J. (1991), *Politics and Public Policy in Scotland* (Edinburgh: Mainstream).

Miller, D. (1995), *On Nationality* (Oxford: Oxford University Press).

Milward, A.S. (1992), *The European Rescue of the Nation-State* (London: Routledge).

Mitchell. J.D.B. (1968), *Constitutional Law* (2nd ed., Edinburgh: Greens).

Monar, J. (1998), "Justice and Home Affairs in the Treaty of Amsterdam: Reform at the Price of Fragmentation" 23 *European Law Review* 320.

Morgan, R. (1985), "Setting the P. A.C.E.: Police Community Consultation Arrangements in England and Wales" Bath Social Policy Papers No.4 (University of Bath).

Morgan, R. (1992), "Talking About Policing", in D. Downes, (ed.), *Unravelling Criminal Justice* (London: Macmillan) pp. 165–183.

Morgan. R. and Newburn, T. (1997), *The Future of Policing* (Oxford: Oxford University Press).

Morison, J. (1998), "The Case Against Constitutional Reform" (1998) 25 *Journal of Law and Society* 510.

Muir, W.K. (1977), *The Police: Streetcorner Politicians* (Chicago, Ill.: University of Chicago Press).

Mulcahy, A. (1999), "Policing History: The Official Discourse and Organizational Memory of the Royal Ulster Constabulary" 40 *British Journal of Criminology* 68.

Mullender, R. (2000), "Negligence, Public Authorities and Policy-Level Decisions" 116 *Law Quarterly Review* 40.

Murdoch, J. (1995), "Police" in *Stair Memorial Encyclopaedia* vol. 16 paras. 1701–1821 (Edinburgh: Butterworths/Law Society of Scotland).

MVA Consultancy (1997), *The 1996 Scottish Crime Survey: First Results, Crime and Criminal Justice Research Findings no. 16* (Edinburgh: Scottish Office Central Research Unit).

Nadelman, E. (1993), *Cops Across Borders; The Internationalization of U.S. Criminal Law Enforcement* (Philadelphia: Penn. State University).

Nairn, T. (1997), "Sovereignty after the Election" (1997) 224 *New Left Review* 3.

Newing, J. (1987), "Perspectives on Accountability" 3 *Policing* No.1.

Northern Ireland Office (1994), *Policing in the Community: Policing Structures in Northern Ireland* (Belfast: HMSO).

Northern Ireland Office (1996), *Foundations for Policing: Proposals for Policing Structures in Northern Ireland* Cm.3249 (Belfast: HMSO).

Northern Ireland Office (2000), *Patten Report: Secretary of State's Implementation Plan* (Belfast: HMSO).

O'Leary, B. (1998), *The British-Irish Agreement: Power-Sharing Plus* (London: Constitution Unit).

O'Malley, P. and Palmer, D. (1996), "Post-Keynesian Policing" 25 Economy and Society 137.

Oliver, D. (1999), *Common Values and the Public-Private Divide* (London: Butterworths).

Oliver, I. (1987), *Police, Government and Accountability* (London: Macmillan).

Oliver, I. (1997), *Police, Government and Accountability* (2nd ed., London: Macmillan).

Palmer, S.H. (1988), *Police and Protest in England and Ireland 1780–1850* (Cambridge: Cambridge University Press).

Pasquino, P. (1991), "Theatricum Politicum; The Genealogy of Capital —Police and the State of Prosperity" in G. Burchell, C. Gordon and P. Millar (eds), *The Foucault Effect* (Brighton: Harvester), pp. 235–250.

Paterson, L. (1994), *The Autonomy of Modern Scotland* (Edinburgh: Edinburgh University Press).

Patten, C. (1999), *A New Beginning for Policing in Northern Ireland: The Report of the Independent Commission on Policing for Northern Ireland.* (Belfast: HMSO).

Peers, S. (2000), *E.U. Justice and Home Affairs Law* (Harlow: Longman).

Pike, M.S. (1985), *Principles of Policing* (Basingstoke: Macmillan).

Police Authority for Northern Ireland (1998), *Listening to the Community: Working with the RUC* (Belfast: PANI).

Policy Studies Institute (1983), *Police and People in London*: Vol. I D.J. Smith, "A survey of Londoners"; Vol. II S. Small, "A Group of Young Black People"; Vol. III D.J. Smith, "A Survey of Police Officers"; Vol. IV D.J. Smith and J. Gray "The Police in Action" (London: PSI).

Power, M. (1997), *The Audit Society: Rituals of Verification* (Oxford: Oxford University Press).

Prosser, T. (1982), "Towards a Critical Public Law" 9 *Journal of Law and Society* 1.

Punch, M. (1979), "The Secret Social Service", in S. Holdaway (ed.), *The British Police* (London: Edward Arnold).

Punch, M. (1983), "Officers and Men: Occupational Culture: Inter-Rank Antagonism and the Investigation of Corruption" in M. Punch (ed.) *Control In the Police Organisation* (Cambridge, Mass.: MIT Press), pp. 227–250.

Regan, D. (1983), *Are The Police Under Control? (Research Report Papers No. 1)* (London: Social Affairs Unit).

Reiner, R. (1978), *The Blue-Coated Worker* (Cambridge: Cambridge University Press).

Reiner, R. (1981), "The Politics of Police Power" in *Politics and Power, Vol. 4* (London: Routledge).

Reiner, R. (1991), *Chief Constables* (Oxford: Oxford University Press).

Reiner, R. (1992a), *The Politics of the Police* (2nd ed., Hemel Hempstead: Harvester Wheatsheaf).

Reiner, R. (1992b), "Policing a Postmodern Society" 55 Modern Law Review 71.

Reiner, R. (1993), "Police Accountability: Principles, Patterns and Practices" in R. Reiner and S. Spencer (eds) *Accountable Policing: Effectiveness, Empowerment and Equity* (London: IPPR) pp. 1–24.

Reiner, R. (1994), "Policing and the Police" in M. Maguire; R. Morgan and R. Reiner (eds) *The Oxford Handbook of Criminology* (Oxford: Clarendon Press) pp. 705–772.

Reiner, R. (1995), "From Sacred to Profane: The thirty years' war of the British police" 5 *Policing and Society* 121.

Reiner, R. (1996), (ed.), *Policing Vols. I and II* (Aldershot: Dartmouth).

Reiner, R. (1997), "Policing and the Police" in M. Maguire; R. Morgan and R. Reiner (eds) *The Oxford Handbook of Criminology* (2nd ed., Oxford: Clarendon Press) pp. 997–1049.

Reiner, R. and Leigh, L. (1994), "Police Power" in C. McCrudden and

G. Chambers (eds) *Individual Rights and the Law* (Oxford: Clarendon Press), pp. 109–144.

Reiner, R. and Spencer, S. (1993), "Conclusions and Recommendation" in R. Reiner and S. Spencer (eds), *Accountable Policing: Effectiveness, Empowerment and Equity* (London: IPPR), pp. 172–191.

Reiner, R. and Spencer, S. (1993) (eds), *Accountable Policing: Effectiveness, Empowerment and Equity* (London: IPPR).

Rhodes, R.A.W. (1985), "Power-dependence, Policy Communities and Intergovernmental Networks" 49 *Public Administration Bulletin*, 4.

Rhodes, R.A.W. (1997), *Understanding Governance: Policy Networks, Governance, Reflexivity and Accountability* (Buckingham: Open University Press).

Robertson, G. (2000), *Crimes Against Humanity: The Struggle for Global Justice* (Harmondsworth: Penguin).

Robinson. C.C., Scaglion, R. (1987), "The Origins and Evolution of the Police Function in Society, Notes Towards a Theory" 21 *Law and Society Review* 1.

Rokkan. S. and Urwin. D. (eds), (1982), *The Politics of Territorial Identity: Studies in European Regionalism* (Sage: London).

Rose, N., "Powers of Freedom: Reframing Political Thought" (Cambridge: Cambridge University Press).

Rose, N. and Millar, P. (1992), "Political Power Beyond the State: Problematics of government" 43 *British Journal of Sociology* 172.

Rose. D. (1996), *In the Name of the Law: the Collapse of Criminal Justice* (London: Jonathan Cape).

Royal Commission on the Police (1962), Final Report, Cmnd.1728.

Royal Commission on Criminal Justice (1993), Report, Cm.2263.

Saulsbury. W., Mott. J. and Newburn. T. (1996), *Themes in Contemporary Policing* (London: Police Foundation/Policy Studies Institute).

Savage. S. (1984), "Political Control or Community Liaison?" 55 *Political Quarterly* January–March.

Savage, S., Charman, S. and Cope, S. (1996), "Police Governance: The Association of Chief Police Officers and Constitutional Change" *Public Policy and Administration* 92.

Saward, M. (2000), "A Critique of Held" in B. Holden (eds) *Global Democracy: Key Debates* (London and New York: Routledge).

Scarman, Lord (1972), *Violence and Civil Disturbance in Northern Ireland in 1969* (Belfast: HMSO).

Scarman, Lord (1981), *The Brixton Disorders*, Cmnd.8427.

Schachter, O. (1991), *International Law in Theory and Practice* (Dordrecht: M. Nijhoff).

Scottish Constitutional Convention (1995), *Scotland's Parliament, Scotland's Right* (Edinburgh: SCC).

Scottish Executive (1999), *Action Plan on the Stephen Lawrence Inquiry* (HMSO: Edinburgh).

Scottish Executive (2000), *Review of Police and Fire Services. Police Review: Interim Report* (Edinburgh: Scottish Executive).

Scottish Office (1995), *Guidance for Members of New Police Authorities and Joint Boards* (Edinburgh: Scottish Office).

Sedley, S. (1995), "Human Rights: A Twenty-First Century Agenda" *Public Law* 386.

Shaw. J. (1999), "Postnational Constitutionalism in the European Union" 6 *Journal of European Public Policy* 579.

Shearing, C. (1992), "The Relation Between Public and Private Policing" in M. Tonry and N. Morris (eds) *Modern Policing* (Chicago, Ill.: Chicago University Press), pp. 399–434.

Shearing, C. (1996), "Public and Private Policing" in W. Saulsbury, J. Mott and T. Newburn, (eds) *Themes in Contemporary Policing* (London: Independent Committee of Inquiry into the Roles and Responsibilities of the Police), pp. 83–95

Shearing, C. and Stenning, P. (1983), "Private Security Implications for Social Control" 30 *Social Problems* 493.

Shearing, C. and Stenning, P. (1987) (eds), *Private Policing* (Beverly Hills, Cal.: Sage).

Sheptycki, J. (1995), "Transnational Policing and the Making of a Post-modern State" 35 *British Journal of Criminology* 613.

Sheptycki, J. (1998a), "Policing, Postmodernism and Transnationalization" 38 *British Journal of Criminology* 485.

Sheptycki, J. (1998b), "The Global Cops Cometh: Reflections on Transnationalization, Knowledge Work and Policing Subculture" 49 *British Journal of Sociology* 57.

Shils, E. (1982), *The Constitution of Society* (Chicago: University of Chicago Press).

Simey, M. (1988), *Democracy Rediscovered: A Study in Police Accountability* (London: Pluto).

Skolnick, J. (1966), *Justice Without Trial* (New York: Wiley).

Smith, A. (1991), *National Identity* (London: Penguin).

Smout, T.C. (1970), *A History of the Scottish People: 1560–1830* (Glasgow: Collins).

Spencer, S. (1985a), *Called to Account: The Case for Police Accountability in England and Wales* (London: NCCL).

Spencer, S. (1985b), "The Eclipse of the Police Authority" in B. Fine and R. Millar (eds) *Policing the Miners' Strike* (London: Lawrence & Wishart), pp. 34–53.

Steedman, C. (1984), *Policing the Victorian Community* (London: Routledge).

Steel, J. and Cowan, D.S. (1994), "The Negligent Pursuit of Public Duty—A Police Immunity?" *Public Law* 4.

Steiner, H. and Alston, P. (eds) (1996), *International Human Rights in Context; Law, Politics, Morals* (Oxford: Oxford University Press).

Stinchcombe, A. (1963), "Institutions of privacy in the determination of police administrative practice", 69 *American Journal of Sociology* 2.

Stone Sweet, A. (1998), "Constitutional Dialogues in the European Community" in A-M. Slaughter, A. Stone Sweet and J.H.H. Weiler (eds) *The European Court and National Courts—Doctrine and Jurisprudence: Legal Change in its Social Context* (Oxford: Hart), pp. 303–330.

Storbeck, J. (1996), "Part of the Union" 2 *Policing Today* Part 1, 28–31.

Storch, R. (1975), "The Plague of Blue Locusts: police reform and popular resistance in Northern England 1840–57" 20 *International Review of Social History* 61.

Sunstein, C. (1996), *Legal Reasoning and Political Conflict* (New York: Oxford University Press).

Taylor, I. (1992), "The International Drugs Trade and Money Laundering: Border Controls and Other Issues" 8 *European Sociological Review* 181.

Teubner, G. (1997), "Global Bukowina: Legal Pluralism in the World Society" in G Teubner (ed) *Global Law Without a State* (Aldershot: Darmouth), pp. 3–30.

Toth, A. (1998), "The Legal Effects of the Protocols Relating to the United Kingdom, Ireland and Denmark", in T. Heukels, N. Blokker and M. Brus (eds) *The European Union after Amsterdam: A Legal Analysis* (The Hague: Kluwer), pp. 227–252.

Tully, J. (1995), *Strange Multiplicity: Constitutionalism in an Age of Diversity* (Cambridge: Cambridge University Press).

Tully, J. (1999), "Identity Politics and Freedom: The Challenge of Reimagining Belonging in Multicultural and Multinational Communities" Paper to Conference on Reimagining Belonging, Aalborg, Denmark.

Turnbull-Henson, P. (1997), "Negotiating the Third Pillar: The Maastricht Treaty and the Failure of Justice and Home affairs Co-operation among E.U. Member States" unpublished paper to the ECSA Conference, Florida, USA.

Turpin, C. (1994), "Ministerial Responsibility" in J. Jowell and D. Oliver (eds), *The Changing Constitution* (3rd ed., Oxford: Clarendon Press), pp. 109–154.

Uglow, S. (1996), Police Act 1996, Current Law Statutes, London: Sweet & Maxwell.

Uglow, S. and Telford, V. (1997), *The Police Act 1997* (Bristol: Jordans).

Uildriks, N. and Mastrigt, H. van (1991), *Policing Police Violence* (Aberdeen: Aberdeen University Press).

Van Maanen, J. (1974), "Working the Street", in H. Jacob (ed.) *The Potential for Reform of Criminal Justice* (Beverly Hills, Cal.: Sage).

Vile, M.J.C. (1967), *Constitutionalism and the Separation of Powers* (Oxford: Clarendon Press).

Vincent, A. (1987), *Theories of the State* (Oxford: Basil Blackwell).

Von Bogdandy, A. (2000), "The European Union as a Supranational Federation: A conceptual attempt in the light of the Amsterdam Treaty" 6 *Columbia Journal of European Law* 27.

Waddington, P.A.J. (1999), *Policing Citizens: Authority and Rights* (London: UCL Press).

Wade, E.C.S. and Bradley, A.W. (1993), *Constitutional and Administrative Law* (11th ed. by A.W. Bradley and K.D. Ewing) (Harlow: Longman).

Wade, E.G.S. and Bradley, A.W. (1997), *Constitutional and Administrative Law* (12th edition by A.W. Bradley and K.D. Ewing) (Harlow: Longman).

Wade, Sir W. (1996), "Sovereignty—Revolution or Evolution?" 112 *Law Quarterly Review* 568.

Wadham, J. (1994), "The Intelligence Services Act 1994" 57 *Modern Law Review* 916.

Waever, O. (1996), "European Security Identities" 34 *Journal of Common Market Studies* 103.

Waever, O. and Kelstrup, M. (1993), "Europe and its Nations: Political and Cultural Identities" in O. Waever, B. Buzan, M. Kelstrup and P. Lemaitre (eds) *Identity, Migration and the New Security Agenda in Europe* (London: Pinter) pp. 40–92.

Walker, N. (1991), "The Middle Ground in Public Law" in W. Finnie, C.M.G. Himsworth and N. Walker (eds) *Edinburgh Essays In Public Law* (Edinburgh: Edinburgh University Press), pp. 57–95.

Walker, N. (1993a), "The Dynamics of European Police Co-operation: The U.K Perspective", in W. Gilmore (ed) *Action against Transnational Criminality* Vol II (London: Commonwealth Secretariat).

Walker, N. (1993b), "The International Dimension," in Reiner, R. and Spencer, S. (eds) *Accountable Policing: Effectiveness, Empowerment and Equity* (London: IPPR) pp. 113–171.

Walker, N. (1994a), "Care and Control in the Police Organisation" in M. Stephens and S. Becker (eds) *Police Force, Police Service: Care and Control In Britain* (London: Macmillan), pp. 33–66.

Walker, N. (1994b), "European Integration and European Policing" in M. Anderson and M. den Boer (eds) *Policing across National Boundaries* (London: Pinter) pp. 22–45.

Walker, N. (1994c), "Reshaping the British Police: The International Angle" 2 *Strategic Government* 25.

Walker, N. (1995), "Police and Government in Scotland," *Scots Law Times,* Issue 22, 199.

Walker, N. (1996a), "Defining Core Police Tasks: The neglect of the symbolic dimension?" 6 *Policing and Society* 53.

Walker, N. (1996b), "European Constitutionalism and European Integration" *Public Law* 266.

Walker, N. (1996c), "European Policing in Transition" in O. Marenin (ed.) *Policing Change, Changing Police: International Perspectives* (New York: Garland) pp. 251–284.

Walker, N. (1998a), "Constitutional Reform in a Cold Climate: Reflections on the White Paper and Referendum on a Scottish Parliament" in A. Tomkins (ed.) *Devolution and the Constitution* (London: Key Haven), pp. 61–88.

Walker, N. (1998b), "Sovereignty and Differentiated Integration in the European Union" 4 *European Law Journal* 355.

Walker, N. (1998c), "European Policing and the Politics of Regulation" in P. Cullen and W. Gilmore (eds) *Crimes Sans Frontières: International and European Legal Approaches* (Edinburgh: Edinburgh University Press), pp. 141–160.

Walker, N. (1998d), "Justice and Home Affairs" 47 *International and Comparative Law Quarterly* 231.

Walker, N. (1999a), "Decoupling Police and State" in E. Bort and R. Keat (eds) *The Boundaries of Understanding: Essays in Honour of Malcolm Anderson* (Edinburgh: International Social Sciences Institute), pp. 59–71.

Walker, N. (1999b), "Situating Scottish Policing" in P. Duff and N. Hutton (eds) *Criminal Justice in Scotland* (Aldershot: Dartmouth), pp. 94–114.

Walker, N. (2000a), "Beyond the Unitary Conception of the U.K. Constitution?" *Public Law* 384.

Walker, N. (2000b), "Flexibility within a Metaconstitutional Frame; Reflections upon the Future of Legal Authority in Europe", in G. de Burca and J. Scott (eds) *Constitutional Change in the E.U.: Between Uniformity and Flexibility* (Oxford: Hart), pp. 9–30.

Walker, N. (2000c), "The Police Complaints System in Context" SCOLAG Bulletin, August, 8.

Walker, N. (2000d), "The Transnational Dimension" in F. Leishman, B. Loveday and S. Savage (eds) *Core Issues in Policing* (2nd ed., Harlow: Longman).

Walker, N. and Telford, M. (2000), *Designing Criminal Justice: The Northern Ireland System in Comparative Perspective* (Belfast: Northern Ireland Office).

Walker, S. (1992), *The Police In America: An Introduction* (2nd ed., New York: McGraw-Hill).

Walters, M. (1999), "Nationalism and the Pathologies of Legal Systems: Considering the *Quebec Secession Reference* and its Lessons for the United Kingdom" 62 *Modern Law Review* 370.

Watt, A. (1999), "The Crown and its Employees" in M. Sunkin and S. Payne (eds), *The Nature of the Crown: A Legal and Political Analysis* (Oxford: Oxford University Press), pp. 283–314.

Weale, A. (1995), "Democratic Legitimacy and the Constitution of Europe", in R. Bellamy, V. Bufacchi and D. Castiglione (eds), *Democracy and Constitutional Culture in the Union of Europe* (London: Lothian Foundation).

Weatheritt, M. (1996), *Policing Plans: A Members' Guide* (London: AMA/COLPA).

Weber, M. (1948), *Politics as a Vocation* (London: Allen and Unwin).

Weiler. J.H.H (1981), "The Community System: The Dual Character of Supranationalism" 1 *Yearbook of European Law* 267.

Weiler, J.H.H. (1991), "The Transformation of Europe" 100 *Yale Law Journal* 2403.

Weiler. J.H.H. (1999), *The Constitution of Europe* (Cambridge: Cambridge University Press).

Weinberger, B. (1991), *Keeping the Peace? Policing Strikes in Britain 1900–1926* (Oxford: Berg).

Weitzer, R. (1995), *Policing Under Fire: Ethnic Conflict and Police-Community Relations in Northern Ireland* (Albany: SUNY Press).

White, R.M. (1998), "Disciplining Chief Constables" Scots Law Times (News), pp. 77–80, Issue. 11, March 20.

Willmott, P. (1987), "Introduction" in Willmott, P. (ed) *Policing and the Community* (London: Policy Studies Institute), pp. 1–6.

Witte, B. de (1999), "Direct Effect, Supremacy and the Nature of the Legal Order" in P. Craig and G. de Burca (eds) *The Evolution of E.U. Law* (Oxford: Oxford University Press), pp. 177–213.

Wright, E.D. (1979), Non-Home Department Police Forces: Report of the Committee of Inquiry into Pay and Conditions, Cmnd.7623.

Zander, M. (1991), *The Police and Criminal Evidence Act 1984* (2nd ed., London: Sweet and Maxwell).

Index

Europol,—contd.
Council, decision-making
authority of, 239, 242
creation of, 14
Drugs Unit,
establishment of, 237
role of, 237–238
framework under Maastricht
Treaty, 235–241
history of birth of, 235–236
institutional competencies in
relation to, 239–240
part of Third Pillar of E.U.,
227
powers, 237–238, 254
structural arrangements under
Third Pillar, 238–239
Third Pillar and, 235–244
Europol Convention,
effect of, 203
powers granted by, 237–238,
254
signing of, 238
Europol Drugs Unit (EDU),
establishment of, 14, 237
role of, 237–238

Fairness, issues of,
police governance, in relation
to, 58–59
**Financial Management
Initiative,** 91
Fisher v Oldham Corporation,
effect on constabulary
independence doctrine, 49–52

GCHQ. *See* **Government
Communications
Headquarters**
Germany,
Basic Law of 1949, 10

Good Friday Agreement. *See*
Belfast Agreement
Governance, police. *See* **Police
governance**
**Government Communications
Headquarters (GCHQ),**
statutory recognition, 221

Health and Safety Executive,
263
History of police service,
autonomy from local
government, of, 47–48
chief constable, of authority of,
46–47
doctrine of constabulary
independence, of, 45, 46–47
First World War, 42–43
integration of police service, of,
42–44
New Police, 41, 278
Northern Ireland, in, 172–178
Scotland, in, economic
development, 151–155
Second World War, 43, 44
Home Office,
chief constable and,
consolidation powers, 80–81
doctrine of ministerial
responsibility,
amendatory accountability
requirements, 17–18
significance of, 16–17
non-Home Office forces. *See*
Non-Home Office policing
Police Department within,
establishment of, 43
police, predominant role, 32
Home Secretary,
Action Plan following
Lawrence Inquiry, 120